KABBALISTIC TEACHINGS
of the
FEMALE PROPHETS

KABBALISTIC TEACHINGS
of the
FEMALE PROPHETS

The Seven Holy Women of Ancient Israel

J. ZOHARA MEYERHOFF HIERONIMUS

Inner Traditions
Rochester, Vermont

Inner Traditions
One Park Street
Rochester, Vermont 05767
www.InnerTraditions.com

Library of Congress Cataloging-in-Publication Data
Hieronimus, J. Zohara Meyerhoff.
   Kabbalistic teachings of the female prophets : the seven holy women of ancient Israel /
J. Zohara Meyerhoff Hieronimus.
      p. cm.
   Summary: "The spiritual teachings of Israel's biblical prophetesses from a kabbalistic
perspective"—Provided by publisher.
   Includes bibliographical references and index.
   ISBN 978-1-59477-227-6 (pbk.)
   1. Women prophets. 2. Women in the Bible. 3. Cabala. I. Title.
   BS1199.W7H54 2008
   221.9'22082—dc22

                                                                              2008013652

Printed and bound in the United States by Lake Book Manufacturing

10 9 8 7 6 5 4 3 2 1

Text design by Jon Desautels and layout by Priscilla Baker
This book was typeset in Garamond Premier Pro with Tiepolo and Delphin used as dis-
play typefaces

To send correspondence to the author of this book, mail a first-class letter to the author
c/o Inner Traditions • Bear & Company, One Park Street, Rochester, VT 05767, and we
will forward the communication.

*Like the scent of goodly oils is the spreading fame
of Your great deeds: Your very name is Flowing
Oil, therefore have nations Loved you.*

Song of Songs 1:3

*Praise HaShem, Host of Hosts
For giving us life and His Torah.*

Contents

Acknowledgments

Without the enduring love of my husband, Dr. Robert R. Hieronimus, and his regard for the spiritual path, I would have been less able to pursue the prophetic lineage of which our age is an inheritor. Love to my Meyerhoff and Hieronimus families, the Hendlers, Rubensteins, Pancoes, Katzes, Schewels, and all their branches for their support, wisdom, and humor; and to my ancestors for their own love of Torah, HaShem, and the People of the Book. May their memory be for a blessing! A special acknowledgment to my great-grandfather Oscar (Asher) Meyerhoff (1864–1946) for informing my heart and soul from above with a love of Chassidut and Torah, and for planting our family tree in America. Thank you to all the women who have taken part in my classes and discussions on the teachings of the seven prophetesses of Israel and for sharing, in joy, these remarkable women. For my daughter, Anna, and stepdaughter, Mare: May the prophetesses guide you in finding peace and purpose in your own lives. Great thanks to Laura Cortner for her constant and tireless assistance in whatever is needed, and to Meghan Bowen and Alden Brigham for taking care of my broadcasting needs. To all the wonderful providers at the Ruscombe Mansion Community Health Center, which I founded in 1984: May your loving attendance of others continue to be blessed.

Gratitude to R. Avraham Brandwein,[1] Samuel Ben-Or Avital,

---

[1] R. before a name stands for the title Rabbi.

R. Noah Shavrick, and R. Simon Jacobson for their guidance in Torah and Kabbalah.

Shalom Shalom to the blessed Chazal (sages) whose teachings illuminate our minds and hearts, bringing us closer to God, Torah, and peace.

I give great appreciation to R. Schneur Zalman (Baal HaTanya, author of *Likkutei Amarim Tanya*); R. Yaakov Ibn Chaviv for his sixteenth-century work, *Ein Yaakov,* and R. Avraham Finkel for his translation of it; and R. Moshe Chayim Luzzatto (the Ramchal, 1707–1747 CE) and R. Moshe Cordovero (the Ramak, 1522–1570 CE) for all of their illuminations. In addition to the Torah, their writings, translated into English, were my primary set of keys, along with Gutman Locks's *The Spice of Torah—Gematria,* in my journey with the seven prophetesses of Israel and the teachings of which they are a part.

Blessings to Inner Traditions International, with special gratitude to Jeanie Levitan, Jamaica Burns, and Elaine Cissi, for their editorial excellence and for making it possible to share the female prophets and their holy lives with others. May the reader benefit by the shining light of their guidance.

Rosh Chodesh, 30 Nissan, 5767
April 18, 2007

Preface

The female prophets are the seven holy women of Israel who lived between the Middle Bronze Age (1880 BCE) and the end of the Persian period (350 CE). A study of their communal lives shows how the holy presence of God reveals itself through prophecy in the world and in our lives and follows a fundamental progression or an archetypal story for all of humanity. Their collective story is one of conception, birth, learning correct moral action, achieving holy spiritual conduct, the existence of royal lineages as a result of both birth and spiritual merit, and the promise of the Moshiach (Messiah) and of the World to Come (Olam HaBa), all culminating in the promise of redemption and resurrection.

The seven prophetesses of Israel are Sarah, Miriam, Devorah, Chanah, Avigail, Chuldah, and Esther. Together, these seven women embody the Creator's presence in Judaism, referred to by the People of the Book as the Divine Immanence of the Creator or the Shechinah. Each prophetess has her own story to tell, and though each woman's nature and apparent purpose is a model for all of us cultivating our own intuition, self-refinement, and closeness to God, an analysis of the combined lives of all the prophetesses, spanning almost two thousand years, creates a system of evolution and development as pertinent to our lives today as it was for the biblical communities in which they originated. The details of their lives are also important to discover, for in them we find the capacity for prophecy, an ability to speak for and with the Creator, as well as the excellence of loving-kindness, leadership, beauty, fortitude, humility, sacrifice and sovereignty in service to the Creator, the word of God, and the goal of personal and global harmony and redemption.

Others have shown correlations between the lives of these women and different aspects of Kabbalah, but not in the manner in which this book explores them. The Holy Sage the Arizal (R. Isaac Luria, 1534–1572) teaches of the relationship between the seven species of Israel (wheat, barley, grapes, figs, pomegranates, olive oil, and date honey) and the Sefirot, or spheres of the Tree of Life. The Holy Sage the Ramak (R. Moshe Cordovero) tells us of the relationship of the seven prophetesses to seven of the overall ten Sefirot of the Tree of Life. These correspondences help us see how our lives are part of a greater spiritual model. In addition, I have included other systems of seven, such as the corresponding days of the week. Doing so gives the reader a helpful guide to focus each day on a particular quality inherent in the divine plan of the Creator reflected as it is in our world.

A comprehensive integration of all of these elements—the prophetesses, the Sefirot, the body, the seven species, the days of the week, and the appropriate texts from the Judaic holy books—shows us a way of living and acting in the world in any given situation in a way most harmonious to the root nature of the Creator in whose image we are made.

These systems of seven manifest as a very specific progressive development for Israel and every human being, symbolically and literally. The story of the seven prophetesses of Israel is the story of every person's journey in general and the spiritual story of the Jewish people in particular. From creation to redemption and ultimately resurrection, it is the story of our entire world's development. It points not only to where we come from, but also to where we are soon to be in the promised thousand years of peace, the messianic age.

THE PROPHETESSES AND THE
TREE OF LIFE (ETZ CHAYIM)

We will study each of the prophetesses' particular role in biblical history and look at how each of them defines a different aspect of life for us individually, for the nation, and for the world. We will see through ancient Kabbalistic teachings that each prophetess is connected to the Sefirot, or vessels, characterized throughout Kabbalah as the Tree of Life (Etz Chayim). They are the Sefirot composing what are called the seven emotions (*middot*):

> Loving-kindness (Chesed)
> Judgment (Gevurah)
> Beauty (Tiferet)
> Victory (Netzach)
> Majesty (Hod)
> Foundation (Yesod)
> Kingdom (Malchut)

The prophetesses' unique qualities and the Sefirot they represent are revealed through a study of Torah,[1] the prophetesses' Hebrew names, and other sources. Correspondences we will study include how the Sefirot of Kabbalah, in addition to their spiritual functions, have accompanying symbolic body parts in the human being. What we learn about each Sefirah and prophetess from this perspective can help us in our repair of the world (*tikkun olam*) to which all of humanity is assigned. Also connected are the holy seven species of the land of Israel, which God gave to the Jewish people (the People of the Book).

The climax of their communal story is the message of our ultimate redemption and resurrection as designed for us by the Host of Hosts, our beloved God (HaShem). His love for us and the created world is boundless,

---

[1] The Torah (Torah preceded by the definite article *the*) generally refers to the Five Books of Moses, whereas Torah (no definite article) refers to all the Jewish oral and written tradition.

and He showers His mercy upon us. With HaShem's blessings, we now join the seven prophetesses of Israel as they show us the way to individual and communal refinement, harmony, and oneness with God as preserved for us in the teachings of the descendants of Abraham and Sarah, the People of the Book.

CHANUKAH, ROSH CHODESH 30 TISLEV, 5767
DECEMBER 21, 2006

1

Prophecy and the Prophetesses

The History of Prophecy in Judaism

The lives and teachings of the women of prophecy, the seven prophetesses of Israel, are rooted in the art and practice of prophecy itself. According to the classical Jewish writings, prophecy has played an important role in Judaism historically as a tool for divine revelation and communal guidance. A person can experience prophecy as a result of great effort and preparation or by divine selection alone. Prophecy is given to a person or a group of people only if their generation is deserving of such revelation.

While it is said traditionally that prophecy left the Jewish people with the destruction of the Second Temple in 70 CE, texts attest to the fact that certain levels of prophecy, such as the Ruach HaKodesh, a gift of the Holy Spirit, ". . . is attainable by any person, at any time or place as long as the person makes himself worthy of it."[1] Many sources suggest

---

[1] R. Moses Ben Maimon (Maimonides; the Rambam), *Mishneh Torah, Hilchot Yesodei HaTorah,* 7:1, 244. Note that R. before a name stands for the title Rabbi.

that prophecy was a counterbalance to idolatry and that when idolatry ceased, so too did prophecy.[2]

Another opinion is that though prophecy of the level during which the Temple stood ceased after 70 CE, prophecy has never left the Jewish people. "Any Torah leader whose works have been accepted by all of Israel, is assumed to have been divinely guided."[3] Prophetic insight continues as demonstrated through the intellect and soul of a scholar or person living a devoted Torah-directed life. According to R. Moses Ben Maimon (Maimonides or the Rambam, 1135–1204 CE), with the exception of Isaiah, every Jewish prophet in the Bible received his gift through his predecessors and is part of a long, unbroken chain of prophecy.

In *The Guide of the Perplexed,* the Rambam explains that God grants the gift of prophecy only for the sake of His people. Even if an individual is worthy, prophecy will not be obtained unless his or her generation is also worthy. The Rambam writes that a prophet must obtain his first prophecy in Israel before obtaining a vision in other lands, and then only if it is absolutely necessary for the sake of Israel. Three of the seven prophetesses—Sarah, Miriam, and Esther—all received their prophecies outside the land of Israel (Eretz Yisrael) showing important exceptions to this for the sake of the entire People of the Book.

PROPHECY: SUPREME LANGUAGE
OF THE SOUL

Prophecy distinguishes itself from all other arts and intuitive talents. It delegates to prophets an unequaled status among their peers as the Creator's representative. They are found to be of good character, wise judgment, and merciful hearts and are righteous and diligent in study, teaching, and practice of their faith.

---

[2] "The Vilna Gaon (R. Elijah Ben Solomon Zalman; 1720–1797) wrote in his Commentary to Seder Olam, 'Until this point there were Prophets—meaning, from the time they eradicated idolatry, prophecy ceased.'" Bezalel Naor, *Lights of Prophecy,* 23.

[3] R. Moses Ben Maimon (Maimonides; the Rambam), *Mishneh Torah, Hilchot Yesodei HaTorah,* 9:2, and R. Aryeh Kaplan, *Handbook of Jewish Thought,* vol. 1, 6:56, 8:52, 102, 165.

Prophecy as the supreme language of the soul is a vehicle by which the Creator instructs His people. Those gifted with prophetic talent are by their very presence performing the role of teacher and guide to the community, no matter how quiet or robust their public standing.

The Rambam explains that a prophet's unusual capacity to hear the word of God through the various faculties of perception results from the combination of a strong intellect and a vigorous imagination. Prophecy is the overflow of the presence of the Holy One to an individual, group, or nation.[4] Required are both the faculty of courage and an aptitude for divination.

TORAH (TEACHING) IS THE BOOK

Torah, from the root *yoreh,* "to teach," is the Hebrew word representing the Book referred to in the name the People of the Book. Torah is also referred to as the Law. The Torah can stand for the first five books of the Hebrew scriptures or the Five Books of Moses, the Pentateuch, or all of the Hebrew scriptures, made up of twenty-four books. The word Torah refers to the written and oral teachings of Judaism that were handed down in an unbroken tradition. "Moses received the Torah from [God who revealed himself at Mt.] Sinai and conveyed it to Joshua; Joshua [conveyed it] to the Elders; the Elders [conveyed it] to the Prophets; and the Prophets to the Men of the Great Assembly. They said three things: 'Be deliberate in judgment; develop many disciples; and make a protective fence for the Torah.'"[5]

Torah gives instructions to us for becoming holy. Chassidut (the Chassidic movement) teaches that the Torah is the blueprint for Creation that the Creator authored prior to creating the world and is a guide for humankind's refinement. This divine map is contained in the Torah and understood through the Jewish spiritual science and art of Kabbalah.

---

[4] R. Moses Ben Maimon (Maimonides; the Rambam), *The Guide of the Perplexed,* part 2, chapters 36–38 (80a–80b), 369, 373.

[5] R. Menachem Davis, ed., *The Pirkei Avot, Ethics of the Fathers,* Avot 1:1, 7.

From the three-letter root (KBL; ק Kof, ב Bet, ל Lamed), Kabbalah means "a received tradition." The rigorous self-discipline it describes for the individual and the community who receive it can lead to prophecy as the natural outcome of attendance to God, love of others, and service in the world in a holy and selfless fashion.

Prophetic visions generally occur in fields and woods, by rivers and mountains—in places uncontaminated by the general population. Prophecy is how the divine will and presence are made known to the individual and the community. It serves as a way for the Creator to instruct and guide the created to come closer to Him and to help the created discern the relationships between the seen and unseen, the physical and the immaterial. Prophecy occurs in different forms and in different intensities. Ultimately, this holy speaking unites humanity and God. *Echad,* the Hebrew word for "oneness," is the process and the outcome of prophecy.

PROPHECY AND TORAH

"The most usual reason that God sends a Prophet is to admonish the people to keep the Torah." Torah is the "foundation of Judaism, without it, Judaism cannot exist."[6] This explains the saying "The gift of divine guidance is granted to those who teach Torah publicly, bringing the people closer to God."[7]

Devotion to God and God's Word (Torah) and dedication to teaching Torah precipitate the capacity for prophecy.

> Inspiration and prophecy are not mere psychological processes in which the human imagination constitutes the main factor, rather they are conditions in which man becomes the instrument through which God exerts His power. They are experiences that are as real as physical sensation, leaving absolutely no doubt as to their authenticity. True

---

[6] R. Aryeh Kaplan, *The Handbook of Jewish Thought,* vol. 1, 8:52, 121. This two-volume set is an anthology of sources on the subjects referenced in this chapter with an excellent compilation from numerous original classical writings.

[7] Ibid., 6:19, 87.

Prophets were therefore even willing to sacrifice their lives for the sake of their teachings.[8]

Prophecy and Torah are inseparable. "It is thus written, 'this book of Torah shall not depart from you . . . and you shall observe everything written in it, for then you shall have good success (Joshua 1:8).'"[9] The accurate prediction of the future and the ability to speak with and for the Creator are outcomes of a Torah-devoted life.

The body and prophecy are inseparable, just as the soul of the prophet is in partnership with the Creator. Prophecy is intended to correct behavior, predict the future, or avert danger from a threat to national defense or natural disasters. Study of Torah (the word of God) and practice of the art of prayer, the service of the heart, condition the body and soul to being a God-attuned vessel through which prophecy can occur.

The teachings of the Chassidic tradition[10] (Chassidut) reveal that God, being a total unity, has no needs but as a form of giving desires to see man's pleasure in becoming God-like. Self-refinement and right action are the hallmarks of the journey. The Torah instructs us about the creation of humankind on the sixth day of God's creation of the world. Our refinement and way to perfection is through closeness to the Creator, which prophecies highlight.

---

[8] R. Aryeh Kaplan, *Handbook of Jewish Thought,* vol. 1, 6:17, 121.

[9] Vayikra Rabbah 35:6.

[10] The Chassidic movement, beginning with Baal Shem Tov (1698–1760 CE), is part of a long lineage of holders of the Kabbalistic tradition. From Abraham's Book of Formation (Sefer Yetzirah) to the Torah revealed to Moses, we can see the progressive addition of holy texts serving generations with their ongoing development and understanding of the hidden teachings of Torah. Other texts include: The Bahir (Sefer HaBahir, or the Book of the Brightness); the Zohar (the Book of Splendor), ascribed to R. Shimon bar Yochai, ca. 120 CE); *Ein Yaakov* (The Wisdom [Eye] of Yaakov) by R. Yaakov Ibn Chaviv, 1460–1516 ; *Shaarei Kedusha* (Gates of Holiness) by R. Chayim Vital, 1543–1620; *Etz Chayim* (The Tree of Life), the teachings of the Arizal, or R. Yitzchak Luria, 1537–1572; *Mishneh Torah* (The Doctrine of Torah) by R. Moses Maimonides, 1135–1204; *Derech HaShem* (The Way of God) by R. Moshe Chaim Luzzatto, 1707–1746; *Likkutei Amarim Tanya* by R. Schneur Zalman, published in 1887); and *HaSulam* (The Ladder) by R. Yehudah Leib Ashlag, 1886–1955.

For almost five hundred years, the sacred teachings of the Aggadah ("the narration," referring to the nonlegal sections of the classical Rabbinic texts) were difficult to find in English.[11] The Aggadah addresses all the subjects of the Talmud, the central body of Jewish teachings and folklore accumulated over a period of seven centuries (200 BCE–500 CE), except for Halachot, the body of Jewish law. *Ein Yaakov,* originally written in the sixteenth century (1516) by R. Yaakov Ibn Chaviv and translated into English by Avraham Yaakov Finkel in 1999, is a compilation of classical and traditional teachings of the Jewish sages and rabbis.[12] For this book, I have drawn from this work extensively.

"Every Prophet has a kind of speech peculiar to him," reveals the Rambam. It is "the language of that individual's, which the Prophetic revelation peculiar to him causes him to speak to those who understand him."[13] As expressions of the outcome of living a Torah-centered life, the prophets and prophetesses are holy figures proving that prophecy is the outcome of God's Torah. Sometimes the prophets are not believed and their prophecies are ignored. Their own courage becomes the foundation upon which their prophecies remain intact and their record preserved.

Classical Judaism teaches that the Torah is the blueprint for God's creation of the world. This is why the People of the Book believe "the authority of the Torah does not come from any miracle, but from God Himself."[14] It is a foundation of faith to believe in the "eternal authority of the Torah." "Things that are revealed to us belong to us and to our children forever."[15] God's creation of the world is embedded in the thought of the world before creating it, and the steps for the refinement of humankind are contained in Torah. If the Creator wanted the

---

[11] The Aggadah is composed of the moral stories, history, ethical statements, and folklore of the Rabbinic tradition. It comprises about one third of the entire Talmud. See Geoffrey Wigoder, *The Student's Encyclopedia of Judaism,* 10.

[12] R. Yaakov Ibn Chaviv, *Ein Yaakov,* Chullin, "The Humility of Our Great Men," 773.

[13] R. Moses Ben Maimon (Maimonides; the Rambam), *The Guide of the Perplexed,* part 2, 60a, 2:29, 337.

[14] R. Aryeh Kaplan, *Handbook of Jewish Thought,* vol. 1, 7:15, 124.

[15] Deuteronomy 29:38.

created to become God-like, to have a personal or even a face-to-face relationship with Him as Moses did, did He not show us the way with His Word?

Baal Shem Tov (1698–1760 CE), founder of the Chassidic movement, teaches in the Torah that God concealed the light from the first day of creation. With this light, we can see from the beginning to the end of time. Studying and living as the Holy Book (the Torah) instructs redeems the world and makes our lives holy.[16] Prophecy itself is the most refined modality for communication between humankind and God, and few human beings attain it. But there are other levels of divine guidance and inspiration that are attainable to this day by all righteous people (such as Ruach HaKodesh, mentioned later in this chapter).

THIRTEEN PRINCIPLES OR ARTICLES OF FAITH

"It is a foundation of our faith that the entire Torah, both written and oral, was revealed to Moses by God."[17] This belief in Torah's singular authenticity is one of thirteen principles outlined by Maimonides (the Rambam) and known today as the Thirteen Principles or Articles of Faith. This credo, as expressed in Yigdal,[18] represents the classical beliefs of the historic People of the Book. It is the foundation of these beliefs that the divine Commandments were given for all times, that all generations are "to keep all the words of Torah."[19] It is forbidden to this day to add or subtract any portion, letter, or note of the Torah.

---

[16] Baal Shem Tov, *The Testament of R. Israel Baal Shem Tov,* footnote 24.

[17] The thirteen principles or articles of faith are called in Hebrew Shloshah-Asar Ikkarim. They were compiled by R. Moses Ben Maimon (Maimonides; the Rambam) from Judaism's 613 commandments found in the Torah and were published in Maimonides' commentary on the Mishnah.

[18] This is a portion of the prayer service.

[19] Deuteronomy 29:28.

Thirteen Principles or Articles of Faith
(Shloshah-Asar Ikkarim)[20]

1. I believe with complete (perfect) faith that the Creator, Blessed is His Name, creates and guides all creatures, and that He alone made, makes, and will make everything.

2. I believe with complete faith that the Creator, Blessed is His Name, is unique, and there is no uniqueness like His in any way, and that He alone is our G-d, Who was, Who is, and Who always will be.

3. I believe with complete faith that the Creator, Blessed is His Name, is not physical and is not affected by physical phenomena, and that there is no comparison whatsoever to Him (i.e. there is nothing whatsoever to be compared to Him).

4. I believe with complete faith that the Creator, Blessed is His Name, is the very first and the very last. (G-d is eternal.)

5. I believe with complete faith that the Creator, Blessed is His Name—to Him alone is it proper to pray and it is not proper to pray to any other.

6. I believe with complete faith that the words of the Prophets are true.

7. I believe with complete faith that the prophecy of Moses, our teacher, peace be upon him, was true, and that he was the father of the Prophets—both those that preceded him and those who followed him.

8. I believe with complete faith that the entire Torah now in our hands is the same one that was given to Moses, our teacher, peace be upon him.

9. I believe with complete faith that this Torah will not be exchanged, nor will there be another Torah from the Creator, Blessed is His Name.

10. I believe with complete faith that the Creator, Blessed is His Name, knows all the deeds of human beings and their thoughts,

---

[20] R. Nosson Scherman and R. Meir Zlotowitz, eds., *The Complete Artscroll Siddur.*

as it is said, "He fashions their hearts all together, He comprehends all their deeds."[21]

11. I believe with complete faith that the Creator, Blessed is His Name, rewards with good those who observe His commandments, and punishes those who violate His commandments.

12. I believe with complete faith in the coming of the Messiah, and even though he may delay, nevertheless I anticipate every day that he will come.[22]

13. I believe with complete faith that there will be a resuscitation [resurrection] of the dead whenever the wish emanates from the Creator, Blessed is His Name and exalted is His mention, forever and for all eternity.

These classical beliefs are the background associated today with Orthodoxy and are considered a reflection of all classical observant lineages held in common with the ancient People of the Book of the times of the prophetesses. By knowing them, we are given a better understanding of the lives of the prophetesses and the concealed spiritual tradition they reflect.

JOY (SIMCHA) AS A REQUISITE FOR PROPHECY

We are told that prophecy does not rest upon a person unless he or she is in a . . .

. . . happy, joyous mood, because prophecy cannot rest upon a person when he is sad or languid, but only when he is happy. Therefore the Prophet's disciples would always have a harp, drum, flute, and lyre [before them when] they were seeking prophecy to create the requisite

---

[21] Psalm 33:15.

[22] The Messiah and the messianic era are not the same as those of the Christian faiths. To better understand the Judaic messianic tradition and the teachings of the coming of Moshiach, refer to R. Moshe Chayim Luzzatto (the Ramchal), *Secrets of Redemption*.

emotional joy. This is what is meant by the expression in 1 Samuel 10:5: "They were prophesying"—i.e. following the path of prophecy until they would actually prophesy—as one might say, "so and so aspires to greatness."[23]

In Chassidic Judaism, which serves as the instructional background to this book, this level of joy—**simcha** שמחה: ש Shin (300) מ Mem (40) ח Chet (8) ה Hay (5)—is not the result of merriment, wine drinking, and frivolity, but of devoted love and awe of the Creator, observance of Torah, and the practice of performing loving acts of kindness.

FOUR QUALIFICATIONS FOR BEING A PROPHET

There are four primary qualities that every prophet must embody, reflecting attributes possessed by Moses. "R. Moshe Yochanan said: The Holy One, blessed be He, allows His Shechinah to rest only on a person who is strong, wealthy, wise and humble . . ."[24] Moses' strength we know in part from his setting up of the Tabernacle on his own and the carrying of the colossal stone tablets. His wealth from the remnants of the tablets, which were his to keep, the material being sapphire. How do we know that Moses was wise? Rav and Shmuel both say: Fifty gates of wisdom were created in this world, and all but one was given to Moses, for it says, "You have made him [Moses] slightly less than the angels, and crowned him with soul and splendor" (Psalms 8:6). In Numbers 12:3, we are told that "Now the man Moses was exceedingly humble."[25] A spiritual vision proceeds from sincere humility.

---

[23] R. Moses Ben Maimon (Maimonides; the Rambam), *Yesodei HaTorah,* chapter 7:4.

[24] R. Yaakov Ibn Chaviv, *Ein Yaakov,* Nedarim, 404.

[25] Ibid., 404–5.

WHO WAS A PROPHET OR PROPHETESS?

In the Kabbalistic writings, the woman is endowed by the Creator with extra Binah, the capacity for understanding, making it possible for numerous women to have divine insight, but only seven women are called prophetesses: ". . . Sarah, Miriam, Devorah, Chanah, Avigail, Chuldah and Esther."[27] Only those whose record of prophecy is written in holy works of the Tanach (the Five Books of Moses or the Torah, the Prophets, and Writings) and whose texts of attestation are apparent and

TIME LINE OF THE PEOPLE OF THE BOOK[26]

Time in World History (Gregorian Calendar)	Historical Age	Occurrence for People of the Book
8000–4000 BCE	Neolithic period	3761 BCE: creation of the world
3150–2900 BCE	Early Bronze Age 1	
2900–2600 BCE	Early Bronze Age 2	
2600–2300 BCE	Early Bronze Age 3	
2200–1950 BCE	Middle Bronze Age 1	2000–1500 BCE: pre-Exodus
1950–1550 BCE	Middle Bronze Age 2	
1550–1400 BCE	Late Bronze Age 1	1500–1200 BCE: Egypt, Exodus
1400–1200 BCE	Late Bronze Age 2	
1200–1000 BCE	Iron Age 1	1200–1050 BCE: Hebrew settlements in the land of Israel
1000–586 BCE	Iron Age 2	1050–920 BCE: period of kings
		586 BCE: destruction of the First Temple
536–142 BCE	Persian and Hellenistic Age	516 BCE:dedication of the completion of the Second Temple

[26] *Encyclopedia Judaica*, charts on pages 766–67.

whom the Torah and other holy writings identify as being so are prophetesses. While the matriarchs and other women showed the ability to perceive what was unseen and in some instances communicated with God's messengers, they are not called prophetesses. Finally, prophetesses (and prophets) were judged by the people for their clarity and explanations of what they had seen or been told, and, most important, by whether their prophecies came true.

The Jewish calendar in use today, according to tradition, was adopted by Adam HaRishon (Adam, the first man) and passed down through the ages. It places the creation of the world in 3761 BCE and the creation of Adam and Eve on the sixth day of Creation. The lives of the seven Jewish prophetesses span fifteen hundred years, beginning with Sarah's life (1802–1675 BCE) in the Middle Bronze Age and ending with Esther's life (ca. 420–355 BCE) in the Persian period. The year 2008 CE is comparable to the year 5768 on the Jewish calendar.[28]

THE ROLE OF PROPHETS AND PROPHETESSES IN THE COMMUNITY

The biblical people turned to their prophets and prophetesses to know God's will for their own lives. These visionaries made communication possible with the one God. Highly treasured by commoner and king alike, the prophets were spiritual nobility; they were mystics who had good insights and were wise and who reasoned well. Their very presence was as much a part of their role as the teachings that were given through them. The prophets and prophetesses told the future, pointed to the dangers of past and present, and gave others hope and faith in the meaning of life. They helped interpret both world affairs and personal predicaments. They were the holy speakers, the mouthpieces of the Creator who were selected by God alone but who were tested by humans: They were judged by whether their prophecies came to be.

---

[27] Megillah 14a.

[28] The many theories concerning these calculations are not included in the scope of this book.

TIME LINE OF THE SEVEN PROPHETESSES

Event	Jewish Calendar[29]	Gregorian Calendar
Sarah		
Birth–death	1958–2085	1802–1675 BCE, Middle Bronze Age
Birth of Yitzchak	2048	1712 BCE
Miriam		
Birth–death	2362–2487	1398–1273 BCE, Late Bronze Age
Exodus from Egypt	2448	1312 BCE
People of the Book enter the land of Israel	2488	1272 BCE
Devorah		
Period of rule	2636–2676	1124–1084 BCE, Iron Age 1
Chanah		
Birth	2702	1058 BCE, Iron Age 2
Prayer at Shiloh	2831	929 BCE
Birth of Shmuel	2832	928 BCE
Avigail		
David (birth–death)	2854–2924	906–836 BCE, Iron Age 2
David's rule	2884–2924	876–836 BCE
Chuldah		
Prophecy	3303	457 BCE, monarchical period, Iron Age 2
Esther		
Feast of Achashverosh	3395	365 BCE, Persian period
Esther crowned Queen	3398	362 BCE
Purim	3405	355 BCE

[29] These dates were compiled by R. Noah Shavrick for this publication. Not all of the prophetesses' births and deaths are known, but dates of significant events in their lives are recorded and sometimes we are told the number of years that they lived.

The Rambam describes how a prophet's reliability was tested:

Therefore, if a person whose [progress] in the service of God makes him fit for prophecy arises [and claims to be a Prophet]—if he does not intend to add [to] or diminish [the Torah], but rather to serve God through the Mitzvot [divine Commandments] of Torah—we don't tell him: "split the sea for us, revive the dead, or the like, and then we will believe in you." Instead we tell him, "If you are a Prophet, tell us what will happen in the future." He makes his statements and we wait to see whether [his prophecy] comes to fruition or not. Should even a minute particular of his "prophecy" not materialize, he is surely a false Prophet. If his entire prophecy materializes, we should consider him a true [Prophet].[30]

A prophet's negative edicts were listened to if he was reliable in past positive predictions, yet people were not to change their lives based on a negative prophetic edict unless they were in counsel with the sages of the time. *Teshuvah,* repentance and change of our conduct, can nullify negative predictions.

In addition to tests of accuracy given in order for a person to secure the title of prophet, when an accepted prophet declared another person a prophet—as Moses did Joshua—the people are to accept the designated prophet.[31] Also, "once a Prophet has made known his prophecy, and his words have proven true time after time, if he continues in the path of prophecy, it is forbidden to doubt him or to question the truth of his prophecy."[32] In addition, a prophet was forbidden "to disregard his own prophecy . . . [or] to withhold a public message entrusted to him by God. If a Prophet does either, he is worthy of death."[33]

---

[30] R. Moses Ben Maimon (Maimonides; the Rambam), *Mishneh Torah: Hilchot Yesodei HaTorah,* 10:5.

[31] R. Moses Ben Maimon (Maimonides; the Rambam), *Yesodei HaTorah,* 10:5.

[32] Ibid., 10:2. See also Aryeh Kaplan, *Handbook of Jewish Thought,* vol. 1, 8:22, 156.

[33] R. Aryeh Kaplan, *Handbook of Jewish Thought,* vol. 1, 8:25, 157.

RUACH HAKODESH

During the time period in which all seven prophetesses lived (1850 BCE–350 BCE), prophecy was relevant in culture. Often, the prophetic talent ran in family lines, yet not all prophets were of equal ability.[34]

For prophets, the primary purpose of exercises and training in meditation, including the repetition of divine names and the chanting of psalms and prayers, was to "isolate the mind from both internal and external thought, leaving it perfectly clear to receive divine influx."[35] While these practices "were helpful, divine inspiration (Ruach HaKodesh) could be attained without them, merely through incessant and fervent study of the Torah. It could also be attained through deep meditation in prayer." As we will see with the prophetesses, Ruach HaKodesh (also called the Holy Spirit, which can manifest as the divine voice) often comes "automatically through a great act of faith or from the observance of a commandment in utter joy."[36]

Divine inspiration is the level of prophecy just above divine guidance. (The Talmud equates divine inspiration with Ruach HaKodesh.) Through Ruach HaKodesh, though a lower level than prophecy itself, an individual "can be aware of future events, as well as other people's thoughts."[37]

The last chapter of this book explores prophecy in detail as it pertains to the Shechinah, the Divine Immanence of the Creator. Without the Divine Immanence, prophecy cannot occur. Described in feminine terms and called the Bride, the Daughter of the King, and the Queen of Israel, the Shechinah is not a separate divine feminine presence in Judaism as expressed in many other religions' theologies. Rather, the Shechinah signifies the indwelling presence or Divine Immanence of the Creator Himself. The Shechinah is one aspect of the Creator when His presence is among us. Though some comparative religion writers might

---

[34] R. Moses Ben Maimon (Maimonides; the Rambam), *Hilchot Yesodei HaTorah,* 7:2.

[35] R. Moses Ben Maimon (Maimonides; the Rambam), *Shaarei Kedushah,* 3:8. See also R. Aryeh Kaplan, *Handbook of Jewish Thought,* vol. 1, 6:23, 90.

[36] R. Aryeh Kaplan, *Handbook of Jewish Thought,* vol. 1, 6:24, 90.

[37] Ibid., 6:17, 86.

refer mistakenly to the Shechinah as the divine feminine, the People of the Book regard God's being as one, not two. The Shechinah also stands for the word of God. All things are ushered from His Word. This is why some have called Torah, Israel, and the world itself the Shechinah.

In the classical teachings of the People of the Book, there are ten fundamental steps through which to progress before attaining divine inspiration (Ruach HaKodesh). Unlike prophecy, Ruach HaKodesh is attainable by any of us anywhere in the world, provided we are worthy of it. We are to assume that every prophetess in this book accomplished at least this. We are told it is how King David was able to write his Psalms and Solomon his Song of Songs. The classical ten steps of preparation are delineated in the Talmud and are explained in the Ramchal's (R. Chayim Luzzattos's) *Path of the Just* and R. Aryeh Kaplan's *Handbook of Jewish Thought*.[38]

1. Constant study and observance of the teachings of the **Torah** (תורה): ת Tav ו Vav ר Reish ה Hay

2. Scrupulous care (**zehirut** זהירות) not to violate a single law: ז Zayin ה Hay י Yod ר Reish ו Vav ת Tav

3. Constant diligence (**zerizut** זריזות) to fulfill every commandment: ז Zayin ר Reish י Yod ז Zayin ו Vav ת Tav

4. Living completely free of sin (cleanliness, **nekiut** נקיות) in thought and in deed: נ Nun ק Kof י Yod ו Vav ת Tav

5. Avoiding even the permissible when it may lead to wrong (abstinence; **perishut** פרישות): פ Pey ר Reish י Yod ש Shin ו Vav ת Tav

6. Purifying ourselves of all sin, both past and present (purification, **tohorah** טהרה): ט Tet ה Hay ר Reish ה Hay

7. Dedication to God far beyond the call of the law (piety, **Chassidut** חסידות): ח Chet ס Samech י Yod ד Dalet ו Vav ת Tav

8. Absolute negation of the self (humility; **anavah** ענוה): ע Ayin נ Nun ו Vav ה Hay

9. Loving God so much as to dread all sin and evil (fear of sin;

---

38 R. Aryeh Kaplan, *Handbook of Jewish Thought*, vol. 1, 88, 89.

yirat chet יראת חטא ('ירא): י Yod ר Reish א Alef ת Tav ח Chet ט Tet א Alef

10. Total negation of the worldly (holiness; **kedusha** קדושה): ק Kof ד Dalet ו Vav ש Shin ה Hay

"Once a person had completed all these steps, he was then ready to engage in the exercise of meditations (Hitbodedut), that were used to attain inspiration."[39]

The Bat Kol: Daughter of the Voice

It is also true that "a Prophet's first experience may be so negligible that he (or she) might not even recognize it as prophecy. The prophecy may consist of a voice indistinguishable from human speech, as in the case of Samuel. It is then very much like a Bat Kol,"[40] a lesser grade of divine presence, called the Daughter (Bat) of the Voice (Kol), through which many events in Torah were confirmed. This level of prophecy is a well-established phenomenon in Torah texts, and some believe it is identical to the Ruach HaKodesh.

Historical Occurrence of the Divine Voice (Bat Kol) in Biblical Times

Examples of the phenomenon of a divine voice are mentioned in the Talmud:

When Yehudah admits his involvement with Tamar, a divine voice announces, "You saved Tamar and her two sons; I will save your three descendants [Chanahniah, Mishael, and Azariah] from the fire": Sotah 10b.

A divine voice confirms Yehudah's statement that he was the father of Tamar's children: Sotah 10b.

Other mountains challenge Mt. Sinai at the presentation of the Torah, and the defense is presented by a divine voice: Megillah 29a.

---

[39] R. Aryeh Kaplan, *Handbook of Jewish Thought*, vol. 1, 6:22–23, 88, 89.
[40] Ibid., 6:58, 103.

"When the Children of Israel [accepted the gift of the Torah and] said 'We will do' before they said 'we will hear,' a Heavenly voice went forth and said: 'Who revealed to my children this secret that is being used by the ministering angels?'": Shabbat 88a.

A divine voice emerges during Moses' burial: Sotah 13b.

A divine voice in Samuel's court confirms that he had never wronged anyone: Makkot 23b.

A divine voice tells King David that he is unable to fulfill the biblical verse of "1 chasing 1000" in war because of the incident with Bat Sheva, a married woman with whom David had relations, and whose husband he sent into war, hoping to eliminate him: Moed Katan 16b.

A divine voice confirms King Solomon's decision as to who is the mother of a disputed child brought before his court: Makkot 23b.

A divine voice tells King Solomon that he can't acquire the forty-nine levels of understanding that Moses had achieved: Rosh Hashanah 21b.

The students of Shammai debate the students of Hillel for three years until a divine voice announces that although the words of both are the words of the Living God, the Law follows the students of Hillel due to their gentle humility: Eruvin 13b.

These examples show us that the Ruach HaKodesh (Holy Spirit) can manifest as a voice (Bat Kol) and is an expression of the Creator's presence and immanence, having a role in determining communal and personal life. Judaism accepts prophecy as a means of knowing the Creator's will. This acceptance is as pertinent today as it was for the People of the Book in biblical times.

ELEVEN DEGREES OF PROPHECY

According to the Rambam's writings on the subject, there are eleven distinct levels of the prophetic experience. Following are brief summaries of these identifiable and distinct processes in the Judaic tradition by which the prophetic experience occurs.[41]

1st Degree. At this level of experience, an individual is moved to great, righteous, and important action by the spirit of God and is referred to as being moved by the spirit of the Lord.

2nd Degree. Another force descends on the person or community and makes him or her speak about the nation (government) or divine matters while awake. It is said that in this way King David composed Psalms and King Solomon composed Proverbs, Ecclesiastes, and the Song of Songs. In addition, Daniel and Job composed their writings in a state of the second degree of prophecy. In cases of this prophecy, an individual or the community as a whole "speaks through the Holy Spirit."

3rd Degree. At this level the prophetic experience occurs through seeing images: Parables in a dream are made clear in the dream itself. It is identified by the saying "The word of the Lord came to me."

4th Degree. Here the person hears a parable in a dream without seeing the speaker.

5th Degree. In this case the prophet is addressed by a man in a dream, much like Ezekiel was: "And a man said unto me." In other words, an individual is aware of who it is that is imparting information, and this information is not in parables.

6th Degree. At this level, the prophetic experience involves angels appearing to an individual in a wakened state. It is often stated in Torah as: "an angel of God said to me . . ."

7th Degree. The prophet at this level has a dream in which the messenger is identified "as the Lord," as is attested by Isaiah's record.

8th Degree. Here the development of the prophet's clairvoyance and clairaudience increases. The prophet's revelation comes to him in a "vision of prophecy" in parable form, as Abraham saw "in a vision

---

[41] R. Moses Ben Maimon (Maimonides; the Rambam), *The Guide of the Perplexed,* chapter 45, book 2, 396, 403.

during the day." Here the prophet is not asleep, but is fully conscious and is shown a vision of parables.

9th Degree. Here the person's clairaudience and clairvoyance are equal—he hears speech in a waking vision.

10th Degree. Joshua at Jericho demonstrated this degree in seeing a man who addressed him in his prophetic vision. At this level, a prophet is awake and has a vision and is aware of being addressed by a human being.

11th Degree. The prophet sees an angel in a dream, as the patriarchs experienced at various times.

The Rambam has differentiated between waking and sleeping states and information brought by messengers and by direct communion with God. Some degrees of prophecy seem more attainable than others, making it easier to interpret the divine messages. For a more developed examination of the subject, turn to the Rambam's work *The Guide of the Perplexed,* from which this summary is taken.

R. Moshe Chayim Luzzatto (the Ramchal) teaches that "when God reveals Himself and bestows His influence, a Prophet is greatly overwhelmed. His body and all his limbs immediately begin to tremble, and he feels as if he is being turned inside out."[42] He clarifies that "the power of prophecy is therefore much greater than that of divine inspiration, even with respect to gaining knowledge. Prophecy can bring about the highest enlightenment possible for man, namely that which is an aspect of his being bound to his Creator."[43]

MOSES: THE GREATEST PROPHET WHO EVER WAS, IS, OR WILL BE

Tradition teaches us that Moses was unlike any other prophet. As it says in Exodus (33:11), "God spoke to Moses face to face, as a man speaks to

---

[42] R. Moshe Chayim Luzzatto, *Derech HaShem* (The Way of God).
[43] Ibid., 209.

his friend." Unlike other Prophets, Moses was always in a potential state of prophecy; he could therefore receive God's revelation at will. Numbers 7:89 says, "When Moses went into the Tent of Meeting [Ohel Moed], he heard the Voice speaking to him." According to Numbers 8:9, when asked an opinion, Moses was able to answer, "Stand by, and let me hear what instructions God gives regarding you." "Moses was able to receive revelation from God at any time and in any place."[44]

At the receiving of the Torah, all of those present reached a state of prophetic consciousness as they heard the same words uttered by the Creator through Moses, the greatest prophet of all. While it is true that Moses heard things others did not, they all heard simultaneously the word of God revealed through Moses. Furthermore, it is said that all present had no regard for themselves but only for each other. Their level of experiencing themselves as one body, as one people united in the experience of being in the presence of God, has been the testimony of the covenant between the Jewish people and God ever since. The Torah received then is the same Torah studied every day of every year by the living community of the People of the Book.

How the Book Was Written

Because we know that the Torah was given through Moses, it is interesting to find out how the People of the Book say the Torah was recorded. A variety of classical Talmudic and Kabbalistic sources describe the process.

> God would dictate each passage of the Torah to Moses and Moses would repeat it out loud. He would then write it down. God would dictate a paragraph to Moses, and then give him a break in order to consider it. These breaks are preserved in the Torah in the form of spacing, dividing the text into pieces or portions (Parshiot). Moses would transcribe each of these portions as a small scroll. Shortly before his death, he combined all portions to form the Torah that we have

---

[44] R. Aryeh Kaplan, *Handbook of Jewish Thought,* vol. 1, 7:11, 123. See also Nefesh HaChaim 3:14; Shemoth Rabbah 2:9.

today. According to another opinion, with the exception of certain portions that were needed earlier, the entire Torah was preserved orally until just before Moses' death when he wrote it all down at once.[45]

Another point of view states that "the entire Torah was given to Moses during two intervals. The first part was given during the year after the Exodus. The rest was given shortly before Israel crossed the Jordan at the end of the 40 years in the desert. Between these two periods, there was a hiatus of 38 years, during which no portion of the Torah was given."[46]

It is also said that before he died, Moses wrote by hand thirteen Torah scrolls. Twelve of these were given to the Twelve Tribes and the thirteenth was hidden inside the Ark of the Covenant.[47] Eventually the Ark was put in the Holy of Holies of the Temple, and only occasionally was the scroll brought out in order to check the accuracy of other scrolls produced. We can hope this holy original scroll is still preserved. It has been hidden since 70 CE and could be revealed at the arrival of Moshiach (the Jewish Messiah), the Davidic prophet king and redeemer who will assist God in bringing world peace.

THE PROPHECY OF THE COVENANT BETWEEN GOD AND THE PEOPLE OF THE BOOK

Prophecy is predicated on conducting our inner and outer life according to very particular guidelines. Because it is not just for the individual, but also for the world, it confirms the oneness of all creation. The Holy Torah begins with Creation and ends testifying to the greatest prophet who ever was, is, or will be, Moses our Teacher (Moshe Rabeinu). If prophecy is inextricably bound up in Torah, then the prophet and the art of prophecy can be viewed as the outcome of Creation itself, the poten-

---

[45] R. Aryeh Kaplan, *Handbook of Jewish Thought*, vol. 1, 7:28, 7:30, 120.
[46] Ibid., 7:32, 129.
[47] Ibid., 7:34, 130.

tial outcome of all the holy teachings of Judaism. Following the Book can produce the prophetic experience.

An observant life today is based on the same teachings given to Moses and the Israelites. The same words held holy and unchangeable as the divine word of God have not been changed nor, as attested to by the Thirteen Principles, can they be altered. Adherence to the Book can lead to union with God and the perfection of humanity, the final outcome and purpose of creation.

The covenant of being "chosen" obligates the Jewish people to self-refinement and communal refinement. It is a covenant demanding internal rigor and the performance of justice and charity leading to the manifestation of a holy nation. Each person, a nation unto him- or herself, is instructed to rely on Torah, the Book, and Kabbalah, the keys to the Book's inner or concealed teachings. Torah organizes our own kingdom or life in the world by giving our ministers (hands, feet, and mouth) moral direction. The observant person attempts to refine and elevate the king (head) and queen (heart) to wise action and to teach his or her children (emotions) total devotion to performing good deeds and refraining from all evil in order to bring into a coherent and humble expression the inner community, the holy family within. This self-refinement benefits the community we live in as well as making us a vehicle by which divine providence and God's will can be known.

Following the spiritual path shown to us by the prophetesses and the People of the Book in relationship to Kabbalah's Etz Chayim (Tree of Life), an outline of the spiritual worlds, which we will examine next, leads to hearing and speaking with and for the Divine Master, our God who is one. The prophetesses and prophets show us the way to holiness, acting as guides for the rest of humanity, testifying by their lives to that of which each of us is capable and for which we were designed. It is this process of self-development, of coming closer to God, that Torah and Kabbalah make available and that the prophetesses show us how to engage.

2

Kabbalistic Treasure Maps

Introducing the Correspondences to the Seven Prophetesses of Israel

To appreciate what the seven prophetesses reveal, a basic understanding of Kabbalah is necessary. The "map" on page 27 contains the majority of correspondences we will examine in the rest of this book. The numbers in parentheses next to the prophetesses' names are their numeric equivalent when their names are spelled in Hebrew using *gematria,* a system of number values assigned to each letter. For more on gematria and how these numbers have been derived, see the sections on gematria later in this chapter and in the chapters following this one. For now, because Hebrew letters have been used in conjunction with "English" spellings of these letters in chapter 1 and will be used in the pages that follow, the following chart shows these correspondences.

SUKKAH REVELATION MAP

The correspondences and relationships among the Sefirot, the seven species attributed to the land of Israel in the Bible, the prophetesses, and the days of the week were first revealed to me while I sat in my *sukkah*

HEBREW LETTER CHART

מ	ח	ז	ו	ה	ד	ג	ב	א
Tet	Chet	Zayin	Vav	Hay	Dalet	Gimel	Bet	Alef
(T)	(Ch)	(Z)	(V/O/U)	(H)	(D)	(G)	(B/V)	(Silent)

ס	ן	נ	ם	מ	ל	ך	כ	י
Samech	Nun	Nun	Mem	Mem	Lamed	Chaf	Caf	Yod
(S)	(N)	(N)	(M)	(M)	(L)	(Kh)	(K/Kh)	(Y)

ת	ש	ר	ק	ץ	צ	ף	פ	ע
Tav	Shin	Reish	Kof	Tzadee	Tzadee	Fey	Pey	Ayin
(T)	(Sh/S)	(R)	(Q)	(Tz)	(Tz)	(F)	(P/F)	(Silent)

(booth) during the harvest festival of Sukkot in 2004 (5764). Tradition teaches us that Sukkot is a harvest festival recognizing the miraculous protection of the Israelites during their Exodus. At that time, I was unfamiliar with both the Arizal's (R. Isaac Luria's) teachings on the Sefirot and the species and the Ramak's (Moshe Cordovero's) teachings on the Sefirot and the prophetesses. As I sat meditating on the seven *tzaddikim* (righteous ones) we traditionally invite into our sukkahs over the eight-day-long festivities, I saw the same pattern of relationships that the Arizal and Cordovero describe.[1] They were shown to me in a combined fashion in a momentary picture in my mind. In addition to intuiting what can be called the historic esoteric correspondences, I was shown a component, represented by the following sukkah revelation map, that served as the impetus for writing this book. It was not until a year and a half later that I learned from my blessed teachers, R. Avraham Brandwein of Jerusalem and R. Noah Shavrick of Baltimore, about the original sources confirming my "woman's intuition."

What I was shown in a single image is that when the prophetesses' lives are combined into a historical sequence, a profound description

---

[1] In the sixteenth century there began the custom of inviting the guests (*Ushpizin*): Abraham, Isaac, Jacob, Joseph, Moses, Aaron, and David are the seven guests welcomed. One guest is added each night until all seven are present the final night. They correspond in chronological order to the Sefirot of Chesed through Malchut in the fashion attributed to the prophetesses in this work.

of the process of development is revealed. This process applies both to individuals and to the global community and the world itself. The story embodied collectively by the seven prophetesses is suggested by the quality of each Sefirah, its purpose as taught traditionally, what is concealed in the narratives of the prophetesses, the Hebrew names of the seven women, and the places they occupy on the Tree of Life. The following sukkah revelation map shows this blueprint of progressive and gradual development as it was shown to me. Under each prophetess's name are descriptive words that, when seen in their totality, describe the revelation I had of the descent of God's Immanence into the history of the People of the Book. For instance, under Sarah are the words *seed* and *creation*. *Deliverance* appears under Miriam, *moral order* under Devorah, *spiritual order* under Chanah, *royal bloodline* under Avigail, *World to Come* under Chuldah, and *redemption* and *resurrection* appear under Esther. When the lives of the prophetesses are put into this allegorical form, as we know them from the Bible, we can begin to understand how the Tree of Life is a divine map for our own and the world's repair. The lives of the seven prophetesses of Israel seem to guide us ultimately on this archetypal and universal journey. They teach us about the properties of the Divine Immanence of the Creator or Shechinah and how the Shechinah is experienced. The prophetesses show us how to unite with the Shechinah—the prerequisite to prophecy itself.

This map and teaching demonstrate that our own and the world's development is a seven-stage process.[2] They reflect the seven-stage descent of the Shechinah into the life of Israel. The story of the prophetesses' collective lives, when explored more deepy, reveals this cosmic map. In it we can see the story of creation and redemption to, ultimately, resurrection. This was the heart of what I learned on that auspicious night of Sukkot.

---

[2] See pages 52–54 in this chapter for more on the seven stages of the light's descent.

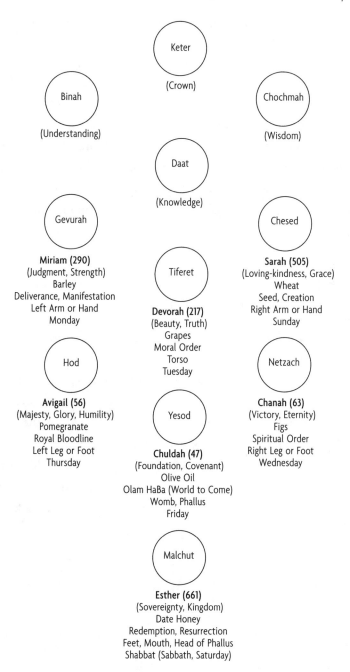

Map 1 (א Alef): Revelation map showing the seven prophetesses of Israel and correspondences (revealed 2004/5764)[3]

[3] Note that the gematria information included after each prophetess on the map was not in the revelation I received. It has been added here for the reader's benefit.

PaRDeS: FOUR WAYS TO INTERPRET TORAH

There are four traditional ways of studying Judaism's Torah. R. Avraham Brandwein[4] describes this traditional teaching in *Classical Kabbalah: The Hidden Teachings of Torah and the Zohar*.[5] He writes: "The Torah is divided into four strata, called 'PaRDeS,' the Orchard, an acronym for Peshat, Remez, Derush, Sod (Literal, Allusion, Homiletical, and Secret). Peshat, the literal translation, is the external form of Torah; Remez, allusion, is internal. Derush, homiletical meaning, is more internal, and Sod, Kabbalah, is the most internal."[6] This book uses a combination of all of these approaches.

THE STORY OF THE SEVEN PROPHETESSES: HUMANITY'S JOURNEY

In the Torah are recorded forty-eight male prophets and Moses, the greatest prophet of all. Though there were thousands of men and women possessing some level of prophetic talent, only seven women of Israel are actually called prophets (prophetesses). If the Creator does everything with purpose, why were only seven prophetesses needed for the development of B'nai Yisrael (Children of Israel)? Why did they come onto the world stage in the order that they did? What is the relationship between the seven prophetesses and the Tree of Life (Etz Chayim), a Kabbalistic "map" describing qualities every human and every world is made of and must refine?

---

[4] R. Avraham Brandwein teaches the classical Kabbalah of the Arizal (1534–1572 CE), from the writings of his father (R. Yehudah Tsvi Brandwein, z'tl) and those of his father's teacher (R. Yehudah Leib Ashlag, z'tl; 1886–1955). R. Avraham Brandwein, the Admor of Stretten, is a direct descendant of the famous first Admor of Stretten. His family tree contains almost all the great Chassidic masters, including the Maggid of Mezritsch, Elimelech of Lizhensk, and Levy Yitschak of Berditshev, who trace their lineage to Baal Shem Tov, the founder of the Chassidic movement and part of the Davidic lineage. Born in Israel in 1945, Rav Brandwein is the seventh generation in his family to live in Israel. His family settled originally in Tsfat, the city of Kabbalists.

[5] R. Avraham Brandwein, *Classical Kabbalah*.

[6] Ibid., foreword by the author.

During Sukkot, each night we invite one of the seven male leaders of Judaism—Abraham (Avraham), Isaac (Yitzchak), Jacob (Yaakov) Moses (Moshe), Aaron, Joseph (Yosef), and David—into the Sukkah, and each is an expression of the lower seven of the ten Sefirot (vessels of light) comprising the Etz Chayim. Could the prophetesses, like the patriarchs, have a similar correspondence, given that there are seven of them? Also, as indicated on map 1, there are seven species attributed to the land of Israel in the Bible: wheat, barley, grapes, figs, pomegranates, olive oil, and date honey. Do they have a connection to the prophetesses and the Sefirot? How might the seven days of the week fit into this correspondence system? This book is an attempt to answer these questions, for they were the ones I asked when I started my own Kabbalistic journey with the prophetesses.

Discovering some of the spiritual teachings of the seven prophetesses of Israel has been a humbling and glorious journey. This community of holy women can help us all work together for the betterment of the world and can lead us to experience God in our hearts and actions. The prophetesses show people from all faiths and traditions how to reach our greatest potential by integrating body, mind, and soul for the repair of the world through human refinement. The Kabbalistic studies of R. Isaac Luria's Tree of Life (Etz Chayim) and the ideas and traditions that come from this root are the tradition from which this book blossoms. Using a combination of traditional methods for our inquiry into the hidden teachings of the seven prophetesses of Israel, we discover that what is revealed in their collective story is the inner journey of every person and all of humanity.[7]

KABBALISTIC TEACHINGS: THE ETZ CHAYIM AND THE DESCENT OF THE LIGHT

Kabbalah is the Hebrew term for "received tradition," stemming from its three-letter root, KBL, or kibel (ק Kof ב Bet ל Lamed). It was an oral

---

[7] The Arizal, "The Lion of Blessed Memory," R. Isaac (Yitzchak) Luria (1534–1572 CE).

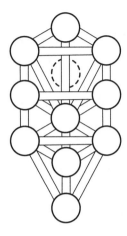

Figure 2.1. The Tree of Life, or Etz Chayim.

tradition for many centuries before ever being written down. It is the secret (*sod*) of the Torah, the Hebrew scriptures of the People of the Book.

Kabbalah's map is called the Etz Chayim, or the Tree of Life, and it is this map that guides us on our journey with the prophetesses themselves.

According to Kabbalah, there are ten Sefirot, or "vessels," differentiated from the light they hold. An analogy would be that a pitcher that holds water is different from the water it holds, yet the function of both is made possible by the combination of the two elements: a vessel and what fills it. According to the Arizal, "The first reference to Sefirot [singular Sefirah] occurs in Sefer Yetzirah [Book of Formation], an early Jewish contemplative text. . . . [It] describes ten entities that it calls Sefirot, which are instrumental in the creation of the world, relating the Sefirah to the Hebrew words safar (to count), book (sefer) and communication (sippur)." Later commentaries added the term for sapphire, brightness (Sappir), an additional meaning of the word Sefirah. These archetypal spheres of action are "metaphysical forces, luminous emanations, the agents of the Deity . . ."[8] in this spiritual blueprint. The Tree of Life is a lifetime itinerary for spiritual development. It is a guidebook for relating to God's divinity and His holy Word and for the refinement of the self and all of humanity.

---

[8] Donald Menzi and Zwe Padeh, *The Tree of Life*, xxiv.

Qualities of Each Sefirah

Here is a brief summary of the qualities of each Sefirah of classical Kabbalah and how we experience each in our lives. There are also numerous books available on the basic attributes of each Sefirah.[9]

> **Keter (Crown):** The light of illumination and the source of all life. We may experience this emanation as the "glow" that occurs in moments of mental, emotional, and spiritual oneness. It is the light of the Creator that flows to us through our body, mind, and soul. It is also called the limitless light (Or En Sof).
>
> **Chochmah (Wisdom):** Called the Father (Abba), wisdom is a type of whole knowing and whole seeing. We see patterns and relationships in a type of "vision" beyond intellectual analysis. It is the flash of divine insight people experience as a "peak" moment, one in which some great issue or question is solved by revelation.
>
> **Binah (Understanding):** Referred to as the Mother (Imma), Binah enables analysis of information, the ability to compare, differentiate, and synthesize various components into an articulated whole. It is referred to commonly as "woman's intuition" and suggests a type of second sense that is rational and intuitive at the same time.
>
> **Daat (Knowledge):** In some sources, Daat is given the attribution of Bat Kol, or the Daughter of the Voice, the hidden but knowable presence of the Creator through the Holy Spirit (Ruach HaKodesh). It is a combination of the quality of wisdom (Chochmah) and understanding (Binah) that produces our knowledge. Daat represents the knowledge we acquire from personal experience and divine guidance. It is not simply information, as knowledge is sometimes characterized.
>
> **Chesed (Loving-kindness):** Chesed is the impulse to do well, to love others unconditionally, to give charity. It knows no boundaries of its own and enables the expansive quality of experiencing all life as one life accentuating inclusiveness. Chesed requires its left-pillar partner,

---

[9] See Simon Jacobson, *The Counting of the Omer.*

Gevurah, in order to express itself properly. (For more on the pillars, see map 2 on page 47.) Just as a river needs its banks, we need to make boundaries for generous behavior.

Gevurah (Judgment, Strength): Strength and judgment proceed from our ability to discern the proper place and time for everything. Gevurah is a type of discipline of evaluation. While Chesed will compel us to act generously or to have an idea, to seed or begin a plan, Gevurah helps us apply the idea or impulse in a beneficial fashion. Gevurah without Chesed could lead to brutality, selfishness, and exclusivity.

Tiferet (Beauty, Truth): Tiferet is the Sefirah where five other Sefirot connect. It is the middle of the middle pillar and represents our ability to integrate, harmonize, and present our actions and ourselves in a beautiful balance, using all of our talents and attributes. As the balance of parts, it is synonymous with truth. This is the secret about truth: Like beauty, truth integrates parts, even opposite ideas, into a balanced whole. Beauty describes how we are to relate to others. Tiferet helps us bring out the best in every situation and person.

Netzach (Victory, Eternity): Netzach is our ability to endure, to apply ourselves tirelessly to some task, to put a plan into action and follow through with it. It is the way the willpower (*ratzon*) of a person is applied to life and leads to victory. Netzach shows us the Creator's tireless participation in the world and how our devotion to Him in any undertaking is what makes His participation manifest in the world of action.

Hod (Majesty, Glory, Humility): Hod is the key to our humility, to our ability to surrender ourselves to God's will, which is inherent in our lives and the world around us. This is the Sefirah that helps us nullify our egos. As the partner to Netzach, Hod keeps our willed action in the world from being overbearing or too demanding of others. Hod and Netzach combined allow us to give the world our ideas in a manner suitable to our abilities and in a lasting fashion. In Hod we experience humility in action, a type of majestic splendor.

Yesod (Foundation, Covenant): Yesod is the place of covenant or bond between the Creator and humanity. Yesod reminds us that all our efforts, indeed all our lives, express not only God's commitment to us, but also our commitment to His will. For a foundation to be successful, it must be built on the qualities mentioned in the Etz Chayim: love, judgment, beauty, enduring will, and humility. The descent of the light is an accumulative developmental description of a way for participating in the world.

Malchut (Sovereignty, Kingdom): Malchut is the physical world in which we live. It is our place of action. It is where the soul and body, as a united partnership with the Creator, use all endowments for the repair of the world (*tikkun olam*) and our own spiritual repair (*teshuvah*). It is a return to unity with God. Using as a totality Chochmah (wisdom), Binah (understanding), Daat (knowledge), Chesed (loving-kindness), Gevurah (strength and judgment), Tiferet (the ability to create harmony, beauty), Netzach (victory and eternity), Hod (humility and selflessness), and Yesod (our covenant with God), we are guided toward becoming holy humans. The stated destiny of the People of the Book is to become a holy nation, a light unto the nations of the world.

A Summary of the Sefirot and Their Attributes

Keter: Crown

Chochmah: Wisdom

Binah: Understanding

Daat: Knowledge

Chesed: Loving-kindness

Gevurah: Judgment, Strength

Tiferet: Beauty, Truth

Netzach: Victory, Eternity

Hod: Majesty, Glory, Humility

Yesod: Foundation, Covenant

Malchut: Sovereignty, Kingdom

CLASSICAL KABBALISTIC SOURCES
AND ETZ CHAYIM

This book uses a combination of already established correspondence systems that, when interpreted as a single story or a unity of parts, contributes to a deeper understanding of the lessons in the lives of the prophetesses. Kabbalah is considered a system of correspondences, and sages (Chazal) over the centuries describe the many ways the world is reflected through the Tree of Life of the Zohar and of Kabbalah in general.[10] The Great and Holy Arizal (R. Isaac Luria; 1534–1572 CE), a principal kabbalist in Jewish history, taught that the Etz Chayim is a guide to understanding all of Torah's concealed wisdom. The Arizal revealed a correspondence between each Sefirah and one of the seven sacred species that the Creator gave to Israel as listed in Deuteronomy 8:8: wheat, barley, grapes, figs, pomegranates, olive oil, and date honey. Map 1 and the chart on page 36 show how each of these species corresponds to each of the seven prophetesses.[11] R. Moshe Cordovero (the Ramak; 1522–1570 CE) revealed a correspondence between each prophetess and one of the seven lower Sefirot. The Ramak's teachings on this subject can be found in a book written by his benefactor and student, Menachem De Fano.[12]

THE SEVEN SPECIES AND THE
TEMPLE SERVICES

In addition to these aspects of the Sefirot and the prophetesses, there is correspondence to the seven species of Eretz Yisrael (the land of Israel) as taught by the great Kabbalistic master R. Isaac Luria, the Arizal

---

[10] The Zohar, a mystical interpretation of the Torah based on the Tree of Life pattern, was written by R. Simon Bar Yochai in the second century after he and his son hid in a cave for thirteen years in order to avoid being killed by the Romans.

[11] In *Sefer Halikutim*, R. Isaac Luria writes of the seven species of the land of Israel and the seven Sefirot.

[12] R. Menachem Azariah De Fano, *Asarah Ma'amarot, Ma'amar Em Kol Hai*. Part 2, Siman/Aleph, 54a–c, offers a correspondence between the seven prophetesses and the seven Sefirot.

HaKadosh (Holy Lion). Not only are these species the elements of Jewish ritual today as they were long ago, but they are also the agricultural products by which the Jewish people's lives have been sustained throughout history.

There is a beautiful text called the Perek Shira, or Song of the Universe, that contains the eighty-five songs of God's animals, plants, and elements. There is no agreement about the author, though some have credited King David, others King Solomon, and yet others the sages of the Mishnah, including R. Akiva.[13] There is also disagreement regarding who sings these songs. One teaching suggests that each creature and element sings its own song. Others say these are songs only the angels sing. Another opinion is that the songs were intended to be neither sung nor spoken but rather are implicit in each of the eighty-five created elements of God's universe.

In examining the Perek Shira relative to our study of the Sefirot, the prophetesses, and the seven species, we can find a song for all of the species except one: the olive tree and its fruit. There is a general song sung by all the trees of the field, but no single song for the olive or olive tree. Given the significance of the olive as the source of the oil that produces the sacred eternal flame in the Jewish Temple and the ritual tradition of lighting Sabbath oil lamps, this absence is a great mystery that I leave to the readers to explore. Perhaps it is because the olive tree (oil) falls in Yesod with Chuldah, which is considered hidden or concealed, and as such, it will have its song at the time of redemption. "In the future, with Moshiach," R. Avraham Brandwein mused when I asked him for his opinion on this mystery I had discovered. Some have even suggested that perhaps the olive tree was the Tree of Life in the Garden of Eden (Gan Eden) forbidden to Adam and Eve. Whatever the reason, Perek Shira has no song for this one holy species, but the other six species (wheat, barley, grapes, figs, pomegranates, and date honey) do have songs. The Perek Shira is a wonderful holy writing for people of all ages and of all faiths. Here, I have included the Torah source for the song of each species.

---

[13] R. Nosson Scherman, *Perek Shira, The Song of the Universe*, 6.

PEREK SHIRA'S BIBLICAL SOURCES FOR THE
SONGS OF THE SEVEN SPECIES

Prophetess	Sefirot	Species	Biblical Source
Sarah	Chesed	Wheat	Psalms 130:1
Miriam	Gevurah	Barley	Psalms 102:1
Devorah	Tiferet	Grapes	Isaiah 65:8
Chanah	Netzach	Figs	Proverbs 28:18
Avigail	Hod	Pomegranates	Song of Songs 4:3
Chuldah	Yesod	Olive oil	No song exists in Perek Shira for the Olive
Esther	Malchut	Date honey	Psalms 92:13

For more on the seven species of Israel and their gematria, see the gematria sections later in this chapter.

INTEGRATING THE ARIZAL'S SPECIES–SEFIROT
CORRESPONDENCE AND THE RAMAK'S
PROPHETESSES–SEFIROT CORRESPONDENCE

To the Arizal's correspondence between the species and the Sefirot and the Ramak's insights into the prophetesses and the Sefirot I have added the traditional correspondences of the seven days of the week to arrive at a basic set of relationships that can assist us in our daily lives throughout the year. When we combine them as a larger system of correspondences, other patterns begin to emerge.

The Sefirot and the Prophetesses
From Sarah, the first prophetess, we learn about Chesed, loving-kindness, the species wheat, and Sunday. From Miriam, the second prophetess, we learn about Gevurah, strength in leadership and judgment, the species barley, and Monday. From Devorah, the third prophetess, we learn about Tiferet, the species grape, and Tuesday and we experience liberation and the art of synthesizing—combining various qualities to make

a balanced harmony in society that reflects truth and beauty. Chanah, the fourth prophetess, and Netzach correspond to the species fig and Wednesday. She shows us how our endurance leads to achieving victory and how to pray and act as a holy partner with God. Avigail, the fifth prophetess, corresponds to Hod, the species pomegranate, and Thursday. She leads us in the act of selfless devotion and peacemaking, showing us the majesty that comes from humility. The prophetess Chuldah, the sixth, and Yesod correspond to the species olive oil and Friday. She shows us the foundational covenant we have with the Creator and His promise of our ultimate deliverance from ignorance and the experience of separateness. Esther, the seventh and final of the seven biblical prophetesses of Israel, is located in the Sefirah of Malchut, whose species is date honey and whose day is Shabbat (Sabbath). She teaches us how to reflect all of the attributes of the Sefirot into an integrated life as a sovereign person and world, leading to redemption from the oppression of selfishness to an experience of unity and closeness to God.

THE SEFIROT, THE ARIZAL AND RAMAK SYSTEMS, AND THE DAYS OF THE WEEK

Prophetess	Day	Sefirot	Quality	Species
Sarah	Sunday	Chesed	Loving-kindness	Wheat
Miriam	Monday	Gevurah	Judgment, Strength	Barley
Devorah	Tuesday	Tiferet	Beauty, Truth	Grapes
Chanah	Wednesday	Netzach	Victory, Eternity	Figs
Avigail	Thursday	Hod	Majesty, Glory, Humility	Pomegranates
Chuldah	Friday	Yesod	Foundation, Covenant	Olive Oil
Esther	Sabbath	Malchut	Sovereignty, Kingdom	Date Honey

A Guide to Daily and Holiday Reflection

Though we will not explore in great depth the implications of the correspondences among the Sefirot, the species, and how they relate to the days of the week and even the hours of the day, this book is useful for daily reflection and for learning more about specific rituals and holidays.

Kabbalah is not a philosophy; it is a description of the workings of the ten-dimensional individual and universe. The correspondences between the days of the week and the Sefirot can help us structure our lives in a pattern that is more attuned to the Creator's plan. They add another dimension to our observance of Torah during the year, in our daily activities, and provide a spiritual structure for aligning ourselves with the divine source. By reading each prophetess's chapter in this book on the day of the week to which she is assigned (i.e., Sarah on Sunday, Miriam on Monday, Devorah on Tuesday, etc.), the prophetesses become our teachers for the days of our lives. For example, the week in Judaism begins on Sunday (Sabbath—Saturday—is the pinnacle of the week before). Sunday is associated with Sarah and Chesed and the species wheat. On Sunday we can focus our attention and intention on the quality and *mitzvot* of loving-kindness, performing charity, or making bread for others. On Monday, associated with Miriam and Gevurah and the species barley, we can work at refining a plan or task by discerning what is good and what needs to be changed or rejected.

Another dimension of the Etz Chayim comes into our lives in a practical and spiritual way when we contemplate each prophetess on her associated holiday (see the following chart for holiday correspondences) and examine the prayers and blessings with which each is associated. If we also apply to prayer and study on holidays the progressive methodology of daily contemplation of the prophetesses and their correspondences, the prophetesses show us a universal road map.

We can also express these spiritual capacities by using the seven species (foods) in a more conscious fashion in our diet. For instance, based on the Tree of Life, wheat (Chesed) and barley (Gevurah) complement one another, just as figs (Netzach) and pomegranates (Hod) are a healthy combination. Olive oil (Yesod) is an apparent foundation for a healthy diet.

Using all the elements presented, the lives of the prophetesses provide a weekly guide for meditation, prayer, right action, and even food combining. Following the attributes assigned to each day of the week gives a spiritual correspondence to the planning of our activities. Following is a chart of correspondences for the prophetesses, Sefirot, species, major Jewish holidays, blessings, and days of the week. Though not all scholars

PROPHETESS–HOLIDAY CORRESPONDENCES

Day of Week	Prophetess	Sefirah	Species	Holiday, Prayer, or Blessing
Sunday	Sarah	Chesed	Wheat	Rosh Hashanah, Rosh Chodesh, challah, candles, Akeidat Yitzchak
Monday	Miriam	Gevurah	Barley	Pesach, Sefirat HaOmer, Mikvah, Tevilat Kellim, Vidui, Tashlich, Havdalah
Tuesday	Devorah	Tiferet	Grapes	Sukkot, blessings on wine, Hallel, Birchat Hamazon
Wednesday	Chanah	Netzach	Figs	Tu B'Shevat, Amidah, blessings on children
Thursday	Avigail	Hod	Pomegranate	Shavuot, Lag B'Omer, Modeh(Ani), Modim in Shemoneh Esrei
Friday	Chuldah	Yesod	Olive oil	Yom Kippur, Chanukah, Kaddish, Brit Milah, Kabbalah, Shabbat
Shabbat	Esther	Malchut	Date honey	Purim, Simchat Torah, Shema, blessings on a wedding, blessings on the Torah

agree on these correspondences, they reflect the content culled from the chapters of this book.

STAGES OF INDIVIDUAL AND GLOBAL DEVELOPMENT

The seven stages of Sefirotic, prophetic, and evolutionary development, which the combined seven lives of the prophetesses represent, are, in their entirety, a description of what each of our lives can fully express. They are a holy manifestation of the Creator's Kabbalistic map, the Tree of Life. Through the prophetesses we are shown the treasure map held by the People of the Book and are shown how to use it to understand Torah and ourselves. I believe it accurately describes personal, global, and spiritual reality.[14]

A brief overview of this developmental progression begins with Sarah as a representative of creation. Miriam brings deliverance. Devorah shows us right moral action. Chanah demonstrates right spiritual decorum. Avigail demonstrates true humility and commitment to a royal bloodline. Chuldah points to our inheritance of the eternal words of Torah and the World to Come. Esther reveals the promise of redemption and ultimately resurrection and what it means to be a holy human in partnership with the Creator. When all are combined, we inherit God's guide for becoming holy humans.

Stages of Individual and Global Development

1. Seed, Creation
2. Deliverance, Manifestation
3. Moral Order
4. Spiritual Order
5. Royal Bloodline
6. World to Come
7. Redemption, Resurrection

---

[14] We can call Kabbalah the original ten-step program and can term an understanding of the seven Sephirot as the method by which we embark on that personal and global journey.

KABBALAH: DECODING THE
CREATOR'S BLUEPRINT

The Torah is the Creator's blueprint for creation. "Blessed are You, God, our God, King of the Universe, Who gave us the Torah of Truth and implanted eternal life within us. Blessed are You, God, Giver of Torah."[15] Kabbalah's Etz Chayim is the decoding map for understanding the secrets of the written and oral teaching of the Torah. The map represents Adam Kadmon, the primordial man from which all of the worlds originate. "This Adam Kadmon acts as a filter through which the light of the Infinite is emanated," says the Arizal, "especially from his eyes, ears, nose, and mouth, representing the human organs of vision, hearing, smell, and speech."[16] Adam Kadmon was how the Creator engendered the four worlds by which the universe is structured: emanation (Atzilut), creation (Beriyah), formation (Yetzirah), and action (Asiyah). Our bodies and souls and all of creation function in these four dimensions.

That humanity is made in God's image explains why Kabbalah's holy map is a sacred tool for humanity's development and refinement. Each of us reflects this sacred pattern in our spiritual and material composition. Using Kabbalah for self-refinement can lead to prophetic union with God and His Holy Spirit, making our life meaningful, joyous, and full of peace.

Prior to settling on the Etz Chayim as a model for the gradual descent of the light from God, the Creator used a variety of methods for distributing His limitless light to the world. The Creator (HaShem)[17] emanated His light (*orot*) directly into vessels (*kelim*) below. Each successive vessel was smaller than the one above it. Unable to hold all of the emanations from preceding vessels, each Sefirah broke in succession. This resulted in what is called in Kabbalah "the breaking of the vessels" (Shevirat HaKelim), producing

---

[15] R. Nosson Scherman, ed., *Tanach*. Blessings of Torah is a blessing said in synagogue after someone reads a portion of the Torah.

[16] Donald Menzi and Zwe Padeh, *The Tree of Life*, xxiv.

[17] HaShem is a term used in place of the word God, and literally means "the name," referring to the unknown and unpronounceable name of the Creator.

the "fallen sparks" that are encased in the shells of evil (*kelipot*). It is from these kelipot or shells that all evil inclinations are derived.[18] The Creator's purposeful event (Shevirat HaKelim) created the opportunity for humanity to use its God-given free will for the repair of all sin. This is what is meant by "choosing good."

Elevating Good and Evil

When we do what is most beneficial according to the divine laws we are given, we elevate the sparks in that situation, person, place, or idea. Each of our spiritual missions includes elevating these fallen sparks of holiness wherever they are found.

> Man was given the task of rectifying all creation in maintaining all things in the state desired by God, man is serving God and doing His work. This is accomplished through man's actions based on the Torah and commandments that he was given. All of this, however, is based on the fact that man is God's servant, and was therefore given the task of rectifying all creation. It is for this reason alone that his deeds can have such an effect and he can thus actually accomplish this. The fact that man has this responsibility is called God's yoke . . ."[19]

. . . or the yoke of Torah.

The 613 divine commandments, the good deeds and blessings that accompany them, and actions we are to restrain from doing rectify the light encased in the kelipot or shells of evil in the world, transforming them, elevating them, and sending them back to the Creator. We live in a world of matter and spirit. The spirit of HaShem vivifies matter, materializing spirit, so to speak—and human beings, birthed into the world of matter, elevate the material realm by spiritualizing it. It is as though we act as an alchemical helper, having the potential to refine everything we come into contact with, and it is through this that even the good within

---

[18] For a more thorough study of the subject, read R. Schneur Zalman of Liadi, *Likkutei Amarim Tanya*, chapter 10.

[19] R. Chayim Luzzatto (the Ramchal), *Derech HaShem* (The Way of God), 297.

evil is elevated. This Lurianic (referring to R. Isaac Luria) frame of reference tells a story of the creation of humankind, its fall, and its ultimate redemption. The seven prophetesses of Israel prove these holy insights.

Lurianic Kabbalah tells this story of creation as a willed contraction—*tzimtzum*—of the Creator and the resulting single ray of emanation this contraction produced, which took the form of the ten Sefirot. According to the Arizal, it is from the ten Sefirot that there was made Adam Kadmon, the primordial man "who is the sole conduit and filter through which energy flows from the Infinite into the finite worlds that are destined to be created in the midst of the void."[20] The Ramchal (R. Moshe Chayim Luzzatto) posits that all of this work (*avodah*) of self-refinement leads to elevating the body itself. The body participates in the soul's eternal glory by choosing good in this world (Olam HaZeh), which will be elevated to a status of immortality at resurrection. The ultimate reward for this accomplishment and of control over our will and desires is in the World to Come (Olam HaBa). Torah and Kabbalah give us the tools for this ultimate purpose of perfection. All of the Lurianic Kabbalah stems from this foundation.[21]

Downward Flow, Upward Flow

The Creator's light flows to us in a progressive and gradual descent of the light (see fig. 2.2a, on page 44), allowing each Sefirah, or vessel (kelim), to hold only so much of the essence above it. The light that fills each Sefirah contains some of the light from every preceding vessel—but not all of it, which protects each Sefirah from breaking.

As shown in figure 2.2a, a little bit of Chochmah (divine wisdom, circle 2) is in every vessel below, but only enough to filter down to each lower vessel. It is for this reason that in Ashlagian Kabbalah (Kabbalah as interpreted by R. Yehudah Ashlag, a twentieth-century derivative of Lurianic teachings as taught by R. Avraham Brandwein in Jerusalem), the denser the vessel, the finer the light. The farther from the source of the original emanation (fig. 2.2a, Keter, circle 1), the denser it is and the more "materialized" it has become. Like a progressive stack of

---

[20] Donald Menzi and Zwe Padeh, *The Tree of Life*, xxxviii.

[21] R. Chayim Luzzatto (the Ramchal), *Derech HaShem*, 391–97.

strainers inside of one another, the finer the mesh (hence, the denser the vessel), the finer the particle that can be sifted through.

We find this same "flow" in the lives and stories of the prophetesses. In the personal teaching and contributions of each chronologically successive prophetess we can find apparent elements of the prophetesses who lived before her. One example of this progressive descent of qualities (light): Sarah, who represents the first of the seven Sefirot we will study (Chesed or loving-kindness; circle 4), lived for 127 years. Queen Esther, who corresponds to the last and most earthbound Sefirah (Malchut, or kingdom and sovereignty; circle 10), ruled over 127 provinces. Such likenesses show up throughout the lives of the prophetesses.

The Tree of Life (Etz Chayim; fig. 2.2b) is a ten-dimensional pictogram. As part of the oral and written Torah, it describes the spiritual and material human, representing the way in which the light of God and Divine Immanence (the Shechinah) reaches us. When we choose good, using our free will for its ultimate purpose—to make a sacrament of all life—we reverse this process and proceed from the bottom Sefirah, Malchut (circle 10), ascending by moving from left to right: circle 9 to circle 8 and so on, until we reach circle 1 at the top. Therefore, life, like the sap in a tree that invigorates it, flows downward from the Creator

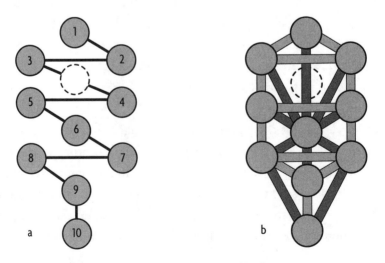

Figure 2.2. (a) A simplified diagram of light's descent,
(b) a dimensional model of the Sefirot.

and then upward in return. This divine energetic pattern is recognized in many cultures, as it is by the People of the Book. Free will is our energy pump, and choosing good adds to the world's perfection. Likwise, choosing its opposite—choosing to do evil—adds to its deterioration or even what is referred to as spiritual "pollution."[22]

This is a brief preliminary explanation of the mechanics of how our thoughts, words, and deeds elevate the sparks in the world by spiritualizing them through good intention and actions. It is also how we will eventually elevate the body to merit an eternal composition, like the soul it houses during life, and it is this thesis that serves as the backdrop to this book. The world itself is ultimately designed to be eternal.[23]

THE THIRTY-TWO PATHS OF WISDOM AND THREE PILLARS

While we acknowledge that the Creator has no form and that the Etz Chayim is only a symbolic representation meant for humanity's use, it is a design that helps us integrate into a harmonious whole our material and spiritual makeup of body and soul. The Etz Chayim is composed of three pillars referred to by the names of three Sefirot: Chesed (lovingkindness) on the right side, Gevurah (judgment and strength) on the left, and Tiferet (beauty and truth) in the middle.

The limitless light of the Creator (Or En Sof) is the source of vitality that fills the Tree of Life's Sefirot and illuminates all life. All existence—day and night, life and death, left and right—is dependent on the Creator. Kabbalah is the method for studying how light changes depending on the vessel it fills. All ten of the Sefirot are distinct vessels with individual qualities and functions. The lower seven Sefirot represent the articulated emotions or *middot,* which means "measured flows" in Hebrew and refers to the Sefirot as ten measures, telling us that the Sefirot are sources of vitality or measures of light. Each Sefirah also has a corresponding quality and body part to which our lives are connected in both the material

---

[22] The world's material pollution reflects humanity's spiritual deterioration.
[23] R. Chayim Luzzatto (the Ramchal), *Derech HaShem,* 393–96.

and spiritual worlds. Between the Sefirot are twenty-two pathways, corresponding to the twenty-two letters of the Hebrew alphabet, the Alef-Bet, connecting them to each other. The combination of these twenty-two paths connecting the Sefirot and the ten Sefirot themselves make up the thirty-two paths of wisdom (figure 2.3). The central column in the Etz Chayim harmonizes the left and right columns, which is why the middle path is regarded as the most difficult but also the most beneficial.

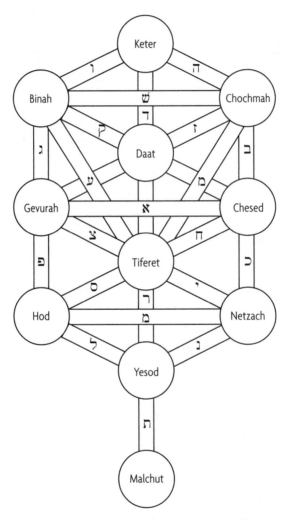

Figure 2.3. The Arizal's Etz Chayim and the Thirty-two Paths of Wisdom. The thirty-two paths are understood as the ten Sefirot and the twenty-two letters of the Hebrew alphabet, as shown here.

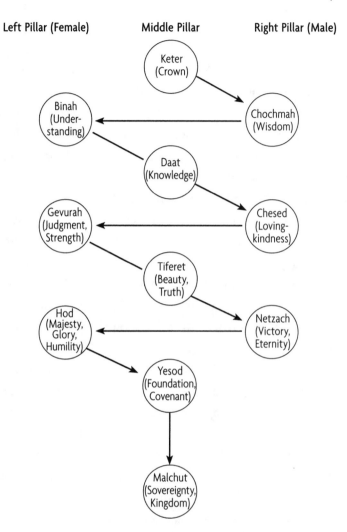

Map 2 (ב Bet): Tree of Life and the Three Pillars[24]
Note that on this map, the descent of light follows the direction of the arrows.

THE TREE OF LIFE AND THE HUMAN BODY

The upper three of the ten Sefirot form a triad called the Sechol, Hebrew for "intellect." They represent different components of the intellectual and spiritual realms and faculties we possess, contributing to our

---

[24] Donald Menzi and Zwe Padeh, *The Tree of Life,* xxxiii, from the Lurianic Kabbalah.

intellectual insight and our understanding and knowing of something. They also represent the faculties of seeing, hearing, smelling, and speaking. You will notice that one Sefirah—Daat—is the third element in the triad including Chochmah (wisdom) and Binah (understanding) when Keter, the crown and the source of all emanations (Or En Sof, limitless light) is excluded. Below the intellect or head is the body, represented by the remaining seven Sefirot with corresponding symbolic body parts. The Sefirot are divided into four levels, or "worlds": Atzilut (emanation), Beriyah (creation), Yetzirah (formation), and Asiyah (action). The worlds have correspondences in the realm of the soul's five components: Nefesh (soul), Ruach (spirit), Neshamah (pneuma or breath), Chayah (life force), and Yechidah (spark of God). The worlds, the Sefirot within them, the five parts of the human soul, the human body, our intellect, and our emotions are all integrated in Kabbalah. For a chart summarizing these correspondences, and for further information on the five parts of the soul, see the section in chapter 10 beginning on page 359.

Opposites are combined in Kabbalah and life to produce balance. The lives of the prophetesses embody the Sefirot's inherent purpose, drawing us to that balance. For example, we use our right and left legs (Netzach and Hod) to walk. The torso (Tiferet) connects the legs at the hips. In Kabbalistic studies, the middle pillar represents the synthesis of the other two pillars, though each pillar has additional unique qualities. Lovingkindness (Chesed, the right hand) and strength or judgment (Gevurah, the left hand) together produce beauty and truth (Tiferet). Victory and eternity (Netzach) combine with majesty and humility (Hod) to produce a solid foundation (Yesod). They are all reflected in the sovereign kingdom of life (Malchut).

Becoming familiar with each Sefirah's qualities, strengths, and purpose gives us a way to measure our own behavior. For instance, when we are asked to do something for someone else, we are told to use both our hands. This means that Chesed (our right hand of loving-kindness) should be combined with Gevurah (our left hand of judgment) to determine how to give, what to give, and to whom.

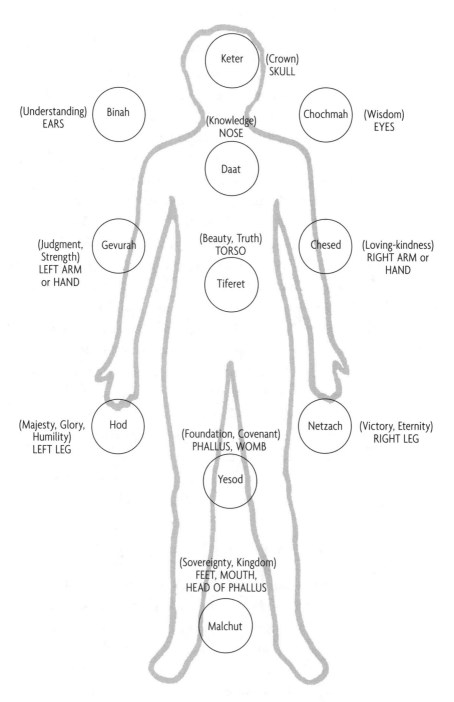

Map 3 (ג Gimel): The Body and the Tree of Life

THE SEFIROT AND THE FAMILY TREE

Also in Kabbalah, the name of the Creator— ' Yod (10) + ה Hay (5) + ו Vav (6) + ה Hay (5) = 26—represents the Partzufim, or personification of archetypal family members. Another methodology used in Kabbalah for describing the individual Sefirah of the Etz Chayim is to link each of them to different family members—these Partzufim (faces), personas, or roles (Partzuf) of the overall family group. While these terms are used sparingly in this work, they serve as a tool for readers who want to explore this aspect of Torah and Kabbalah more fully. Described by the Arizal in this fashion, the Tree of Life also becomes a pattern for understanding familial relations. Keter is related to the Great-Grandfather or Ancient One (Arikh Anpin), also referred to as Long Face or Patient One. Father and Mother (Abba and Imma) are the permanent male–female union of Chochmah and Binah and are often called "lovers" or "friends" in Kabbalah. Zeir Anpin, the Son, is also called the Small Face or Impatient One and is composed of the six Sefirot of Chesed through Yesod. Nukvah, the final Partzuf, represents the female as Wife, Daughter, and Shechinah in the realm of Malchut.[25] If we look at the Etz Chayim from this perspective, we can understand why we each reign over a kingdom, a particular life, and a body. We are all part of a dynamic cosmic arrangement of correspondences, making it clear how life on earth is a spiritual as well as a physical reality.

THE STORY OF THE PROPHETESSES

Now that we have examined the basic design of the Tree of Life of Kabbalah, its corresponding days of the week, seven species, and stages of personal and global development, a brief examination of each Sefirah's additional qualities and meanings as they are expressed by the collective lives of the prophetesses will support the coming chapters. This developmental story is the premise of this book: The combined lives

---

[25] Donald Menzi and Zwe Padeh, *The Tree of Life,* xxxiii.

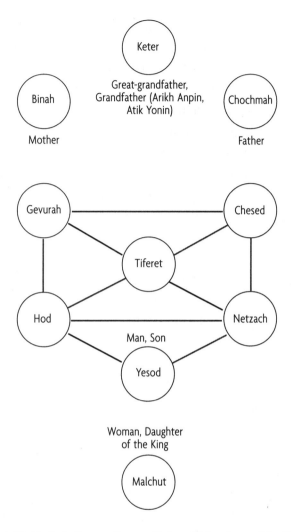

Map 4 (ד Dalet): Partzufim, or Roles of Members of the Family

of the seven prophetesses teach us how to use the Etz Chayim (Tree of Life). They are themselves the expressed manifestation of the Creator's Immanence (Shechinah) in its gradual descent into the world of B'nai Yisrael (Children of Israel) and the rest of the world. The prophetesses' progressive story describes the journey of every person's efforts toward living a holy life.

The Sefirot and the Shechinah are one. Accepting that all of the

Sefirot are aspects of a single entity, that within each Sefirah are qualities of all the others, then it is logical to view all seven prophetesses as aspects of a single form. That singular form is the Shechinah, the presence or Divine Immanence of the Creator. This embodiment is sometimes called the King's Daughter.[26] In his *The Palm Tree of Devorah,* the Ramak shows us that the Sefirot are the garments that the Creator wears in order to make His presence known to us.[27] We can say that the seven stages of development presented here are the stages in our personal and communal relationship to the Creator's divine presence, a description of His descent and our ultimate ascent. It is an ever-deepening manifestation of His presence and our realization and participation in His divinity on earth.

The teachings of R. Yehudah Loew of Prague (the Maharal, 1512–1609 CE) explain why we have physical bodies. In the spiritual realm, opposites such as good and evil and night and day cannot be integrated. They remain separate from each other. On earth, it is the human being that can act as a conduit through which these polarities are made manifest as a balance. It is the incarnate soul that presses the body into service to do some of the "heavy lifting" of matter, making it realized in the name of God. This is the same as elevating the fallen sparks encased in the kelipot (see earlier in the chapter). The soul and body in partnership elevate the spirit in all matter.

The following summary of the Sefirotic story of the prophetesses is developed more fully in the following chapters focusing on each individual woman.

Sarah–Chesed (Seed, Beginning): Every idea, every action, every relationship has its beginning. Our first stage of existence and hence the first stage in creating anything is conceiving it with the intention of love, just as we were conceived by God. It is important to endow these initiatives with loving-kindness. The Creator's

---

[26] R. Moshe Cordovero (the Ramak), *The Palm Tree of Devorah.* In this text, he examines the "Thirteen Supernal attributes of Mercy mentioned in Micah 7:18–20."
[27] Ibid., xii.

love for us is abundant, and so too should our love be for all of creation. The seed of all life is love.

Miriam–Gevurah (Deliverance, Manifestation): After we conceive an idea, begin a relationship, or start to work at something, the manifestation should include loving-kindness and discrimination. In manifestation we learn to separate the holy from the unholy. Our second stage of development is the manifestation of this love beginning to work on our self-refinement, to remove from our nature that which is unholy, making boundaries and limits productive to development in ourselves and in our surroundings.

Devorah–Tiferet (Moral Order): In the third stage of personal and global development, the individual joins with the community to create moral order, to have relationships built on love and holiness. Proper boundaries harmonized with considering the welfare of others makes a beautiful, moral society. In this third stage the Shechinah binds us together, requiring that we focus on integrating everything in service to God as a communal consciousness.

Chanah–Netzach (Spiritual Order): After we or society learn to conduct ourselves in a just and compassionate manner, we or the society must take the next step of group refinement into a disciplined devotion to the Creator. Just as the individual does this in Gevurah, the second stage, the community does this in Netzach, the fifth stage. In this way the community takes part in birthing Moshiach (the Messiah), in bringing God's kingship to earth. Spiritual discipline gives us the endurance to persevere in greater and greater refinement.

Avigail–Hod (Royal Bloodline): A group guided by love, holiness, and oral and spiritual discipline is capable of receiving the Creator's chosen redeemer. In our own lives it means we anoint our soul to guide us—the body is no longer the ruler but the servant to the presence of the Shechinah in each one of us. Through our humility, we merit becoming members of the royal family: holy humans. We are from the royal bloodline dating back to Adam and Eve.

Chuldah–Yesod (World to Come): At this sixth stage in a community or global life, recognition of the interconnection between the material and spiritual worlds makes it possible to prepare for a society reflecting attachment to the eternal and disengaging from temporal values. In the individual, this means completeness in serving the world and God and in being a connector to the holy covenant, which includes our redemption from ignorance and separation from God.

Esther–Malchut (Redemption, Resurrection): In the final stage of personal or community or global development, return is made possible to the source of seed and God alike. Here, the person or world group reflects all that has come before the final stage in the descent of the Creator's presence, the making of the earth person, or the elevated queen herself. The soul is anointed while in the body, making the body a vessel capable of reflecting back on the chain of development. All people who repair themselves and the world of which they are part can redeem the sparks in the material realm back to their spiritual root, completing the work, which in Hebrew is called *avodah* (work, labor).

WHAT THEIR NAMES TELL US

"Let their voices be heard" I was instructed that first night of Sukkot in 2004, when the map of correspondences was shown to me (see map 1, page 27). Using Kabbalah's gematria (the method of turning letters into numbers and calculating their value by various procedures) to explore the letters composing the name of each prophetess allows us to add remarkable insight to the lives and prophecies of these women. This system of analysis has its roots in Judaism's ancient esoteric history and the Hebrew alphabet's inherent multiple applications.

The Hebrew language is referred to in Judaism as the holy language, the Lashon HaKodesh. The belief of the People of the Book is that the Hebrew alphabet is God's tool kit for creation. The twenty-two letters of the Hebrew alphabet (Alef-Bet) are called foundation letters or, in Hebrew, *otiot yesod*. From these letters, Kabbalah teaches us that the universe was made and is sustained. The Book of Formation, or Sefer Yetzirah, one of the oldest Kabbalistic sources (accredited to the patriarch Abraham himself), says of the letters, "[W]ith them He depicted all that was formed, and all that would ever be formed."[28] The Talmud tells us that Betzalel, the builder of the Tabernacle and great-grandson of the prophetess Miriam, knew "how to permute the letters with which heaven and earth were made."[29] We also learn that Adam, who is sometimes called the first Kabbalist, was able to name all living things because of this similar capacity.

Names are not simply words to identify things. They are a series of holy letters. The very letters themselves are units of energetic uniqueness describing the function of each created entity. In Hebrew, each letter is associated with a common form: Alef is associated with ox, Bet with house, and so on. These are rudimentary symbols for their natures, and the Alef-Bet chart (Hebrew Letters and Corresponding Numbers, page 56) supplies this information, but their deeper and more profound makeup can be discovered only by studying them directly. Practicing the art of gematria affords a relationship with the letters, creating a spiritual discipline with great rewards. One of my teachers, Samuel Ben-Or Avital, suggests a meditation for twenty-two days on each of the twenty-two letters of the Alef-Bet. I did this: For twenty-two days I focused attention on Alef, and then for the next twenty-two days on Bet, and so on until I reached the final letter, Tav. This amounted to a commitment of 484 days meditating on the Hebrew alphabet—and such a meditation brings us into rapport with the letters and enables us to appreciate their interior natures expressed by their forms.[30] They are living letters whose presence affects the nature of every word. The quality of a word is also affected

---

[28] R. Ayreh Kaplan, *Sefer Yetzirah,* 2:2, 100.

[29] Exodus 31:3 describes what the Creator says about Betzalel: "I will fill him with the Spirit of God. With wisdom, with understanding, and with knowledge." (This means Chochmah, Binah, and Daat perfected.)

[30] For more such exercises, read Samuel Ben-Or Avital, *The Invisible Stairway: Kabbalistic Meditations on the Hebrew Letters,* and R. Yitzchak Ginsburgh, *The Alef-Beit, Jewish Thought Revealed through the Hebrew Letter.*

HEBREW LETTERS AND
CORRESPONDING NUMBERS

Name	Book	Cursive	Hand	Number	Sound	Literal Meaning
Alef	א			1	silent	ox, bull
Bet	ב			2	b/v	tent, house
Gimel	ג			3	g	camel
Dalet	ד			4	d	door
Hay	ה			5	h	window, fence
Vav	ו			6	v	nail
Zayin	ז			7	z	weapon
Chet	ח			8	Ch	fence, hedge, chamber
Tet	ט			9	t	to twist, a snake
Yod	י			10	y	closed hand
Caf	כ			20	k	arm, wing, open hand
Lamed	ל			30	l	cattle goad, staff
Mem	מ			40	m	water
Nun	נ			50	n	fish (moving)
Samech	ס			60	s	a prop
Ayin	ע			70	silent	eye
Pey	פ			80	p	mouth
Tzadee	צ			90	ts	fishhook
Kof	ק			100	q/k	back of the head
Reish	ר			200	r	head
Shin	ש			300	sh/s	teeth
Tav	ת			400	t	sign, cross

by where in a word a letter is positioned. The names that the first man of earth (Adam HaRishon) used in naming the creatures God had created were based on their hidden purpose and inner essence, which Adam could discern through prophetic insight.

Though there are twenty-two distinct Hebrew letters, we are taught that there were only ten instruments of creation and only ten utterances that created the world.[31] This aspect of creation is related to Kabbalah in that it describes the Tree of Life's essential nature: a combination of ten qualities through which all life is made manifest. In Kabbalah these ten vessels comprise the Etz Chayim, the Tree of Life, a patterned description of creation that, as we have learned, the world and each individual reflects.

HEBREW LETTERS TELL US ABOUT PROPHECY

Every letter of the 304,805 letters in the Torah is placed for a particular reason and is in a sequence for a particular purpose. It is inspiring to learn that originally the Torah was given to Moses orally, without any punctuation. All the letters of the Torah were in a long, unbroken chain in much the same way that our own lives are each part of a long unbroken chain of human development.

The Creator's holy language of twenty-two letters, the cosmic DNA, is what made all and what sustains and will make all. It is told in Chassidut that the Torah was created before the world, meaning that the Torah is the world's blueprint. We are also taught that the Jewish people were created to receive the Torah beginning with Adam and Eve (Adamah and Chava). When God offered His holy Torah to the world, all the nations rejected it. Only the Jewish people were willing to say, "We will do and we will listen," to which the Creator replied, "Who revealed the Angels' Secret to my Children?"[32] On the merit of Abraham, the Jewish people

---

[31] R. Yaakov Ibn Chaviv, *Ein Yaakov,* Chagigah, 342: "R. Zutra b. Tuvyah said in Rav's name: With ten things the world was created: With wisdom, understanding, knowledge, strength, rebuke, might, righteousness, and judgment, kindness and compassion."

[32] Shabbat 88a. A divine voice asked this when the Jews said, "We will do and we will listen."

were able to nullify themselves enough to become the guardians of this sacred and eternal blueprint. Preserving and living these teachings is the fundamental task and destiny of the People of the Book.

GEMATRIA: FINDING TREASURE AND SPIRITUAL ARCHAEOLOGY

Gematria's number system is a Kabbalistic tool for uncovering what is hidden in the letters of any name or word. Samuel Avital calls gematria "spiritual archaeology." After transposing each letter of a Hebrew word into its number value, there are numerous ways to calculate the letters' relationships. The method used throughout most of this work is called *mispar hechrachi,* and is accomplished by way of simple addition.[33] This classical system of gematria essentially turns letters into numbers and gives the student a variety of ways to research the meaning of those number values. This is a traditional method of revealing what is concealed in any word or sentence of the Torah, the concealed essence of all creation. The mispar hechrachi is one of the simplest of the gematriatic systems—it is based on the simple addition of each letter's value and is akin to a periodic table in chemistry. It gives us the keys to understanding the concealed nature of anything on which we focus. Using this method, we can discover what Adam, Abraham, Betzalel, and other Kabbalists could do naturally: see the deeper essence of everything. If the Torah describes God's kingdom or palace, then the systems of gematria provide some of the keys to the palace. Kabbalists have been using gematria for centuries to discover hidden (*sod*) stories concealed within the more apparent (*peshat*) narratives of the Torah.

Gematria works because names are vessels whose letters are qualities of energy. Each letter in the Alef-Bet is a unit of cosmic energy. The order of the letters affects what they mean. We will use this basic process of gematriatic simple addition to unveil each of the prophetesses in the chapters that follow.

---

[33] Gutman Locks, *The Spice of Torah—Gematria,* xxii. For a more comprehensive overview of the various systems of numeric interpretation, read the introduction to Locks's book by R. J. Immanuel Schochet, Ph.D.

How to Practice Basic Gematria

To practice the technique of gematria and make use of this book most fully, you will need the following tools:

- **English–Hebrew dictionary.** I use The New Bantam Meggido Hebrew and English Dictionary (New York: Bantam Books, 1975).
- **A cipher codebook.** A guide such as *The Spice of Torah—Gematria* by Gutman Locks (or a computer program that does the same) shows which words and expressions in the Torah have the same numeric value and where to find them in the Torah itself.
- **An English–Hebrew Tanach** (the Jewish Torah, Prophets, and Writings). I use R. Nosson Scherman, ed., *Tanach* (New York: Artscroll, Mesorah Publications, 2003).

Here are the steps involved in practicing gematria for a given word or words.

Step 1. In a Hebrew–English dictionary, look up any English word you want to study.

Step 2. Write down the Hebrew spelling in Hebrew letters.

Step 3. Look on the chart of Hebrew Letters and Corresponding Numbers (page 56) to assign the numeric values of each Hebrew letter, and then add all the numbers together. Example: **Sarah** = Shin ש (300) + Reish ר (200) + Hay ה (5) = 505

Step 4. Look up the total number (in this example, 505) in the *Spice of Torah—Gematria* or a similar cipher codebook. Listed there will be numerous words and their specific locations in the Torah. Select as many words as you want, though it's best to begin with only a few.

Step 5. In the Torah (Tanach), look up the selected words listed as equal to 505, and then note the situation in which the words or phrases appear. Example: The words or phrases given for Sarah include **gave** (Genesis 5:12), **shall you finish it** (Genesis 6:16),

given (Genesis 38:14), and **the wing** (Exodus 38:14). We can use these clues to uncover a deeper story concealed in Sarah's name by reading the text around the actual place in the Torah where the words or phrases appear.

This describes the particular process I used in researching the prophetesses, and it works for studying anything and everything, "everywhere and everywhen."[34] Here are the number values of each prophetess's name. In each of the following chapters devoted to particular prophetesses, we will explore the details of where some of the corresponding words are found in the Torah and what they add to our understanding of the spiritual teachings these seven holy women embodied and have given to the world.

THE PROPHETESSES AND ALEF-BET GEMATRIA

Prophetess	Alef-Bet Gematria
Sarah שרה	ש Shin (300) ר Reish (200) ה Hay (5) = 505
Miriam מרים	מ Mem (40) ר Reish (200) י Yod (10) ם Mem (40) = 290
Devorah דבורה	ד Dalet (4) ב Bet (2) ו Vav (6) ר Reish (200) ה Hay (5) = 217
Chanah חנה	ח Chet (8) נ Nun (50) ה Hay (5) = 63
Avigail אביגיל	א Alef (1) ב Bet (2) י Yod (10) ג Gimel (3) י Yod (10) ל Lamed (30) = 56
Chuldah חלדה	ח Chet (8) ל Lamed (30) ד Dalet (4) ה Hay (5) = 47
Esther אסתר	א Alef (1) ס Samech (60) ת Tav (400) ר Reish (200) = 661

Here is another example using gematria: The word for "love" in Hebrew is **ahava** אהבה = א Alef (1) ה Hay (5) ב Bet (2) ה Hay (5) = 13. A Hebrew word for God in Kabbalah is **Havaya** יהוה and is spelled

---

[34] An expression used by a teacher of mine, the late Terry Edward Ross, a world-renowned dowser, regarding the continuity of life, which is accessible to knowing.

' Yod (10) ה Hay (5) ו Vav (6) ה Hay (5) = 26. It is said that two hearts together are two in love: (13 +13) = 26 shows us that when we love one another, we experience the essence of God, which is love. This example shows how gematria is used as an interpretive art to learn the deeper truths in any subject we wish to study. This process makes it possible for anyone to investigate anything in the universe through the lens of the Torah as either a telescope or microscope.[35]

Other Words Have the Numeric Values of the Prophetesses

The following lists a number of words that share the numeric value of each prophetess as defined using the system of gematria outlined above.[36]

Sarah שׂרה: שׂ Shin (300) ר Reish (200) ה Hay (5) = 505

Gave, shall you finish it, given, the wing, you shall offer up, trials

Miriam מרים: מ Mem (40) ר Reish (200) ' Yod (10) ם Mem (40) = 290

Fruit of, your neighbor, fresh corn, bitter, and for a vow, stirs, awakens, the [red] heifer

Devorah דבורה (Deborah): ד Dalet (4) ב Bet (2) ו Vav (6) ר Reish (200) ה Hay (5) = 217

And have dominion, my errand, my word, the river, by a wind, they shall rule, and the mountains

Chanah חנה (Hannah): ח Chet (8) נ Nun (50) ה Hay (5) = 63

Prophet, sacrifices, free will offering, nations, as a lioness, we are undone

---

[35] The microscope and telescope analogy is from my private coversation with Samuel Ben-Or Avital in 2003.

[36] To find the words in Hebrew with their number values, see Gutman Locks, *The Spice of Torah—Gematria* 225, 138, 109, 29, 50, 18, 265 (beginning with Sarah, 505, and ending with Esther, 661).

Avigail אביגיל (Abigail): א Alef (1) ב Bet (2) י Yod (10) ג Gimel (3) י Yod (10) ל Lamed (30) = 56

And they knew, and King, your servant, and water, the angel, to your tents

Chuldah חלדה: ח Chet (8) ל Lamed (30) ד Dalet (4) ה Hay (5) = 47

His/its mother, unto him, to shear, the jubilee, to good, let dip, in the tents of

Esther אסתר: א Alef (1) ס Samech (60) ת Tav (400) ר Reish (200) = 661

Shall I be hid, their bones, your word, and you will bring down, the lamps

SPECIES GEMATRIA

The numeric values of the seven species of the land of Israel can be determined by gematria, both collectively and separately.

Seven Species (Shevat Ha'minim שבעת המנים): ש Shin (300) ב Bet (2) ע Ayin (70) ת Tav (400) = 772; ה Hay (5) מ Mem (40) נ Nun (50) י Yod (10) מ Mem (40) = 145; 772 + 145 = 917

In Deuteronomy 8:6–8:9, Moses reminds B'nai Yisrael that "[y]ou shall observe the commandments of God, your God, to go in his ways and fear him, For God, your God, is bringing you to a good Land; a Land with streams of water, springs and underground water coming forth in valley and mountain; a Land of wheat, barley, figs, and pomegranate; a Land of oil-olives and date honey; a Land where you will eat bread without poverty—you will lack nothing there . . ."

The seven species represent the fertile and bountiful Eretz Yisrael. Once settled in Canaan, the Jewish people were commanded to bring their first fruits (*bikkurim*) to the priests (the Levites). On Shavuot, the holiday commemorating the receiving of Torah, which occurs in the spring, forty-nine days after Passover (Pesach), they carried the first harvest from their villages to Jerusalem.

As we have seen, the seven sacred species have their counterparts in the days of the week, the prophetesses, the body parts, and the meanings attached to the Sefirot in which they find their home. Following is an explanation of each species as it relates to the People of the Book and the role of each in ritual Judaism. Also provided is the numeric value of the name of each species for gematriatic reference. These will allow you to look in the Torah for other words and phrases of equal value.

wheat חטה (Sarah–Chesed): ח Chet (8) ט Tet (9) ה Hay (5) = 22

> *Where there is not Torah, there is no Flour.*
> PIRKEI AVOT 3:21

Wheat is a symbol of settled agrarian life and was an export product of ancient Israel. Wheat is superior to barley and is harvested after it, from April to June. It requires a great deal of winter rain (equated with Chesed) for its growth. Wheat is primary in Judaism, in which bread is considered the staple of life. Not only is it the key ingredient for the daily offerings and the Sabbath bread, symbolizing manna and mercy, but in its unleavened state, it composes the Passover (Pesach) *matzah,* the symbol of the Israelites' hardship and God's deliverance of B'nai Yisrael from Egypt. Wheat is the main ingredient in most of the daily grain offerings made during the holidays and afternoon services (*mincha*). Some offerings are voluntary and others are obligatory, some are for the individual and some are for the community. Wheat offerings are mixed with oil and are baked in ovens, scalded in hot water, or fried in a pan or on a griddle. Parts of the offering were given to burn on the altar—these were called the *chometz* and were often mixed with frankincense, or *levonah*—while the remainder of the offering was given to the High Priest (Kohen Gadol) to eat.

barley שעורה (Miriam–Gevurah): ש Shin (300) ע Ayin (70) ו Vav (6) ר Reish (200) ה Hay (5) = 581

> *Bring before me the Omer Offering on Pesach so that the grain in the fields will be blessed.*
>
> ROSH HASHANAH[37]

In biblical times, barley bread was a staple of the Jewish people. Later it was replaced with wheat, and barley became associated with the food of the poor, suitable as an animal grain. It is the first grain to ripen in the spring and represents the season of spring itself. In ancient times, barley was reaped on the second day of Passover (Pesach) and comprised what is called the Omer offering, which included a quantity of barley to fill three fingers wrapped around it in a cupped hand.[38] The barley was then brought to the Temple. For forty-nine days between Pesach and Shavuot, individuals perform the Counting of the Omer.[39] The book of Ruth, read on Shavuot, takes place during the barley harvest. As an offering, it "symbolizes ascent, mourning, remembrance, spiritual fulfillment, transition and vulnerability."[40]

grapes ענבים (Devorah–Tiferet): ע Ayin (70) נ Nun (50) ב Bet (2) י Yod (10) ם Mem (40) = 172

> *Your wife shall be as a fruitful vine, in the innermost parts of your house.*
>
> PSALM 128:3

---

[37] R. Yaakov Ibn Chaviv, *Ein Yaakov,* Rosh Hashanah, "Two Loaves and the Pouring of Water," 243.

[38] Omer offering: From the second day of Passover until Shavuot, the Jewish people count seven weeks—seven times seven days—to refine themselves individually for the receiving of Torah as well as "to commemorate the time period between the Exodus from Egypt and the revelation of Sinai." During these seven weeks, each of the holy seven species comes into a critical phase of development. "Olives, grapes, pomegranates and dates come into flower; figs begin to develop; and wheat and barley kernels fill with starch. Their survival depends upon a balance of north and south winds. It is during this vulnerable period that the fate of Israel's harvest is determined." From Ellen Frankel and Betsy Platkin Teutsch, *The Encyclopedia of Jewish Symbols,* 123.

[39] Sefirot HaOmer: To find the Hebrew prayer for this forty-nine-day ritual, see R. Nosson Scherman and R. Meir Zlotowitz, eds., *The Complete Artscroll Siddur,* 312. For a more detailed understanding, see R. Simon Jacobson's *Counting of the Omer.*

[40] Frankel and Teutsch, *The Encyclopedia of Jewish Symbols,* 124.

Throughout the ancient world, the grapevines of the Holy Land were highly prized for their quality and quantity. Grapes remain a vital part of Israel's economy. In Genesis 9:20–21, the grapevine is the first cultivated plant mentioned in connection to Noah. Grapes often represent the fertility of the land. When the twelve spies returned from Canaan, it took two of them to carry on a pole a single cluster of grapes. Besides being a symbol of fertility, the grapes are what elevate all the other foods in a meal when the blessing (Bracha) on the wine is made. In this way, it is said that the grape and its wine are a symbol of God's blessings and our obligation to bless Him. They are eaten especially on the holiday of Tu B'Shevat, which celebrates the new agricultural season, the holiday of the first fruits. Grapes are also hung in the fall in the sukkah (booth or shelter used during Sukkot).

figs תאנה (Chanah–Netzach): ת Tav (400) א Alef (1) נ Nun (50) ה Hay (5) = 456

> *The Fig tree has formed its first small figs, ready for ascent to the Temple. Their vines are in blossom, their fragrance declaring they are ready for libation, Arise My Love, My fair one and go forth!*
> SONG OF SONGS 2:13

In both ancient and modern Israel, many homes cultivate at least one fig tree. They provide ample shade and sweet fruit twice each summer, ripening in June and August. In Genesis 3:7, the fig is the very first fruit mentioned. It was fig leaves that Adam and Eve used to cover themselves after eating of the forbidden fruit in the Garden of Eden. The prophet Micah (4:4) assures us that in the coming messianic age, we will all sit under the vine and fig tree, and none will be afraid. Figs are also a fruit associated with love, and in the Song of Songs they are featured as a gift to the beloved. Like grapes, figs are eaten on the holiday of Tu B'Shevat, symbolizing peace, redemption, and blessings.

pomegranate רמון (Avigail–Hod): ר Reish (200) מ Mem (40) ו Vav (6) ן Nun (50) = 296

> *As many as a pomegranate's seeds are the merits of*
> *your unworthiest within your modest veil. The Queenly*
> *offspring of Abraham . . .*
>
> SONG OF SONGS 6:7

Like the fig, the pomegranate is featured in the Song of Songs as an image of royalty. The fruit's outer shape mirrored that of the bells on the robes of the High Priests. The pomegranate and lilies adorned the tops of the Temple columns. According to the oral teachings as recorded in Talmud (Hagigah 15b), there are 613 seeds in the pomegranate, symbolizing the divine commandments (*mitzvot*) given in Torah. On the Jewish New Year, Rosh Hashanah, the pomegranate blesses the tables when we pray: "[M]ay my merits be as numerous as their seeds."[41] The pomegranate sits atop many Torah scrolls in synagogues worldwide, decorating the ends of the rod or staff called Etz Chayim (Tree of Life), around which the scrolls are wound. These finials are known as the *rimonim,* and most also have small bells attached to them, reminiscent of a priest's royal robes fringed by bell-like pomegranates. Like the grape, the pomegranate was shown to Moses by the returning spies as a sign of the land of Israel's (Eretz Yisrael's) fertility.

olive oil זית שמן (Chuldah–Yesod): **olive** = ז Zayin (7) י Yod (10) ת Tav (400) = 417; **oil** = ש Shin (300) מ Mem (40) ן Nun (50) = 390; 417 + 390 = 807

> *Like the scent of goodly oils is the spreading fame of Your*
> *great deeds:*
> *Your very name is Flowing Oil, therefore have nations*
> *Loved you.*
>
> SONG OF SONGS 1:3

---

[41] Frankel and Teutsch, *The Encyclopedia of Jewish Symbols,* 128.

The olive tree can live more than a thousand years, and thus it often stands for immortality and longevity. As a mainstay in historic and modern-day Israel's economy and diet, olive oil is prized worldwide for its great variety in hue and taste. Olive oil is also valued as the source of our spiritual light, filling the holy lamps in each synagogue and home. Additionally, it is a medicinal remedy and culinary foundation used internally and externally. It was the olive branch that was the sign of dry land in the epochal Noah story: The bird of peace returned to Noah's ark with an olive branch in its beak. Classical writings teach that this olive branch came from the Mount of Olives above Jerusalem. This may have an important connection to the two Moshiachs (Messiahs) that the People of the Book expect to usher in a thousand years of peace.[42]

The dove's purpose as a messenger of peace bringing the olive branch is a sign of the promised redemption. The oil of the olive (tree) is the shine of the Jewish teachings (Torah) and the hidden essence of Yesod. Like the seed of man that combines with the woman's egg to produce life, our willingness to have faith in the covenant acts as the womb for Moshiach's existence. We all draw light from this covenant or this promise as the illumination from the Creator. The People of the Book are like the olive tree, an evergreen that survives and flourishes in less-than-perfect settings. We are all tasked to refine ourselves, to amplify the light of our souls. The ego, pressed by self-nullification, is diminished in order to produce our spiritual light just as the olive is pressed to render oil. When we accomplish this self-refinement, we add our shine to the world and become more like the Redeemer's shine, creating a pull below or a vessel for the Creator's descent through a redeemer. Diminishing the ego elevates the soul.

---

[42] It is reasonable to suggest from this hint of the dove that it may be from the Mount of Olives that Moshiach (Ben Joseph) will present himself publicly as the predecessor to the ultimate and long-anticipated redeemer, Moshiach (Ben David) of the Davidic lineage, who will become known in Jerusalem. Moshiach Ben David's purpose as the ultimate redeemer and peacemaker for the world will be revealed. It is said that he will enter Jerusalem through the eastern wall of the city, via the Gates of Mercy, a double-arched entryway that is currently sealed.

(date) honey רבש (Esther–Malchut): **honey** = ד Dalet (4) ב Bet (2) ש Shin (300) = 306

(Date fruit is implied, so is not part of the total of 306 for date honey.)

> *I am my beloved's and he longs for my perfection.*
> SONG OF SONGS 7:11

> *The righteous shall flourish like the date palm.*
> PSALMS 92:13

The palm tree's great height and longevity associate it with beauty and fruitfulness. In Exodus 3:8 we learn of the land "flowing with milk and honey" and that this honey is the syrup made from the fruit of the date palm tree. Today, dates remain delicacies and an export item from the Holy Land, and hearts of palm are a Mediterranean specialty used worldwide. Performing good deeds or coming closer to God is likened to pouring honey from the fruit of the date palm tree. The tzaddikim, or righteous ones, are compared to palm trees (Psalm 92:13). On Sukkot, in the Tabernacle of the Booths, the unopened palm branch known as the *lulav* forms part of the four species carried in procession at synagogue and waved symbolically in the sukkah (booth or shelter). It represents our spine, which must be flexible and humble. Like the lulav when it is shaken close to the ear, our spirit sounds like the wings of a bird in flight. So should our love and passion for doing good elevate us to the heights of the date palm. The palm tree is often the herald of a sacred oasis in the midst of desert terrain, just as the Torah is our oasis whose sweet fruit confirms our relationship of love and intimacy with the Creator.

The Species and the Prophetesses

We have already discussed the correspondence between the species of the land of Israel and the prophetesses, but these can be examined further through gematria.

GEMATRIA OF SPECIES AND PROPHETESSES
SHEVAT HA'MINIM B'ERETZ YISRAEL

Species	Prophetess
Wheat = 22	Sarah = 505
Barley = 581	Miriam = 290
Grapes = 172	Devorah = 217
Figs = 456	Chanah = 63
Pomegranates = 296	Avigail = 56
Olive oil = 807	Chuldah = 47
Date honey = 306	Esther = 661

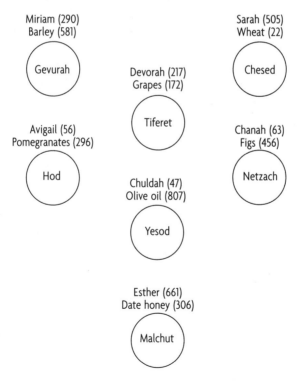

Map 5 (ה Hay): Prophetesses and Species Gematria

HOW THE CHAPTERS ON THE PROPHETESSES ARE DESIGNED

Now that we have reviewed the basic elements of some classical Kabbalistic maps and added new correspondences unique to this book, the majority of the remaining chapters will examine these elements in deeper detail as we focus on each prophetess.

Each chapter, 3–9, begins with the name and numeric value of the prophetess, her title, family affiliations, place in history, correspondences, and other elements important to understanding her. Other elements presented at the start of each prophetess's chapter include her associated holidays, symbols, rituals, prayers, text of prophecy or song, and the shine of the future that her life reflects. Also, for each prophetess is included her phase of development; life principle; world action; spiritual action; meaningful work; day focus; association with a particular species of the land of Israel; particular texts applicable to her, including prayers and portions of the Torah; and the teachings concealed in her name using gematria's number permutations. In addition, dozens of beautiful teachings from the People of the Book are woven into each chapter, composing the wedding dress of the Shechinah, decorated in the gems and pearls of Torah.

The following references are the locations in the Torah for the prophetesses' important contributions—their prophecy, prayer, or song, resulting from the prophetic spirit.

> **Sarah.** Genesis 21:10: ". . . the son of that slave woman will not inherit with my son." Genesis 21:12: ". . . whatever Sarah tells you, heed her voice."
>
> **Miriam.** Exodus 15:20 (the song of Miriam): "Sing to God for he is exalted above the arrogant . . ."
>
> **Devorah.** Judges 4:4–5:31: ". . . behold God, the God of Israel has commanded . . ." Judges 5:1–31 (the song of Devorah): "When vengeances are inflicted upon Israel . . ."
>
> **Chanah.** Samuel 1, 1:12: "God, Master of Legions . . ." Samuel 1, 2:1–10 (the song and prayer of Chanah)

Avigail. Samuel 25:23–44: "Let my Lord not set his heart against this base man . . ."

Chuldah. Kings 22:11–20: "Thus said God, God of Israel."

Esther. Megillat Esther 4:16: "Assemble all the Jews . . . and fast for me . . . then I will go in to the king."

THE BEGINNING OF TORAH

The Sefer Yetzirah (Book of Formation), mentioned earlier as one of the earliest Kabbalistic texts, instructs us clearly about the relationship between creation (beginnings) and endings, telling us that they are forever connected. As we learned in chapter 1 regarding the Ten Sefirot of Nothingness: "[T]heir end [is] embedded in their beginning, and their beginning in their end, like a flame in a burning coal. For the Master is singular, he has no second, and before one, what do you count?"[43] Because this book is based on what the Torah and Kabbalistic sources teach about the prophetesses and prophecy, it is relevant for us to examine the beginning and ending of the Torah, for they are profoundly connected to the issue of prophecy.

The very first line of the Torah in Genesis begins with the Hebrew word *bereshit* (creation), or "created six." The first sentence of the Torah in Parshat Bereshit 1:1–15 reads: "In the beginning of God's creating the heavens and the earth—when the earth was astonishingly empty, with darkness upon the surface of the waters—God said 'Let there be light,' and there was light. God saw that the light was good, and God separated between the light and the darkness. God called to the light: 'Day,' and to the darkness He called: 'Night.' And there was evening and there was morning, one day."[44]

This is how we are told the Creator began His handiwork in making the world. The same holy Torah ends in Deuteronomy with a description of Moses' prophetic stature as the greatest prophet who ever was, is, or will be. Here, in the final chapter of the Five Books of Moses

---

[43] R. Ayreh Kaplan, *Sefer Yetzirah,* 1:7, 57.
[44] Genesis 1:1–15.

(Deuteronomy 34:10–12), we read: "Never again has there arisen in Israel a Prophet like Moses, whom God had known face to face, as evidenced by all the signs and wonders that God sent him to perform in the land of Egypt, against Pharaoh and all his courtiers and his land, and by all the strong hand and awesome power that Moses performed before the eyes of all Israel."

If the Torah is the Creator's holy blueprint for all of life and living and in it we find every science and art, why, then, does the Creator's holy blueprint begin with creation and end with Moses' prophecy and a summary of the miracles of redemption?

THE END OF TORAH

Following the traditional guidance of the Sefer Yetzirah—the end is embedded in the beginning—we can see that perhaps creation and prophecy are bound up in each other, one being the beginning of the Torah and the other its end. Does creation, then, seem to be for the ultimate purpose of producing a humanity composed of holy prophets? Learning from the Jewish people's own journey toward refinement, we wonder if these prophets will also fulfill God's plan of perfection. Is the state of prophecy our natural and divine inheritance, our natural state of being in the world, albeit a degree less than that of Moses? On an individual level, the guidance that the end is embedded in the beginning tells us to be mindful of all our beginnings. Our intentions in performing any action are like seeds being planted in the material world, watered and tended by our will. The ends, therefore, are concealed in the beginnings. A fundamental goal of esoteric Judaism is to understand the material world—why and how things manifest—as well as to create a better understanding of the relationships between the material and spiritual realms. We should look at the beginnings and endings of things, or at least try to estimate the potential outcomes of our efforts. Ultimately, though, we surrender what comes of our good actions to God.

If the Torah teaches us that prophecy is the natural outcome of creation and of the human experience, then the descent of spirit into matter serves as a training ground for the God-like human. Will humankind's redemption herald its resurrection, making the soul and the body eternal? If prophecy contributes to our redemption, the ending of our exile, our separateness from the Creator, was the founding of the State of Israel in 1948 the beginning of the end? Did Esther, like all the other prophetesses, point to this in prophecy?

BEGINNINGS AND ENDINGS: A KEY TO KABBALAH AND PROPHECY

Each of our own lives in the physical world begins with the birth of the physical body and ends with the body's death, making our beginnings and endings connected by the living that takes place between them. Our physical births can be seen as the original exile from the Creator, a separation that in itself is likened to a form of death. On the other hand, when the physical body has fulfilled its purpose of acting as a vessel for the soul's journey on Earth and it perishes, it is considered a rebirth into the spiritual domicile. The physical and spiritual worlds are interconnected at one end of the spectrum, being representative of birth, and at the other, its polar opposite, being a station of death. As this book suggests, together the ultimate outcome of such a journey is what the People of the Book refer to as both immortality and resurrection. This will be discussed further in the chapters on Chuldah and Esther.

Our bodies and souls are both beginnings and endings, partners through which God and humankind are united. In the story of the prophetesses, Sarah begins what Esther completes. What begins in Chesed (Sunday, Seed, Wheat, Loving-kindness) ends in Malchut (Sabbath, Redemption, Date Honey, and the Kingdom). Just as life (creation), our beginning, is one kind of descent, at our death we begin the ascent back up the "ladder of light," using the Zohar's classical term for the Tree of Life (Etz Chayim), to reunite with the Or En Sof, from which all emanates. In this sense, at the death of the physical body, we experience prophecy, knowing unity with God. Prophecy is the death of the ego and redemption is the death of identifying ourselves as the body. In revelation we can see the beginning of time by the light of creation reflected from the end.[45]

With our Kabbalistic treasure maps and sacred Torah in hand, let us join the seven women of prophecy as they guide us in the seven stages of development in God's perfect design, of which we and the world are part.

---

[45] Berachot 57b. "There are five things considered one sixtieth of something else, namely fire, honey, Shabbat, sleep, and a dream. Fire is one sixtieth of Gehinnom (hell). [The pain caused by a burn is only one sixtieth of the anguish of Gehinnom.] Honey is one sixtieth of manna, Shabbat is one sixtieth of the delight in the World to Come. Sleep is one sixtieth of death. A dream is one sixtieth of prophecy." Included in this framework is the mysterious subject of resurrection, which suggests a revival of the dead. Does this mean a revival of those dead to Torah? Does it suggest that the bones of the dead will have, through prophecy, as some texts suggest, the addition of sinew and flesh? The subject is a deep mystery in Kabbalah that the Sefirah of Malchut holds.

3
Sarah
Chesed · The Seed of Life Is Love

I will bless her and she shall give rise to nations; kings of peoples will rise from her.

GENESIS 17:15

Sarah שרה

ש Shin (300) ר Reish (200) ה Hay (5) = 505

Sefirah Correspondence: Chesed

Titles: Matriarch and First Prophetess, Keeper of the First Tent of Holiness

Family: Daughter of Haran, wife of Abraham (Avraham), mother of Isaac (Yitzchak), grandmother of Jacob (Yaakov)

Time Period	Jewish Calendar	Gregorian Calendar
Life (birth–death)	1958–2085	1802–1675 BCE
Birth of Isaac	2048	1712 BCE

Developmental Stage: Seed

Day: Sunday

Sacred Species: Wheat

Body Correspondence: Right arm or hand

Rituals: Making challah, Mikvah

Holidays: Rosh Chodesh (New Moon), Rosh Hashanah (New Year)

Symbols: Hovering cloud of glory, tent, Sabbath candles

Prayers: Lighting Sabbath candles, the Akeidat Yitzchak

Shine of Sarah–Chesed: The promise of the conception of Moshiach or the messianic age

Prophecy Source: Genesis 21:10, ". . . the son of that slave woman will not inherit with my son." Genesis 21:12 ". . . whatever Sarah tells you, heed her voice."

SEFIRAH: CHESED

The first in the constellation of the Sefirot referred to as the emotions, or *middot* (in Hebrew), Chesed (Sarah) receives its shine directly from Binah (understanding) before it on the left pillar and Chochmah (wisdom) above it on the right pillar. Chesed illuminates Daat, Gevurah, Tiferet, and Netzach in the descent of the Tree. Representing the right pillar and also called Chesed, the Sefirah, like the matriarch Sarah, is the first in a dynamic group of Sefirot.[1]

Phase of Development: Holy creation begins in love. Anything that is birthed properly—a child, an idea, an undertaking—should be conceived with this feeling. Sunday, the beginning of the new week, is illuminated by Shabbat, making it conducive to selflessness. The seed of life is love.

Life Principle: Sarah teaches us that loving-kindness added to everything we do is the spiritual root of life. Beginnings guided by selfless intention bring the greatest reward.

World Action: Sarah as Chesed demonstrates generosity, hospitality, and

---

[1] The triad made by Chesed (Sarah), Gevurah (Miriam), and Tiferet (Devorah). The Etz Chayim's other two triads are commonly thought of as Chabad (Chochmah, Binah, and Daat or Keter, Chochmah, and Binah). The bottommost of the Tree's triads is made up of Netzach (Chanah), Hod (Avigail), and Yesod (Chuldah).

kindness as a way of life, including opening our homes to others for meals and education and opening our hearts to the needs of others.

Spiritual Action: Chesed is a disposition of the heart as unconditional love. It is the soul being in oneness with all life. In prayer it is a unity with God that flows from boundless love and awe.

Meaningful Work: The work of Chesed is one of nurturance in service fields, home care, and family and providing communal well-being.

Day Focus: Perform your day with love invested in your actions. Do a kind deed for another you know or for a stranger. Teach others through generosity of spirit.

Species: Wheat is an offering for a person's elevation and the elevation of someone's prayers. Wheat is a species endowed with wisdom (Chochmah), and it is a food of primary sustenance.

SARAH'S STORY

Note: The bold words in the following section correspond to headings in the subsequent section called Symbolism of Sarah. This device exists in all prophetesses' stories so that the reader can delve deeper into the bold topics appearing in each initial narrative.

Sarah, the **daughter of Haran,** lived during the Middle Bronze Age between 1802 BCE and 1675 BCE and died when she was 127.[2] She lived in Ur Kasdim before becoming Abraham's (Avraham's) wife and traveling toward **Canaan.** As the first in the progressive descent of the presence of the **Shechinah** (the Divine Immanence of the Creator), Sarah reveals how the seed and vessel of love give birth to an entire nation. She is considered the matriarch of the People of the Book, just as Abraham is the patriarch.

Her **beauty** was well known: She is described as one of the most beautiful women in the world, a woman with vision. Sarah was **abducted** twice by **foreign rulers** and then returned to Abraham unscathed.

---

[2] Abraham died in 1639 BCE, when he was 175 years old.

Chronicled in her story are both her long ordeal with **Hagar,** a woman who was a gift from Egypt's pharaoh and who became Abraham's concubine, and Sarah's prophecy regarding the fate of Ishmael, the son of Hagar, who, she determined, would not inherit with Isaac, "this son of mine."

Tradition teaches that the Shechinah hovered by the door of Sarah's tent[3] and describes Sarah as a guardian and instructor of women. (She converted and educated the women of the desert and Abraham educated the men.[4]) She taught the Israelite women about attachment to God through loving-kindness (Chesed) and about family purity (*niddah*) and, as the Zohar tells us, instructed them in the ritual use of immersion (Mikvah).[5] She taught the Israelite women elements of holiness and keeping Shabbat: She was the first maker of *challah* (sacramental bread) and was responsible for the first lighting of the Sabbath candles, and established generosity as a cornerstone of Judaism. Under Sarah, the New Moon was observed for the first time as the timekeeper of the Israelites' lives.

We are told that her prophecy was greater than that of Abraham. Her tent was the first communal tent where God visited and the Shechinah rested at her door—the prelude to the Holy Tabernacle itself. Sarah is the only matriarchal prophetess and mother of the patriarch Isaac, but she laughed when God spoke to her directly and told her that she would conceive. After Isaac was born, the **women tested Sarah** because they did not believe that Isaac was her own child. It is said that on the day that Abraham went up the mountain to sacrifice their son Isaac **(the Akeidah),** Sarah died. She was buried in the **Cave of Machpelah,** the burial place of the matriarchs and patriarchs. It was selected by Sarah and purchased by Abraham after her death.

---

[3] Bereshit Rabbah 60:16. "Throughout the years that Sarah was alive, a cloud [signifying the divine presence] hovered at the entrance to her tent, the doors [of the house] were open wide, her dough was blessed, and lamp burned [in her tent] from one Sabbath eve to the next. When she died, all these ceased, but when Rebecca came, they all returned."

[4] Pirkei Avot 12:8. "The Patriarch Abraham confounded [the views of] people and brought them under the wings of the divine presence [i.e., he converted them]. Sarah did the same."

[5] Zohar 1:102b.

SYMBOLISM OF SARAH

Daughter of Haran

We first meet Sarah as the daughter of Haran and the daughter-in-law of Terach. Terach was the father of Abraham and Nachor. Nachor's wife was Sarah's sister Milcha. At the beginning of her chronicle, she and her family depart "from Ur Kasdim (said to be the birthplace of Abraham) to go to the land of Canaan; they arrive at [a place called] Haran and they settle there."[6]

Sarah's Beauty

Sarah's name was also Iscah (Yiskah),[7] from the word *gaze,* because she could see things through divine inspiration and "because all gazed at her beauty."[8] She was considered one of the most beautiful women in the world[9] and was called both princess[10] and chieftainess. According to R. Isaac, "The beautiful image of Eve was transmitted to the heads of the generations (some very righteous and prominent women are blessed with beauty that resembles Eve), but [Sarah] was very beautiful,[11] more than the image of Eve."[12]

Sarah and Abraham Go to Canaan

From Ur Kasdim, Sarah, Abraham, Lot (the son of Haran), and all their households "go to Canaan." It is here that Abraham is told by God, "To your offspring I will give this land."[13] They proceed to Beit El and to Ai, where they make altars to God, and then they continue southward into Egypt.[14]

---

[6] Genesis 11: 31.

[7] Genesis 11:29.

[8] Megillah 14a.

[9] Megillah 15a, "There were four beautiful women in the world: Sarah, Rahab, Avigail, and Esther."

[10] Berachot 13a, "At first she was a princess to her people; then she became a princess to the whole world."

[11] Genesis 12:14.

[12] Bereshit Rabbah 40:5.

[13] Genesis 12:7.

[14] Genesis 12:9.

Foreign Rulers and Abduction

Sarah's dramatic story is set in motion in Canaan. Abraham asks her to pretend to be his sister while they are in Egypt, explaining that if the Egyptians think she is his wife, they will kill him and abduct her. As Abraham predicts, Pharaoh's men capture Sarah, "and the woman was taken to Pharaoh's house."[15] Abraham and Sarah's trickery works initially, and the pharaoh "treated Abraham well for her sake."[16] It is said that the pharaoh does not have conjugal relations with Sarah because God afflicts his house with a skin disease. The pharaoh then summons Abraham to ask him why he pretended that Sarah was his sister. Abraham explains his dilemma, saying their deception was necessary to protect their lives. Fearing that God's wrath would escalate, the pharaoh says wisely, "Now, here is your wife; take her and go."[17]

Sarah as Queen and Abduction

Sarah is captured a second time in the kingdom of Avimelech. The king tries to disguise her by giving her a royal garment (Esther is given such a garment by the king of Persia almost fifteen hundred years later) to signify his plans to make her queen. He thinks this will prevent other men from approaching her and perhaps discovering her true identity.

As on the occasion of her first abduction, Sarah is set free, which demonstrates her courage, patience, and trust in God, who helps each of us when we are abducted temporarily by our desires or a situation that is foreign to us. Both Sarah and Esther elevate the sparks hidden deep within the kelipot. Both prophetesses, infused with God's holy radiance, make it possible to elevate a situation from evil to good. The story of Sarah is a parable for each of us. Everything we experience in life is for the refinement of all creation.

---

[15] Genesis 12:15.

[16] Genesis 12:16. This suggests a role reversal of Abraham and Sarah. In this instance, the natural receiver, the woman, becomes the emanator. This term is used in Kabbalah to suggest the light that is emanated to a vessel, rather than the vessel that receives the light. In general, women are considered receivers.

[17] Genesis 12:19.

The Shechinah and the Foreign Rulers

The theme of being taken into the foreign ruler's house is repeated throughout the Israelites' numerous exiles and in the life of Esther, the last prophetess of B'nai Yisrael. Sarah's and Esther's identities and marital status are concealed. The foreign kings (who practice idolatry and self-worship) attempt to steal the prophetesses of Israel.[18] In the stories of both the first and last prophetesses, the foreign kings (representing the kelipot) try to capture the Shechinah.

From the abduction of Sarah to the forced marriage of Esther, the plight of the prophetesses reflects the story of the Shechinah. When society inhibits the freedom of women or their intuitive natures, the Shechinah and therefore prophecy are also suppressed. In Kabbalah, this state of remoteness or separation from God is called *geulah,* or exile.[19]

Concealing Identities

When the good inclination (*yetzer tov*) is abducted by the king of the animal nature or evil inclination (*yetzer hara,* the kelipot), infusing us with desires other than closeness to God, we conceal the light of the soul. When we become captive to carnal and selfish desires of the body and ego, even dressed up as beautiful queens, the light of glory is evicted.

Sarah's first abduction and her second abduction by Avimelech suggest that when a woman's identity is hidden, the entire community suffers. When women are treated improperly, the Shechinah is sent into exile. When we suppress our intuition (our feminine quality of Binah), our kingdoms and lives suffer. The consequent geulah (exile) and disharmony between our left and right ministers or sons can lead to destruction.[20] Any desecration of the holy temple or body comes from an unbridled ego destroying the place where there occurs the holy union

---

[18] Malchut, the Sefirah Esther occupies, is sometimes referred to as the Daughter of the King.

[19] We will examine the indwelling presence of the Creator, the Shechinah, in the final chapter of this book, which discusses how the People of the Book refer to the exile of the Queen of Israel and our own separation from the Creator.

[20] Recall that all six middot, or Sefirot, from Chesed to Yesod, are called the Son, Zeir Anpin.

between humankind and divinity. Arrogance destroys the temple or our own life. Fundamentally, selfishness is a weapon of destruction.

Hagar

When Sarah and Abraham leave Egypt, they are given Hagar as a gift. Hagar is a princess, one of Pharaoh's daughters, who is transformed overnight into a servant. We can imagine how Hagar feels, being given to foreigners traveling to a foreign land—no longer a princess but a maidservant.

Hagar's debased status (from princess to maidservant) is reflected in the conception of her offspring: Yishmael, the "wild ass of a man," the expert archer. He is a product of a woman acting as a vessel of another woman's (Sarah's) desire for her husband to bear seed. Abraham and Hagar produce a hunter.

Sarah and Abraham Receive Tithing from the King of Sodom

Next in Sarah's story are the nine wars of the kings. Sodom is defeated and Lot is taken captive. Abraham rescues Lot, and the king of Sodom, Malkizedek (who, according to some, was Noah's son Shem), blesses Abraham in Salem (Jerusalem), saying, "Abraham of God the most high, who has delivered your foes into your hand . . ." Abraham is then given a tenth of everything the king owns.[21]

Sarah Is Barren and Gives Hagar to Abraham

"Now Sarah, Abraham's wife, had borne him no children," begins the section on Sarah's plight of barrenness. It weighs heavily on Sarah's heart. The oral tradition tells us that Sarah "did not have a womb, and the Holy One, Blessed is He, formed one for her."[22] In addition, "Abraham and Sarah had undeveloped reproductive systems."[23] It is more than just their age that makes a miracle of the subsequent conception of Isaac.

Before Sarah conceives, however, she gives Hagar, her maidservant, to

---

[21] Genesis 14:18–20.
[22] Yebamoth 64a.
[23] Bereshit Rabbah 53:5.

Abraham. Sarah asks Abraham to "consort" with Hagar, and Hagar conceives a child (Yishmael) and then begins to show Sarah great disrespect. Sarah condemns Abraham, telling him that it is his fault that Hagar has grown to have contempt for her, and she asks that "God judge between me and you!"[24] Some rabbis say that Sarah had forty-eight years taken from her life for this retort.[25]

Hagar Is Sent Back to Sarah

Eventually, Hagar is expelled from Abraham and Sarah's family, but after the first of two separations, Hagar runs away because "Sarai dealt harshly with her."[26] An angel of God finds Hagar by a spring and asks her, "Where have you come from and where are you going?" She replies "[I am] running away from Sarah, my mistress."[27] The angel tells Hagar to return and submit to Sarah's domination. In addition, Hagar is told that she will have many children who will not be "counted for abundance."[28] She will bear a son to be called Yishmael, "and he will be a wild ass of a man: his hand against everyone, and everyone's hand against him; and over all his brothers shall he dwell."[29] The Well of the Living One Appearing to Me is the name Hagar gives to the place where she has these encounters with the angels of the Creator. It is located between Kadesh and Bered.[30]

The Covenant Is Made and Sarai Becomes Sarah

When we remember that Sarah stands for the Sefirah Chesed and the seed of life as love, it is interesting to note that it is not until Sarah and Hagar are separated and the Creator's angels tell Hagar to return that Sarah and Abraham have their names changed. God then speaks to Abraham and makes the promise of the covenant: "You shall be a Father of a multitude of nations . . . I will ratify My covenant between Me and

---

[24] Genesis 16:5.
[25] Bereshit Rabbah 45:5.
[26] Genesis 16:6.
[27] Genesis 16:8.
[28] Genesis 16:10.
[29] Genesis 16:12.
[30] Genesis 16:14.

you and between your offspring after you, throughout their generations, as an everlasting covenant, to be a God to you and to your offspring after you."[31] Circumcision is demanded,[32] and Abram's and Sarai's names are changed to Abraham and Sarah, each gaining the letter Hay at the end of his or her name.

Once Hagar is separated and returned by divine intervention and told her proper place, Sarah can take hers. First, upon her return to Sarah, the angels demand that Hagar submit to Abraham's wife, and then Sarah is elevated. Regarding the name change, God tells Abraham[33] ". . . as for Sarah[34] your wife, do not call her name Sarai. For Sarah is her name. I will bless her; indeed, I will give you a son through her; I will bless her and she shall give rise to nations; kings of peoples will rise from her."[35]

Hearing this from God, Abraham "throws himself upon his face and laughs" at the notion that a ninety-nine-year-old man and a barren eighty-nine-year-old woman could give birth.[36] God assures him that Sarah will have a son to be called Isaac, and that it is to be through Isaac, not Yishmael, that the everlasting covenant is to be made.[37]

Sarah Laughs

Abraham does not tell Sarah of God's visit. She learns of her impending conception from three angels who visit, posing as men in need of water and food. Just like Abraham, Sarah laughs out loud when she is told, first by an angel, that she will bear a son. Sarah denies that she laughed when God himself confirms that in one year's time she will bear a son, and although Abraham is not reprimanded for laughing, Sarah is chastised by

---

[31] Genesis 17:4–8. The covenant, including the promise of all of Canaan as an inheritance, is a beautiful testimony to God's enduring love and commitment to the Jewish people. For those interested, there are other secrets hidden in God's words to Abraham.

[32] Read Genesis 17:1–14 for the details of the covenant regarding circumcision.

[33] It is tradition not to refer to Abraham as Abram nor to Sarah as Sarai because the letter Hay added to their names is a spiritual elevation from which they did not fall.

[34] Genesis 17:15, Rashi, and Berachot 13a say that Sarai means "princess" and Sarah means "princess to all the nations of the world." R. Nosson Scherman, ed., *Tanach.*

[35] Genesis 17:15.

[36] Genesis 17:17.

[37] Abraham is told that Yishmael will be fruitful and father twelve princes (a counterbalance, perhaps, to the Twelve Tribes of Abraham's people).

the Creator for doubting His power and His Word. "And Sarah laughed at herself saying, 'After I have withered shall I again have delicate skin? And my husband is old?' Then God said to Abraham, 'Why is it that Sarah laughed, saying, 'Shall I in truth bear a child, though I have aged?' Is anything beyond God? At the appointed time I will return to you at this time next year, and Sarah will have a Son.'"[38]

God Speaks to Sarah Directly

God speaks to both Sarah and Abraham and they both hear Him. Of all seven prophetesses, tradition teaches that Sarah is the only one to whom God spoke directly, even though the other prophetesses tell, in their songs, what God said to them.[39]

Sarah's role as the only matriarch who is also a prophetess[40] shows us that each subsequent prophetess benefits as the light of her actions descend, as explained in the discussion of the descent of the light in chapter 2. Sarah's life shows us that the Shechinah and prophecy attend those who possess the attributes of Chesed (loving-kindness) tempered by Gevurah (the act of expelling Hagar). Creating boundaries is an aspect of a well-proportioned love.

Conception of Isaac

Sarah conceives Isaac on Rosh Hashanah, the Jewish New Year.[41] This reflects Chesed's relationship with conception and the "head" or *rosh* of the year. We see this aspect of creation in the way a child is born, entering the world headfirst. It also gives us clues as to why the holiday Rosh Hashanah and the monthly festival of the New Moon are represented by Sarah, the first of the seven prophetesses of Israel.

In God's great mercy and due to the merit Sarah earns when she

---

[38] Genesis 18:12.

[39] LeKach Tov, Bereshit 23:1: "We do not find that the Omnipresent spoke [directly] with any woman except for Sarah." Yerushalmi Sotah 7:1: "The Holy One blessed is He, spoke to all [other] righteous women through an angel, but to Sarah [he spoke] through divine communication."

[40] Berachot 16b, "Only four women were called Matriarchs: Sarah, Rebecca, Rachel, and Leah."

[41] Berachot 29a.

conceives through divine intervention, "many barren women conceived with her, many deaf became capable of hearing, many blind became capable of sight, and many madmen became sane at that time."[42] As the recipient of the additional flow of God's essence from Keter to Chochmah (or from God to Abraham to Sarah), Sarah is not the only one to experience greater light. The increase in Binah, the essence of understanding, affects other women as well. In her role as a vessel for the descent of the Shechinah, the entire world receives extra Binah through Sarah. B'nai Yisrael also receives an extra capacity for understanding and hearing the word of the Creator (Atzilut, emanation), which makes the women better vessels of conception (Beriyah, to create). These miracles are attributed to Sarah's life and relationship to the Creator. The influx of additional Chochmah (wisdom) affects sight. Chochmah and sight are related to the realm of emanation (Atzilut). The additional influx of Binah (understanding) connected to Beriyah (creation) influences hearing.

These events teach us that everyone is an emanator (one who gives light to others) and a receiver of light. It is not always what we do for others that is our gift to them; it is often simply the fact that we *are* for others. Our mere presence and regard for others is sometimes the greatest gift we have to offer others and the world.

The Birth of Isaac

The next time we meet Sarah in the Torah is after she has given birth to Isaac. "God has made laughter for me; whoever hears will laugh for me."[43] And she adds, "Who is the One who said to Abraham, 'Sarah would nurse children'? For I have borne a son in his old age!"[44] Sarah's declaration precedes the final expulsion of Hagar and Yishmael from the tent of Sarah and from the People of the Book.

Sarah's offspring, Isaac, implanted through divine intervention, is a scholar, whereas her maidservant Hagar's son is a "wild ass of a man." The women's polarization reflects the future centuries of difficulty between the

---

[42] Bereshit Rabbah 53:8.
[43] Genesis 21:1–3.
[44] Genesis 21:7.

Israelites and other communities. Sarah's initial experience of childlessness results in the wife (Binah) giving to her husband (Chochmah) another woman's body (Malchut) and womb (Yesod); thus Yishmael can be seen not as the outcome of the emanations of Chochmah and Binah in partnership (Father, wisdom, with Mother, understanding), but rather as Chochmah looking for its reflection in Malchut, the Kingdom. It is a contraction (*tzimtzum*) of the pathway between Chochmah and Binah, diminishing Chesed.[45] Put simply, Hagar's conception of Yishmael is initially a diminishing of Sarah, but it leads to Sarah's ultimate perfection and conception of Isaac. So, too, enmity between some of the descendants of Yishmael and the rest of the world will be for the eventual elevation of humanity.

Tradition tells us that Sarah notes the negative influence of Yishmael on Isaac, the future father of B'nai Yisrael. "Sarah saw the son of Hagar, the Egyptian, whom she had borne to Abraham, mocking. So she said to Abraham, 'Drive out this slave woman with her son, for the son of that slave woman shall not inherit with my son, with Isaac!'"[46] These are Sarah's final words in the Torah and highlight the prophecy of Sarah. Suppositions about Sarah's reasoning range from the fact that Hagar and Yishmael are idol worshippers to the fact that Yishmael practices homosexuality and eats from animals that are not fully dead, which is forbidden.

Because God tells Abraham to listen to Sarah, this drama has an element of the prophetic in it. Sarah and Hagar represent different aspects of life. Perhaps there is a parallel between the repair (*tikkun*) of our "inner Hagar," our experiences of being diminished by circumstances around us or by our own *yetzer hara,* or selfishness, and the elevation of the sparks of light, which can occur by removing the kelipot encasing them (i.e., removing pride and arrogance from our nature). Hagar leaves Sarah and Abraham twice; the second time leads to her final expulsion with Yishmael. These two events seem related to the two times Sarah is abducted until her own final emancipation. Both women experience a loss of station and freedom, each eventually being put in her proper place by divine intervention.

---

[45] One of the mysteries concealed in the word Chesed itself is revealed through gematria. Chesed in Hebrew is equal to the number 72, the number of names of the Creator himself in Kabbalah.

[46] Genesis 21:9–10.

The Women Test Sarah

At the time of Isaac's weaning, Sarah invites to the celebration other women and their husbands who doubt that Isaac is the son of Sarah and Abraham. To test Sarah, each woman brings an infant without its wet nurse. By some miracle, Sarah has enough milk to nurse all of the infants present. This unusual demonstration proves her status as the true mother of Isaac, discounting claims that she had stolen the child or bought him in the marketplace.[47]

"All the proselytes and the God-fearing people in the world descended from those who suckled Sarah's milk."[48] Chesed is the vessel of the Creator's milk from which our progeny will endure. Chesed is a spiritual state of selflessness, an emanation of Chochmah (wisdom) and Binah (understanding) integrated with the desire to give.

A mother who breast-feeds her children gives them her love and protection, creating a spiritual shield for her children beyond the established health benefits. She endows them with her spiritual attributes. Chesed is an emanation of love. It is also why the right hand must be used only for acts of goodness, including the fierceness of self-preservation.

The Akeidah and Sarah's Death

Our final encounter with Sarah is her death after Abraham's journey to Mt. Moriah with Isaac as his intended sacrifice. "After Abraham bound his son Isaac [on the altar] then Satan came and told Sarah that Abraham had slaughtered his son Isaac. She cried out in grief and died."[49] Others teach that Sarah had lived out her full number of years already allocated to her by God and that if her life was shortened, it was due to the earlier incident when Sarah said to Abraham, "God judge between me and you!" (Genesis 16:5). Some say that forty-eight years of her life were withheld for that retort.[50] Sarah was eighty-nine years old when she conceived Isaac, ninety when she gave birth to him, and 127 years old when she died. The

---

[47] Bava Metzia 87a. See also R. Yishai Chasidah, *Encyclopedia of Biblical Personalities*, 525.

[48] Pesikta Rabbati 42:23.

[49] Targum Yonatan Bereshit 22:20.

[50] Bereshit Rabbah 45:5.

Figure 3.1. Right: Statue of Faith; detail (below) shows the Akeidah. Sculpture by Daniel Kafri, Abrashah Park, Jaffa, Israel.

binding of Isaac (the Akeidah) corresponds to the death of Sarah, which makes it a central element and climax of Sarah's life. Because it coincides with her death, and if we see the end as embedded in the beginning, the suggestion is that her birth was, in part, for the purpose of the Akeidah.

Etz Chayim Is Rectified by the Akeidah

The Akeidah, a pivotal historic event in the lives of the People of the Book, is a receptacle of the future light on Mt. Moriah. The earth is the vessel of Malchut. Prior to recitation of the Shema prayer each morning, these holy events are recalled. The Akeidah stands as a merit for all Jewish people and affirms the eternal covenant, when God replaced Isaac with a living ram. Mt. Moriah became the Holy of Holies of love grown from sacrifice; it is the shine of redemption, which comes from a total commitment to God and the willingness to use everything in our possession for that service. What Sarah begins in Chesed as the seed of life and the sacrifice of Isaac is completed by Esther in Malchut and the erection of the Third Temple on Mt. Moriah.

The Sacrifice of Isaac and Rectifying the Tree of Life

Traditionally, Sarah's husband, Abraham, is associated with the quality of Chesed. The Father (Abba) in Kabbalah is Chochmah (wisdom), and the Kabbalah calls Isaac, the Son in the ancestral family, Zeir Anpin or Tiferet, implying the other five Sefirot: The Son represents the six middot (Sefirot Chesed through Yesod) or emotional qualities that all humans are in the process of developing and refining. This shows us that the Akeidah (the binding of Isaac) recounted in daily prayers reflects the participation of the family constellation concealed in the Etz Chayim, the Tree of Life.

Chochmah is wisdom, Father, and Abraham; Binah is understanding, Mother, and Sarah; Tiferet is Zeir Anpin, Son, and Isaac, which includes Chesed (loving-kindness), Gevurah (judgment), Tiferet (beauty), Netzach (eternity, victory), Hod (humility, glory), and Yesod (foundation). The only one of the Partzufim (members of the divine family) seemingly missing is Malchut, the Daughter. Yet Malchut is represented by Mt. Moriah, where the holy act is performed. We can see, then, how the Akeidah could be said to be a rectification of the entire Etz Chayim—why it is taught that the prayers that the observant say to commemorate the event are their rectification (forgiveness of sin). All of the Sefirot of these individuals—including the Sechol, the upper Sefirot of the intellect—are engaged in an elevation.

In this way, the Akeidah itself (or the sacrifices any of us make) is a correction of the Original Sin of Adam and Eve's disobedience and a pre-rectification of the sin of the golden calf—the sin of self-worship—which occurs during the life of the next prophetess, Miriam. As we will learn in the next chapter, the women of the Exodus do not take part in building the golden idol. Just as Sarah is pivotal in the Akediah and as she precedes the other six prophetesses of Israel and therefore shines on them, all seven of the prophetesses are in some way connected to the Akeidah. Like the prophetesses, we each receive from Israel's first family an emanation of their faith and love of God revealed at Mt. Moriah.

The Cave of Machpelah

> *While Sarah was alive, the people of the country were*
> *successful in all their ventures [in her merit]. After she*
> *died, [everyone perceived the magnitude of the loss to such*
> *an extent that] they wept in mourning and distress, until*
> *Abraham the Patriarch arose and spoke soothingly to them.*
> MIDRASH HAGADOL, BERESHIT 23:3

Seeing far into the future, Sarah selects Machpelah (in Mamre, or Hebron) as the place where she and the other matriarchs and patriarchs will be buried. Abraham and Sarah, Isaac and Leah, Jacob and Rebecca, and, it is said, Adam and Eve are buried there.[51] Sarah, as the first prophetess and mother of Israel, understood the importance of the burial site as a historical marker showing future generations that the biblical people existed, that their stories are true stories that can be known.

---

[51] Zohar 3:164a: "The burial arrangement in the cave of Machpelah is as follows: women are buried beside women, men beside men, Adam is at the head, with Eve beside him; Sarah is next to Eve, with Abraham beside her..."

R'Benaah [was marking off the precise location of the burial places in the Cave of Machpelah] when he encountered Abraham's servant Eliezer, who was standing before the entrance of the cave, and asked him, "What is Abraham doing now?" [Eliezer] replied, "he is lying in Sarah's arms and she is examining his head" [as she might be doing when both were still alive], to show that Sarah was the mainstay of Abraham's house.[52]

We are told in Proverbs 31:7, "[S]he envisions a field and buys it." Sarah has planned on purchasing the Cave of Machpelah, but Abraham buys the holy resting place of the Jewish people's blessed forefathers and -mothers from Ephron, son of Zohar, after Sarah dies. This is a delightful testimony that Abraham does in fact do what Sarah tells him to, just as God had instructed. Whether it is the eviction of the Egyptian Hagar and Abraham's son Yishmael or buying Machpelah, Sarah's extra Binah, her understanding of the hidden relationships between the spiritual and physical realms, is elevated enough to guide her husband and the Children of Israel.

We have now briefly reviewed the primary junctures in the Torah where Sarah's life is profiled. The oral tradition has built a great wealth of interpretation around a few paragraphs of actual text in which her life is mentioned.

GEMATRIA

An Interpretation of Sarah

Sarah's life reflects the story of the root of creation, the seed of Israel. It is the story of the first mother of Israel. She embodies the Shechinah in the first stage of its descent, which might account for some of her hardship along the way, as she held the emanation of the Creator at a very high level of Beriyah (creation). Shin, the last of the three mother letters in the Hebrew language (Alef, Mem, Shin), is the first letter of Sarah's name and the first letter in the word Shechinah. A simple rule in gema-

---

[52] Maharsha, Bava Batra 58a.

tria is to note the first letter of a name as we would the head of a person's body in order to identify a person's uniqueness or similarity to others. Sarah is the fire of the Holy One, his seed in the womb, the fire in water. She merits the hovering cloud of glory at her tent, Shabbat candles, and holy bread. Her entire life is a testament to the presence of the Creator's loving-kindness.

The Akeidah: What Did Sarah Know?

To best understand Sarah and Chesed, let us examine the day of Sarah's death, the Akeidah. In Genesis 23:1, the Torah portion Chayei Sarah (Life of Sarah) says that we can count thirty-seven years from the day Isaac was born until his binding on the altar. What does the number 37 reveal in this context?

In the Jewish prayer book (Siddur), we recount this monumental event as if we ourselves were the participants in this holy drama of the first family of B'nai Yisrael. The Arizal (Isaac Luria) teaches that when we recite the Akeidah prayer, it brings about atonement "to someone who repents sincerely, for he identifies himself with the two patriarchs who placed loyalty to God above all other considerations."[53] Sarah also shows her ultimate faith in God, though this seems to be overlooked by the commentators in general. She is willing to let her husband and son go up into the hills together, and given Sarah's prophetic talents, it is difficult for us to assume she could see nothing of her husband's intentions. We are told for a fact that her prophetic skill is greater than Abraham's. When we apply gematria to the age of Sarah at the time of Isaac's binding, we discover that she may have seen clearly the events to come, including her own death.

127 and 37: Parshat Chayei Sarah

Using the method of gematria described in chapter 2 (mispar hechrachi), we can investigate the numbers 127 (the length of Sarah's life) and 37 (the age of Isaac at the time of Sarah's death and the Akeidah).

In Chayei Sarah (Genesis, chapters 23–25), the portion of the Torah named in Sarah's memory, she is commemorated by her death rather than

---

[53] R. Nosson Scherman and R. Meir Zlotowitz, eds., *The Complete Artscroll Siddur,* 205.

by her birth. It begins: "Sarah's lifetime was one hundred years, twenty years, and seven years; the years of Sarah's life." The end of her life is embedded in the beginning. Her death becomes a statement of her living legacy.[54] The Hebrew words that begin the chapter named for Sarah in Torah, **And the life,** add up to the number 37:

And the life ויהיו (Genesis 32:1, Zohar 1:123a): ו Vav (6) י Yod (10) ה Hay (5) י Yod (10) ו Vav (6) = 37

The last thirty-seven years of Sarah's life are also the first thirty-seven years of Isaac's life up until the Akeidah. It seems that all the preceding years are in preparation for these thirty-seven years.[55] We are told by the sages (Chazal) that Sarah's twenty-five years of barrenness with Abraham and her ordeal with Hagar were God's way of purifying her nature to ready her as the holy matriarch and the only matriarchal prophetess of the Jewish people.[56]

127: *Reflections Elsewhere in the Torah*

And he offered him up ויעלהו (Genesis 22:13): ו Vav (6) י Yod (10) ע Ayin (70) ל Lamed (30) ה Hay (5) ו Vav (6) = 127

As we have seen, the Akeidah is central to Sarah's life. The phrase **And he offered him up** refers to this monumental moment in the Torah when Abraham offers Isaac as a sacrifice on Mt. Moriah. Isaac agrees willingly to be sacrificed to God once he realizes his father's intentions. **And he offered him up** in Hebrew is equal to the numeric value 127. This astounding correlation between Sarah's length of life and the action of the Akeidah means that Sarah's lifetime carried within it the destiny of this act by which B'nai Yisrael merited being "lifted out of Egypt" by the strong hand of God—God's right hand, Chesed. We can see why

---

[54] Genesis 23:1.

[55] Zohar 1:123a, "Thirty-seven years from the day Isaac was born until the moment he was bound (on the altar)—were years of 'life' for Sarah. [Thirty-seven is] the numeric value of 'The life of Sarah was' (Genesis 23:1)."

[56] Pesikta Rabbati 43:38, "The Holy One, blessed is He, tried and refined Sarah [by withholding children from her] for twenty-five years from the time she came to the Land of Israel."

God tells Abraham that Sarah will give rise to nations and that nations of kings will be born from her.

The Akeidah is reflected in every *aliyah*—in the synagogue, going up to the Bimah to read the Torah, or a return to the land of Israel, both types of spiritual elevation—which draws vitality from this seminal act on Mt. Moriah.[57] Prayer offerings take the place of the actual Temple rituals, animating their spiritual origin. Words of prayer become vital enactments of holy processes.

Sarah's spiritual purpose and the Shechinah's first stage of descent are hidden in the first line in the Torah portion called by her name. Sarah's beginning and ending of life and the number of years of her life, 127, are fulfilled in the Akeidah. That Sarah may have foreseen what was to come seems highly probable given the keys provided by the Torah and gematria in addition to her prophetic gaze. This is why we can say with confidence that the Akediah reflects the sacrifice of Abraham, Isaac, and Sarah.

It is noteworthy that the other right-pillar prophetess Chanah offers her son Samuel to the priesthood. Both prophetesses—mothers—surrender their sons to the service of God.

There are a few more words in the Torah equal to the number value 127, the number of years of Sarah's life, revealing the illumination or the shine that comes from Chesed and the first prophetess of Israel, upon whom God's Divine Immanence rested:

the kindness הֿחֿסֿדֿיֿם (Genesis 32:11): ה Hay (5) ח Chet (8) ס Samech (60) ד Dalet (4) י Yod (10) ם Mem (40) = 127

Jacob says to God, "I have been diminished by all the kindness and by all the truth that You have done Your servant." Then he pleads to be rescued from the wrath of Esau (his brother). Having crossed the Jordan, he says, "[N]ow I have two camps," or, in other words, how can I bring peace between these two aspects of my family? The pairs of brothers and

---

[57] It is possible to see how the Akeidah was the elevation of the sparks in the branch—the branch as Yishmael and his descendants rectified through Yishmael's father, Abraham, and his brother Isaac surrendering their lives to God (Judaism), one situation balanced by the other. This pattern is seen in both Hagar's two exiles and Sarah's two captivities.

family divisions in many of these situations represent how each individual beseeches God for peace between the divine soul and the animal soul, between physical needs and spiritual needs.

upon Your Face לאפיו (Genesis 48:12): ל Lamed (30) א Alef (1) פ Pey (80) י Yod (10) ו Vav (6) = 127

Joseph (and his offspring) is seen by his father, Israel (Jacob), for the first time in twenty-two years and Jacob says, "I dared not accept the thought that I would see your face [upon your face], and here God has shown me even your offspring." Equal to the value of Sarah's length of life, the moment highlights the power of Chesed in hurdling even the greatest obstacles. As the matriarch of these families, Sarah radiates the effluence of God's loving-kindness, engendering eventual repair of the branches of her tree. This is the hallmark of the first Sefirot of the middot called Chesed and of the life of Sarah. She is the optimal epitome of loving-kindness balanced by discernment (Gevurah, judgment), fitting for the birth of a holy nation.[58]

Sarah (Chesed) and Esther (Malchut) Are Related through 127

The beginning of Israel's existence in Sarah (Chesed) is fulfilled in Queen Esther (Malchut), the final Sefirah of the Etz Chayim. Applying the guide of Sefer Yetzirah (the Book of Formation, attributed to Abraham)—the end is embedded in the beginning—we discover many relationships between Sarah and Esther. Sarah lived 127 years and Esther ruled over 127 nations.[59] As Kabbalah teaches, the light descends from one Sefirah to another, leaving some of its presence in those below as it descends. Chesed (Sarah) is seen in Malchut (Esther). Sarah, Abraham,

---

[58] We often associate Gevurah with Sarah: Abraham himself is given the attribute of Chesed and Sarah is his balance. Yet in the context of the seven prophetesses, the seven Sefirot, and the seven species, Sarah stands for the vessel of the seed of the Creator. Chesed and the Akeidah are the root of the elevation offerings and are why an *aliyah* is called a "going up" or an elevation.

[59] Bereshit Rabbah 58:3, "Let Esther, descendant of Sarah—who lived 127 years—come and reign over 127 provinces."

and Isaac show total faith in God, which is echoed in the life of Esther. Together, Chesed of Malchut represents the promise of redemption and the building of the Third Temple during the prophesied messianic age, the final outcome of the Akeidah.

37: Reflections in the Torah

Continuing this deeper examination of the Akeidah, we can find words and expressions that have the numeric value of 37, the age of Isaac at the time of Sarah's death: ל Lamed (30) + ז Zayin (7).

and they became ויהיו (Genesis 2:25): ו Vav (6) י Yod (10) ה Hay (5) י Yod (10) ו Vav (6) = 37

We learn about the unity of Sarah and Abraham in this phrase. The phrase **and they became** refers to Adam (Adamah, Adam HaRishon, Adam the first man) and Eve's (Chava's) first awareness of each other after the creation of Eve. We are told "that they were both [and they became] naked, and they were not ashamed." In this way, we also see the unity between Sarah and Abraham: In being aware of each other's entire natures, they still do not view themselves as separate from each other. In union we experience a wholeness and closeness to God.

Abel הבל (Genesis 4:2): ה Hay (5) ב Bet (2) ל Lamed (30) = 37

In the story of Abel, the conflict of two is resolved through Chesed. "And additionally she bore his brother Abel. Abel became a shepherd and Cain became a tiller of the ground." Highlighted here is the pattern for conflict between brothers (nations) and between the animal soul and the divine soul in the individual.

In the Torah there are several conflicts between brothers, notably between Cain and Abel, between Yishmael and Isaac, and between Jacob and Esau. Through them we learn the challenge of overcoming polarization and making harmony from variation, as the kind that exists in the relationship between Cain and Abel. The firstborn (Cain) is a tiller of the earth, suggesting a lower spiritual station (Asiyah)—working with the mineral and plant kingdoms. His younger brother, Abel, is a shepherd who gathers and leads the animal kingdom (Yetzirah). The fact that the elder brother in each of these pairs (Cain, Yishmael, and Esau) represents the physical world of Asiyah, where physical action takes place, suggests that we must be cognizant in prophecy of the various worlds. Abel, Isaac, and Jacob stand above this plane of action, engaged in the worlds of formation (Yetzirah). While one in each relationship works on refining the physical world, the other is dedicated to the spiritual worlds taking shape in the lives of those around him. Both are necessary for the repair of the individual and the world.

great גדל (Genesis 26:13): ג Gimel (3) ד Dalet (4) ל Lamed (30) = 37

"The man (Isaac) became great and kept becoming greater until he was very great." Sarah's son, Isaac, becomes a model of greatness. He has a quality of refinement that is a beacon of leadership for the community. Greatness (*gadlut*) is a measure of the light we contain and emanate, and thus Sarah's son is a great beacon for all generations. His desire to share in the Akediah teaches us about closeness and faith in God. With Chesed as emanator, when we show great faith, we are rewarded with great emanations from the Creator above.

Later, in Deuteronomy 26:8, we read, "God took us out of Egypt with a strong hand and with an outstretched arm, with great awesomeness, and with signs and wonders." It is this important act that underpins the holy celebration of Pesach—a holiday associated with the next prophetess, Miriam. It is an act remembered in our prayers every day of the week and on every Sabbath. God is the conductor of our enslavement and our emancipation, and Sarah is rescued by the strong arm or hand of God, which the Sefirah of Chesed represents.

And El ואל (And God, Genesis 28:3): ו Vav (6) א Alef (1) ל Lamed (30) = 37

"And may El Shaddai [And God] bless you, make you fruitful and make you numerous, and make you be a congregation of peoples." This is Isaac's blessing of his son Jacob, Sarah and Abraham's grandson. Here, it becomes clear that when God blesses Sarah with Isaac, God's promise to Abraham is fulfilled: He will father a nation of people as numerous as the stars.

benefited וייטב (Exodus 1:20): ו Vav (6) י Yod (10) י Yod (10) ט Tet (9) ב Bet (2) = 37

In the next Torah portion related to the age of Isaac at the Akeidah, God ensures proliferation of His chosen people. "God benefited the midwives" refers to the population increase of B'nai Yisrael when the midwives facilitate all births, even when the pharaoh orders them to kill B'nai Yisrael's newborn sons. The seed of Sarah, the seed of creation, is preserved and proliferated. Chesed, the seed of Creation, shows us that what is conceived in love has the capacity for regeneration.

they gazed ויחזו (beheld, Exodus 24:11): ו Vav (6) י Yod (10) ח Chet (8) ז Zayin (7) ו Vav (6) = 37

The presence of the Shechinah is reflected in the phrase **And they gazed.** Moses, Aaron, Nadav, Avihu, and seventy elders ascend Mt. Sinai. "They saw the God of Israel and under his feet was the likeness of sapphire brickwork, and it was like the essence of the heaven in purity" (Exodus 24:10). "Against the great men of the Children of Israel, He did not stretch out His hand, they gazed at God, yet they ate and drank" (Exodus 24:11).

Sarah's refinement is what allows God to speak to her directly and why she merits the hovering cloud of glory and the holy light in her tent from Sabbath to Sabbath. Just as visitors and householders can be in the immanence of God in her tent (*ohel*) and eat and drink, so too can Moses and the elders see the Creator's immanence and still carry on with strengthening the physical vessels occupied by their souls. This level of refinement makes it possible to be in the presence of the Shechinah while remaining in possession of our body. Our will and faculties reflect a high level of prophecy. Also, we know that Sarah's name, Yiskah (or Iscah, meaning to watch or gaze), is related to her prophetic vision.

banner דגל (flag, Numbers 2:3): ד Dalet (4) ג Gimel (3) ל Lamed (30) = 37

"Those who encamp to the front, at the east, shall be the banner of the camp of Judah according to their legions." The east is the direction of the holy city of Jerusalem, signifying its leadership and the tribe of

Judah. Because Sarah is the leader of her people and initiates teaching the women of early Jewish practices, her life is a banner for B'nai Yisrael.

505: The Numeric Value of Sarah's Name

Sarah שרה: ש Shin (300) ר Reish (200) ה Hay (5) = 505

God tells Abraham, "Do not call her Sarai, Sarah is her name" (Genesis 17:15), signifying an elevation in refinement. Sarah's body is the vessel from which the generations of Jewish people originate. Chesed is a vessel of life and regeneration. Through Chesed, reunion is made possible and closeness with God is achieved. By examining who is speaking in each of the following portions of the Torah, what they are speaking about, and to whom they are speaking, we see a dramatic revelation about Chesed and Sarah. This proves the power of names, the significance of name changes, and why naming children is a holy undertaking.

shall you finish it תלכנה (it = the Ark and Chesed, Genesis 6:16): ת Tav (400) כ Caf (20) ל Lamed (30) נ Nun (50) ה Hay (5) = 505

Noah is told by God to complete the window in the Ark: "to a cubit [shall you] finish it from above." The window is a portal of sight, suggesting the realm of emanation (Atzilut). The Ark ensures the survival of human-kind and general living things, much like the womb of Sarah conceals the future generations of B'nai Yisrael. When we seek shelter in the Ark (Torah), we are assured a safe view and a sustaining higher vision.

your land אדמתכם (the land to grow on, Genesis 47:23): א Alef (1) ד Dalet (4) מ Mem (40) ת Tav (400) כ Caf (20) מ Mem (40) = 505

Sarah's grandson Joseph speaks to the Israelites: "Look, I have acquired you this day with your land for Pharaoh; here is seed for you, sow the land." Joseph negotiates that all the land of Egypt be sold to the pharaoh, except for that of the Egyptian priests. He also negotiates that one fifth of the harvest will go to the pharaoh and four fifths will go to the sharecroppers. Here, the land becomes the general vessel for life and the theme of planting seeds is reiterated, as represented by Sarah's life and the purpose of Chesed as the seed of God's love.

Southward תימנה (Southside, Exodus 26:18): ת Tav (400) י Yod (10) מ Mem (40) נ Nun (50) ה Hay (5) = 505

God speaks to Moses about making the Tabernacle: "You shall make planks for the Tabernacle; twenty planks for the Southside." The Tabernacle is another vessel or dwelling place of the Shechinah. Sarah's name shares this attribute with these other vessels for holy life: the Ark, the land, and the Tabernacle.

priesthood לכהנת (Exodus 40:15): ל Lamed (30) כ Caf (20) ה Hay (5) נ Nun (50) ת Tav (400) = 505

God speaks to Moses about creating B'nai Yisrael's priesthood and introduces the concept of an eternal bloodline with particular obligations: "you shall anoint them as you had anointed their Father, and they shall minister to me, and so it shall be that their anointment shall be for them an eternal priesthood for their generations."

The appointment of Aaron's sons as priests is the act of God making a covenant with them as he does with Sarah and Abraham. Flowing from Chesed, the covenant is the Creator's endowment to these people, enabling their performance of holy acts for the community. The priesthood is Chesed balanced by Chochmah (wisdom), Binah (understanding), and Gevurah (judgment). Laws different from those ruling the conduct of other men and women rule the *kohanim* (priests) and the Kohen Gadol (High Priest). Through this law, which is more stringent and involves more limitations, we see that when Chesed is balanced by proportioned limitation (Gevurah), the holy blessings of the Creator have a vessel in which to reside.

their iniquities פשעיהם (sins, Leviticus 16:21–22): פ Pey (80) ש Shin (300) ע Ayin (70) י Yod (10) ה Hay (5) ם Mem (40) = 505

Just prior to the first erection of the Tabernacle, God speaks to Moses: "Aaron shall lean his two hands upon the head of the living he-goat and confess upon it all the iniquities of the Children of Israel, and all their rebellious sins among all their sins, and place them upon the head of the he-goat, and send it with a designated man to the desert. Then the he-goat will bear upon itself all their iniquities to an uninhabited land, and he should send the he-goat to the desert."

The confession of the Kohen Gadol (High Priest) for the people's sins acts as a national confession. The scapegoat acts as the vessel effecting the community's atonement. By sending the he-goat into the desert, all of Israel's sins are forgiven. This he-goat reflects the offering of Isaac by Abraham and Sarah as the sacrificial gift to God from which we derive an emanation whenever we recite the Akeidah prayer. This communal sacrifice on Yom Kippur and its recitation in prayer invigorates the shine of the Third Temple to be built on Mt. Moriah. Once again, we see an element of Sarah's personal history concealed in her name itself.

test המסה (trials, Deuteronomy 7:19): ה Hay (5) מ Mem (40) ס Samech (60) ת Tav (400) = 505

Moses recounts the miracles God did for Israel: "The great test [trials] that your eyes saw, and the signs, the wonders, the strong hand and the outstretched arm, God your God took you out—so shall God your God do to all the peoples before whom you fear." We see the reiteration of Chesed as the outstretched arm of God.

The Words of Sarah's Inner Story in the Torah

Sarah's inner story, concealed in words and expressions equal to the numeric value of her name, revolves around the instruments through which God preserves life and makes himself present. We find 505 reflected in the Ark after the Flood; in the appointment of Aaron's sons; in the Tabernacle that accompanied them throughout their wanderings—a precedent to the Beit Hamikdash;[60] and in individual and communal atonement, just as Sarah's tent was personal and communal.

The promise of emancipation and the shine from the promise of the Third Temple on Mt. Moriah are concealed in Sarah's life story. Sarah as teacher of the women merits the miracles of the hovering cloud, the

---

[60] This all-inclusive description of the Temple reflects that the resting place of the divine Shechinah is in the holy Temple and its instruments.

eternal lamp, the perfect dough for making challah out of wheat, birth for all women, hearing the angels speak, hearing God speak, and seeing and selecting the burial place of the matriarchs and patriarchs. Her tent precedes the Tabernacle, showing us how Chesed in our lives is the quality of God's presence represented by the nurturing wife–mother–grandmother of the patriarchs. Sarah reveals how Chesed exists in the world and in our lives.

72: The Numeric Value of Chesed

Chesed חסד: ח Chet (8) ס Samech (60) ד Dalet (4) = 72

In this chapter's final look through the lens of gematria, we find several expressions linked to the numeric value of Chesed, or 72. There are several examples to explore more fully.

their heart לבם (Genesis 42:28): ל Lamed (30) ב Bet (2) ם Mem (40) = 72

Your son בנכ (Exodus 10:2): ב Bet (2) נ Nun (50) כ Caf (20) = 72

to his tent לאהלו (Leviticus 14:8): ל Lamed (30) א Alef (1) ה Hay (5) ל Lamed (30) ו Vav (6) = 72

The words in these examples show us a key commonality among the stories of Sarah's tent, son, and heart. Also interesting to note is that there are seventy-two names of the Creator, suggesting that all of his attributes derive from love.

THE TRADITIONS SARAH ORIGINATED

Now that we have examined the hidden mysteries of Sarah's life and purpose, let us close by looking breifly at the traditions that, according to the Torah, originated with Sarah.

Sarah's Tent: The First Sanctuary

Sarah's tent (*ohel*) is the precedent for the Tent of Meeting and for the Tabernacle as the Holy of Holies, reflecting the light of the Or En Sof (the endless light) of Keter. Keter is the crown and source (emanation) of all life—Atzilut. Using vessels as the recipients and distributors of the Holy Spirit's life force, we bring down the light into the action of the physical kingdom (Malchut, Asiyah).

Sarah is the first holder of the holy lamp. In Sarah's ohel, a lamp burns from Sabbath to Sabbath, making her tent the first sanctuary. Sarah is the first holder of the eternal flame now prominent in every Jewish synagogue in the world. It is her flame that precedes the flame that remained lit while the First and Second Temples stood. As a symbol for Chesed, the unlimited light suggests the presence of the Shechinah. Sarah's tent, like those of the Israelites after the tenth plague in Egypt, is always full of light, while the Egyptian tents are shrouded in darkness.

During Sarah's life, the divine presence hovers in the form of a cloud at the entrance to her tent, just as the hovering cloud exists on the merit of Aaron, Miriam's younger brother, during the Exodus. We are taught that when Sarah dies, all these miracles cease until Rebecca, Sarah's daughter-in-law, arrives as Isaac's wife. Through Sarah and the other primary women in the tent (the other matriarchs as told in Judges 5:24), along with Rebecca, Rachel, and Leah, we are shown the place of God's meeting even before Moses was born. God's Divine Immanence or Shechinah was present in the women's tent.

In addition, with the monthly observance of the New Moon—Rosh Chodesh—the new (head) of the month begins with Sarah and the women of her time. It is a beautiful image to regard the seven prophetesses as the holy women of the New Moon. The moon, representing Malchut and the Shechinah fully embodied in the world, will one day be equal to the sun. There will be two great lights in the sky.

Diminishing for an Eventual Aliyah

This beautiful teaching, presented in more detail in chapter 10, is the cosmic story of humanity's diminishment, like Sarah's initial diminishment, for the sake of a greater elevation (*aliyah,* "going up"). We see this again in the lives of Miriam, Chanah, and Esther—and we have likely experienced this in our own lives.

In Ashlagian Kabbalah, an initial diminishment for an eventual elevation is a process of refinement. We see this holy pattern in the origins of humankind's epic biblical story. After the sin of eating from the Tree of Knowledge, all of humanity took part in being diminished. No longer would everything be easily provided; we must work for our daily sustenance. Rather than having, by the gift of God, an eternal body as a companion to the eternal soul, we have acquired this garment of the soul, built as it is on the thought, speech, and action of each person's free will.

The epic journey of humanity is to restore eternal life to the body, the vessel of the soul. By the merit of every person's love of the Creator and attachment to the process of elevating everything in life to its greatest potential through proper self-management according to Kabbalah, this is what is the outcome of living a Torah-centered life. The People of the Book are to walk the middle path, the middle of the Tree of Life, showing others a way for completing our purpose as God-like human beings. Each Sefirah makes this possible. Each prophetess reflects the components we are made of and also reflects the world's composition.

Sarah's Sabbath Obligations

Being familiar now with the essence of Chesed, let us look at the Jewish woman's Sabbath obligations. These rituals, like prayers, are spiritual tools for building a holy life. Performing them creates a vessel filled with the presence of the Shechinah. When a woman performs her Sabbath rituals in joy, she reflects Chesed's capacity for loving-kindness and mercy, the ultimtate barometer for justice and goodness in the family and community. These qualities are embodied through the holy candles and the Sabbath bread.

Chesed is the first gate of self-refinement—loving-kindness mixed with wisdom (Chochmah), understanding (Binah), and knowledge (Daat). Loving-kindness makes the woman "like" the Creator—an emanator—even though her general purpose is as a vessel (kelim), if we distinguish between the light (emanator, or) and vessel (receiver, kelim).

The Sabbath candles. Lighting the Sabbath candles can be compared to lighting the flame of love in our heart or in the ohel, the Tent of Meeting in the body. Sarah's holy lamp, which remains lit from Sabbath to Sabbath, adds to the world's shine of the heart. As it is said in Chassidut, the body is the wick and the soul the oil that is lit, and it is the heart that fans that fire. The light in us and on the Sabbath table represents the eternal covenant between God and His created beings. The two lit candles tell us of the inherent equality between the sun and the moon, which we will examine in detail in the sections on Esther and the Shechinah (chapters 9 and 10). The Sabbath candles represent the primary teaching that we should remember (*zachor*) and guard (*shomer*) and perform Shabbat. The flames stand for the Shechinah, whose presence is above and below, and thus we are shown that peace (shalom) comes from the proper balance of two elements, such as Chochmah and Binah, Chesed and Gevurah, Netzach and Hod. The two candles reflect the combined light of each pillar, bringing the presence of God's completeness into every home and heart. At the close of Sabbath, a three-wick candle is lit with the accompanying Havdalah prayer of Gevurah, separating the holy from the secular but also, as Sarah shows us, elevating the secular to its holy purpose. This is the middle path—when the pillars of the Etz Chayim are combined in balance in our life journey.

The song of wheat and the importance of challah. The Perek Shira, the Song of the Universe mentioned in chapter 2, adds another confirmation of Sarah's role in the Sefirah of Chesed. According to Psalms 130:1, "A Song of ascents. From the Depths I called you, God."[61]

The Arizal (R. Isaac Luria) equates Chesed with the species of wheat, and the Ramak (R. Moshe Cordovero) places the prophetess Sarah in the Sefirah of Chesed. Both of these teachings are reflected here, as we have explored. Sarah's home or tent (ohel) is always open to strangers. It is taught that Sarah's dough (wheat) for the Sabbath, challah (sacramental loaves), is blessed. Regardless of the number of guests, she never lacks dough for bread. With wheat in the Sefirah of Chesed and the grain used to make challah, Chochmah—the Sefirah of wisdom above Chesed on

---

[61] "Jews do not despair! There is always hope, because we have a God of mercy!... This is the message of the wheat sheaf. Its future is brightest when it is smashed and dismembered— because that is when its kernels are gathered from the chaff and are milled to make the flour that will nourish man" (Perek Shira, 54).

the right pillar—flows directly into Chesed. The ritual bread is a product of wisdom, and the challah dough of Sarah is the precedent for the miracle of manna, which feeds B'nai Yisrael in the desert during their forty years in the wilderness after their emancipation from Egypt. It is interesting that this very sequence of challah becoming manna and then matzah (unleavened bread, the bread of Gevurah) is represented in the story of the second prophetess of Israel, Miriam.

The Sabbath bread reminds us that manna is not just a physical food, a gift God bestows on the wandering Israelites, but is an overflow of Chochmah (wisdom) to Chesed (loving-kindness). Manna is the light of the Creator manifested as created sustenance. It does not grow from the earth, but rather is showered downward from heaven. It is created as Chochmah in the realm of Atzilut as God's merciful food—the limitless light as root—and as Chesed in the realm of Beriyah, or creation. The two loaves of sacramental bread blessed at the Sabbath table represent the double portion of manna the Israelites collect the day before Shabbat. Acts of loving-kindness, or perfecting our Chesed, result in a double portion of good fortune.

Making challah for sacramental loaves teaches us how to prepare ourselves as an offering to the Creator. We are to plant the grains (seeds) of Torah in our lives, to work our lives toward self-refinement, turning over the ego, digging deeply, and praying for rain (God's merciful love) in its proper time. We are to harvest what we produce by separating the wheat from the chaff in ourselves. We are to mix it with oil (soul pressings) or water (Torah) with kneading actions (refining work with our hands). In the same way that we make bread, we are to shape our lives. Binah, the Mother (Imma) and the root of mercy (*rachamim*),[62] flows to Chesed and receives endowment from Chochmah (Father, Abba), wisdom.

Sarah's challah as an eternal shine from Chesed is reflected as the loaves shared during the Sabbath that the High Priests consecrated when the Temples stood. The loaves of bread made for Shabbat by the women of the community are divine representations of loving-kindness from the Creator and represent manna. That Sarah's dough is endless shows

---

[62] Personal discussions with Rav Avraham Brandwein, July 7, 2006.

the presence of the Shechinah, that which creates unlimited bounty, the flowing of Chesed from Binah (understanding) and Chochmah (wisdom), the efforts of both the Mother and Father of the Etz Chayim combined to feed their children (lower middot).

Wheat requires that we separate the chaff from the grain in the same way that we are to remove from ourselves what is coarse and unrefined in order to reveal the grain of truth implanted in each one of us. The Temple rituals during the time period of prophecy included wheat offerings as part of the daily meal offering. These showbreads were made from wheat, both in the Temple and, since that time, on our Sabbath tables. If not properly balanced by other foods, such as barley (Gevurah), grapes (Tiferet), figs (Netzach), pomegranates (Hod), olive oil (Yesod), and date honey (Malchut), wheat can lead us to feel too expanded or ungrounded. Eating wheat abundantly without the other species and their vitalities can lead to illness, just as Chesed without boundaries can lead to an expansion beyond our borders—in other words, to sins such as gluttony, jealousy, and incest.

Sarah (Chesed) Corresponds to the Right Hand

As we saw earlier, in the numeric value of Sarah's name (505) there is a direct value pertaining to Chesed as God's strong right arm and hand. Because most people are right-handed, we equate the right hand with the hand of action, with the hand that initiates what we do.

Chesed also represents God's mercy and the strong hand or strong arm that takes us out of captivity, one of the expressions concealed in the numeric value of Sarah's name. Because mouth, hands, and feet are considered in Chassidut to be the body's ministers, this correspondence instructs us to rely on loving-kindness in all that we do. In our prayers, the right hand is represented by the name Adonai, a name of loving adornment, and the left hand (Gevurah) is designated Elokim, or judgment and rectification of error. In our lives, Chesed signifies engaging the world with a charitable heart.

The oral tradition teaches that when we are lost, we should turn to the right. When we are in doubt about how to behave, turn toward Chesed: Do what is most generous given the situation. It is a navigation tool for living.

SUMMARIZING THE IMPORTANCE
OF SARAH

We learn from the miracles attending Sarah—the eternal light, the challah dough, the New Moon blessings, the hovering cloud, the birth of Isaac, the participation in the Akeidah, and more—that prophets and prophetesses do not simply tell others what God has said. Their very presence in the community changes it and contributes to its refinement. Their lifetime dramas and accomplishments are part of their roles as seers and leaders. Sarah's marriage, her ordeals of being abducted, teaching women, overseeing the ritual bath for women, talking with the angels and God, the birth and willing sacrifice of her son—all of these elements in her personal life became the events through which the community related to her. The women of prophecy had a deep involvement in the community's welfare both spiritually and physically.

We find that Sarah's presence, along with that of Abraham and Isaac, plays a role beyond her lifetime, guiding us toward the messianic days we are approaching. It shows us the importance of Chesed in the world. In Baba Metzia, a tractate from the Talmud, we learn of an incident involving R. Yehudah Hanasi: It is said that Elijah would often appear at his school and place of study (*yeshiva*) and that one day, on Rosh Chodesh, the New Moon, the first day of the new month:

> Rabbi waited for Elijah, but he did not appear. [When he did come] Rabbi asked him, "Why did you not come until now?" Elijah replied, "[I was busy.] I had to wake up Abraham, wash his hands, allow him to pray, and he would have to go to sleep afterward. I had to do the same for Isaac and again for Jacob." Questioned Rabbi, "Why not wake them all up at the same time?" Replied Elijah, "if they all prayed simultaneously, they would inject so much mercy into the world that Moshiach would come before his time. That is why I am not allowed to wake them up at the same time."[63]

---

[63] R. Yaakov Ibn Chaviv, *Ein Yaakov,* Baba Metzia, 539.

Through our prayers, God's mercy and judgment, sweetened by Chesed, will bring Moshiach at the appropriate time. Chesed showered upon the world as a result of personal atonement will bring redemption. Chesed accomplishes its influence by being balanced with the next step in the Shechinah's descent into the world through Gevurah—or Miriam— whom we will study next.

As observed in Sarah's life and the concealed wisdom in her name, we are shown how to bring the Creator's blessings through Chesed. We have seen how the length of Sarah's life and the events that occur during her life are found through the story of the letters composing her name. We have seen how the love of God, the willingness to separate the pure from the impure in ourselves and in our environment, and observing the holy mitzvah of honoring the Sabbath as the outcome of Creation all contribute to a holy life and the presence of the Shechinah, hence the capacity for prophecy.

The End and the Beginning

The end is embedded in the beginning. In Sarah's life are reflected the beginning (creation) of B'nai Yisrael and the promise of redemption (the end of our refinement). In Chesed (Sarah), we find the source of redemption (Malchut, Queen Esther) and the promise of the Third Temple (the light of Mt. Moriah), where the Akeidah occurred.

In all that we do, we are to invest love (Chesed) in the kingdom of the world (Malchut) and in our actions (Asiyah). This is referred to in Kabbalah as Chesed of Malchut of Asiyah. To do this without being taken captive by the kelipot (the shells of evil), we must first attach ourselves to God and, with loving intention, give to others. It is this intention that reflects the wisdom and will of the Creator so that our deeds are themselves as numerous as the stars, like Abraham and Sarah's descendants. When we act in the world through our generous nature, through selflessness, the countless blessings of the Creator are ushered from above to below in response. Sarah shows us that the seed of life is love, that the light of Chesed is life itself.

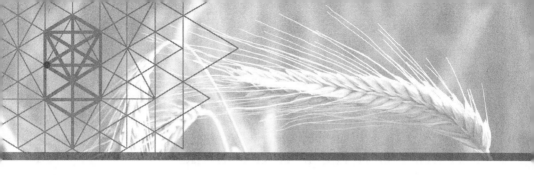

4

Miriam

Gevurah · The Waters of Deliverance

*As a reward for the righteous women who lived in that
generation, our forefathers were delivered from Egypt.*
SOTAH, R. YAAKOV IBN CHAVIV, *EIN YAAKOV*,
"THE MERIT OF THE RIGHTEOUS WOMEN"

Miriam מרים

מ Mem (40) ר Reish (200) י Yod (10) ם Mem (40) = 290

Sefirah Correspondence: Gevurah

Titles: Prophetess, Midwife, Leader

Family: Daughter of Yocheved and Amram, older sister of Moses and
  Aaron, wife of Calev, grandmother of Betzalel

Time Period	Jewish Calendar	Gregorian Calendar
Life (birth–death)	2362–2487	1398–1273 BCE
Exodus from Egypt	2448	1312 BCE
Entered land of Israel	2488	1272 BCE

Developmental Stage: Deliverance

Day: Monday

Sacred Species: Barley

Body Correspondence: Left arm or hand

Rituals: Repentance, midwifery, song and dance

Holidays: Pesach (Passover) and Sefirat HaOmer (Counting of the Omer)

Symbols: The miracle of the "traveling" well, the red heifer

Prayers: Vidui, Tashlich, Tevilat Kelim, Havdalah

Shine of Miriam–Gevurah: The birth of the messianic age, Moshiach's birth

Prophecy Source: Exodus 15:20

Miriam's Song: Exodus 15:20, "Sing to God for he is exalted above the arrogant . . ."

SEFIRAH: GEVURAH

The Sefirah of Gevurah is commonly referred to as the place of judgment and strength. It is the Sefirah of boundary-making epitomized by Miriam's role among her people as a prophetess midwife and leader. Her capacity for self-refinement through atonement teaches us the deeper spiritual meaning of deliverance and judgment.

Phase of Development: After the seed (Chesed) is planted and the light proceeds to the next Sefirah of Gevurah, what is holy is separated from the unholy. Appreciation and attendance to disciplined behavior arise. This awareness facilitates the process of repentance (*teshuvah*) and a return to the path of a balanced life.

World Action: Gevurah helps us to lead others and to use the divine will and soul for control of our animal nature and selfish desires. It exercises the influx of Chesed, loving-kindness with judgment, discriminating where to serve, whom to serve, and how to serve.

Spiritual Action: Gevurah requires that we add mercy to our judgment: Gevurah with Chesed. Acts of loving-kindness balanced by proper discernment describe this Sefirah. In prayer it is applied will to self-refinement, a type of spiritual forbearance or strength necessary in repentance. Gevurah teaches us how to nullify our egos.

Meaningful Work: Gevurah enables leadership in new ventures that take courage to administer or positions of decision making as a disciplined visionary or with work in justice, grassroots activities, or entrepreneurship.

Day Focus: Gevurah facilitates sorting through our life, belongings, and feelings and deciding what to keep and what to discard. This life review takes a spiritual form each night before we go to bed, when we look through our day and ask for forgiveness not only for what we have done now, but also for what we have done in other incarnations.

Species: Barley as a grain offering or a wave offering was the first product of the year to be taken to the Temple. Barley also is integral to the ritual process that takes place between the second night of Pesach and the eve of Shavuot, a forty-nine-day process called Sefirat HaOmer (Counting of the Omer).[1]

MIRIAM'S STORY

Other than Esther, Miriam is the only prophetess about whose childhood we know something. She was the older **sister of Aaron and Moses,** who was not yet born when she was a young girl. She accompanied her mother, Yocheved, as a **midwife,** and together they defied the pharaoh. Miriam, strong-willed and attached to God, **challenged her father, Amram,** about his separation from her mother's bed. After going to the council of elders (Sanhedrin), Amram returned and remarried Yocheved. **Miriam danced** around her mother during the wedding ceremony, leading her younger brother Aaron in celebration. She prophesied Moses' birth and status as a redeemer and exemplifies the **courage** and strength of a prophetess, having faith in her prophecies even when others doubted her. She engineered Moses' safe return to his mother, who acted as his

---

[1] This Kabbalistic ritual traverses, one week at a time, all seven Sefirot we are studying. The purpose is self-refinement and self-repair in order to enable the Shechinah to rest within us so that we are able to receive the Torah on Shavuot. The Torah is the Shechinah's body (*guff*) and her soul (Neshamah) the shine of God's brilliance within it.

wet nurse, after putting him **into the Nile.** Later, after the Jews were delivered from Egypt, Miriam acted as midwife to the people, bringing them to a new stage of consciousness.

She epitomizes leadership, guiding the women across **the Red Sea,** where her famed **Song at the Sea**—considered her prophecy—took place. From Miriam's merit, the people always had God's presence and mercy in the traveling well of Miriam, which provided water to the Israelites. Her entire life is characterized by the meaning and power of **water,** Torah, and **repentance** (teshuvah) in both a personal and a communal setting. Later, when she challenged God's choice of Moses as spokesman for the people and chastised Moses for marrying a Cushite woman, she was punished by God and stricken with **leprosy.** She healed in a week, and B'nai Yisrael waited for her return to health before moving forward in their journey.

Miriam's repentance (teshuvah) shows us a **three-stage process** in which we come back to God. She taught the people the importance of personal and communal repentance. Miriam lived eighty-six years, and over her the angel of death had no power. She died first in the same year her two brothers, Moses and Aaron, died. None entered the Holy Land.

SYMBOLISM OF MIRIAM

A broken and humbled heart, O God, You will not disdain.

PSALMS 15:19

Sister of Aaron and Moses

We first meet Miriam, also called Puah, when she is five years old and accompanies her mother, Yocheved (Shifrah), as a midwife attendant. They are the midwives summoned in Egypt by the pharaoh.[2] He tells them, "when you deliver the Hebrew women, and you see them on the birth stool; if it is a son, you are to kill him, and if it is a daughter, she

---

[2] Shemot Rabbah 1:13, Exodus 1:15. The Hebrew midwives were Yocheved and Miriam. Miriam, who was only five years old at that time, went with Yocheved to assist her.

shall live."[3] Miriam and her mother "feared God and they did not do as the King of Egypt spoke to them, and they caused the boys to live."[4] The pharaoh summons them again and asks why they did not follow his orders, to which they reply: "[T]he Hebrew women are unlike the Egyptian women, for they are experts; before the midwife comes to them, they have given birth."[5]

This is an act of group rebellion in the Torah, and Miriam is the youngest leader. The Israelite women's collective rebellion against the pharaoh, even under threat of death, is a commitment to God. "God benefited the midwives and the people increased and became very strong. And it was the midwives who feared God that he made them houses."[6]

Gevurah as Return to God

"R. Avira expounded: As a reward for the righteous women who lived in that generation, our forefathers were delivered from Egypt. When the women went to draw water, the Holy one, blessed be He, prepared for them small fishes in their jugs so that their jugs would come up half full of water and half full of fishes."[7] The righteous are called fish, as are Moses and Joshua, for like fish, their eyes are always open to the light as they swim in the sea of Torah.

Miriam Challenges Amram

We see Miriam's courage and strength displayed again, prior to Moses' birth, when she confronts her father for divorcing her mother and departing from her mother's bed and for instructing the Israelites to leave their wives because they fear producing sons who will be killed by the Egyptians. Miriam says, "Father, your decree is harsher than Pharaoh's. Pharaoh's decree is directed only against the males, whereas yours [by preventing the birth of newborn children] is directed against the males

---

[3] Exodus 1:16.
[4] Exodus 1:17.
[5] Exodus 1:19.
[6] Exodus 1:20.
[7] R. Yaakov Ibn Chaviv, *Ein Yaakov*, Sotah, "The Merit of the Righteous Women," 447.

and females."[8] While only six years old at the time of this incident, the divine spirit, Ruach HaKodesh, infuses Miriam. Her father, Amram, so astounded by her "voice," takes Miriam before the Sanhedrin, the high court of seventy Jewish elders. They say that he is the one forbidding marriage and thus, likewise, could permit it. "What do you advise?" asks Amram, "Shall we marry quietly?" They reply, "then who will make it known to all Israel?"[9]

Dancing around the Shechinah

Amram remarries his wife, Yocheved, seating her for a wedding procession. "Aaron and Miriam sang and danced before her [happy that the savior of Israel would be born to their mother] when married to their Father."[10] Here we witness Miriam and her younger brother, Aaron, who will become the leaders of Israel, celebrating their parents' reunion. Aaron shows his faith in Miriam's prophecy concerning their parents' giving birth to the promised redeemer. We are told that at that moment "the ministering angels said, 'The Mother of children is joyful.'"[11] The Shechinah is seated on the throne and the guardians of B'nai Yisrael are rejoicing.

This celebratory dance by Aaron and Miriam is a holy convocation. Dancing is an act that uses the entire body for joyous celebration, creating a vessel for prophecy to occur. Here, Gevurah is elevated to Binah above it on the left pillar, receiving the direct shine of Or En Sof from Keter in the realm of Atzilut (emanation) preceding it, showing us the elevation of both children, Aaron and Miriam. Aaron is later appointed High Priest of Israel and merits the protective cloud of glory during the Exodus. Miriam merits the miracle of the well, which provides water to the Israelites during their sojourn.

Together, their attendance is re-created in their adulthood in the

---

[8] Sotah 12a.

[9] Pesikta Rabbati 43:27. See also R, Yishai Chasidah, *Encyclopedia of Biblical Personalities,* 338.

[10] Sotah 12a, Bava Kama 120a. See also R. Yishai Chasidah, *Encyclopedia of Biblical Personalities,* 338.

[11] Sotah 19a, Psalms 113:0. See also R, Yishai Chasidah, *Encyclopedia of Biblical Personalities,* 338.

dance at the Red Sea. Both times their joyous dancing causes an arousal from below, an *itaruta delitata*, creating a vessel to be filled. This is followed by a reciprocal arousal from above, an *itaruta deliayla*, or God's response of filling that vessel with light. Kabbalistically, "God's flow of benevolence [is] termed *mayyim duchrin* (masculine waters); man's obedience to God and fulfillment of the divine commandments are viewed as a stream rising from man to God, [and are] termed *mayyim nukvin* (feminine waters); the former may come as an act of pure grace,"[12] or by the result of our positive actions. Baal HaTanya shows us why "the God–man relationship in Kabbalah is often symbolized in terms of the meeting of the streams of water."[13]

Miriam as Midwife

Miriam is the midwife of B'nai Yisrael. Gevurah is painful in the same way that childbirth contractions are painful, but the birth of the child causes great joy. We live in the time period referred to as the "birth pangs of Moshiach." As with Miriam and the Israelites before us, will the world's messianic age revolve in large measure around water—both its bounty and its scarcity?[14] In terms of the Shechinah, the midwife is expert in aiding even the smallest opening to expand to give birth. This process is evident in childbirth and is experienced spiritually in teshuvah (repentance).

It is interesting that Miriam's early prophecies, according to the oral tradition and her communal position, all revolve around the issue of birth. Beginning at the age of five, she helps her mother deliver Hebrew babies. Gevurah can represent a severe contraction or that which is called, in Kabbalah, *tzimtzum,* a Hebrew term referring to God's act of withdrawing himself in order to create the universe. Developmentally, Sarah is the seed of creation and Miriam represents deliverance, the manifestation of

---

[12] R. Schneur Zalman of Liadi, *Likkutei Amarim Tanya,* part 1, glossary, chapters 4, 10, 53.

[13] Ibid.

[14] As the world begins its final descent from the current age of Yesod to the age of Malchut, we, like Miriam, are the midwives of Moshiach. We must "sweeten the bitter waters" with our prayers and proper actions.

that seed. Sarah is the mother of Israel; Miriam is Israel's midwife. Her first prophecy, according to the oral tradition, foretells Moses' birth: "My Mother is destined to bear a son who will redeem Israel."[15] When Moses is born, "the whole house was filled with light." Miriam's father, Amram, "kissed her on her head and said 'My Daughter, your prophecy has been fulfilled . . .'"[16]

Just as healthy childbirth takes place nine months after incubation in the womb, so Gevurah gives us the discipline to prepare for the deliverance, the manifestation of any idea, task, or belief.

Miriam's Courage

Miriam's courageous actions on behalf of the Creator and the truths of Torah she learns are astonishing examples of bravery and how our courage inspires others. Setting boundaries, the essential purpose of Gevurah, makes it possible for us to keep our place. Miriam is a shepherd who keeps the flock in order, making sure that things that flow down the Nile arrive at their appointed destination. Like Sarah, Miriam is a teacher of the women;[17] both are the grandmothers of holy leaders.

It is said that Betzalel's wisdom is in Miriam's merit. As Exodus 1:21 says, "It is written [God] made them houses, the priesthood and the monarchy. Miriam received wisdom. She produced Betzalel and from her issued David."[18] Betzalel is the architect and maker of the Tabernacle and its instruments. David, of course, becomes king, the lineage from which Moshiach will descend, the human vessel for Moshiach's holiness and presence to descend to earth.

Moses Is Placed into the Nile

Three months after the birth of Moses, we meet Miriam at the water's edge. Hoping to save him from being put to death by the Egyptians, Miriam and Yocheved place Moses in a basket in the Nile. Then "her

---

[15] Megillah 14a.
[16] Megillah 14a.
[17] Targum Michah 6:4.
[18] Shemot Rabbah 48:4.

mother slapped her on the head and said, "My daughter, where is your prophecy?"[19]

Miriam waits a little while for Moses' discovery. With an obvious plan from the start, staying by the water's edge, "his sister stationed herself at a distance to know what would be done with him."[20] The pharaoh's daughter comes "to bathe by the river" and sees the basket among the reeds. She has her servant pull out the basket, and then the pharaoh's daughter opens it and finds the child crying. "She took pity on him and said, 'This is one of the Hebrew Boys,'"[21] who were easily recognized by their circumcision.

Miriam then asks the princess, "[S]hall I go and summon for you a wet nurse from the Hebrew women, who will nurse the boy for you?"[22] Miriam retrieves her mother, Yocheved, who is reunited with her son, the prophet and emancipator of the Israelites. Miriam, as receiver and enabler of God's Word, shows complete faith in God. This epic moment in Torah history suggests a story yet to unfold anticipating the birth of Moshiach and the messianic age. From each Sefirah's roots grow elements of the past, present, and future.

Miriam's Song at the Sea

Miriam and her brothers are destined to lead Israel together. "Three good leaders arose for Israel; Moses, Aaron and Miriam."[23] After Moses is raised as a prince of Egypt in the pharaoh's house, demonstrating the descent into the kelipot for the eventual elevation of the Israelites and the Egyptians, our next encounter with Miriam occurs during the Exodus. On the Israelites' behalf, God performs the miracle of separating

---

[19] Shemot Rabbah 1:22. (In some references it says it was her father who slapped Miriam.) This instance is a wonderful example of the kind of courage the Rambam (Maimonides) speaks of as an element of prophecy. In this case, Miriam, who is only a child of six, has to have courage and faith in God to know that what she is shown and what she knows in her heart are true—so true, in fact, that while her mother and father ridicule her, we find that next she carries out her prophetic mission, securing Moses as a prince of Egypt.

[20] Exodus 2:4.

[21] Exodus 2:6.

[22] Exodus 2:7.

[23] Exodus 15:2.

the waters, whereupon the entire Egyptian army is swallowed by the sea. Just as Miriam had saved the Israelite sons from death, here she leads the mothers, daughters, and sisters of Israel in a jubilant song and dance of triumph after they have crossed the Red Sea. Called Miriam's Song, the following verse is taken from the first line (Exodus 15:20; see appendix 1 for the complete text): "Miriam the Prophetess, sister of Aaron, took the drum in her hand and all the women went forth after her with drums and with dances. Miriam spoke up to them, 'sing to God for He is exalted above the arrogant, having hurled horse with its rider into the sea.'"

Here, the theme of rejoicing and praising the Creator is re-created. It is the second stage of the manifestation of Miriam's prophecy. The first is when she helps to restore peace in her family's household in order to set the conditions for Moses' birth. Now, with God's help, Moses has fulfilled his role as emancipator of B'nai Yisrael. Miriam leads these two public ritual dances, marking the events with her very bones, making dance and song a sacred ritual by which the Shechinah can be aroused and the Ruach HaKodesh summoned. Crossing the Red Sea, Miriam as leader of women shows us the nature of courage the Rambam speaks of as necessary in prophecy. Sarah teaches faith and generosity, and Miriam teaches the addition of courage and discernment. Here, these two teachings combine to accomplish deliverance (*geulah*).

The Bitter Waters and Waters of Deliverance

The parting of the Red Sea, which precedes the successful crossing of the Israelites out of Egypt, can be compared to the breaking of the waters in childbirth. It is only after this that the child is born. Miriam is midwife to the entire people, helping them reach a new stage of development. Miriam's well, like womb waters, sustained the Israelites during their epochal forty-year process of incubation.

After crossing the Red Sea, B'nai Yisrael continues toward Israel for three days without water. "They Came to Marah—but they could not drink the waters of Marah, because they were bitter; therefore they named it Marah."[24]

---

[24] Exodus 15:23.

The community then calls out to Moses, "What shall we drink?" Moses cries out to God—and God shows "him a Tree; he threw it into the water and the water became sweet. . . . There he established for the Nation a decree and an ordinance and there he tested it. He said, 'If you hearken diligently to the voice of God your God and do what is just in His eye, give ear to His commandments and observe all of His decrees, then any of the disease that I placed in Egypt, I will not bring upon you, for I am God your healer.'"[25] The next line in Torah tells us that the Children of Israel are rewarded for all their ordeals. Did those whose thirst was quenched by the sweetened waters of the bitter exile merit being brought into the land of milk and honey in the same way that those who suckled from Sarah were descendents of the righteous? Did they reach a spiritual apex of the covenant for their generation? Perhaps they brought down the Shechinah from the highest source of the Creator (Atzilut, emanation) to the physical world of the kingdom (Asiyah, action)—a model for every human being then and now. Was Miriam's well, like Sarah's milk, a source of the Creator's Divine Immanence?

". . . They arrived at Elim, where there were twelve springs of water and seventy date-palms; they encamped there by the water."[26] The twelve springs have great significance. Having already learned that the relationship between God and man in Kabbalah is represented by the meeting of the streams of water, the twelve springs represent the Twelve Tribes of Israel, which are commemorated again after the people cross the Jordan River. The seventy date palms are symbolic of the Sanhedrin, the council of elders, represented by Devorah and Tiferet. The number 70 is the Hebrew letter Ayin and is also the word for "eye," suggesting the vision gained from Torah for rendering justice.

"They encamped there by the water" suggests a place of arrival. A month and half later, "fifteen days of the second month,"[27] the Children of Israel speak to Moses and Aaron, saying, "If only we had died by the hand of HaShem in the land of Egypt, as we sat by the pot of meat, when

---

[25] Exodus 16:26.
[26] Exodus 15:27.
[27] Exodus 16:1.

we ate bread to satiety, for you have taken us out to this wilderness to kill the entire congregation by famine."[28]

The Creator tells Moses, "Behold—I shall rain down food from the heaven," which is manna, and then He gives the laws pertaining to its collection, showing His love of His people. But God creates a test to find out "whether they will follow My teaching or not."[29] The Israelites are told to collect a double portion of manna on Friday and are prohibited its collection on Sabbath. Those who collect extra manna at night discover that by morning it is infested. Also, each person has only the amount needed, regardless of how much manna each has collected. Still, God fulfills His Word, raining down manna and quail at night.

Here we see how Chesed, the Sefirah of Sarah, representing overflowing beneficence and preceding Miriam and Gevurah, commingles with the harsh experience of exile. This demonstrates the descent of the light and how elements of every prophetess and Sefirah are embodied in those who follow and in the light's ascent—and why it is said that we stand on the shoulders of our ancestors.

Miriam Is Punished by God

The next time we hear of Miriam after the crossing of the Red Sea, after the bitter waters, and after the miracle of manna is in Numbers 12:1–4. "Miriam and Aaron speak against Moses, regarding the Cushite woman he had married . . ."[30] They ask, "Was it only to Moses that God spoke? Did he not speak to us, as well?" And God hears. "Now the man Moses was exceedingly humble, more than any person on the face of the earth. . . .[31] God said suddenly to Moses, to Aaron, and to Miriam, 'you three go out to the Tent of Meeting.' And the three of them went out."[32]

This is the only time all three of these siblings are addressed as one unit in the Torah and are separated from the rest of B'nai Yisrael.

---

[28] Exodus 16:3.

[29] Exodus 16: 26.

[30] Numbers 12:2.

[31] Numbers 12:3.

[32] Numbers12:4.

God then descends in a pillar of cloud and stands at the entrance to the tent. He summons Aaron and Miriam, and to them He says: "Hear now my words. If there shall be Prophets among you, in a vision shall I, God make myself known to him; in a dream shall I speak with him, not so with my servant Moses; in my entire House he is the trusted one. Mouth to mouth do I speak to him, in a clear vision and not riddles, at the image of God does he gaze. Why did you speak against my servant Moses?"[33] Then God's wrath rises up and He departs: "The cloud had departed from atop the tent, and behold, Miriam was afflicted with Tzaras [tzarat], like snow! Aaron turned to Miriam and behold, she was afflicted with Tzaras [tzarat]."[34]

Leprosy and Repentance

> R. Shmuel b. Nachmani said in the name of R. Yochanan:
> Because of seven things the plague leprosy is brought down
> on people, namely slander, bloodshed, false oath, incest,
> arrogance, robbery and envy.
>
> ARACHIN 16a

Furthermore, we are taught, "The Holy one, blessed is He, accorded Miriam great honor at that time. He said, "I [will serve as] a priest [for her]; I will quarantine her, I will declare her a leper, and I will discharge her."[35]

God himself ministers to Miriam for the entire week of her quarantine, benefiting all of B'nai Yisrael. The Akeidat Yitzchak (the prayer related to the sacrifice of Isaac) in Sarah's life becomes the merit by which all of Israel benefits to this day and in which is concealed the promise of the building of the Third Temple on Mt. Moriah (the Temple Mount of modern-day Jerusalem). So, too, Miriam's teshuvah helped elevate all of B'nai Yisrael as they prepared to enter Israel. Her diminishment, as we see in Sarah's life of barrenness, is for all of Israel's eventual elevation and for the Israelites' removal from Egypt by the strong arm of God.

---

[33] Numbers 12:6.
[34] Numbers 12:10.
[35] Zevachim 102a.

Teshuvah: Foundation of Redemption and Deliverance

Free will is the foundation of teshuvah. As a teacher, Miriam is an example to her people. Gevurah expresses the process we each go through in choosing right action through humility. Her quarantine expresses this process of repentance by which all of B'nai Yisrael benefits. The Rambam's *Hilchot Teshuvah* says:

> [E]ach person is fit to be righteous like Moses, our teacher, or wicked like Jerobam. [Similarly] he may be wise or foolish, merciful or cruel, miserly or generous, or [acquire] any other character traits. There is no one who compels him, sentences him or leads him towards either path. Rather, he, on his own initiative and decision, tends to the path he chooses. This was [implied by the prophet] Jeremiah who stated [Eichah 3:38]: "From the mouth of the most High, neither evil or good come forth."[36]

We cause our own losses. Self-discipline is the cornerstone of the observant person's life, making it possible to choose wisely. "Behold, I have set before you today life and good, death and evil."[37] There is also always hope. Repentance acts as a corrective force. When we recall our failures in judgment and actions and ask for forgiveness, we are, with God's mercy, sweetening the bitter waters of our emotions. Prayers of repentance act as a spiritual remedy for the body and soul. It is for this reason that Chazal (sages) teach, "All the Prophets commanded [the people] to repent. Israel will only be redeemed through Teshuvah."[38] R. Eliezer declares: "If Israel repents, she will be redeemed. If they do not [repent] they will not be redeemed."[39]

---

[36] R. Moses Maimonides (the Rambam), *Mishneh Torah, Hilchot Teshuvah,* chapter 5.

[37] Ibid., *Hilchot Yesodei,* chapter 5, 3; Deuteronomy 30:15. Deuteronomy 11:26 adds, "[B]ehold, I have set before you this day, the blessing and the curse." This implies that the choice between good and evil is in our hands.

[38] R. Moses Maimonides (the Rambam), *Mishneh Torah, Hilchot Teshuvah,* chapter 7, 5. See also Yoma 86b and Sanhedrin 87b, which states that "[a]ll the appointed times for [the messianic redemption] have passed and the matter is only dependent on Teshuvah."

[39] Sanhedrin 87b.

The Six Remembrances

From the daily prayer book used by observant Jewish men and women, at the end of the morning prayers (Shacharit) we recite the Six Remembrances. The first five are the Exodus from Egypt, receiving the Torah at Mt. Sinai, Amalek's attack as the Israelites were leaving Egypt and the killing of the weaklings, the building of the golden calf, and Miriam. The Siddur (prayer book) states, "Remember that which God your God did to Miriam on the way when you were leaving Egypt." The sixth remembrance is the Sabbath ("Remember the day of the Sabbath to sanctify it").

Concerning the fifth remembrance—Miriam: Why aren't the People of the Book counseled to remember Miriam for the miracle of the well or for her midwifery and bravery? Why is she not remembered for her leadership or prophecy? She was the greatest prophetess of her time. Of the six daily remembrances, two are remembrances of something negative: Amalek's murder of the old and infirm at the end of the caravan leaving Egypt and the Israelites' building of the golden calf. One of these is focused on what was done to the Israelites by the evil Egyptian leadership and the other is focused on what Jewish men did in a collective rebellion of evil against the Creator. Three of the remembrances form the pillars of the Jewish people's existence: the Exodus from Egypt, receiving the Torah at Mt. Sinai, and remembering and keeping the Sabbath.

While Miriam has attained the same status as Abraham, Isaac, and Jacob, she is remembered in the Siddur (prayer book) for the most Gevurah-like quality in her life story: challenging God's selection of Moses as the exclusive voice of the Almighty's will and the consequences of her action—her subsequent affliction and teshuvah. Though her momentary arrogance and subsequent *tzarat* (leprosy) form one purpose of this remembrance—to remember what God did to her—a deeper lesson is that God attends the penitent as He did the second of B'nai Yisrael's prophetesses during her teshuvah. God attends each one of us who returns to Him in sincerity. Teshuvah is a disposition of the heart originating in the desire for closeness with God.

The Sefirah directly above Gevurah on the left pillar—Binah, which stands for Mother—flows down to Gevurah. When Imma (Mother) and

Gevurah (judgment) are balanced, there is a proper measure that flows into Tiferet (beauty), the Sefirah following Gevurah in the descent of the light. Loving-kindness (Chesed) mixed with sound judgment (Gevurah) produces truth (Tiferet). Beauty, like truth, is the proper mixture of opposites. Both require a selflessness in which our egos are not invested with some notion or desire for a specific outcome. Instead, we humble ourselves to serve as a vessel for the Creator's will. Devorah and Tiferet, the focus of the next chapter, exemplify this capacity.

Gevurah as Teshuvah: The Narrow Return

Gevurah represents a form of self-evaluation and self-nullification. This teshuvah, and the consequent return to closeness with the Creator, is an ongoing life process. The Baal Teshuvah is a person who returns to Torah of his or her own choosing; those who do stand higher than even the *tzaddikim* (righteous men and women). Why? The tzaddikim, we are told, are born with this inclination to aspire to live righteously and are most often raised for this purpose. The Rambam teaches that the tzaddikim never have the kind of lack that motivates the repentant in their search for God and therefore cannot progress from the level of lack to gain the reward that the Baal Teshuvah does. The Baal Teshuvah chooses by free will to put on the "yoke of Torah," which, by its nature, is more defined by limitations we would not otherwise observe. We are rewarded for the effort put into learning and living the word of the Creator.

Teshuvah: A Three-stage Process

As we have learned, Sarah represents the head of the week as Sunday, the New Year, and Rosh Hashanah, during which is blown the shofar, made of the ram's horn and symbolizing the Akeidah. The three notes blown a total of one hundred times represent three stages of teshuvah that every person experiences in an effort to come closer to God. Expressing the combination of Gevurah and Chesed, the penitent is reminded that this "thing is very near to you, in your mouth, and in your heart, to do it."[40] The Torah refers to the Jewish New Year holiday as the "day of Teruha,"

---

[40] Deuteronomy 30:11–14.

the middle of the three shofar notes blown ritualistically. The teshuvah that we undergo on this holiday is a three-stage process and gives us clues to our own return.[41]

First, we must use our mouth to repent. We must say what we have regrets about. Then we must "wail" and truly feel the broken heart of having sinned. In the third step of our repentance, we are elevated by the change in intention and desire for a new beginning. The broken-hearted are most likely to experience the glory of teshuvah.[42] The shofar calls everyone to return. The shofar was blown when Torah was received at Mt. Sinai[43] and will herald the arrival of Moshiach. "And it shall be on that day a great shofar will be blown . . ."[44]

In the Talmud we are reminded that "the Holy Blessed One said: 'Blow before Me on the shofar of a ram so that I will remember to your credit the Akeidah of Yitzchak the son of Abraham. I will accept your Teshuvah, and I will rescue you from your enemies and adversaries.'"[45]

Teshuvah as the Spiritual Tikkun Olam

In Kabbalah, teshuvah represents the return of the final Hay to the first Hay in the tetragrammaton for the name of God (Havayah יהוה): י Yod ה Hay ו Vav ה Hay. The first Hay represents the Mother, the final Hay stands for the Daughter, Vav represents the Son, and Yod stands for God or Father. The name of God, which we do not pronounce, is the embodiment of the holy family. All the Partzufim are engaged together. (See map 4 on Partzufim, in chapter 2.) Every teshuvah is a correction of an entire world. The act of teshuvah is a full return, a completion represented by closeness to the Creator. A single person returning to a Torah-based life is a rectification of the collective Tree of Life. This explains why we are told that when a single life is saved, it is as if the entire world is saved.

---

[41] Bambidar 29:1.
[42] R. Yitzchak Abohav, *Menoras Hamaor: The Ten Days of Teshuvah*, 38.
[43] Shemot 19:90.
[44] Yeshayahu 27:13.
[45] R. Yitzchak Abohav, *Menoras Hamaor*, Rosh Hashanah 16a, 41.

The Process of Gevurah

Deliverance is an act of God, one of four aspects of the Israelites' emancipation from Egypt[46] commemorated with the four cups of wine during Pesach (Passover), to which Miriam and Gevurah relate.[47] The four promises made by God are:

1. "And I will bring you out from beneath the suffering of Egypt . . ."
2. ". . . and I will save you from their enslavement [of you] . . ."
3. ". . . and I will deliver you . . ."
4. ". . . And I will take you for me, as a Nation, and I will be, for you, the Lord."[48]

The third statement by the Creator, "and I will deliver you," suggests that He and the Shechinah will midwife the birth of the nation of Israel. Unlike other nations, which are born of familiar tribes and then are territorially consolidated, the nation of Israel was created by divine decree. It attests to God's promise that if the People of the Book live by the Book, God will keep His people as a nation intact. As R. Avraham Brandwein reminds us, in the Zohar written by R. Shimon bar Yochai more than eighteen hundred years ago, we learn that "[t]he holy One Blessed be He, the Torah, and Israel are one."[49]

Purification

Prior to Miriam's affliction with tzarat and as if to prepare the nation for her affliction, Torah instructs the Israelites on the method of purifica-

---

[46] Exodus 6:6.

[47] R. Avraham Brandwein, *Classical Kabbalah,* 11.

[48] It is noteworthy that after the Israelites are redeemed, the men are given the mitzvah of putting on *tefillin* before prayer each day except for Sabbath. These phylacteries, or two prayer boxes with leather straps, are worn on the forehead and the left forearm of those who are right-handed and represent the heart (left arm, Gevurah) and head (mind, Chochmah and Daat) being brought together in prayer. Men wear tefillin during the weekday morning prayers. Tefillin symbolize the Holy of Holies of the Temple and contain four passages from the Torah: Exodus 13:1–10 and 11–16 and Deuteronomy 6:4–9 and 11:13–21, which proclaim the existence and unity of God and serve to remind the wearer of the liberation from Egypt.

[49] R. Avraham Brandwein, *Classical Kabbalah,* 11.

tion for those afflicted with disease or those who have become contaminated by handling or encountering anything that is dead. We learn the significance of the ash of the red heifer (the ash acquired from burning the red heifer): It is a remedy for purifying the contaminated, but the ash also contaminates those who prepare it. Torah details the washing and immersing of clothes, utensils, household, and body, as well as the length of time quarantine must be observed, ranging from one day to seven days or longer. Discussed are numerous kinds of skin afflictions, the degree of contamination that can occur, and what signs of healthy healing are determined by the Kohen Gadol (High Priest) through inspection of every person and his or her household.

When Miriam is afflicted and set apart from the congregation, the Israelites have no water, and if they travel without her, there is no guarantee that they will find some. Since their collective experience at Marah with the bitter waters, the Israelites depend on Miriam's traveling well, said by some to be a rock. While she lived, God provided water through this rock. Miriam as Gevurah is sternly judged and afflicted by the Creator. Yet Miriam's repentance, like our own, affects the mercy (Chesed) of the Creator. It is said that rain is the Chesed of God and snow his Gevurah. Describing Miriam's leprosy as snow suggests frozen waters that fall from heaven, a statement of stern judgment (Gevurah as Elokim) by the Creator.

Moses begs God, "Please, God, heal her now." God tells Moses that were she to have spat in her father's face, would she not have been "humiliated for seven days? Let her be quarantined outside the camp for seven days, and then she may be brought in."[50]

Miriam is punished in a visible way so that all of Israel can see the outcome of God's judgment and can conclude that, surely, if such punishment applies to Miriam, it applies to everyone. Her seven days of repentance is a communal restoration; Miriam performs the function of communal repentance that a High Priest performs in the Temple. "Because Miriam waited a little while for Moses [showing her trust in

---

[50] Numbers 12:13–14.

God that he would be saved when he was placed in a basket on the Nile, she was rewarded in that] Israel waited seven days for her."[51]

Miriam is the literal and metaphorical midwife of B'nai Yisrael. Her quarantine serves as an analogy to the seven days after childbirth when a woman is considered impure and in the usual seven-day menses after which a woman immerses in the ritual bath (the Mikvah) to be purified. In addition, if a woman has given birth to a son, it is on the eighth day that he is circumcised, as the covenant with the Creator requires.

Miriam's Death and the Sin of Moses and Aaron

The final part of Miriam's story spoken of in the Torah is at her death. "The children of Israel, the whole assembly, arrived at the Wilderness of Zin, in the first month and the people settled in Kadesh, Miriam died there and she was buried there."[52] But then we learn immediately afterward that "there was not water for the assembly, and they gathered against Moses and Aaron."[53] With Miriam gone, the miracle of the well stopped. It is here that the congregation says, "If only we had perished as our brethren perished before God. Why have you brought the congregation of God to this wilderness to die there, we and our animals? And why did you bring us up from Egypt to bring us to the evil place? Not a place of seed, or fig, or grape, or pomegranate; and there is not water to drink!"[54] This statement is fascinating. Beyond the apparent massive rebellion by the people, Moses and Aaron are asked where there are to be found the qualities God gives us—seed (Chesed), grapes (Tiferet), figs (Netzach), pomegranates (Hod). Where are these holy attributes and their corresponding foods that the Israelites were promised to find in the land of Israel (Eretz Yisrael)?

We are then told that Moses and Aaron "went from the presence of the congregation to the entrance of the Tent of Meeting and fell on

---

[51] Sotah 9b.
[52] Numbers 20:1.
[53] Numbers 20:2.
[54] Numbers 20:3–5.

their faces. The glory of God appeared to them."[55] Moses and Aaron ask God to help them. They hear God tell Moses to "[t]ake the staff and gather together the assembly, you and Aaron your brother, and speak to the Rock before their eyes and give drink to the assembly and to their animals."[56]

Moses and Aaron go before the assembly, as they are told, but then Moses decides instead to strike the rock two times, saying, "'Listen now, O rebels, shall we bring forth water for you from this rock?' Then Moses raised his arm and struck the rock with his staff twice; abundant water came forth."[57] While some Rabbinic scholars suggest Moses does this because he cannot find the "proper rock" (the rock referred to as Miriam's well; it had become indented), Torah suggests that Moses' decision is disobedient. As a result of this single act, Moses and Aaron are both told by God summarily, "Because you did not believe in Me to sanctify Me in the eyes of the children of Israel, therefore you will not bring this congregation to the Land that I have given them. They are the waters of strife, where the children of Israel contended with God, and He was sanctified through them."[58]

Just as Miriam is punished for challenging God's authority to decide who would speak on His behalf and for criticizing Moses for marrying a Cushite woman, now her two brothers are told that they will not enter the Promised Land. In all three instances we learn that the closer we are to the Creator, the greater is our sphere of influence in the spiritual realms. Moses', Miriam's, and Aaron's punishments are extremely severe, expressing the deepest nature of Gevurah—but we may ask why Aaron is punished for Moses' independent decision. The answer: Aaron does not attempt to stop Moses from disobeying God, just as he does not prevent the men of the assembly from erecting the golden calf in Moses' absence. We are responsible for not only our wrong actions, but also the wrong we do not attempt to prevent. This is an obligation that the Sefirah of Gevurah embodies.

---

[55] Numbers 20:6.
[56] Numbers 20:7.
[57] Numbers 20:10–11.
[58] Numbers 20:12–13.

The Waters of Kedusha

When Miriam dies at the age of eighty-six,

> Moses and Aaron were busy with her burial, [while] the people of
> Israel were searching in vain for water [since the well that supplied
> them with water had stopped functioning]. Moses and Aaron were sit-
> ting and mourning Miriam. Forthwith, the entire congregation gath-
> ered against them. Seeing their angry faces, Moses and Aaron fled to
> the Tent of Meeting. "Public servants," said the Holy One, Blessed is
> He, "go out of here quickly. My sons are dying of thirst, and you are
> mourning over [Miriam]?"[59]

The story of B'nai Yisrael unfolds once again around water, both its
Chesed-like nature of life and bounty and its Gevurah aspect as judgment before deliverance. As the Creator makes clear, the living take precedence over the deceased.

Our next encounter concerning water, the echo of Miriam's purpose,
was documented in a book that no longer exists, the Book of Wars of
God. It recounted the many battles the Israelites fought on their way to
the Promised Land after Miriam died.

The Israelites Sing to the Water

Once Miriam, who merited the well, is deceased and the roles of Moses
and Aaron, who together can summon the water to rise, begin to wane,
the Israelites themselves must merit the same miracles as those merited
by their three great sibling leaders.[60] It is worth noting that after Miriam
dies, it is due to the merit of Aaron and Moses together that the water
is restored. But the people now realize that they themselves must do the
work of asking for God's help.

Continuing their sojourn, Moses and Aaron lead the people during
the wars against the rulers of the territory, including Amalek. During

---

[59] Yalkut Shimoni, Chukat 763.

[60] Deuteronomy 30:7: "You shall return and listen to the voice of HaShem, and perform
all his commandments that I command you today."

this process, many of the Israelites who lose heart and speak out against God die from the bite of fiery snakes. The people then repent and God tells Moses to make a fiery serpent and put it on a pole. Any of those who have been bitten and who look at it will be cured.[61] It is in Arnon "which is in the wilderness" that this statement is made:

> The gift of the Sea of Reeds and the rivers of Arnon; the outpouring of the rivers when it veered to dwell at Ar, and leaned against the border of Moab. And from there to the well—it is the well of which God said to Moses, "assemble the people and I shall give them water. . . ."[62]

> Then Israel sang this song: "Come up, O well! Call out to it! Well that the princes dug, that the nobles of the people excavated, through a lawgiver, with their staffs. A gift from the Wilderness—the gift went to the valley, and from the valley to the heights, and from the heights to the valley in the field of Moab, at the top of the peak, overlooking the surface of wilderness."[63]

This well is "a gift from the Wilderness," rewarding B'nai Yisrael's communion with God and nature. The entire congregation of Israel speaks to the well together to merit God's mercy, whereas during Miriam's lifetime, she alone merits the Creator's benevolent participation in watering His seeds of creation. After she dies, her two brothers make it possible for the Israelites to drink. Now, for the first time since leaving Egypt, they merit as a community God's downflow of loving-kindness in the form of nourishing water. Miriam's midwifery of her people reaches its apex. Everyone is elevated to a new station.

Joshua Ben Nun and the Jordan River

We have now seen how many significant events occur around water during Miriam's life and shortly after, leading up to the final crossing into

---

[61] Numbers 21:6–8.

[62] Numbers 21:14–15.

[63] Numbers 21:17–20.

Eretz Yisrael. Every human being is composed of 90 percent water, and our emotions affect these waters. This is one reason it is important to learn how to control the flow of our emotions, much as a farmer learns to irrigate a field properly. If we recall that the middot (the Sefirot of Chesed through Malchut) or emotions are also referred to as "measured flows," we can see that Gevurah and Miriam prove that repentance and living a holy life provide us with living waters. At the time of Miriam's death, we are told she is eighty-six, and we know that she left Egypt when she was forty-six. In the year that Miriam dies, both of her brothers die as well. Therefore, in a single year, three righteous people die.

If we skip ahead in the Torah narrative, we find that after the deaths of Aaron and Moses, Joshua (Moses' protégé), the one whom Moses appointed at God's command, becomes leader of the people. The leadership has moved to a new generation of those born in the desert during the Exodus. Having built the Tabernacle according to God's instructions through Betzalel's (Miriam's grandson's) facilitation of a holy union with the Shechinah, the kohanim (priests) instead of the Levites, who usually carry the elements of the Tabernacle, are told to go first into the Jordan River, carrying the Tabernacle.[64]

As soon as their feet hit the water and they are immersed "in the edge of the water . . . the waters descending from upstream stood still and they rose up in one column, very far from Adam, the city that is near Zarethan; and the [water] that descends to the sea of the plain, the Dead Sea, ceased, and was cut off; and the people crossed opposite Jericho."[65] Joshua instructs each of the Twelve Tribes to choose one man who will select and bring a boulder with him to commemorate the miracle of the waters being held back, a phenomenon we also saw in the crossing of the Red Sea. After each man places his stone on dry land in the riverbed, Joshua himself takes twelve stones and places one at the feet of each of the kohanim, who then leave the dry riverbed.

---

[64] In the subsequent generation of leadership (Joshua, Betzalel, and Samuel, who anoints the first two kings, Saul and David), we hear the echo of the lives of Moses, Miriam, and Aaron.

[65] Joshua 3:14–17.

As soon as they do, "the waters of the Jordan returned to their place and flowed—as they had yesterday and before yesterday—upon all its banks."[66]

This ritual seems to be connected to the twelve streams at Elim after the Israelites had crossed the Red Sea, and now they have crossed the Jordan—and both are stages of deliverance. We might say that crossing the Red Sea is what is known in labor as "transition" and crossing the Jordan, when the people finally arrive in Israel, is the actual "birth" of a new nation. This aliyah (going up) for all of Israel can be said to be the outcome of Moses', Miriam's, and Aaron's leadership as commanded by God. All of Israel is elevated.

The Benefits of Quarantine

In the Parshiot in which Miriam's life plays a part, we see elements of what is holy and what is not, what is required of us, and what miracles are promised by our attendance to God's Word: water, fruit, God's loving care, our duty of burning the red heifer to obtain the ash for purification rituals, our Omer offering, and other peace offerings. In addition, on two occasions in the story of Miriam, we are shown a sort of spiritual medicine whose principles seem to underly a more modern medical science called homeopathy: A bitter tree sweetens the bitter waters and the ash resulting from the burning of the red heifer purifies the contaminated and contaminates the pure. In this sense, we are being instructed that if we keep the commandments, we will not face death by plague (with plague being an ever-enlarging circle of malaise and self-interest).

God is our healer. Quarantine and rest are effective restorative tools. This cutting ourselves off from those habits, ideas, and actions that are contaminating our soul's vessel is what we do when we give up bad habits. We cut ourselves off from them because of the damage they do to our kingdom. There is no middle ground; there is only purification. Gevurah as teshuvah is the birth of the newly returned person, hence the term for such a person: the Baal Teshuvah. The sacrificial obligations of the red

---

[66] Joshua 4:18.

heifer,[67] the grain offering, and our own teshuvah keep us healthy and under the loving care of God, who is our healer.

Miriam Revives

Miriam's role in Gevurah and as midwife is both a physical and a spiritual midwifery. She and the presence of Shechinah that rests in her are both life-giving and spiritually restorative. The red heifer as a symbol of Gevurah tells us that hidden in this concealed sacrifice—whose meaning we are told not to try to understand, but which is part of the Temple service—is something vital for our repentance and return to God. Even those contaminated by the dead—which requires a seven-day cleansing period—are given a remedy (ash of the red heifer) for immediate purification. Because this remedy is connected to Miriam directly, we should ask ourselves if our soul is dead in our body when we sin, when we behave with arrogance and selfishness. Is being contaminated by the dead also a parable of the danger of being dead to God's Word? As tradition teaches, not only does Miriam (Puah, which means to make sounds with one's mouth) revive dead children by whispering (Malchut, Asiyah) into their ears (Binah, Beriyah), but she also revives those who have been dead to God's Word. The well is the living fountain of eternal life contained in the Creator's Word. Torah is like water, our source for being guided toward eternal life.

It is interesting that, as in modern homeopathic medicine, an element that heals the sick when given to a healthy person will cause the ailment it is meant to treat in the ill person. Those who manufacture the ritual ash of the red heifer will be contaminated, but those who are defiled by the dead are cleansed by it. The bitter waters that exist after crossing the Red Sea are treated by Moses similar to the homeopathic methodology for purifying the contaminated person. In homeopathy, it is said that the water holds the etheric (realm of Yetzirah, formation) imprint of the

---

[67] The creating and using of the ash of red heifer (the ash resulting from the sacrifical burning of the red heifer) constitutes one of the enigmatic mitzvot. We are instructed not to ask "Why are we to do this?" Some commandments, we are told, are beyond reason. Faith must be exercised in doing even what we do not understand.

material put into it—that is, water holds the signature of anything put into it, whether physical, emotional, or spiritual. For the Jewish person, a blessing on the water precedes every drink of water. When we rise in the morning, the first thing we do after thanking God for restoring the pure soul in our body is to wash our hands ritually and say another blessing.[68] Before prayer, the observant purify their hands with water and a blessing. It is also said that our tears in prayer take the place of the water rituals performed by the High Priests during the time of the Temples.

Prophecy and the Well

Throughout the Torah, wells, rivers, and seas are central elements around which revolves much of the Israelites' story. Miriam merits the miracle of the well throughout the Israelites' forty-year journey in the wilderness. "R. Chaya said: 'if you want to see the well of Miriam, climb to the peak of Mount Carmel. When you look down toward the sea you will see a round rock, shaped like a sieve. That is Miriam's well.' Rav said: a moveable well is tahor (ritually pure), and, like a Mikvah, may be used to cleanse people and utensils of tumah (contamination) by immersing them in it. The only moveable well in existence is the well of Miriam. It [the rock] miraculously followed the children of Israel through the wilderness, thanks to the merit of Miriam."[69] "When Miriam died, the well stopped functioning."[70] We are told that it is in the Sea of Galilee, and that at the time of Moshiach, it will be found again.

The Angel of Death Has No Power over Miriam

It is interesting that we know nothing particular of Miriam's birth from the written Torah, nor do we know about Sarah's birth, but we do know that Miriam's death holds a holy status afforded no other woman in all of the Torah.

---

[68] It is said that the kelipot (shells of evil) attach themselves to our hands when we sleep, which is why we do not touch our bodies after we rise until we have cleansed our hands of the kelipot with a special prayer and water ritual.

[69] Shabbat 35a,

[70] Sifri Nitzavim, 305.

Along with being one of the great leaders of Israel, Miriam is the only woman over whom it is said the angel of death had no power. Her unique status signifies the level of the embodiment of the Shechinah she possesses. According to the Torah, the angel of death has no power over six individuals: Abraham, Isaac, Jacob, Moses, Aaron, and Miriam. She dies on the tenth of Nissan[71] with a "kiss."[72] Many people celebrate Miriam's memory on Rosh Chodesh, the New Moon of April.

According to *Likkutei Amarim Tanya,* after we die, the soul goes through a period of cleansing while the body disintegrates.[73] Saying that the angel of death had no power over these great leaders of Israel means they did not need the requisite time of life review and preparation for the World to Come that most of us will experience. They went directly from living in the mortal body to eternal living, that which is promised for all righteous humans in the messianic period. Further testifying to Miriam's bodily endowment of eternal light, we are told that "worms had no power over [the bodies] of seven [that is, their bodies did not decompose]: Abraham, Isaac and Jacob; Moses, Aaron, Miriam and Benjamin."[74]

Shechinah as Present Light

As we now know, the Shechinah can be evidenced by the quality of light present. It can be seen in the face of an individual, as we have seen with the righteous and with Moses and as we have seen in Sarah's tent and in the illumination in her beauty. Of Miriam it is also said, "Her face became [as radiant] as the sun at noon."[75] Some have suggested her other name was Zohar due to this "splendorous light." This supports why Miriam left her body through unity with the beloved Creator (through a kiss). The soul infused the vessel of the entire body with the divine light of the Or En Sof. Each of the six who departed as Miriam did had made of his or her body the holy Tabernacle, where the Holy of Holies—the

---

[71] End of Megillat Ta'anit.

[72] Bava Batra 17a.

[73] R. Schneur Zalman of Liadi. *Likkutei Amarim Tanya.*

[74] Bava Batra 17a.

[75] Sotah 12a.

heart—like the Torah itself, is full of God's glory. Miriam's death shows us that the body is designed for eternal life, a concept we will explore in chapters 9 and 10.

Gevurah as Opposition toward Resolution

Miriam as Gevurah is constantly analyzing, separating the holy from the unholy, the necessary from the unnecessary. Gevurah, unlike Chesed, is not designed to flow unimpeded. It is designed to balance the flow with judgment, establishing what is worthy and what is not, what is good and what is bad. It is like the riverbanks that hold the water in its proper channel. It is an ongoing process of discernment, and it attempts to balance the desire to give with the desire to receive. For each person, Gevurah establishes that there is a time and place for everything.

The Counting of the Omer

As mentioned earlier, the ritual of the Counting of the Omer, which begins the second night of Pesach and continues for forty-nine days, until Shavout on the fiftieth day, facilitates a spiritual journey through each of the seven lower Sefirot of the Etz Chayim for a period of one week.

Though we have learned that blessings rest on those things that remain uncounted, in this case blessings come as a result of counting. Why? This manner of self-purification parallels the forty-nine gates of Binah, or wisdom, which, it is said, Moses entered. Each of us is thus shown how the Shechinah's many qualities are manifested in the Etz Chayim. We begin our count with Chesed of Chesed. Then we progress to Gevurah of Chesed, Tiferet of Chesed, Netzach of Chesed, and so on until we reach Malchut of Chesed. The second week, we move to the primary Sefirah of Gevurah. The first night of Gevurah is Chesed of Gevurah, then Gevurah of Gevurah, and so forth. Finally, the very last night of Sefirat HaOmer, the forty-ninth day of counting, we experience Malchut of Malchut (Malchut B'Malchut), where all the prior Sefirot have endowed Malchut with aspects of their nature, making each person an entire nation ready to receive the holy Torah. This falls on the fiftieth day after counting the barley offering for forty-nine days and nights.

Tashlich and Selichot

Tashlich is a ceremony performed on the first afternoon of the Jewish New Year, Rosh Hashanah, when the observant throw small pieces of bread into the water while reciting verses from the prophets Micah and Isaiah. According to Micah 7:19: "You will cast all their sins into the depths of the sea." Here is an action of ablution and repentance of sin. This ritual reflects the inner teachings shown to us by Miriam's life. Selichot, as part of the Shemoneh Esrei, is a daily prayer of repentance during which worshippers strike their chest with their right hand (the hand that lifts us out of bondage) and ask God for forgiveness. A longer version of Selichot is said on certain fast days. The daily prayer said as part of the Shemoneh Esrei includes: "Forgive us our Father, for we have erred, pardon us, our King, for we have willfully sinned; for a pardoner and forgiver are you. Blessed are you God, the gracious One who abundantly forgives."[76]

The Mikvah

The Mikvah was created by Abraham and Sarah, suggesting the nature of Chesed, the loving-kindness of God's purifying water. In the structure of the Mikvah itself, the housing for the water is Gevurah. The ritual immersion in which we are cleansed of spiritual impurities is a mitzvah that must be honored at certain times. This reflects the nature of Gevurah. Everything has its proper time and place.

The blessings recited in the Mikvah, praising the Creator and the mitzvah of immersion, assist in our attaining bodily health and spiritual renewal. Through complete immersion, we experience Gevurah, receiving the emanations from Keter, Chochmah, Binah, and Chesed. The full immersion required for those who recite the blessings shows us the importance of the Crown (our heads), which must be submerged fully three times to receive the light of wisdom inherent in the ritual. In

---

[76] The Rambam (Maimonides) teaches us that the community should come together to fast, pray, and beg for God's mercy when faced with natural or man-made disasters. After the sin of the golden calf, Moses is told by God that when the people sin, they should say this prayer in its order. Based on the thirteen attributes of mercy (examined in chapter 1), it remains a part of the daily recital of prayer of the People of the Book. Exodus 34:6–7 is the source for the thirteen attributes of mercy.

addition, being submerged in His mercy (the waters themselves) causes Binah and Chesed to flow into Gevurah. The waters of purification are endowed with the essence of the upper Sefirot. The Mikvah thus functions as a method for the body and soul to harmonize through prayer, reflecting total submersion in humility and nakedness before God. Kitchen articles are also purified ritually (*tevilat kelim*) in a separate Mikvah for this purpose.

GEMATRIA

The Lessons of Water

As we discover, water is one reason there is war or peace. Water eliminates or sustains life. In this we are given a holy lesson for our own times and for the future. In Genesis 1:29, the numeric value of the expression **to you** or **for you** לכם is ל Lamed (30) כ Caf (20) ם Mem (40) = 90, which is equal to the numeric value of the Hebrew word for **water** מים (mayim): מ Mem (40) ' Yod (10) ם Mem (40) = 90. We are told that the Creator has given us every "herbage yielding seed that is on the surface of the entire earth," showing us that water is the source of bringing all life (the seeds of life) on earth to fruition. While obvious from a physical point of view, this is also a spiritual teaching of the relationship between Sarah and Chesed (as seed-bearer) and Miriam and Gevurah (the deliverer who delivers through self-refinement). The teachings of Torah are the living waters that sustain the soul and refine the body.

90: The Gematria of Water

Having noted the importance of water in Miriam's life as recounted in the Torah and its action when in Gevurah, let us take a moment to look more deeply at this enigmatic word—*water*—in Hebrew and its numeric (gematriatic) meaning.

water מים (mayim): מ Mem (40) ' Yod (10) ם Mem (40) = 90.

The letter Mem is considered one of Hebrew's mother letters: ש Shin (300) א Alef (1) and מ Mem (40). The value of the letter Mem (40) always stands for the womb waters, the forty years in the wilderness, the forty days of Noah's travail, and the forty units of water for the ritual baths (Mikvah). In other words, the first Mem of **mayim** is open like the sea, which allows the tide to come in and go out. The open Mem, like the womb, has an exit. The Mem that is closed (the final Mem), the last letter of **mayim** (water), is like the cranium: The *mochin* (brain) is housed there in a closed chamber, but through it insight is given and communication occurs.

Between the first and last Mem is the Yod (10), which is God's creative seed, the Ten Commandments and the ten utterances that created the world. Yod is the letter in God's holy name that begins His name: י Yod ה Hay ו Vav ה Hay. It is therefore the first signifier of His living presence. Water is the means by which the living presence of the Creator circulates on earth and in our bodies. Water is a holy element in which are imprinted the Creator's intentions. Water is the foundation of all life. Without it, the seed cannot grow, and with too much water, it will drown. In this sense, Chesed without Gevurah will be flooded. The seed, properly watered by measured restraint or receiving rains at the proper time, brings forth life, bounty, and longevity. Our actions in proper measure lead to a purposeful life. Water's bounty becomes the vehicle for bringing life and peace—and conversely, its lack can bring war in the world. Torah replenishes our soul; lacking Torah brings about disorder.

God has been called the source of living waters. In the history of the Jewish people until today, ritual immersion in water (the Mikvah) plays a vital role in communal and personal development. The Mikvah itself is a holy vessel of purification. The first time water is mentioned in the Torah is in Genesis 1:6, recounting the second day of creation: "God said, 'Let there be a firmament in the midst of the water, and let it separate between water and water.'" The Torah explains that this is a separation between the waters below and the waters above the firmament. "God called to the firmament: 'heaven.'" We are reminded in this very first instance of water being mentioned in the Torah that there are boundaries (Gevurah) in God's elements that make up the created world. Gevurah facilitates each element's purpose.

*Figure 4.1. (a) The Mikvah outside the Temple and
(b) seen from a distance, near the Southern Wall.*

Using gematria, let us examine other words that have the same numeric value as **mayim.** Water certainly contains deeper Torah secrets. Here is an abbreviated list and the context in which the words appear.

king or **royal** מלכ (Genesis 14:1): מ Mem (40) ל Lamed (30) כ Caf (20) = 90

The context in which this appears refers to the war of the kings detailed in the lost Book of Wars, mentioned earlier, recounting the Israelites' battles after Miriam's death.

goblet הגביע (Genesis 44:12): ה Hay (5) ג Gimel (3) ב Bet (2) י Yod (10) ע Ayin (70) = 90

The goblet is the one Joseph placed in the sack of his youngest brother, Benjamin, suggesting the Gevurah necessary to reunite the family of Jacob.

I redeem אפדה (Exodus 13:15): א Alef (1) פ Pey (80) ד Dalet (4) ה Hay (5) = 90

God speaks of the redemption of B'nai Yisrael. Waters of Gevurah sweetened by Chesed bring redemption. This reveals that the redemption that comes through the waters of Gevurah (judgment) can be sweetened by Chesed.

sea מים (Exodus 15:22): מ Mem (40) י Yod (10) ם Mem (40) = 90

The Torah describes Moses causing the Israelites to journey from the Sea of Reeds to the wilderness of Shur, going for three days without water, followed by their arrival at the bitter waters (Marah). That **sea** is equal to 90 suggests that the righteousness B'nai Yisrael achieved was due to their communal repentance and humility engendered by their lack of water. Like the Baal Teshuvah, who elevates the community, it is from prior lack that their thirst for Torah and God becomes so intense as to merit closeness and return to God. This principle hints at why even a sin can be elevated for goodness or why exile or enslavement can precipitate emancipation and freedom and why our hardships are worthwhile.

the Ephod הָאֵפֹד (Exodus 28:6): ה Hay (5) א Alef (1) פ Pey (80) ד Dalet (4) = 90

Here, the Torah describes the priestly garments, including the Ephod, the top apron wore by the High Priest, suggesting that this garment performs a spiritual function, conducting spiritual powers in defined and particular ways.

they teach ילמדו (Deuteronomy 20:18): י Yod (10) ל Lamed (30) מ Mem (40) ד Dalet (4) ו Vav (6) = 90

The phrase **they teach** refers to the obligation of the People of the Book to teach their children the lessons of Torah. Because Torah is also referred to as living waters, teaching Torah to others performs the same function as getting water from Miriam's well. Gevurah, the ability to separate the pure from the impure, the bitter from the sweet, enables our emancipation or deliverance from drought or evil.

knew him ידעו (Deuteronomy 34:10): י Yod (10) ד Dalet (4) ע Ayin (70) ו Vav (6) = 90

Here we learn that Miriam's youngest brother, Moses, is concealed in the mystery of water. These words refer to God knowing Moses.

When we study these and other words and expressions that have the same value as the word **water,** we find the essential elements of Miriam's life and the events in which she was pivotal. This makes both Miriam's life and the "deliverance" of any of us from exile dependent on humility and teshuvah.

148: The Gematria of Living Waters

living waters מים חיים (mayim chayim): **chayim** = ח Chet (8) י Yod (10) מ Mem (40) = 58 + **mayim** = מ Mem (40) י Yod (10) ם Mem (40) = 90; 58 + 90 = 148

The following words and expressions are equal in value to the numeric value of the word **chayim** (living, 58).

the Garden הַגָּן (Genesis 2:9): ה Hay (5) ג Gimel (3) ן Nun (50) = 58
Noah נֹחַ (Genesis 5:29): נ Nun (50) ח Chet (8) = 58
grace or **favor** חֵן (Genesis 6:8): ח Chet (8) ן Nun (50) = 58

Chai, the number 18—ח Chet (8) י Yod (10)—stands for **life** in general. **Tzadee** (צ), the letter, is equal to the numeric value of the letters in the Hebrew word for **water**—90—and represents the righteous, the tzaddikim. Simply, living waters are the flow of wisdom through the righteousness in us and in our communities. The righteous are the vessels for the presence of God, for the Shechinah. Living waters are the living expression of the Divine Immanence of the Creator. This reminds us of the Rambam's teaching: We can achieve prophecy in nature, such as by a river or lake or in some place away from the community. Water as the outer expression of the Creator's love is the living divine presence of the Creator. We can say that the Shechinah is present in all living water and that water is vitalized by circulation.

The following is also equal to the numeric value of **living waters.**

my doctrine לִקְחִי (Deuteronomy 32:2): ל Lamed (30) ק Kof (100) ח Chet (8) י Yod (10) = 148

This phrase refers to the commandments and teachings that the Creator gave Moses and that were given to the People of the Book. We can see why Chazal (sages) have referred to Torah as "living waters."

86 Years: The Length of Miriam's Life

Using gematria as we did to discover the importance of the length of Sarah's life and the age of Isaac at the time of the Akeidah (a time period that corresponded with Sarah's death), we can find Miriam's Sefirotic essence as Gevurah (also called *din,* or judgment).[77]

---

[77] See Gutman Locks, *The Spice of Torah—Gematria,* 44, for other Hebrew phrases equal to 86, such as: **and he circumcised** (Genesis 17:23); **and tents** (Genesis 25:27); **the throne** (Genesis 41:40); **the bondage, work, service** (Exodus 2:23); **and the priest** (Leviticus 5:16).

God, master אלהים (Elokim) (Exodus 7:1): א Alef (1) ל Lamed (30) ה Hay (5) י Yod (10) ם Mem (40) = 86

"God said to Moses, 'See I have made you master over Pharaoh, and Aaron your brother shall be your spokesman.'" Here the limitations placed on Pharaoh represent the diminishment of our egos. Humility is the precursor to teshuvah and redemption. In this we see that Miriam is the quintessential representative of Gevurah and Elokim, as Sarah was of Chesed and Adonai.

to Elim אילמה (Exodus 15:27): א Alef (1) י Yod (10) ל Lamed (30) מ Mem (40) ה Hay (5) = 86

Here, in Elim, as reviewed earlier in Miriam's story, the Israelites find the twelve springs and seventy date palms. In this instance, a story concerning Miriam is revealed in the gematria of her years of life, just as the words **offered him up,** referring to the Akeidah and Sarah's son, Isaac, are revealed in the gematria of Sarah's years of life.

and they learn ולמדו (Deuteronomy 31:13): ו Vav (6) ל Lamed (30) מ Mem (40) ד Dalet (4) ו Vav (6) = 86

This refers to the children of every generation learning the word of God.

In addition, the ritual of circumcision found in Genesis 17:12 equals 86. By examining these numeric correspondences, we can begin to see how every name and the length of every life conceals a story. The name is the key to the vessel's nature and makeup. In the length of our life, the vessel's time serving the individual soul, we find keys to our place in the world. This concealed reality in our names and years of life helps to explain why it is said that at our death, all the good we have done illuminates the world, and it is this shine of the soul that is remembered on earth and in heaven on the annual anniversary of our physical death.

290: *The Numeric Value of Miriam's Name*

In the numeric value of Miriam's name, 290, we find explicitly the concealed importance of judgment (Gevurah or din) and repentance (teshuvah). We have already seen that God's name as judge, Elokim, is concealed in the name Miriam, being equal in value to Miriam's name. Din, or judgment, signifies return, and it **stirs** and **awakens** (Deuteronomy 32:11), words that are also equal to the value of Miriam's name and are found in the song of Moses, in which he expresses God's kindness to Israel, making it clear that it is God who facilitates deliverance and emancipation.[78] Also, the numeric value of the word **bitter** is equal to numeric value of Miriam's name, 290, and refers to Exodus 15:23, when God tests the Israelites at Marah, where the waters are bitter. All of these phrases and many others show us that what we find in the text of a person's Torah story is also rooted in that person's name. This is miraculous proof of Hebrew's vitality as a living language, reflecting the Creator's blueprint.

Just as we learned that Sarah's name defines her great prophetic talents, we discover that Miriam's name tells of an entire period in which she lived. **Maror** refers to the bitterness in Egypt.[79] **Bitter** מ Mem (40) ר Reish (200) י Yod (10) ם Mem (40) = 290. Maror is a bitter herb, one of the elements of the Pesach table ritual commemorating the bitterness of the Israelite's life in Egypt.

Another opinion is that her name is Miriam because "at the time [of her birth] the Egyptians began to embitter the lives of the Children of Israel."[80] Miriam, though, was also called Puah, a name that means to coo or produce sounds with one's mouth, referring to her midwifery talent of reviving babies by cooing in their ears; "she gave the newborns wine and restored the babies to life when they appeared to be dead; she lit up Israel before God [by teaching the women] . . ."[81]

---

[78] The eagle in the shield of America's national coat of arms suggests a relationship between Teshuvah or humility and God's attending protection.

[79] Seder Olam Rabbah, 3.

[80] Yalkut Shimoni, Shemot 165.

[81] Shemot Rabbah 1:13.

Before we note the Torah words and expressions equal to the numeric value of Miriam's name, we can note how many of these portions of the Torah actually define Miriam's journey as already presented. This proves the nature of the Torah as a blueprint for creation. We see demonstration of the cosmic harmony between things that might seem dissimilar—yet their natures are actually intimately related, as shown by their equal numeric values.

fruit פְּרִי (Genesis 1:11, 1:29): פ Pey (80) ר Reish (200) י Yod (10) = 290

"On the third day of Creation, God said, 'Let the earth sprout vegetation; herbage yielding seed, fruit trees yielding fruit each after its kind; containing its own seed on the earth,' and so it was." Fruit is the product of seed (Chesed); thus in this sense, the Sefirah Gevurah brings forth the seed.

your fellow רֵעַ (your neighbor, Exodus 2:13): ר Reish (200) ע Ayin (70) כ Caf (20) = 290

Moses sees two Egyptian men fighting, and he kills the wicked one of them: "He went out the next day and behold! Two men were fighting. He said to the wicked one, 'Why would you strike your fellow?'" The next day, two Hebrew men are fighting, and one says to Moses, "Do you propose to murder me as you murdered the Egyptian?" Moses, realizing that his murderous act was witnessed and now afraid for his own life, flees from Pharaoh and settles in Midian. Here he saves the seven daughters of Yitro (Jethro), his future father-in-law, the priest in Midian, who gives his daughter Tzipporah to Moses as a reward.

This moment in Moses' life precedes his encounter with God in the burning bush. The seven daughters he saves suggests a rectification of the Etz Chayim. They may reflect the refinement of Moses' own middot: The seven daughters suggest a refinement of Moses' understanding of how we use our place in the world properly and how we use our sense of justice.

Miracle of Crossing the Red Sea

Miriam מרים (Exodus 15:20): מ Mem (40) ר Reish (200) ' Yod (10) ם Mem (40) = 290

"Miriam the Prophetess, the sister of Aaron, took her drum in her hand and all the women went forth after her with drums and with dances." Miriam speaks to them, "Sing to God for he is exalted above the arrogant, having hurled horses with its rider into the sea."

Thousands of years after this historic act, Miriam is best known for her dance and song with the women at the deliverance of the Israelites. Pursued by the Egyptians, men, women, and children are forced to wade into the sea, which opens up for them miraculously. The water rises to both sides like glass walls, allowing them all to pass through. Once they reach the other side of the sea, it is Miriam who leads the women in celebratory dancing and singing while they watch as the waters engulf all of the Egyptian horses and riders who have pursued them.

Miriam is midwife in Egypt, and the miracle of the parting of the Red Sea is like the breaking of the waters in childbirth, a moment that precedes the active stage of delivery. Here, all of Israel is delivered out of Egypt. Just as Miriam and Aaron once danced as children around their mother, Yocheved, Miriam dances again—this time with all of the female Israelites, therefore fulfilling at the midpoint of her life her childhood prophecy of Moses' role as redeemer. Miriam spends the next forty years with B'nai Yisrael in the desert, acting as their midwife and seer.

bitter מרים (Exodus 15:22): מ Mem (40) ר Reish (200) ' Yod (10) ם Mem (40) = 290

"Moses caused Israel to journey from the Sea of Reeds and they went out to the Wilderness of Shur; they went for a three-day period in the wilderness—they didn't find water. . . .[82] They Came to Marah—but they could not drink the waters of Marah, because they were bitter; therefore they named it Marah."

Then the people call out to Moses, "[W]hat shall we drink?" Moses,

---

[82] This is why the Torah is read on Mondays and Thursdays—so we never have three days between studying the Torah, for the lack of water was due to lack of the Torah.

in turn, cries out to God—who then shows Moses a tree, which is bitter, and tells him to throw it into the water. Moses throws it into the water, which is sweetened by the bitter tree. "There He established for [the nation of Israel] a decree and an ordinance and there He tested it. He said, 'If you hearken diligently to the voice of God your God and do what is just in His eye, give ear to His commandments and observe all of His decrees, then any of the disease that I placed in Egypt, I will not bring upon you, for I am God your healer."[83] Here too is revealed a portion of the story of Miriam as a component of her name. Here, prior to the miracle of her traveling well, the bitterness suggests that Gevurah is an aspect of the covenant with the Creator: Difficulty in our lives brings us closer to the Creator, and the Torah is the living waters that can purify our lives.

ripe ears כרמל (fresh corn or groats, Leviticus 2:14): כ Caf (20) ר Reish (200) מ Mem (40) ל Lamed (30) = 290

"When you bring a meal offering of the first grain to God; from ripe ears parched over fire, ground from plump kernels, shall you offer the meal-offering of your first grain." The meal offering is for the process of self-refinement: giving up something precious. On the second day of Pesach, the first offering of the new grain crop was brought to the Temple as a barley offering or a meal offering. We see that in Sefirat HaOmer (the Counting of the Omer) we are instructed to count from the barley harvest to the first wheat harvest, and this measures forty-nine days. In this sense, we see that the discipline of observance is a process for self-refinement, giving up the precious fruits of our labors and recognizing that all belongs to God.

(the red) heifer הפרה (Numbers 19:5): ה Hay (5) פ Pey (80) ר Reish (200) ה Hay (5) = 290

"Someone shall burn the cow [the red heifer] before his eyes—its hide, and its flesh and its blood with its dung shall he burn." Here we

---

[83] Exodus 15:26.

encounter the sacred and enigmatic red heifer, which, when burned as a sacrifice, provides ash that purifies those who have come in contact with the dead while contaminating those who prepare the ash that the Kohen Gadol, the High Priest, burns. The heifer is embedded in Miriam's story, as just prior to her affliction with leprosy, its cure, involving the ash of the red heifer, is revealed to the people, as we have already examined. Here once again, Miriam's name hides her life story, containing the secret of the red heifer as purification for contacting the dead and repentance for being dead to Torah. Both are remedies for body and soul.

arousing יְעִיר (stirring, awakening, Deuteronomy 32:11): י Yod (10) ע Ayin (70) י Yod (10) ר Reish (200) = 290

This song of Moses describes God's loving care: "He was like an eagle arousing [stirring, awakening] its nest, hovering over its young, spreading its wings and taking them, carrying them on pinions."

MIRIAM, SARAH'S SUCCESSOR

Sarah's tent is the vessel of the holy spirit. Miriam's well is the source of living waters. The bread of life is in Sarah's tent. Miriam merits the waters that sustain life. Sarah is obedient. Miriam is courageous. Miriam challenges all authority, while Sarah is an obedient authority in her community.

In the simplest terms, what Chesed implants in the world as the Creator's beloved creation Gevurah brings forth. Sarah is the seed bearer of B'nai Yisrael, Miriam is the midwife of that creation. Miriam and the women who follow her across the Red Sea are the flowering of Sarah's teachings about the Creator being the Redeemer—as she experiences when she conceives Isaac at age eighty-nine. The first tzaddikim's successor, Miriam, sister of Moses, the greatest prophet, is herself the vessel through which God's waters of mercy (emancipation) and bitterness (enslavement) are tasted.

Sarah and her tent bring about the miracles of the holy presence, resulting in the celebration of the New Year; the New Moon; and the Shabbat rituals of making bread, lighting the candles, and serving the stranger. Miriam's life revolves around the community's observance of the mitzvot of the Mikvah, Sefirat HaOmer, and Pesach and the role of teshuvah. From Sarah of the eternal flame—often symbolized by the letter Shin (ש), the first letter of Sarah's name—we move to Miriam and the holy waters of libation and birth. In Miriam's name the first and last letter, Mem (מ/ם)—also called a mother letter—signifies water. Sarah is the fire in Miriam's water.

Miriam's Barley to Sarah's Wheat

Wheat is Chochmah (wisdom) and Chesed (loving-kindness). Barley, which later becomes animal feed, is called a wave offering. Used in repentance, barley reflects the emanation of Binah (understanding) and Gevurah (strength). Wheat has an expansive influence on the body; barley has a contractive and consolidating one. A diet that balances the two grains and those who balance both attributes lead to a beautiful (Tiferet) life.

SUMMARIZING THE IMPORTANCE OF MIRIAM

Sarah shows us the first step of our lives and how we are conceived in love; Miriam shows us our next stage of development and teaches us about our birth. From their combined lives and the combination of Chesed and Gevurah, the individual and the nation must act, rooted in love with merciful judgment, and then we can manifest our intentions (*kavanah*) with the proper balance of generosity and restraint, humility and strength.

Miriam and the Sefirah of Gevurah tell us that our rebirth as individuals and humanity occurs through our heartfelt repentance of arrogance and error. Miriam is the prophetess who predicts the birth of Moses and his role as redeemer. She is instrumental in preserving the Jewish people by refusing to follow the pharaoh's orders to kill the newborn Israelite boys. As guide and midwife of the next generation in the Exodus, the expression of Chesed in the world protected by boundaries of right action, she is guardian of the miraculous "traveling rock" or well that provides the nation with water for forty years. We remember Miriam for leading the Israelites into freedom from the pursuing Egyptian army and for demonstrating the importance of teshuvah (repentance) and return to the Creator. For all of this and more, we recognize the promise her life gives to us: Moshiach will be born and there will arrive the age of redemption, when all of Israel returns to a love of the Creator and His Torah.

From Chesed we inherit the promise of the Third Temple and the messianic age; from Gevurah we glean the fact of the Redeemer's birth. Miriam and the Torah show us that water can be instrumental in global conflict and harmony in the days preceding Moshiach's birth. This adds meaning to the Chazal's traditional teachings that say of the age in which we currently live: We are the generation of the birth pangs of Moshiach; we exist in the age of Yesod, which precedes the messianic age of Malchut. In Miriam's story there are answers to what our conduct must exhibit: We function collectively as midwives to the birth of our redeemer, the Divine Immanence (Shechinah) of the Creator embodied in the descendant of the Davidic bloodline and in humanity's hearts.[84] Prophecy occurs, as we now know, only if the generation is deserving of it. May we merit in our days the Moshiach's speedy arrival.

Beauty Comes from Combining Chesed and Gevurah

In Devorah, the next prophetess, and the Sefirot of Tiferet, we will encounter the moral order that unites the individual (seed and community that has blossomed) and a code of law. Combining Chesed, the right hand, and Gevurah the left hand, we arrive next at beauty and the balance among all parts, resulting in a moral and well-ordered society or individual.

---

[84] It is noteworthy that Avigail—also on the left pillar, under Miriam—contributes to the actual, physical bloodline of the Davidic kingdom, from whence the Redeemer will come.

5

Devorah

Tiferet · The Beauty of Moral Order

Judge your fellow fairly.

LEVITICUS 19:15

Devorah דבורה

ד Dalet (4) ב Bet (2) ו Vav (6) ר Reish (200) ה Hay (5) = 217

Sefirah Correspondence: Tiferet

Titles: Prophetess, Judge, Military Leader, Entepreneur, Mother of Israel

Family: Wife of Barak (Lappidoth)

Time Period	Jewish Calendar	Gregorian Calendar
Period she is judge	2636–2676	1124–1084 BCE

Developmental Stage: Moral order

Day: Tuesday

Sacred Species: Grapes

Body Correspondence: Torso

Ritual: Blessings on wine

Holiday: Sukkot

Symbols: Palm tree of righteousness, lulav, wine

Prayers: Hallel, Birchat Hamazon

Shine of Devorah–Tiferet: Establishment of Sanhedrin in messianic times, Ark of the Torah in the Temple

Prophecy Source: Judges 4:4–5:31 ". . . behold God, the God of Israel has commanded . . ."

Devorah's Song: Judges 5:1–31, "When vengeances are inflicted upon Israel . . ."

SEFIRAH: TIFERET

As the middle of the Etz Chayim, Tiferet elevates everything to its greatest potential. It is a place of synthesis, balance, and order. It is the center, drawing its vitality from and distributing it to the other Sefirot of the Etz Chayim. It is like the hub of a wheel. Tiferet (Devorah) represents the melding of all the attributes found in Sarah–Chesed, Miriam–Gevurah, Chanah–Netzach, Avigail–Hod, and Chuldah–Yesod, integrating all of them for their connection to Malchut (Esther) at the bottom of the middle pillar, below Devorah.

Phase of Development: Tiferet is the establishment of moral order. Moral and legal order endows a society with harmony, representing the Creator's plan for us. Devorah guides the Israelites after the Exodus, when we leave Miriam, and shows us how to create a society that is founded on law and order. The physical world (Asiyah) reflects the spiritual laws or "courts" of God (Yetzirah).

Life Principle: Devorah reflects the life principle of beauty and integrated leadership in truth. Tiferet elevates everything by consideration of its purpose and uniqueness, resulting in harmony among the parts. Beauty of the whole will be greater than the sum of its parts. Beauty and truth nurture the soul and world.

World Action: Tiferet integrates many points of view and people, showing us how to balance all our emotions properly into a harmonious unit. In leadership, it emphasizes the ability to guide many—just as Devorah does as a judge, business owner, and military leader—and to do so with fairness. Tiferet engenders peace.

Spiritual Action: Tiferet shows us that a beautiful home or idea or group of people comes from the same integration of parts that respects and honors each thing for its own unique contribution. Devorah recites the Hallel, a great song of praise, reflecting the harmony of God and Israel.

Meaningful Work: Activities related to Tiferet deal with improving situations, environments, or groups of people. Tiferet benefits everything when we bring out the best in each situation and person. Artists, social entrepreneurs, interior designers, and mediation counselors all are rooted in Tiferet.

Day Focus: Tuesday as Tiferet is ideal for making some area more beautiful and harmonious during the day, whether we are at home or in the office or the area is in our hearts (feelings), actions, or words. On this day we do something with a focus on beauty, balance, and harmony. The source of peace is in Tiferet and culminates in Hod (Avigail).

Species: Grapes as the sacramental offering tell us that Tiferet, the center of the Etz Chayim, elevates everything. We say the Bracha (blessing) with wine for our Sabbath meals and holidays. Pressing grapes results in wine. In our own lives, what is precious inside of us is the result of pressing our natures for their refinement. We find a similar trait in Yesod, also on the middle pillar and which stands for olive oil, and in Malchut, date honey. All three—Tiferet, Yesod, and Malchut—represent a refinement of something in order to produce their holy elements.

DEVORAH'S STORY

We meet Devorah as a woman married to Lappidoth, who was either a wickmaker or General Barak (and Lappidoth another of his names). Devorah was a remarkable woman whom we learn from the **Torah** was a prophetess and a judge. Devorah was also a **business owner** of at least four enterprises: palm trees, apple orchards, olive oil, and white earth.

Not only was Devorah independently wealthy, but also she was the only **judge of Israel** in her day who actually sentenced people for their crimes. Later in life, she was told by HaShem (God) to lead an army for which she herself would be considered a **military general.** With Barak, she waged a successful war on Mt. Tabor against the Canaanite king during which **six miracles** were said to have occurred. After their victory, Devorah sang her **song of prophecy,** including the Hallel, a great prayer of praise. It is said by some that Devorah was arrogant for calling Barak to come to her rather than going to see him after God instructed her to wage war. As an example of the holy spirit, Ruach HaKodesh, abandoning her (though there are other ways to interpret this event), these interpreters cite: **"Awake, awake, Devorah."**

Devorah teaches that we **structure time** based on a holy pattern of the six directions of space and that moral order brings certain beauty and peace. We do not know her length of life or where or when she died, but we do know that she sat as a judge and guardian of the people for forty years.

SYMBOLISM OF DEVORAH

Devorah and the Mandate to Establish Justice
We begin our study of Devorah, the Sefirah of Tiferet, and the mandate to establish a justice system with an inspection of the commandment itself. Learning that Devorah is the first judge to be called a prophetess and the only judge of her days whom the people go to for rendering judgment, we are given information about the nature of Tiferet as the third Sefirah in this journey of attributes.

"Our Rabbis taught: Seven commandments were given to the descendants of Noah [i.e., all mankind]: the duty to establish a justice system; the prohibition of blasphemy; idolatry; adultery; bloodshed; robbery; eating flesh cut from a living animal."[1] From where do the sages derive these directives? According to R. Yochanan, the directives come "[f]rom

---

[1] Sanhedrin 56a.

the verse 'The Lord God commanded the man [Adam], saying; 'You may freely eat from every tree in the Garden.'"[2] (The command was given to Adam and therefore to all mankind.) "[C]ommanded the man" refers to the establishment of a justice system; and so the quote goes on, "For I have loved him, because he commands his children and his household after him that they keep the way of God, doing charity and justice."[3] The word *command* is associated with justice,[4] and of all the laws God gives to humanity, establishing a justice system is the first obligation. Tiferet embodies this teaching as the core around which holy life occurs in the individual and the world.

For the People of the Book, establishing a justice system overrides all other issues at the founding of the nation of Israel.

> Judges and officers shall you appoint in all your cities—which God your God gives you—for your tribes; and they shall judge the people with righteous judgment. You shall not pervert judgment, you shall not respect someone's presence [be influenced by status], and you shall not accept a bribe, for the bribe will blind the eyes of the wise and make just words crooked. Righteousness, righteousness shall you pursue, so that you will live and possess the land that God, your God, gives.[5]

Righteousness, an ingredient of justice, is a prerequisite for the possession of the land by the People of the Book. Our inheritance in this world and the World to Come (after death or after the coming of Moshiach) is based on our righteousness.

A Balance of Parts

Beauty and truth form an equilibrium among parts. In the Torah, God gives the Torah to the People of B'nai Yisrael in parts and later gives land in parts through Moses to the different tribes that merit it. In the

---

[2] Genesis 2:16.
[3] Genesis 18:19.
[4] Sanhedrin 56b.
[5] Deuteronomy 16:18–20.

spiritual kingdom, there is balance of parts as there is on earth and in our bodies. A beautiful painting, piece of music, or life is a well-proportioned one. In the twelve months of judgment, the parts of the year, like the Twelve Tribes, have their purpose.[6]

Justice and Charity Bring Beauty, Harmony, and an Elevation

How are judgment and commandment connected to beauty, truth, or mercy? The 365 negative commandments and the 248 positive ones, which have a correspondence in the human body, comprise the 613 commandments for instituting and keeping justice, and it is by these that the Jewish tradition is structured. These 613 parts represent all of Torah's laws.

Significantly, judgment also comes in parts. R. Akiva said, "There are five things that lasted twelve months: 1) the judgment of the generation of the flood; 2) the judgment of Job; 3) the judgment of the Egyptians; 4) the judgment of Gog and Magog in time to come will last twelve months; 5) the judgment of the wicked in Gehinom will continue for twelve months. For it says, 'it will be from one month to the same month a (year later).'"[7]

A well-ordered community, like justice, balances the parts of any given medium or situation. There are twelve stones on the breastplate of the Kohen Gadol (High Priest) representing the Twelve Tribes and the spiritual qualities of the months of the year with which they are associated.

An element of the rectification of sparks is evidenced in administering justice with charity. This charity also shows up in judgment. Beit Hillel, referring to the school of Hillel the Elder, or Hillel HaZaken (70 BCE–10 CE), says, "If a person's merits and failings are evenly balanced, He who is full of mercy will tip the scales of justice towards the side

---

[6] Recall the ceremonial act when the Children of Israel crossed over the Jordan and marked their arrival with twelve stones on earth (*gilgal*) and twelve stones hidden in the river, as an expression of Tiferet in Gevurah.

[7] R. Yaakov Ibn Chaviv, *Ein Yaakov*, Eduyot 4b, 725.

of mercy."[8] We learn, in addition, that "praiseworthy are those who act justly, who do charity at all times."[9] Charity is an equal part of justice. The justice served, the remedy of immorality, in part rectifies the light that is concealed in the evil of an act or situation. Tiferet suggests that action includes an intention, and so we are judged for our intentions in the process of rectification. Intention is the heart of a word, thought, or action, which is why we try to "judge the heart of the situation" or "get to the heart of the matter." We are told to "judge our fellow fairly" with a mixture of mercy (Chesed) and appropriate severity (Gevurah).

The Golden Rule

The golden rule—not to do to your neighbors that which you would not want them to do to you—is the basis of moral order. When it is adhered to, the community forms a potentially beautiful society. Through justice, our deeds and intentions are held accountable. The remedy is balanced by the act of sentence. For the People of the Book, the death penalty is considered neither immoral nor too harsh; though rarely used, it originated in the Law that God gave Moses.

Beauty and moral order utilize deliberate elimination of that which would corrupt harmony, while also making possible methods of restitution. For justice to elevate the sparks, the light encased in the shells of evil (kelipot), justice must be sweetened with charity, which produces mercy, another name for an essential quality of Tiferet. A judge must attempt to rectify the harm of someone's actions against another or toward the Creator's Word by establishing proper remedy. Just as Miriam shows us that repentance is the spiritual remedy for sin, Devorah teaches us that justice is the remedy for immoral action.

The Middle Path

Tiferet as beauty, truth, and mercy suggests a harmonizing of opposites, the classical meaning for the most difficult of the esoteric paths: the middle path. As the middle of the middle pillar of the Tree of Life, Tiferet

---

[8] R. Yaakov Ibn Chaviv, *Ein Yaakov,* Rosh Hashanah, 246.
[9] Psalms 106:3.

establishes the ability to integrate and elevate. Because she is a woman already endowed with extra Binah, or understanding, Devorah's unique role is as the first judge to be called a prophet and the only woman to have such a role in the life of the People of the Book. Just as Sarah's life holds the shine of the Third Temple and the holiday of Rosh Hashanah and Miriam's life holds the promise of self-refinement, the holiday of Pesach, and the promise of the birth of the redeemer, Devorah's life teaches us about communal moral order: an emancipation from tyranny leading to self-rule by the self-governed and a beautiful order according to the Creator's Word. Devorah's life shows us the importance of following God's Law and practicing charity and justice. Tiferet is the promise of the reformation of the Beit Din, the official court of law, reflecting the integration of society's parts and the placement of men and women together among the counsel of elders (Sanhedrin) when the Temple is restored.

Charity and justice are pillars of Jewish life. Charity is represented by the right pillar or Chesed (Sarah) and repentance and return are represented by Gevurah (Miriam). The lives of these two prophetesses and the phases of development they embody are seen as the combined virtues exemplified in the life of Devorah, their immediate successor. Devorah the judge balances the scales in the society according to the spiritual laws of justice. A prophet who is a judge best exemplifies these two bodies of influence: prophecy (Chesed) and obedience (Gevurah) to the teachings of Torah. Devorah's life shows us how to refine ourselves in order to receive prophecy through the Ruach HaKodesh for the benefit of the world.

Devorah in the Torah

Appropriate to Devorah's great prophetic and professional role as a prophetess judge, we meet her first in the Torah in Judges 4:4–5. "Devorah was a Prophetess, The wife of Lappidoth, she judged Israel at that time. She would sit under the date palm of Devorah, between Ramah and Beith-El on Mount Ephraim, and the children of Israel would go up to her for judgment." Devorah is the "first judge be to be described as a Prophet and as a decider of questions of law for the nation."[10]

---

[10] Judges 4:4; R. Nosson Scherman, ed., *Tanach,* 4:4 footnote 590.

Devorah as Business Owner

Devorah comes from the tribe of Naphtali[11] and lives in the city of
"Atarot . . . She was independently wealthy; she owned palm trees in
Jericho, orchards in Ramah, oil-producing olives in Beit-El, and white
earth in Tur Malka."[12] Though we learn of her wealth, we do not know
how she is able to accumulate these businesses if, as some scholars say,
her husband is only a wickmaker named Lappidoth. It is more likely that
Barak, the powerful military leader, is her husband, as other scholars suggest, and the name Lappidoth, which means "fiery" or "flash," is another
of his names. Some even attribute to Devorah the occupation of wickmaker, which can be seen as a metaphor for leading others to arouse their
inner fire.

We are asked to imagine Devorah presiding over several businesses
simultaneously and having the ability to cultivate important domestic
and trading commodities: date honey, apples, olives for olive oil, and
white earth for ceramics.

A Judge of Israel

For a biblical woman, property ownership was rare. But Devorah's talents
go beyond industry. She is also a judge, prophetess, and military leader.
To be a female judge at the time was remarkable, but even more amazing
is that Devorah was the only judge who actually made decisions about
cases. Perhaps her independent wealth made her a good judge, because
she couldn't be bribed. In Deuteronomy, Moses describes the appointing
of elders as Judges:[13] "You shall not show favoritism in judgment, small
and great alike shall you hear, you shall not tremble before any man, for
the judgment is God's; any matter that is too difficult for you, you shall
bring to me and I shall hear it."

Some commentators find fault with Devorah's role as judge, suggesting that a woman should not hold such a position. Some Rabbinic scholars
also fault her for calling Barak to come to her before going to war against

---

[11] Yalkhut HaMechiri, Tehillim 22:1.
[12] Targum Shoftim 4:5.
[13] Deuteronomy 1:17.

the Canaanites. Critics say that this "man's" position of emanation—of acting as judge and warrior—is inappropriate for a woman. Nevertheless, God selects the prophetess Devorah to stand as B'nai Yisrael's leader and judge. As the Torah shows, the community of her day is supportive of her role. Perhaps Devorah, like Sarah and Miriam, as a leader for humanity's redemption, presages the time when women will be the primary emanators, which some Kabbalists predict for the time of Moshiach.

The Prophetess's Reported Arrogance

"There were two women," it is said, "who were arrogant, and both had unpleasant names: Devorah (bee) and Chuldah (mole)."[14] Is their arrogance significant or has there been a historic tendency in scholarship by previous generations of male writers and teachers to diminish the biblical women's centrality and historic leadership? Subsequently, has women's equality in the culture of Judaism been undermined? Is this part of God's plan, an initial diminishing of women for their eventual elevation and therefore the elevation of the world?

Devorah's Seat of Justice

> *The Righteous will flourish like the date palm.*
>
> PSALMS 92:13

We learn from the Torah that Devorah's seat of justice is on top of a hill under a palm tree in the southern extremity of Ephraim, between Beit El and Ramah.[15] We are taught traditionally that she positions her seat here to avoid seclusion with men[16]—that "since a woman must not secure herself with men in the house, she sat in the shade of a palm tree, teaching Torah to the public."[17] While this may be one reason for Devorah's choice, we can consider others. The open-air forum allows greater numbers of people to come and go and possibly hear how proper judgment

---

[14] Megillah 14b. Chuldah can also mean "weasel," suggesting an animal that preys on those smaller than itself, or "rat," which feeds on refuse.

[15] Judges 4:5.

[16] Megillah 14a.

[17] Yalkut Shimoni, Shoftim 42.

is made. When teaching, Devorah can reach more people in a single sitting than would fit in a house. Also, Devorah's prophecy occurs through Ruach HaKodesh when she judges, and this is more easily contacted in nature, as the Rambam shows us. Seated under the palm tree in nature's embrace, Devorah accesses the Holy Spirit.

Knowing that part of Devorah's wealth comes from palm trees, we can also say she has an affinity for the palm tree and the angels that oversee their growth. We are taught that angels are assigned to each and every plant and blade of grass and to all that lives.

Devorah's Wealth and the Etz Chayim

Devorah's wealth comes from products of the earth, with two of them among the seven holy species of the land of Israel: olive oil (Yesod) and date palm honey (Malchut). Interestingly, these species are both on the middle pillar of the Tree of Life, as is Devorah with her personal symbol of the palm tree and as is the holy species for Tiferet, the grape. Amazingly, Devorah, the prophetess in the middle of the middle path, reflects life engagement with all three species inherent in its parts by the enterprises she owns and the sacred species of Tiferet, which she embodies.

Spiritually, then, Devorah and the elements in her life reflect the hidden and interior nature of the entire middle path or pillar, which extends from the source of the loving and almighty God as Keter or Crown (the sun that makes things grow) to Daat, the seat of the Bat Kol (Daughter of the Voice or prophecy and knowledge), to Tiferet (grapes), then to Yesod (olive oil), and finally to Malchut (date honey). The grape, the species associated with Tiferet, elevates the olive oil and date honey just as Devorah, Tiferet, elevates everything we do to a harmonious beauty when we include all parts. Devorah, Tiferet, is where the ascending light and the descending light commingle most clearly. In Tiferet we emanate and receive, ascending and descending the Etz Chayim.

Judgment before Creation or Incarnation

Torah, as the outcome of creation and the laws it prescribes, shows us that justice and mercy were created before the world itself. In the same way, the heart or nature of a person's soul is created in between lives, before the formation of the body, and our attributes and deficits are measured in the afterlife and a course of rectification is set. Our hearts are "established" before the soul can incarnate, reflecting as it does the aspects of ourselves that are complete and those parts that need rectification. The Shechinah does not rest on the corrupt individual. In the same way, without justice, the Shechinah has no "public" house in which to rest.

Qualifications of a Judge

We learn in Baraita (meaning "outside," and referring to those Mishnaic teachings outside of the codified writings of R. Yehudah Hanasi), "R. Yose said: Initially there were not many disputes in Israel; there was one Beit Din (house of Judgment) of seventy-one judges that sat in the Hall of Hewn Stones, and there were two courts of twenty-three judges—one sitting at the entrance of the Temple Mount, and one sitting at the entrance of the [Temple] Courtyard, and other courts of twenty-three-judges were sitting in all cities throughout Eretz Yisrael."[18] The Sanhedrin decided the qualifications of the local judges, saying that "[w]hoever is wise, humble, and well liked by the people should be appointed judge in his city."[19] Devorah fits all of these qualifications, acting as the sole judge, just as Moses does for all of Israel during the Exodus.

Tiferet is traditionally referred to as the seat of Jacob (Yaakov) in the Tree of Life, which represents Israel as a nation, and is where the heart has its seat in the body. Devorah's life, like that of Moses and Jacob, acts as the central organ of unity and life among B'nai Yisrael; she is a mother of Israel who is a living example of the fulfillment of the commandments. Tiferet reflects love and discrimination or judgment (Chesed and Gevurah), the will inherent in victory and eternity (Netzach), and

---

[18] Sanhedrin 88b.
[19] Sanhedrin 88b.

humility (Hod) through the *brit* (a circumcision of the heart) and culminates in the brit milah of the regenerative organs of the male (Yesod), in service to God's Law.

The Nature of Zeal

To have zeal in our desire to perform the mitzvot or the commandments is a desirable quality in those who aspire. "The man whose soul burns in the service of the Creator will surely not idle in the performance of his Mitzvot, but his movements will be like the quick movements of fire; he will not rest or be still until the deed has been completed."[20] The Ramak (R. Moshe Cordovero) says that performing good deeds with speed in the limbs encourages an inner flame. Yet if we are "sluggish in the movements of the limbs, the movement of his spirit will die down and be extinguished." Experience testifies to this. We learn then that "outer movements awaken inner ones."[21]

As both a deeper teaching regarding the role of justice in a society's development and a person's evolution, Devorah displays this multifaceted zeal. In other words, the heart inspires the limbs, the ministers of our will. Tiferet, expressing the zeal of the heart to keep life in the body, is the same zeal of the soul when we use the body in service to the Creator. "It is known that what is most preferred in divine service is desire of the heart and longing of the soul."[22] "My soul longs and goes out for the courts of God."[23]

Pirkei Avot: Ethics of the Fathers

In Pirkei Avot, the Ethics of the Fathers, we are told, "Which is the proper path that a man should choose for himself? . . . Consider three things and you will not come into the grip of sin: Know what is above you—a watchful Eye, and attentive Ear and all your deeds are recorded in

---

[20] R. Moshe Chayim Luzzatto (the Ramchal), *The Path of the Just* (Mesillat Yesharim), chapter 6, 80.
[21] Ibid., chapter 7, 91.
[22] Ibid., 89.
[23] Psalms 84:3.

the Book."[24] The words, *eye, ear,* and *book* give us hints about the deeper or secret (sod) meaning of this advice and how it pertains to Tiferet, Devorah, and the laws of a just society.

The eye is represented by the Sefirah of Chochmah, or Father, joined to the ear, which is Mother or Binah. When we recite the Shema prayer, which begins with "Hear oh Israel," Tiferet (Israel) can "hear" the word of God and gain understanding (Binah). The book of heavenly records, the ending of the three things one is advised to consider to avoid sinning, reflects the soul's afterlife disposition. In the Torah, we are given access to wisdom (sight) and understanding (hearing) so that our record is illuminated by right thought and action (speech). If we listen to the voice of the soul within, controlling what happens in our kingdom (through the ministers of thought, speech, and action), we will be blessed in the World to Come, represented by Yesod, the next Sefirah on the middle path in the descent of the light.

Devorah as a Military General

How the Bible records Devorah's role: "She led Israel at that time." It goes on: "She used to sit under the palm tree of Devorah . . . and the Israelites would come to her for judgment."[25] Devorah is a judge of great repute. She is also a renowned military leader who fights a war of liberation, winning her people independence. Symbolically, this suggests that when we are free from the evil inclination, we are liberated. Devorah promotes the war of liberation from Jabin (Yavin), king of Caanan,[26] a war that Joshua completes several generations later in his battle at Jericho. (It is interesting that Devorah herself owns property in Jericho.) The great military leader Barak trusts and desires Devorah's counsel. While Barak is strongly admired, he goes to his wife and prophetess Devorah for advice and support. We learn

---

[24] R. Moshe Lieber and R. Nosson Scherman, eds., *The Pirkei Avos: Ethics of the Fathers, The Sages Guide to Living,* chapter 2:1, 80. Pirkei Avot "is the only tractate in the Mishnah that is not halachic [pertaining to the Law] in nature."

[25] Judges 4:4.

[26] Judges, chapter 4.

that Barak makes the following statement to Devorah regarding the war God tells Devorah they must undertake: "If you go with me, then I will go."[27] Barak refers to going up to Mt. Tabor to wage war.

Devorah leads this war of rebellion and self-defense. She calls for Barak to come to her prior to war, an event for which she has been criticized by Rabbinic scholars. Why, the rabbis ask, should she call for a man to come to her? Given her pressing life obligations as the sole judge of the people and as a property owner of enterprises, Devorah is a busy woman. Some critics have stated that when she calls for her husband to come to her, it is an insult to all husbands. This analysis evidences itself in centuries of Torah commentary, and perhaps this too will be broadened with other interpretations.

Devorah, Barak, and the Just War

All of the prophetesses in the Bible are either married to a great man or related to one by events, showing the balance of male and female in the life of the People of the Book. Sarah is known primarily as Abraham's wife and Miriam is known as the sister of Aaron and Moses. As we will see, Chanah is related to the High Priest Eli, and to her son, the prophet Samuel; Avigail is related to King David; and Chuldah is related to King Josiah. Even Esther, who saves the Jewish people from Haman's attempted genocide, is guided by her relationship to Mordechai. Devorah stands in partnership with Barak.

A century or so after the Israelites' entry into Canaan, King Jabin (Yavin) of Chatzor (Hazor) controls the valley in which Devorah and her tribe live. During Devorah's time, we are told, "[t]he children of Israel continued to do what was evil in the eyes of God, once Ehud died. God delivered them into the hand of the Yavin, King of Canaan, who reigned in Chatzor. The children of Israel cried out to God, for [Sisera] had nine hundred iron chariots, and he oppressed the Children of Israel forcefully for twenty-years."[28] In the next line in the Torah, we are told:

---

[27] Judges 4:8.
[28] Judges 4:1–3.

"Devorah was a Prophetess, the wife of Lappidoth;[29] she judged Israel at that time."

Devorah summons Barak to tell him her prophecy: "God has commanded, 'Go and convince [the people to go] toward Mount Tabor, and take with you ten thousand men from the children of Naphtali and from the children of Zevulun . . .'"[30]

Barak's response to Devorah shows the high esteem in which this prophetess is held: "If you will go with me, I will go; if not I will not go . . . since the divine inspiration rests upon her, in her merit I will be saved and will suffer no injury."[31] "Very well [indeed], I will go with you," Devorah consents; and having already seen in prophecy the reason for their victory warns him, "[B]ut the path on which you have chosen to go will not be for your glory, for God will have delivered Sisera into the hand of a woman."[32]

Here Devorah, the great female judge and prophetess of Israel, tells the military general that our victory cannot be predicated on your ego or desire for retribution. Having been shown the outcome of the war prior to waging war as instructed by God, Devorah knows how the Canaanite general, Sisera, will be killed. This ability to look into the future through prophecy is reflected in the lives of all the prophetesses and similarly in the life of Avigail, when her words prevent David from doing injury to his royal bloodline by a revengeful killing.

Because the battle on Mt. Tabor occurs during the rainy season, Sisera's chariots become stuck in the mud. The Israelites are able to overwhelm Hazor's army and inflict heavy casualties. Sisera, the general, fleeing on foot, escapes to the Kenite camp, where Yael, the clan leader's wife, invites him to stay. He falls asleep in her tent, whereupon Yael lifts a mallet and drives a tent peg through his head. The famed song of Devorah in Judges 5 (see appendix 1) exults in the breaking of the Canaanite stranglehold over much of the country: "When vengeances are

---

[29] Considered by some scholars as another name of Barak.
[30] Judges 4:6.
[31] Zohar 3:21a.
[32] Judges 4:8–9.

inflicted upon Israel and the people dedicates itself to God—Bless God . . . So may all Your enemies be destroyed, O God! And let those who love Him be like the powerfully rising sun. And the land was tranquil for forty years."[33]

Devorah's Song of Prophecy

It is through prophecy and the Ruach HaKodesh that Devorah learns beforehand of the victory over Sisera. She is shown his mother peering through the window, wondering why her son has not returned from the battle. Seeing future events prior to battle, Devorah describes what she has witnessed. "Through the window the mother of Sisera looked forth and peered. Why is his chariot so long in coming?"[34] The words spoken by Sisera's mother are revealed to Devorah through divine inspiration. She replies, "Wait no longer for your son Sisera, So may all God's enemies perish!"[35]

Devorah's song of prophecy reflects the purpose of prophecy: to warn of natural or man-made disasters and to bring the People of the Book back to Torah and closeness to God. Devorah on the middle pillar, like Esther below her, is instrumental in preventing the deaths of the Israelites. This suggests that the middle pillar, which receives the direct emanation of Keter, the Crown of glory or God, enables prophecy on a level different from that of the right and left pillars. Here, Devorah as a military leader uses Gevurah (strength and judgment) as a weapon for victory or Netzach, the Sefirah following and embodied by Chanah. She reflects awareness of the covenant with God, Yesod, as the ultimate foundation for victory over evil.

Physical Liberation

Devorah gives us lessons about physical liberation from tyranny. While Chanah in Netzach guides us toward spiritual liberation, Devorah, preceding Chanah historically and Sefirotically, guides us toward physical

---

[33] Judges 5:1–31.
[34] Judges 5:28.
[35] Midrash HaGadol, Bamidbar 11:6.

liberation from injustice, using both military might (Gevurah), mercy (Chesed), and legal justice (Tiferet). The war that Devorah and Barak wage together results in the creation of a city strategy for security: "Unwalled cities ceased in Israel."[36] "The small towns that had been laid waste in the days of Sisera became important cities after Devorah arose."[37] This too suggests that when we are victorious over our evil inclinations, peace follows.

In Devorah's time, it was not typical for a woman to lead men into battle, but Devorah did. Here we see the courage of Miriam brought to a new plateau of taking back the land that is the Israelites' to inherit once Miriam has succeeded in bringing them to the edge of Israel. Now in Israel it is Devorah who leads them to victory over the Canaanites, who are oppressing them. It is significant that it is the prophetesses who play such a central role in Israel's redemption from the Egyptians, the Canaanites, and, as we will see with our examination of the life of Esther, the evil of Haman, the Persian viceroy and reincarnation of Amalek, who killed the weak and infirm at the rear of the Exodus community as they left Egypt.

Tiferet: Development as Community

As a continuation of our developmental story, we have moved from Sarah's seed of loving-kindness to proper boundary-making with Miriam to Devorah's action in a moral framework, which shows us how to integrate all the parts according to a moral order. The war she wages, though an offensive one, can be called a just war. This lesson from Devorah tells us that we are obligated to honor the word of God, as she does when she is instructed to wage war. We have moved beyond simply our own role in the world to the community's role in world refinement. From Gevurah, our entry into Tiferet moves us out into community, into each other's part in the whole.

---

[36] Judges 5:7.
[37] Shocher Tov 3:3.

The Six Miracles

On the day that Devorah and Barak commit to waging war to fight against the Canaanites, "six miracles were wrought that day; the people of Israel came [to Devorah], she sent [for Barak] and he [mustered troops], they waged war, Sisera was slain, they divided the spoils, and they sang the song of Praise—all on the same day."[38] During Sukkot, as we shake in the six directions the lulav (palm) and other sacred species of the *etrog* (citron), myrtle, and willow, we utter a prayer of six components. Tiferet is the middle of six Sefirot (Chesed through Yesod) called the Son or Zeir Anpin, and, similar to Tiferet's expression in these six Sefirot, the Kabbalistic Sefirot are expressed in the holidays and rituals of the People of the Book. This deepens our appreciation for Kabbalah as a tool for interpreting the Torah, leading to self-refinement and the fulfillment of prophecy in the Torah.

The Merit of the Women

As we see with Miriam and the women who cross the Red Sea and then sing and dance in celebration, attributing the crossing to God's strong hand, which "took us out" of Egypt, Devorah and Chanah are credited with the greatest praise ever sung to God: "Two women said praises to the Holy One, Blessed is He, that all the men in the world did not: Devorah and Chanah."[39]

Devorah in victory over the Canaanites and Miriam in victory against the Egyptians show us their merit. "In the song of Devorah, the women preceded the men, because here the redemption came through women: Devorah and Jael."[40] As we have learned in Miriam's story, her song and dance reflect creating a vessel below for the light of God to fill. Devorah's Hallel repeats this powerful relationship between God above (Keter) showing mercy (Tiferet, Chesed, and Gevurah) and below, victory (Netzach) and the humble (Hod) people (Malchut) receiving His blessings. Hallel represents

---

[38] Koheles Rabbah 3:14.

[39] Zohar 3:19b; Judges 5:7

[40] Lekach Tov, Shemot 15:20. Perhaps the women went first because they arouse the mercy of God.

the Tree of Life rectified, a battle won. Reciting the Hallel is a spiritual reen-actment of a historic event, revealing the power of commemorative rituals.

Awake, Awake, Devorah!

In Devorah we see a repetition of the complaints by Rabbinic com-mentators against Miriam in Gevurah: We are told that "[i]f a Prophet is haughty, his [her] prophecy departs from him [or her]. We learn this from Devorah [after she boasted] 'Until I Arose, Devorah.'[41] [Her proph-ecy departed and she cried], 'Awake, awake, Devorah!'"[42]

Though we can respect that this is a traditional teaching, we might view the situation differently. Perhaps Devorah's statement "Awake, Awake! Devorah" is a declaration she makes as a personal reminder to elevate, to pay attention, to be entirely present to the Shechinah. Perhaps she makes the testament "until I arose a Mother in Israel," which was a true statement, in order to summon the Shechinah. Perhaps it is not a statement of pride, but a personal remembering of her divine and animal soul coming together to serve God.

Given Devorah's credit for composing the greatest praise of God—greater, even, than that of King David—why would it be in her nature to be arrogant? Perhaps what she speaks is true: that until she arose a mother in Israel, they were not victorious. Perhaps, rather than a state-ment of pride, it is spoken to benefit the other women so that they may know their capacity as leaders, as redeemers, as prophetesses and mothers of Israel. Or perhaps she is suggesting that until we sacrifice ourselves as mothers for our children, we will not be victorious. Perhaps Devorah's words are a statement of the woman's role as the vessel in which the awake Shechinah resides. Perhaps the declaration is about the Shechinah's presence and is not intended as a deflation of the male stature, as the Rabbinic commentators suggest. The criticisms of Devorah's intent are only several of the seventy faces of interpretation said to be apportioned to all things. Perhaps, as the only judge who made decisions and as the

---

[41] Judges 5:7.
[42] Judges 5:7, Pesachim 66b.

leader of a successful military assault for her people, she declares "arise Shechinah, for you the Shechinah [the Divine Immanence of the Creator] are the Mother of Israel!"

Perhaps this is revealed in the mystery of Devorah's name. Calling out her name summons all the qualities inherent in the name's power—qualities that she is obligated by God to embody. Have we not ourselves occasionally called out our own names to awaken ourselves to mindfulness?

Tiferet as Sukkot

Just as we learned that Sarah and Chesed are associated with a major Jewish holiday—Rosh Hashanah, the Jewish New Year—and Miriam is associated with Pesach, commemorating the Exodus from Egypt, Devorah and Tiferet represent the holiday of Sukkot, the festival of the booths. The mitzvah of dwelling in the sukkah and the rituals performed there involve our entire bodies.

The eight-day holiday of Sukkot commemorates the protection that the Creator gave B'nai Yisrael in the wilderness. The sukkah itself honors God's protective mercy, the hovering cloud, an attribute associated with the Sefirah of Tiferet. While a temporary dwelling with a "roof" through which we must be able to see the stars, the sukkah is a dwelling place of the Shechinah, a place the Ruach HaKodesh can inhabit.

During Sukkot, the mitzvot include shaking in six directions the combined native species of Israel. Its four ceremonial elements or "four species" are from the land of Israel: the etrog (lemonlike citron), a palm branch (lulav), two myrtle (hadassim), and three willow branches (aravot), all of which are regulated by several overriding principles. Each species used in ritual in the sukkah should be as beautiful as possible and in its whole, natural state. Because the elements will be unified, each must be complete in itself, instructing us about our own self-refinement and its importance in the world. The myrtle (hadassim) represent the eyes and wisdom and the Sefirah of Chochmah; the aravot (willow branches with their leaves) represent the mouth (Malchut) or Kingdom; the etrog represents the heart (Tiferet and Binah); and the lulav (palm branch) is the spine or middle pillar of the Etz Chayim, connecting all elements and integrating and elevating the body, mind, and soul in their attachment to God. The lulav itself is the tallest element around which the others revolve, like the letter Lamed in the Alef-Bet, the letter that begins the word *lulav.* It teaches us suppleness and strength, flexibility and order. As we perform the prayer of the six directions, suggesting Tiferet's center in the six Sefirot of the middot (emotions), the directions in space that we consecrate each of the days of Sukkot suggest that our head (Keter, Chochmah, Binah) and arms and legs (Chesed, Gevurah, Netzach, and Hod) carry out the will of the heart (etrog).

Tiferet and the Structure of Time

In his book *The Palm Tree of Devorah,* the Ramak teaches that Tiferet is the place of beautification and harmonization, the place where the soul is seated in unity with Malchut and Yesod (the other Sefirot on the middle pillar, below Tiferet). The Ramak's treatise supplies Sefirotic affiliations for the parts of the day:

> On rising at midnight, he should wash his hands of the kelipah (evil) that dominates them, remove the evil from his flesh, and recite the blessing. He should then restore the Shechinah through Torah study. About this, it is written (Mishlei 6:22), "when you lie down, it will guard you" from the forces of evil, and "when you awaken, it will speak with you" and be bound to you, and you to it. Then, his soul will rise to Gan Eden together with the Shechinah, which enters there with the righteous. Tiferet will also come there to delight with the righteous, and with him in their company, for they all listen to his voice. This way, a person journeys together with the Shechinah from a state of sleep and death to the secret of Supernal Life, where he becomes bound up in the mystery of Gan Eden, and Tiferet, which shines upon the righteous in Gan Eden, begins to Shine upon him. This is the explanation of the Zohar on "Terumah."[43]

---

[43] R. Moshe Cordovero (the Ramak), *The Palm Tree of Devorah,* 136.

The illumination from the Sefirah of Tiferet is the light that emanates to the righteous in their nightly ascension through prayer and meditation. Tiferet is the place from which the Creator emanates the "shine of righteousness"—the beauty of moral behavior, thought, and contemplation. Righteousness is the source of peace among a person's body, mind, and soul, its glory and its splendor.

In *The Palm Tree of Devorah,* the Ramak also presents a set of keys to understanding the Torah and its commandments. The Ramak is of Spanish descent and originally from Cordovero, Italy. His work on the Sefirot and the prophetesses shows up in a *sefer* (book) authored by his benefactor and student, Menachem DeFano, whose contribution has already been cited here. It is Cordovero who teaches the correspondences between the seven Sefirot and the seven prophetesses, as was shown to me in my sukkah revelation map in 2004 (5762). His work applies the thirteen attributes of mercy mentioned in Micah (7:18–20), which are analyzed in detail in his book *The Palm Tree of Devorah.* Their primary purpose is to teach B'nai Yisrael the importance of emulating the Creator. "It is proper for man to emulate His Creator, for then he will attain the secret of the Supernal Form in both image (Tzelem) and likeness (Demut) . . . thus it is proper that man's actions imitate the Thirteen Supernal Attributes of Mercy."[44]

We are encouraged to read and study the beautiful holy book of Micah during the ten days between the New Year, Rosh Hashanah, when Chesed opens the gates to life, and Yom Kippur, when the world (Malchut) is judged and the book of life is sealed for the coming year. The sages teach us that by doing this, we rectify one Sefirah each day until all ten days and all ten Sefirot have been properly understood and reflected within us. The thirteen attributes of mercy are primary keys to the secrets of Tiferet. Together, they are a tool for our revelation in Gan Eden (Garden of Eden) now and in the World to Come, for they are the attributes accorded a merciful Creator, in whose image we are made and whom we are instructed to emulate.

---

[44] R. Moshe Cordovero (the Ramak), *The Palm Tree of Devorah,* 2.

Thirteen Attributes of Mercy[45]

1. Who is a God like you,
2. Who pardons iniquity and
3. overlooks (forgives) transgression, for the
4. remnant of His heritage?
5. He does not maintain his wrath (anger) forever,
6. for He desires (delights in) kindness.
7. He will once again show us mercy (compassion),
8. he will suppress (vanquish) our iniquities.
9. You will cast all their sins into the depths of the sea.
10. Grant (show) truth (faithfulness) to Jacob,
11. kindness to Abraham,
12. as you swore to our forefathers
13. in days of old.

The Ramak then goes on to describe how each part of the day has a particular Sefirotic attribute instructing faithful adherents about the benefits of becoming aware of the Sefirot and their attachment to certain parts of the daily prayer cycle. When we become aware of this and use this pattern in our lives as a source of understanding, we can align a proper action with its proper or natural time. Through this conscious alignment, we become more like the Creator: Our waking and sleeping life are bound up in devotion to God.

"At dawn, he prepares to enter the Beit Knesset, binding himself to the three Patriarchs. At the entrance to the Beit Knesset, he should recite the verse, 'And I, through your abundant kindness, come in to your house; I bow toward your holy sanctuary in awe of you.'"[46] We merge ourselves with the secret of Tiferet, for we comprise Chesed, Gevurah, and Tiferet, and we enter the Beit Knesset (which is Malchut) and meditate with the qualities of the three patriarchs when reciting this verse:

---

[45] R. Nosson Scherman, ed., *Tanach,* Micah, 1385.

[46] Psalms 5:8.

"Your abundant kindness" corresponds to Abraham. "I bow toward your holy sanctuary" corresponds to Yitzchak, for bowing—that is, lowering our stature toward the attribute of judgment and allowing ourselves to be pushed aside by it—comes from the aspect of Yitzchak. Then our prayer will be at a propitious time, for the outflow of compassion will be drawn downward upon this attribute to sweeten it. "In awe of you," corresponds to Jacob, who said, "How awesome is this place . . ."[47]

The Ramak continues to show the student how the day itself has certain Kabbalistic potentials. "For in the morning he binds himself to Chesed in his prayers, during the day to Tiferet, and towards evening Gevurah. Coming to the Beit Knesset to perform the mystical unification of Gevurah, just as he does in the morning prayer with Chesed. All this is according to the quality of the 'day.'"[48]

Ending this section of *The Palm Tree of Devorah,* the Ramak reminds us that after . . .

. . . the time of afternoon prayer has passed, and he has been bound to Gevurah, he should wait for night, until Tiferet descends to Malchut. Thus, he is with Malchut from the beginning of the night. He should bind himself to Malchut and enter the Beit Knesset with this intention. As he binds himself below, Tiferet comes to its place of lodging. When he exits the Beit Knesset, he should unite himself with Malchut alone, according to the secret of accepting the Yoke of the Kingdom of Heaven.[49]

Just as each prophetess brings a Sefirotic quality and developmental stage of unfoldment to the generation of which she is part, so too are these brought to history—the time of day, the day of the week, the month of the year, the year in the millennium. Each is a building block

---

[47] R. Moshe Cordovero (the Ramak), *The Palm Tree of Devorah,* chapter 10, 138.
[48] Ibid.
[49] Ibid., 140.

of correspondence from heaven to earth, fulfilling the maxim "As above, so below."

All these actions—binding ourselves to the Creator through one or various faculties and deeds—comprise what in Chassidut are called collectively "the garments of the soul." Devorah with Tiferet is where the kingdom is united and Gan Eden is entered. "This is how a person merges himself with these qualities in thought, speech and action, for thought is the meditation . . . Speech is reciting the verse, and action is coming to the Beit Knesset and bowing towards the sanctuary."[50]

Tiferet and the Six Dimensions

The People of the Book teach that there are ten categories of existence from nothingness through which all life is ushered by the Creator. These categories, corresponding to the ten Sefirot of the Etz Chayim, include the spirit of the living God, air, water, and fire, which were sealed "with spirit and fastened to His great name and sealed with six dimensions."[51] This relationship is summarized thus: "These are the ten spheres of existence out of nothing. From the spirit of the living God emanated air, from air, water, from water, fire or ether, from the ether the height and the depth, the East and West, the North and South."[52]

Tiferet as an expression of six Sefirot brought into harmonious balance (Chesed, Gevurah, Tiferet, Netzach, Hod, Yesod) demonstrates the created world's unification of parts. During the Sukkot holiday, we are directed to shake the elements that are united in our two hands—the etrog, lulav, willow, and myrtle—three times in all six directions, equaling a total of thirty-six movements. Knowing that movement of the limbs inspires the heart and vice versa, we can see how this ritual can be viewed as a Kabbalistic formula for invoking the Ruach HaKodesh in our ohel (tent) and in our heart, the Holy of Holies in the Temple of ourselves. This formula is why, in the ritual, the etrog (heart) is held in one hand and united with the other three elements

---

[50] R. Moshe Cordovero (the Ramak), *The Palm Tree of Devorah*, chapter 10, 138.
[51] R. Aryeh Kaplan, *Sefer Yetzirah,* chapter 1, section 8, 66.
[52] Ibid., section 9, 68.

(the eyes, the mouth, and the spine or will), and why these are dedicated to the six direction of space, which come from the elements air, water, and fire.

GEMATRIA

Phrases Related to Tiferet

judge, judgment שפט: ש Shin (300) פ Pey (80) ט Tet (9) = 389

The soul seeks justice, longing for the balance of all the parts. The Hebrew word at the root of **judgment** means to judge, to create order and harmony.[53] The root letters personify Tiferet readily when seen in this way. If we study other words and phrases that equal 389, we garner additional clues to the nature of justice and judgment, as we would using the technique Stones and Houses, explained in appendix 2.[54]

truth אמת (emet): א Alef (1) מ Mem (40) ת Tav (400) = 441

Truth, or *emet* in Hebrew, is another word associated with describing the Sefirot of Tiferet, because it refers to the severity of *din* (judgment), discernment in Gevurah, and the boundless outpouring of love in Chesed, combined with judgment leaning toward mercy. Tiferet produces truth based on merit.

The first letter in **emet** is Alef, the beginning of the Hebrew alphabet, followed by Mem, in the middle of the Alef-Bet, and Tav, the final letter of the Alef-Bet. Truth therefore comprises the beginning, middle, and end of all things. So too, Tiferet contains within itself the beginning, the middle, and the end of the Tree of Life, the Etz Chayim. The middle path leads to truth.

The word **emet** first appears in Genesis 24:48, when we encounter Elazar, Abraham's servant who has gone to seek a wife for Abraham's

---

[53] Matityahu Clark, *Etymological Dictionary of Biblical Hebrew,* 268; Deuteronomy 16:18, Psalms 7:9.

[54] **rinsed** (Genesis 13:11), **and he that lets go** (Genesis 16:26), **Shaphat** (Numbers 13:5), and **they be destroyed** (Deuteronomy 7:23). See Gutman Locks, *The Spice of Torah—Gematria,* 179, for other Hebrew words and phrases equal numerically to 389.

son, Isaac. Elazar recounts that it is God who "led me to take the daughter of my master's brother for his son." This moment revolves around the finding of Rebecca, who replaces Sarah (Chesed) as the female guardian of the holy light of Israel. We find truth when we follow God's lead. In Exodus 7:4, the phrase **by judgments** ב Bet (2) ש Shin (300) פ Pey (80) ט Tet (9) י Yod (10) מ Mem (40) = 441), equal in value to the word **truth,** refers to the judgment that comes out of the forty days and forty nights of the Flood in Noah's time, reflecting the period of twelve months in which Noah's generation is judged.

Other words and phrases with the same numeric value of **emet** (truth, 441) and **Torah** (which is called "the truth," 611) are:

them אתם (Genesis 1:17): א Alef (1) ת Tav (400) מ Mem (40) = 441

This refers to the setting of the sun and moon, the luminaries in the sky, giving us day and night, two opposites that combine to produce life on earth.

Torah תורה: ת Tav (400) ו Vav (6) ר Reish (200) ה Hay (5) = 611

Torah's purpose is to help guide humanity in its journey toward perfection. Moral and ethical conduct is the foundation on which this accomplishment is built. Torah itself can be thought of as Tiferet.

The word **Torah** appears first in Exodus 12:49, when the Law (Torah) is given to B'nai Yisrael: "one law shall there be for the native and the proselyte who lives among you." The same Law is for everyone, the cornerstone of a just society. Another word equal to the value of the word **Torah** is **apron,** which refers to Adam and Eve making aprons to cover their nakedness,[55] suggesting that following the Law requires modesty. Also equaling the numeric value of the word Torah:

is bound up קשורה (Genesis 44:30): ק Kof (100) ש Shin (300) ו Vav (6) ר Reish (200) ה Hay (5) = 611

This describes how Jacob's (Israel's) soul (which represents Tiferet

---

[55] Genesis 3:7.

as a Sefirah) and that of his youngest son, Benjamin, are bound up in each other. If Joseph forces his brothers to return to their father, Jacob, without his youngest son, their father will die. Each generation's soul is connected to the that of the prior generation. Torah remains in the soul of every generation. Torah, God, and the Jewish people are inseparable. Tiferet contains within its Sefirah the truth of Torah as the Law for everyone. It is this Law that brings beauty and moral order to the world. Devorah, the third prophetess of Israel, accomplishes this.

65: *The Numeric Value of Hallel*

Hallel הלל: ה Hay (5) ל Lamed (30) ל Lamed (30) = 65

The Hallel (praise) is the declaration Devorah and Barak make as a prayer after Sisera attacks. The declaration "Not to us God, not to us, but to your Name give Glory" is the entreaty of total self-nullification, the prerequisite to prophecy, as discussed more fully in chapter 10.

Devorah and Barak recite Hallel prior to the commencement of the war against the Canaanites. "They said, 'Not to us, God, not to us, but to your Name give Glory.'"[56] The spirit of holiness replies, "For my sake, I will do it."[57] This event reveals the importance of the earlier instances of the prophets' or the people's ability to hear the voice of God, and that prophecy is for the well-being of all of Israel.

The Hallel is said on all the major holidays except those of judgment (Yom Kippur, Pesach, Purim) and after major events of being delivered from evil. The full Hallel is "recited on 18 days each year in the land of Israel: [Note that 18 is the number representing the word for "life," **Chai**—ח Chet (8) י Yod (10)] on the eight days of Sukkot, the eight days of Chanukah, both days of Shavuot, and the first day of Passover. It is generally recited in the morning service before the Amidah (the standing prayer of Praise) and the reading of the Law (. . . the Torah portion of the day)."[58] Like the blessing on the wine, which precedes all the other foods,

---

[56] Psalm 115:1.

[57] Pesachim 117a; Isaiah 48:11.

[58] Geoffrey Wigoder, *The Student's Encyclopedia of Judaism*, 157.

the Hallel precedes the other elements of praise prior to the reading of Torah.[59]

Looking in *The Spice of Torah—Gematria,* we find many words suggesting locations, tools, and aspects of praise:[60]

the high הגבהים‎ :ה Hay (5) ג Gimel (3) ב Bet (2) ה Hay (5) י Yod (10) ם Mem (40) = 65

the south הנגבה‎ (negev): ה Hay (5) נ Nun (50) ג Gimel (3) ב Bet (2) ה Hay (5) = 65

Lord, my Lord (master) **Adonai** אדנ׳‎ :א Alef (1) ד Dalet (4) נ Nun (50) י Yod (10) = 65

mandrakes דוד׳אם‎ (violets, jasmine): ד Dalet (4) ו Vav (6) ד Dalet (4) א Alef (1) י Yod (10) ם Mem (40) = 65

staff והמטה‎ (rod): ו Vav (6) ה Hay (5) מ Mem (40) ט Tet (9) ה Hay (5) = 65

its vessels כל׳ה‎ :כ Caf (20) ל Lamed (30) י Yod (10) ה Hay (5) = 65

have power ה׳כל‎ :ה Hay (5) י Yod (10) כ Caf (20) ל Lamed (30) = 65

your might מאדכ‎ :מ Mem (40) א Alef (1) ד Dalet (4) כ Caf (20) = 65

---

[59] Geoffrey Wigoder, *The Student's Encyclopedia of Judaism,* 157: "There are three forms of Hallel: Hallel Ha Gadol, The Great Hallel, Psalm 136, recited on the morning service of the Sabbath and festivals, as an additional psalm for the last day of Passover, and as part of the Haggadah (the book used for the Passover Meal and ceremony); Hallel (Full Hallel, Psalms 113–118, the standard version of Hallel. And the Half Hallel or Chatzi Hallel."
[60] Gutman Locks, *The Spice of Torah—Gematria,* 30–31.

As ordained by the prophets, Hallel is said in times of deliverance from national peril. Tradition teaches that the Hallel's five psalms are selected for this purpose because they contain five fundamental elements from the living experience of the People of the Book: the Exodus, the splitting of the Red Sea, the giving of the Torah on Mt. Sinai, the future resuscitation of the dead, and the promise of the coming of Moshiach.[61] In Devorah as Tiferet, we see how all aspects of the primary beliefs of the People of the Book commingle. This is evidenced in part by the recitation of Hallel after the victory over Sisera just as it is recited by Moses and Israel, who sing Hallel after their victory over the pharaoh and the Egyptian army; by Joshua for his victory at Jericho; by Esther and Mordechai when Haman rises against them; and by others in their efforts to overcome an enemy of B'nai Yisrael.[62]

70: The Numeric Value of Sacramental Wine

Tiferet represents the species of grape that is the source of wine used in all ritual blessings, whether at a marriage, birth, wedding ceremony, Holy Day celebration, or on Shabbat, and the blessing on the "Creator's fruit of the vine" that precedes all eating and drinking and the blessing on the bread on Shabbat. The wine and the Bracha (blessing) over the wine offer us other clues about Devorah and the Sefirah of Tiferet.

wine יי״ן: י Yod (10) י Yod (10) ן Nun (50) = 70

Some say that wine, representative of the Sanhedrin during the time of the Temple, can help elevate the heart to kindness and wise insight.

sod סוד (secret or counsel): ס Samech (60) ו Vav (6) ד Dalet (4) = 70

This word has the same numeric value as wine made from grapes. Tradition says, "[A]s soon as wine goes in, counsel and discernment perish. But the person who keeps a cool head while drinking does not lose his discernment and has the characteristics of the seventy elders."[63]

---

[61] R. Nosson Scherman and R. Meir Zlotowitz, eds., *The Complete Artscroll Siddur,* 632.

[62] R. Yaakov Ibn Chaviv, *Ein Yaakov,* Pesachim (117a), 176.

[63] Ibid., Eruvin 152.

According to *Ein Yaakov,* "R. Ila'I said: There are three things by which you can tell whether a person has a decent character: by his cup (if his mind is at ease after he drank wine), by his purse (by the way he deals in money matters), and by his anger (if he controls his temper.) Some say by his laughter too."[64]

In the Perek Shira, in which all the species associated with the Sefirot except the olive have their own song, the song of the grape is: "Thus says God: When the wine is found in a cluster, and someone says, 'Do not destroy it, because there is blessing in it,' so will I do for My servants, not to destroy everything."[65]

The Four Species of Sukkot Represent the Name of the Creator

In Kabbalah the four species used during Sukkot each represent a letter in the name of God: **aravah** (willow) is Yod (10), **lulav** is Hay (5), **hadas** (myrtle) is Vav (6), and **etrog** is the final Hay (5).

Miriam shows us that repentance (teshuvah) reunites the Father (Yod or Chochmah and wisdom) and the Mother (the first Hay or Binah) with the Son (Vav or Zeir Anpin) and the Daughter (the final Hay or Malchut). In this same way, the ritual of the four elements in the sukkah reflect the name of the Creator and the unification of the family in which all aspects of the community and ourselves are celebrated in joy on Sukkot. This entire family or all of B'nai Yisrael can, by performing the mitzvah of Sukkot in total joy, come into rapport with God through the prophetic spirit of the Ruach HaKodesh associated with the sukkah itself. Personal experience confirms this truth.

68: The Numeric Value of Lulav (Palm Branch)

lulav לולב: ל Lamed (30) ו Vav (6) ל Lamed (30) ב Bet (2) = 68

The palm tree has long been considered the sign of the tzaddik (righteous Torah scholar), who learns and teaches others. This is one of Devorah's symbols, because her place of administering justice in the community is

---

[64] R. Yaakov Ibn Chaviv, *Ein Yaakov,* Eruvin, sayings about wine, 152.

[65] Isaiah 65:8.

Figure 5.1. Palm tree, west coast of Israel, Jaffa.

under a palm tree. As the source of the ceremonial lulav (palm branch) used in Sukkot, it stands for an erect yet supple spine whose branches, when shaken close to the ear, sound like a bird in flight, suggesting the spirit of God (Ruach HaKodesh) in our midst and in the sukkah itself.

wise חכם: ח Chet (8) כ Caf (20) ם Mem (40) = 68

This word, representing the Sefirah of Chochmah,[66] is equal in value to the lulav, the tallest of the four species of Sukkot ritual. As the middle pillar of our anatomy, the spine also suggests Devorah's centrality to the people of Israel. (She is a wise woman who sits under the palm tree.)

shall lead ינהג (Deuteronomy 4:27): י Yod (10) נ Nun (50) ה Hay (5) ג Gimel (3) = 68

---

[66] Deuteronomy 4:6.

This refers to God leading the people into exile for their failure to live a Torah-based life.

prophet הנביא (Deuteronomy 13:4): ה Hay (5) נ Nun (50) ב Bet (2) י Yod (10) א Alef (1) = 68

This word as used counsels the people not to follow the words of a false prophet. Devorah sitting under the palm tree and judging Israel embodies wisdom, leadership, and unity.

376: The Numeric Value of Shalom

peace שלום (shalom): ש Shin (300) ל Lamed (30) ו Vav (6) ם Mem (40) = 376

Tiferet, as the place of meeting, like the Tent of Meeting and the sukkah on Sukkot, also called the Tabernacle of Booths, is the source of peace for the year. Shalom habayit, peace in the home, is a treasured quality. The gematria for the word **shalom** tells us everything we need to know about Tiferet as the place where peace is made.

I will make or **do** אעשה (Genesis 2:18): א Alef (1) ע Ayin (70) ש Shin (300) ה Hay (5) = 376.

The Creator decides that it is not right for Adam to be alone. "God said, 'It is not good that man be alone; I will make him a helper corresponding to him." Peace in the home is found in the creation of Eve. Peace arises from the partnership between man and woman and is at the root of the relationship between the created and the Creator.

from his youth מנעריו (Genesis 8:21): מ Mem (40) נ Nun (50) ע Ayin (70) ר Reish (200) י Yod (10) ו Vav (6) = 376

God promises: "[I] will not continue to curse again the ground because of man, since the imagery of man's heart is evil from his youth; nor will I again continue to smite every living being as I have done. Continuously, all the days of the earth, seed time and harvest, cold and heat, summer and winter, day and night, shall not cease."

Esau עשו (Esav): ע Ayin (70) ש Shin (300) ו Vav (6) = 376

As a hidden teaching of shalom (peace) connected to Tiferet, we can note the list of partnered opposites. **Esau,** first appearing prior to the birth of his brother Jacob, with whom he fights much of his life, suggests that the ultimate peace achieved between brothers is essential to peace in the world.[67]

The word **peace** itself appears just prior to Jacob meeting Rachel at the well.[68] The well is often the place where the Israelites find their mates: Elazar (Abraham's servant) finds Rebecca; Moses meets Tzipporah. Water, like wisdom, is hidden (in the ground) and must be drawn to the surface. "The Wisdom of women builds her home."[69] In this moment in Torah, Elazar is asking if it is well with Laban: "[A]nd they said, 'It is well [**shalom**] and see—his daughter Rachel's coming with the flock.'"[70]

Shalom is also promised by the Creator as the outcome of Torah for the individual, for Israel, and for the world. In Uktzin, the final chapter of the Aggudut of the Talmud, it is written, ". . . the Talmud points out the heavenly rewards that [are] in store for those who diligently and reverently [study] the Torah." In Uktzin we learn the great insight of R. Shimon ben Chalafta: "The Holy one, blessed be he, found no vessel that could hold His blessing for Israel except peace, as it says, 'God will give might to His nation, God will bless His nation with peace.'"[71] According to *Ein Yaakov,* "Tosafot Yom Tov explains: God wants to restore strength and might on his people. How does he accomplish this? By blessing them with peace. For the entire blessing in the world will endure only if there is shalom. Shalom, peace, truly is the most fitting ending of the Talmud."[72]

---

[67] Genesis 25:25.

[68] Genesis 29:6.

[69] Proverbs 14:1.

[70] Genesis 29:6.

[71] Psalms 29:11.

[72] R. Yaakov Ibn Chaviv, *Ein Yaakov,* Uktzin, "God Will Bless His Nation with Peace," 803.

217: The Numeric Value of Devorah

Devorah דבורה: ד Dalet (4) ב Bet (2) ו Vav (6) ר Reish (200) ה Hay (5) = 217

As we have learned so far, in Tiferet the parts are joined and opposites harmonize; moral order is established and truth and peace are made possible. These are the hallmarks of Tiferet and Devorah.

Summarizing each of the polarities mentioned in the Parshiot included here, we see that Tiferet and Devorah are proved as the scales of justice, our experienced closeness to or distance from the Creator, the skill of identifying what forces are operating in any given situation, knowing what is blessed and what is not, and knowing what is holy and what is unholy.

Concealed in the name of the third prophetess are day and night, life and death, blessing and no blessing, hail and no hail, darkness and illumination, divine presence and the absence of the divine presence, and curse and blessing. There is no ambiguity in any of these parts identified in the Parshiot, and in all of them, it is clear that God's presence is made manifest. These polarities found in words equal to Devorah's name and hidden story show us that justice harmonizes light and dark, day and night, blessings and no blessings—opposites are distinct, with different purposes, their balance requisite to prophecy, beauty, and truth. We should assume that the process of judgment leading to justice, truth, glory, and peace is the presence of the divine Shechinah, which explains why Devorah is the only judge who actually judges or makes decisions and why she does so. The Shechinah, as Barak makes clear, rests with Devorah.

In Devorah (the Sefirah of Tiferet); in the torso (where the heart is housed); and in beauty, truth, and peace, there is the ability to hold opposites in balance. Tiferet does this and brings the kingdom to glory. We see that the divine presence is with Devorah, just as it is in the fire of glory before B'nai Yisrael. We also learn that the order in which things must be done is precise and with purpose. The Parshiot point us to the purity of differences and the ability to distinguish clearly among our natures: among Jacob (Judaism), Ishmael (Islam), Esau (Christianity);

between freedom from our stubbornness (Pharaoh) and being set free (Moses); between traveling with God's glory and traveling in the darkness of ego; between being beset by plagues of evil and being free from them. If we participate in ritual service, the Shechinah can be received. All of these qualities tell us about justice and beauty and why we should not tremble before anyone. The judgment is ultimately God's.

Just as we have done with Sarah and Miriam, let us close with the Parshiot concealed in Devorah's name. The following words and expressions have the numeric value of 217. Here is an interesting assortment of references between opposites, just as Devorah the judge determines what is right and wrong, who is guilty or innocent, and the proper restoration or tikkun (repair) to facilitate the elevation of the sparks in every situation.

saw וירא (looked, beheld, Genesis 1:4–5): ו Vav (6) י Yod (10) ר Reish (200) א Alef (1) = 217

Genesis 1:4–5: "God saw that the light was good, and God separated between the light and the darkness—God called to the light: 'Day' and to the darkness he called: 'Night.' And there was evening and there was morning, one day." Here the two parts that make a twenty-four-hour period, day and night, are brought into balance as life principles in all of creation.

on dry (dried) land בחרבה (Genesis 7:22): ב Bet (2) ח Chet (8) ר Reish (200) ב Bet (2) ה Hay (5) = 217

"All in whose nostril was the breath of the spirit of life, of everything that was on dried land, died." All things on the earth are dying. We learn of life and death, the two parts that make for the body and soul experience, mortality and immortality, respectively.

fear חרדה (wonder, perplexity, Genesis 27:33): ח Chet (8) ר Reish (200) ד Dalet (4) ה Hay (5) = 217

"Then Isaac trembled in very great perplexity, and said 'Who—where–is the one who hunted game, brought it to me, and I partook of all when you had not yet come, and I blessed him? Indeed, he shall remain blessed.'" In this instance the story of Esau and Jacob is high-lighted, showing us the mysterious way in which the Creator can make His presence known and can establish justice. In this case, the younger son, Jacob, instead of the eldest, Esau, receives their father's blessing of lineage. The older but cruder elder son receives a blessing, but not inheritance. Awe of God renders the proper judgment.

and the hail וְהַבָּרָד (Exodus 9:29): ו Vav (6) ה Hay (5) ב Bet (2) ר Reish (200) ד Dalet (4) = 217

Here, another coupling of opposites is evident: hail and no hail. Moses tells the pharaoh (after the seventh plague of hail): "When I leave the city I shall spread out my hands to God; the thunder will cease and the hail will no longer be, so that you shall know that the earth is God's." As the Ramak teaches us, Tiferet is the entry to Gan Eden. Because the heart is housed in the torso, like the Torah in the Ark, it is bound to the Creator, who opens the door to supernal wisdom (Chochmah). The entire world is determined by this closeness to or distance from the Creator. Hail, frozen water, is a judgment or Gevurah, as we learned in the chapter on Miriam. Running water, Chesed, is its opposite. Here, as Devorah teaches us, wisdom is rooted in our faith in God.

and it gave light וַיָּאֶר (illuminated, Exodus 14:20): ו Vav (6) י Yod (10) א Alef (1) ר Reish (200) = 217

"It came between the camp of Egypt and the camp of Israel and there were cloud and darkness—while it illuminated the night—and one did not draw near the other all night." In this instance, we learn of the illumination of the camp of Israel by the presence of the Creator and of the lack of light in the Egyptian camp. Here, too, opposites are combined in the epic narrative. Darkness and illumination are highlighted. As story elements, this occurs just prior to the splitting of the Red Sea (Exodus 14:21) when "Moses stretched out his hand over the sea, and God moved the sea with a strong east wind all the night, and he turned the sea to damp land and the water split. . . . And the water was a wall for them on their left and on their right . . ." We are once again shown the Creator's hand in everything from a hovering cloud to splitting the Red Sea to stopping the hail. Likewise, Tiferet as justice teaches us that the vital challenge is to distinguish between good and evil and right and wrong in all actions, thoughts, and events. This is also why Tiferet can represent free will, the choice between good and evil.

and shall appear וירא (will appear, Leviticus 9:6): ו Vav (6) י Yod (10) ר Reish (200) א Alef (1) = 217

Moses said, "[T]his is the thing that God has commanded you to do; then the glory of God will appear to you." Glory is Hod, as we will see in the upcoming chapter on Avigail. Aaron and his sons remain in the Tent of Meeting for seven days while Moses inaugurates the priestly service by erecting and deconstructing the Tabernacle and performing the service himself during that time. He is told to do this in order for the heavenly fire to descend. This descending fire refers to the Shechinah. In this instance, B'nai Yisrael is being shown that the Creator fulfills His promise when we do our part, and He unites with us through the presence of the Shechinah, as we will see in chapter 10. Thus Tiferet has the capacity to bring down the Shechinah so that she rests in the Tabernacle of the Temple of our hearts.

is accursed יואר (Numbers 22:6): י Yod (10) ו Vav (6) א Alef (1) ר Reish (200) = 217

Balak (son of Tzippor, king of Moab), who dislikes the Israelites, calls to Balaam (a Mesopotamian prophet): "So now, please come and curse this people for me, for it is too powerful for me; perhaps I will be able to strike it and drive it away from the land. For I know that whomever you bless and whomever you curse **is accursed.**" In this famous scene, we learn that Balak's evil intention is remedied by the fact that Balaam instead blesses Israel. We are also shown that God uses nature to try to stop us from putting ourselves at risk. The she-donkey Balaam is riding is stopped three times by angels; and later, when God opens the mouth of the donkey who speaks to Balaam asking why he has beat the donkey, Balaam realizes God's purpose and blesses Israel. Here, just as the judge must hear the case and apply the law, life too is revealed as having either a curse or a blessing.

SUMMARIZING THE IMPORTANCE OF DEVORAH

Tiferet, the central point through which five of the other Sefirot and prophetesses are connected, should show signs of qualities from each of the other Sefirah. It is in part for this reason that the blessings after the meal are associated with Devorah, for Tiferet distributes nourishment (elements) to all parts of the body, making Tiferet the proper Sefirah for Birchat Hamazon (blessings said after a meal).[73]

In the chapter on Sarah, we learn of planting the seed of creation. In the prophetess Devorah we see the community tended to in her tireless service as judge. In Miriam we see the action of teshuvah and repentance; in Devorah we see leadership in her song after she is victorious over the Canaanites. We will learn that Chanah, the next prophetess to lead B'nai Yisrael, teaches us about enduring will and union with the Creator through prayer, and she shares with Devorah the distinguished place of speaking the greatest praise ever to the Creator. She calls the Creator "Host of Hosts." Avigail, committed to right action, says to David, "[D]o not forget your maiden," much like the glory spoken of by Devorah—"until I arose a mother in Israel"—which can be seen as a declaration of emancipation from the self and subsequently becoming a mother, who gives up her own well-being for that of her children. Devorah—like Chuldah, whose knowledge of the Torah is superseded by no other prophetess—shows her total adherence to the Law and administration of the Law among the People of the Book. From Esther is gained the similar capacity to save the Jewish people from destruction. In Devorah we see elements of all the other prophetesses and of the Sefirot they occupy. As the middle of the middle pillar, Devorah and Tiferet balance all elements in a harmonious union.

In Birchat Hamazon (blessings after the meal), an action associated with Tiferet and said after partaking of bread and other food, we bless

---

[73] Prayer for Nourishment: Netzach and fig.

the land as our second blessing after the blessing for nourishment. The blessing itself has four parts, corresponding to the four worlds in which we and our soul are rooted. Therefore prayer, represented by the fig and the Sefirah of Netzach, provides us with our spiritual nourishment.

The prayer's four parts are:

1. Blessing for nourishment: God nourishes the entire world
2. Blessing for the land we have been given through our forefathers
3. Blessing for Jerusalem, the resting place (heritage) of God's glory
4. Blessing for God's goodness and bountifulness to us

Devorah teaches us that Tiferet is the place of adjustment between parts, an elevation to balance within and without. The laws of beauty include the laws of moral order, a balance of unique but interdependent parts and events brought into equilibrium. The individual and the community must live by a moral order. The vine produces the sacramental wine with which we bless the Creator and His abundance. The blessings said over the wine—the grape is the species of Tiferet—remind us that under the vine we will sit in harmony and peace and in redemption. When we adhere to an inner and outer order, predicated on the word of God as presented in Torah and as shown by Devorah's life and conduct, the society itself has the ability to elevate the sparks and help bring Moshiach and redemption to the individual and the world.

Just as the other Sefirot seem to reflect from within them some aspect of the time of Moshiach and redemption, Tiferet can be considered the revival of the traditional Sanhedrin (the council of seventy elders) that will precede Moshiach and the Ark that sits in the Temple in which is housed the Torah and the sacred implements. Tiferet reflects the shine of the Temple Ark as the heart within each of us. Through our love of God, we become one house united from which the flame of zeal for performing God's Word illuminates the world with its righteousness and beauty.

We learn from Devorah how to take part in elevating the community to moral order, and the next prophetess, Chanah, teaches the Israelites the true meaning of victory as an outcome of prayer.

6

Chanah

Netzach · The Victory of Spiritual Discipline

The gates of prayer may be closed, but never the gates of tears.

Berachot 32b, Psalms 39:13

Chanah חנה (Hannah)

ח Chet (8) נ Nun (50) ה Hay (5) = 63

Sefirah Correspondence: Netzach

Titles: Prophetess, Mother of Samuel

Family: Wife of Elkanah; mother of Samuel; counterpart to Eli, the High Priest

Time Period	Jewish Calendar	Gregorian Calendar
Birth	2702	1058 BCE
Prayer	2831	929 BCE
Birth of Samuel	2832	928 BCE

Developmental Stage: Spiritual order

Day: Wednesday

Sacred Species: Fig

Body Correspondence: Right leg

Rituals: Prayer, offerings to the Temple

Holiday: Tu' B'Shevat

Symbol: Shiloh

Prayers: Amidah, Sabbath blessing on the children

Shine of Chanah–Netzach: The rituals restored in the Third Temple

Prophecy Source: 1 Samuel 1:25–28, "Please, my Lord! By your life my Lord, I am the woman who was standing by you here praying to HaShem. This is the child that I prayed for; HaShem granted me my request that I asked of him."

Chanah's Song: 1 Samuel 2:1–10, "Then Chanah prayed and said: My heart exults in HaShem, my pride has been raised through HaShem; my mouth is opened wide against my antagonists, for I rejoice in your salvation."

SEFIRAH: NETZACH

Netzach is the source of our endurance, our spiritual will. It is called *victory* and *eternity,* reflecting Chanah's spiritually active life in pursuit of having a child and in her devotion to God at the Temple at Shiloh. Like this Sefirah of great and steadfast action, Chanah discovers through her devotion the mysteries of prayer.

Phase of Development: Chanah shows us how to be consistent in our efforts in our relationships to God and the world. She teaches us a quality of prayer that is full of heartfelt devotion. Spiritual order in our life makes the physical body a vessel for the holy to fill and unites the material and the spiritual. Following Tiferet and Devorah, Netzach develops our inner spiritual will to make it an addition in the community, which helps the community practice faith in action.

Life Principle: As endurance and eternity tells us, Netzach is a principle of effort. Just as the Creator is always working on the world's behalf, we too must make an effort in the world in an enduring, consistent, and committed fashion. Overcoming our own failures and whatever obstructs our progress takes determined action.

World Action: Netzach endows a moral society with eternal spiritual guidelines. Here, the individual moves away from an ego-centered life to an altruistic one. A moral framework guides our human relationships (Tiferet). The next level of maturity is our relationship to the Creator. In all that we do there should be praise and awareness of the Creator as Master of All, Host of Hosts.

Spiritual Action: Using prayer, Netzach is the spirit's call to action. Endowed with mercy and charity, it emphasizes our ability to be constant in our attachment and devotion to God and God's plan for creation. Netzach is our victory over our lower impulses.

Meaningful Work: Netzach enables physically demanding jobs, such as those in the military and in various institutions. It enables excellent managers, entrepreneurs, and leaders.

Day Focus: Do something you have put off or something that requires a great deal of energy—reconnect with people from the past who are important but overlooked or commit to a long-term goal and make a plan of action to accomplish it.

Species: The fig blooms twice each summer, in June and in August.

CHANAH'S STORY

Chanah was the wife of Elkanah, a Godly man. For nineteen years, Chanah petitioned God in her **desire for children.** She eventually conceived, at the age of 130, but before this holy event occurred, Chanah devised a number of methods to conceive and in the process led a **spiritual revolution,** teaching the Israelites to **rely on prayer and not miracles.** She **endured** the taunting of her husband's other wife, Peninah, whom Chanah brought into the household with the thought that it would rouse her own womb to jealousy. Peninah had many children, while Chanah remained barren. She decided she would pretend to have committed adultery, and after the tests for this would prove her innocence, God would give her a child. She went to the **Temple at Shiloh to pray,** but Eli, the High Priest, saw her moving her lips yet heard no words coming from her and thus mistook **Chanah's conversation with God** as the mumblings of a drunken women. She explained her petition to God and promised that if she conceived, she would dedicate her son as a **Nazarite.**

In addition to conceiving the prophet Samuel and four other children, Chanah brought into the world the name of God as **Host of Hosts:** God says, "You have multiplied my Hosts [by calling me Host of Hosts] . . . I will multiply yours."[1] In addition to motherhood, Chanah teaches us spiritual devotion and what would become the structure of the Amidah, the standing prayer recited several times each day in Judaism.

SYMBOLISM OF CHANAH

Right Pillar and Desire for Children

Like Sarah, her predecessor above her on the right pillar of the Tree of Life, Chanah is barren for many years. Chanah's story revolves around her desire to conceive a child and what she does to accomplish that goal. Her life is a dramatic telling of devotion to God, Torah, and the Temple. Her story begins with her supplication to bear children. She ultimately conceives at the age of 130, subsequently giving birth to four more of her own children (three boys and two girls), with her two additional children being her two grandsons, whom she lives to see born.[2]

Like Sarah, Chanah decides that though she herself is unable to bear children, she should not prevent her husband from fathering offspring to increase the family. She also thinks jealousy might arouse her womb to conception, and thus she hatches a plan: "[W]hen Chanah saw that she was not bearing children, she thought, 'I will tell my husband to bring another wife into my house, so that the Holy One, Blessed is He, will see that I

---

[1] R. Yishai Chasidah, *Encyclopedia of Biblical Personalities,* 196. See also 1 Samuel 1:11; Chronicles 25:5; Midrash Shmuel, ed. Buber, 2:5.

[2] Pesikta Rabbati 44:7. This is one explanation for the statement "A barren woman bore seven." See also R. Yishai Chasidah, *Biblical Personalities,* 197.

have brought a rival into the house and will grant me conception.'"[3] It is forbidden to create rivalries between women deliberately, and there are legal prohibitions against two sisters being married to the same man at the same time. Indeed, biblical women show us the anguish it causes in their lives, yet if all is God, then these antagonisms or polarizations are for the eventual rectification of both the individuals and the community.

Chanah's Spiritual Revolution

In Netzach we learn how to pray "for one thing at a time."[4] Chanah's persistent efforts to bear offspring can be seen in her challenges to the Creator, for which she is later rewarded. She is strong-willed and demonstrates that the greater our plea for help—the plea being the vessel that the light can fill—the more likely we are to be answered. Genuine prayer comes from the heart, nullifying ourselves to make room for God's presence. Becoming pregnant with the light, we proclaim prayers not from lack, but from praise of God.

Rely on Prayer, Not on Miracles

God tells Abraham that his people are not controlled by the stars (astrology) and our destiny can be changed from bad to good through prayer.[5] The Rambam (Maimonides) teaches that all the miracles wrought by the prophets are the result of their prayers.[6] "By virtue of sincere prayer, Joshua stopped the sun and Elijah and Elisha resurrected the dead. Even the greatest prophets were not endowed with mysterious supernatural powers; rather, their prophetic spirit brought them closer to God so that they could pray with great intimacy and trust in the almighty."[7] This shows us that we may not rely on miracles when in danger. Instead, we are to rely on prayer, for "prayer is not a miracle."[8]

---

[3] Pesikta Rabbati 43:6. See also R. Yishai Chasidah, *Biblical Personalities*, 196.

[4] Taanit 8b.

[5] Shabbos 156a: "No star controls the destiny of Israel."

[6] Deuteronomy 34:10, the Rambam commentary.

[7] R. Avrahom Chaim Feuer, *The Shemoneh Esrei*, 15.

[8] Ibid., 115.

Chanah's Refinement

Despite Chanah's pleas, the "Holy One, Blessed is He, purified Chanah through suffering for nineteen years: ten years of marriage during which she did not bear children (after which Elkanah married Peninah, who bore him ten sons [in] eight years), and one year of carrying and bearing Samuel."[9] As Hagar troubles Sarah, Peninah troubles Chanah. "Her rival vexed her":[10] "Peninah would rise early and say to Chanah, 'aren't you going to get up and wash your children's faces so they can go to school?' And at midday [Peninah] would say 'aren't you preparing to welcome your children home from school?' When they sat down to eat [Peninah] would say to Elkanah, 'Give this son of mine his portion . . . you did not give that son of mine his portion.'"[11] We learn from the Torah, "But to Chanah he [Elkanah, her husband] gave a double portion, for he loved Chanah and God had closed her womb."[12]

Endurance

In an active way, Chanah seeks spiritual remedy for her barrenness. She uses Jewish Law in some of her plans and ritual in others. She speaks to God as a contemporary with whom she is angry or whom she loves or from whom she needs help. Nowhere do we have the feeling that Chanah is speaking to a Creator that is distant, remote, or inaccessible. Netzach as eternity shows us our fundamental closeness to God, that we are connected to Him at the hip, like a child who is carried by its mother.

Peninah's ongoing taunting of Chanah over her barrenness is HaShem's well-intended way to provoke Chanah to prayer. God uses Peninah's unmerciful behavior for Chanah's good. Because Peninah is cruel, however, all ten of her children perish while Chanah goes on to conceive five of her own children, including Samuel. We are told that

---

[9] Deuteronomy or 1 Samuel 44:5

[10] 1 Samuel 1:6.

[11] Pesikta Rabbati (end of chapter 43).

[12] 1 Samuel 1:5, referring to the double portion Elkanah gave to Chanah in celebration on the occasions of his annual Temple offerings.

"Chanah prayed" means she does so with prophetic inspiration.[13]

When we look at the prophecies of the prophetesses thus far, we see a progressive line of descent to the royal House of David, our next Sefirot of Hod and Avigail. Sarah sees the destiny of Isaac and Jacob as the foundation on which rests all of Israel; Miriam foretells the birth of Moses and his role as prophet and redeemer; Devorah foretells the victory of the Israelites against the Canaanites; and Chanah foretells, in prophetic prayer, that "[m]y son Samuel is destined to be a prophet in Israel, and in his days Israel will be miraculously saved from the Philistines. My Great Grandson Heman, Son of Joel, together with his fourteen sons, is destined to sing hymns with lyres and harps among their fellow Levites in the Temple."[14]

As a single story reflecting the true nature of the Sefirot of the Etz Chayim, the prophetesses' lives and teachings reflect the story of each individual's progressive ascent spiritually, which, paradoxically, involves becoming progressively more immersed in the physical world.

Chanah and the High Priest Eli

In the story of each prophetess, the prophetess has a male counterpart as husband or collaborator or both. Sarah has Abraham; Miriam has her brothers, Moses and Aaron; Devorah has her husband, Barak (or Lappidoth). Who does Chanah have? We learn her husband's name, Elkanah, and that he is a devoted spouse and an observant man. But it is Eli, the priest at Shiloh, who seems to be Chanah's counterpart in her Sefirotic importance as Netzach. Eli is like a spiritual brother to the prophetess Chanah. His life is synonymous with the Temple at Shiloh; he is responsible for raising Chanah's first son, Samuel, who becomes judge, ruler, and prophet of Israel.

Chanah's life story revolves around the Temple of Shiloh, where Eli and Chanah first meet as strangers. Eli and Chanah's stories are interwoven. Chanah and Samuel, a mother and son, each gifted in the holy art of prophecy, become the instruments by which God, through the High

---

[13] 1 Samuel 2:1.

[14] R. Yishai Chasidah, *Encyclopedia of Biblical Personalities,* 198 (Targum Shmuel 1:2:1).

Priest, can anoint blessings. Netzach is a receptacle for the blessings of holy action. While Tiferet holds peace within it, Netzach has the ability to confer on others the qualities it inherits. This is why we see the Kohen Gadol, the High Priest of Netzach, being able to confer the blessings of God on the people. Who confers the blessings on the priests? God administers the blessings on the Kohen Gadol: "I will bless those who bless you."[15]

Chanah's Prayer at Shiloh

In the Torah, Eli, the High Priest at Shiloh, where the Tabernacle is housed, "sees this woman [Chanah] mumbling and hearing no words, mistakes her for a drunkard."[16] But we know that "Chanah rose after she ate in Shiloh and after the drinking"; he drinks, but she does not.[17]

It happens that as she continues to pray before God, Eli observes her mouth. Chanah is speaking to her heart—her lips move, but her voice is not heard—so Eli believes she is drunk. Eli says to her, "How long will you be drunk? Remove your wine from yourself!" Chanah answers, "No my Lord, I am a woman of aggrieved spirit. I have drunk neither wine nor strong drink, and I have poured out my soul before God. Do not deem your maidservant to be a based woman—for it is out of much grievance and anger that I have spoken until now." Eli then responds, "Go in peace, the God of Israel will grant the request you have made of Him." She said, 'May your maidservant find favor in your eyes.' Then the woman went on her way and she ate, and no longer had the same look on her face."[18]

Chanah's Spiritual Strategies

During her nineteen years of barrenness in her marriage, one of Chanah's plans is to create a situation by which she will be tested for

---

[15] Genesis 12:3; Chullin 49a.

[16] 1 Samuel 1:2–7; 19.

[17] Ketubot 65a.

[18] 1 Samuel 1:12–18.

adultery and then found innocent, for Halacha (Jewish Law) tells us: "[I]f the woman be guiltless, then she shall be cleared and shall conceive seed."[19]

In this scheme, Chanah tells God that she will pretend to lie with a man other than her husband, Elkanah, whom she will tell in advance of her plan, though he will object to it.[20] She will then be put through the ordeal of an adulteress and will be forced to drink the Sotah waters—from which a guilty woman will die and an innocent woman live. Chanah tells the Holy One, blessed is He: "When a woman's life is in danger, she is checked in three areas to see whether she is worthy of surviving. [These three areas are] family purity, separation of challah from the dough, and kindling of the Sabbath candles." She asks: "Have I transgressed [in] a single one of them?"[21]

Chanah's knowledge of Halacha (Jewish Law) and her determined will are hallmarks of victory. She knows how, when, and where to apply her will and, ultimately, how to surrender her own will to that of the Creator.

Prayer and Conception

Just as God closes Chanah's womb, He opens it, like the Holy of Holies that the Kohen Gadol enters only once a year, on Yom Kippur, the Day of Atonement. It is said that Chanah, like Sarah, conceives on Rosh Hashanah, the New Year. The Torah tells us of this moment: "They arose early in the morning and prostrated themselves before God: then they returned and came to their home, to Ramah. Elkanah knew Chanah his wife and God remembered her."[22]

Tradition tells us of that day:

Chanah arose after eating in Shiloh and after drinking; and Eli the Kohen was tilting on the chair, near the doorpost of the Sanctuary

---

[19] Numbers 5:28, Berachot 31b.
[20] Berachot 31b.
[21] Numbers 5:28, Berachot 31b.
[22] 1 Samuel 1:19.

of God. She was feeling bitter, and she prayed to God, weeping continuously. She made a vow and said, "God, Master of Legions [Host of Hosts], if you take note of the suffering of Your maidservant, and You remember me, and do not forget Your maidservant, and give Your maidservant male offspring, then I shall give him to God all the days of his life, and a razor shall not come upon his head."[23]

Every year, Chanah and Elkanah go up to Shiloh together to make their annual offerings, at which time Eli blesses them, "'May God grant you offspring from this woman,' because of the request that he [Elkanah] had made of God . . . For God had remembered Chanah and she conceived and gave birth to three sons and two daughters. And the boy Samuel grew up with God."[24]

The child given Chanah as a result of her prayers is named Samuel (requested of God) whom Chanah knows prophetically to be a son of Israel, not a "son of her own." This prophetic knowledge likely explains her willingness to commit him to the priesthood even before he is conceived. Ultimately, we are assured that Chanah is "granted conception in the merit of [her] prostration [before God]."[25] After Eli mistakes her mumbling for that of a drunkard and rectifies his error by blessing Chanah, we learn of Chanah's prophetic talents: "[F]or this child I prayed."[26] "May it be His will that when he grows up, he will strive to serve God as he does now as a child."[27] Samuel eventually rules Israel, first alone for ten years, then two years with Saul, and then David reigns in Hebron for seven years.

---

[23] 1 Samuel 1:9–11.
[24] 1 Samuel 2:20–2:21.
[25] Yalkut Shimoni, Shmuel 80.
[26] 1 Samuel 1:27.
[27] R. Yishai Chasidah, *Encyclopedia of Biblical Personalities*, 198. See also Zohar Chadash 7a.

The Nazarite and the Priestly Blessing

Chanah promises her unborn son to the service of HaShem as a Nazarite.[28] The Bible speaks of two people who were lifelong Nazarites: Samson (Judges 13:3–7) and Samuel (1 Samuel 1:11).[29] After learning the Nazarites' ritual obligations, the Torah next teaches the blessing of the Kohen Gadol (High Priest)—the priestly blessing that "God spoke to Moses saying: 'Speak to Aaron and his sons, saying: So Shall you bless the Children of Israel, saying to them: 'May God bless you and safeguard you. May God illuminate His countenance for [upon] you and be gracious to you. May God lift his countenance to you and establish peace for you. Let them place My Name upon the Children of Israel, and I shall bless them.'"[30]

The instructions given to the High Priests to create the proper vessel to hold God's blessings include that of shalom (peace), a central quality of Tiferet. This tells us that the individual in a state of peace is a vessel for God's blessings. These directives precede the day that Moses finishes erecting the Tabernacle, which he anoints and sanctifies—both the altar and its utensils—just as he did the leaders of Israel—the leaders of the tribes. Moses' accomplishment of building the Tabernacle is the shine for all the Temples, including Shiloh, just as the words of prayer are the shine of our Holy of Holies, our hearts.

The only time Chanah does not ascend to Shiloh for the annual offerings is after Samuel is born. She makes clear that when she does go up to the Temple, it will be at the time of Samuel's weaning, when she will offer him to the priesthood—to the care of Eli.

---

[28] Geoffrey Wigoder, *The Student's Encyclopedia of Judaism*, 247: "A Nazarite, from the Hebrew word *nazar*, means 'to dedicate.' The Nazarite could be a man or a woman who vows to stay pure and dedicate themselves to the Creator with associated abstinence from any wine, grape or anything derived from grapes. Also, he (she) was forbidden from cutting their hair, it being holy for their chosen designated role. Also, a Nazarite was forbidden from coming into contact with the dead, even those bodies of their family were forbidden to them. When a Nazarite's period of abstinence was over, generally a period of thirty days, afterwards they would bring an offering to the Temple, shave their hair, and burn it on the altar. Then the Nazarite could return to their normal status and could drink wine."

[29] Numbers 6:22–27.

[30] Numbers 6:23–27.

Host of Hosts

Miriam challenges all earthly authority as well as that of God. Devorah challenges earthly oppressors and helps establish guidelines by which society should live. Chanah's will is focused on the Creator; she uses the abilities of Miriam and Devorah to elevate the material world to a new plateau, conquering any spiritual adversary we have in our hearts, which is ultimately the source of our doubt in God.

The nature of Chanah's praying is new to B'nai Yisrael and the world. Her declaration to the Creator—"Host of Hosts" (Master of Legions)—has attracted multiple commentaries over the centuries. One interpretation of her declaration is that "[f]or the festival, Chanah went up to the Tabernacle where she saw all of Israel, (gathered). 'Master of the universe,' she said, 'all these hosts are Yours, and not even one among them is mine!'"[31]

In her pleas for conception, Chanah is the first human to call the Creator "Host of Hosts." When Chanah describes her longing for conception, she speaks for all women in her conversations with God regarding her barrenness, telling the Master of the Universe that He created no part of her body in vain: "For what are these breasts that you placed on my heart if not to nurse with? Give me a son to nurse!"[32] The Shechinah is the immortal mother aspect of God who nurses her young humanity and Israel.[33]

Another perspective is that from the day God created the world, no person had ever called him "Host of Hosts" until Chanah came along. According to Chanah: "Of all the hosts that you created in your world, is it hard for you to give me one son?"[34] The sages suggest that Chanah uses her reasoning with God. "Master of the Universe," Chanah says, "there is a host in heaven and a host on earth, and I do not know to which I belong. If [I belong] to the Host of heaven I should not eat, drink, procreate, or

---

[31] 1 Samuel 1:11.

[32] Berachot 31b. When Sarah conceives Isaac at the age of ninety, reflecting the influx of extra Binah, all the deaf can hear—the organ of hearing is Binah. The infertile become pregnant, and the entire community possesses greater understanding.

[33] Berachot 31b.

[34] Berachot 31b.

die, and I should live forever. And if I am of the earthly host, I should eat, drink and also procreate!"[35] "The holy one, blessed is He, said to her 'You have multiplied my Hosts [by calling me Hosts]. I will multiply yours.' Thus it is written, all these were the sons of Chanah."[36]

Prayer and Humility

Prayer increases the flame of spiritual will. Regardless of our stature in the material world, the birthright of the crown, our inner closeness to the Creator, our ability to talk with and for the Creator, determines our ability to have the Shechinah, God's Divine Immanence, rest upon us. Chanah leads us through the gate of prayer. Prayer (tefilah) and song (shira) are both conductors of prophecy and play an equal role in the spiritual life of the People of the Book.

Knowing as we do that humility is the keynote of prophecy, we understand that bowing in prayer has its source of power in surrendering to God's will. "Rabbi Yitzchak said: Everything happens only in the merit of bowing. Abraham returned from Mt. Moriah in peace only because he bowed to God, as it says: 'We will bow down and return to You.'"[37] "Similarly, the Jews were redeemed from Egypt. . . . They received the Torah, Hannah's prayers were answered. . . . The exiles will be ingathered. . . . The Temple will be rebuilt . . . the dead will be resurrected, in the merit of bowing down before God."[38]

Everyone's heart is the entrance to the gate of prayer. This gate is either closed or open. Chanah shows us how to open the gate of prayer and the gate of tears, which is a higher gate than prayer. Tears stand for the ablutions made on the altar, the water rituals of purification. They can be the sign of humility in both joy and awe, the fundamental love Chassidut teaches, bringing us to oneness with God. Chassidut shows us that in nature and in our environment, rain is withheld as result of gossip and slander, of sin and neglect of Torah.

---

[35] R. Yishai Chasidah, *Encyclopedia of Biblical Personalities*. See also Pesikta Rabbati 43:3.

[36] R. Yishai Chasidah, *Encyclopedia of Biblical Personalities*, 196. See also 1 Samuel 1, Chronicles 25:5.

[37] Genesis 22.5.

[38] Bereshit Rabbah 56:3.

Just as the rains bless the land with nourishment and bounty, so too in our personal lives, tears of repentance nourish the entire body with the Creator's mercy and love. Chanah shows us this, as does Netzach. Netzach applies the will not just to the world we live in, but also to the world to which we are rooted in heaven. "May the expressions of my mouth and the thoughts of my heart find favor before You, God, my Rock and my Redeemer."[39]

We are shown from various perspectives that Chanah speaks not a formulated prayer from the intellect, but one from her heart. When Eli, the High Priest, mistakes her silent prayers for drunkenness, she responds, "No, my master, you are not a master in this matter, and divine inspiration does not rest upon you if you suspect me [of being drunk]."[40]

Chanah and Devorah's Connection in Prayer

In the Zohar we learn that "there were two women who uttered songs and praises to the holy one blessed is He such as no man in the world ever uttered. Who were they? Devorah and Chanah."[41] The sequence between Devorah in Tiferet (beauty) and Chanah in Netzach (eternity and victory) shows us that praise as prayer or in song makes us victorious over the forces of darkness and engenders an opportunity for prophecy.

Chanah shows us how to speak from our hearts. Just as Devorah pronounces judgments, declaring who is guilty and who is innocent, Chanah declares her heart's desire to the Creator. Devorah's is a declaration of moral order and Chanah shows a purpose of spiritual speech and how to induce the Shechinah's presence. Baal Shem Tov teaches that the correct use of speech will hasten the ending of our exile.

Prayer Is Eternity in Speech

Netzach shows us the potential return of the light and shows us that prayer facilitates an aliyah, a going up or elevation of the soul. Using speech to praise the Creator is the ultimate use of words. As vessels of

---

[39] Psalms 19:15.
[40] 1 Samuel 1:15.
[41] Zohar 3:19b.

eternal living truth, these words embody the Shechinah in our lives and in the spiritual worlds from which our souls derive their power and glory. Prayer is eternity in speech.

Prayer in speech endows the world with the shine of the Or En Sof, from the end to the beginning. From the shine of our mouths comes the light of eternity. Prayer is the highest form of speech, and Netzach, through Chanah, shows us its purpose. Part of living a holy life is to develop and proliferate through prayer. We receive Chesed (seed) love of the Creator in our hearts (Holy of Holies), the material womb of prayer.

Prayer as Victory

How is prayer an element of victory? Through prayer (spiritual endurance), we conquer our own shortcomings and enter a relationship with the kingdom of heaven and the power of Hod, the splendor of God. We are readied for contact with the divine presence in Hod. So begins the Shemoneh Esrei credited to Chanah: "My Lord, open my lips, that my mouth may declare Your praise."[42]

Receiving the element of loving-kindness from Sarah, the strength and discernment of Miriam, and the skills of just action from Devorah, Chanah gives herself over to all of them, demonstrating that faith and prayer are forerunners to the royal bloodline (Avigail), redemption (Chuldah), and Moshiach (Esther).

Chanah's Song of Prayer

Chanah and Devorah praise the Creator as no other humans. Devorah's song occurs after the overthrow of the Canaanites, a triumph over evil in the material world. Chanah's song is declared just after she "brought the child to Eli."[43]

Chanah then says to Eli, "Please, my lord! By your life, my lord, I am the woman who was standing by you here praying to God. This is the child that I prayed for; God granted me my request that I asked of Him.

---

[42] Psalms 51:17.
[43] 1 Samuel 1:25.

Furthermore, I have dedicated him to God—all the days that he lives he is dedicated to God." "He [Samuel] then prostrated himself to God."[44]

This precedes Chanah's song of prayer, a triumph over her spiritual challenge of keeping faith in the Creator. Chanah shows us that a communal place of worship is as important for the individual as it is for the community. As we saw earlier, a place is blessed by our presence. Netzach teaches us that our enduring efforts in refining the material world are part of the work we must do to prepare a place for the Creator's presence. Our offerings, material or spiritual (prayers and sacrifices), are keys that open the gates of prayer. It is the song of the heart that opens the gates of tears, which are never closed. Through our good deeds and prayers, life's conditions can be altered. This is our victory. This is an eternal and enduring truth highlighted by Chanah's life. Chanah leads us to victorious prayer.

Chanah's regular participation at the Temple in Shiloh is the reason we are given for her ultimate conception of the prophet Samuel (Shmuel HaNavi): "Because Chanah went up regularly to the Tabernacle, [where she] prayed and pleaded before the Holy One, Blessed is He, He heard her prayer and granted her conception."[45] Chanah, like other women in our holy lineage (the matriarchs Sarah and Rachel), is also granted conception on Rosh Hashanah.[46] New Year's day signifies that each of their sons will be a leader of something new, the head of something important. When the book of life is first opened on Rosh Hashanah, and closed on Yom Kippur, which occurs ten days later, the womb of each is opened by the mercy of the Creator on B'nai Yisrael's behalf. Because they stand on the right pillar, it is only fitting that we see this downflow of mercy, love, and abundance to Sarah and Chanah—and on such an auspicious day of the year. New Year's day in Judaism is when we are told the shine of the light of life illuminates all our heads with blessings. It is a day to praise the Creator's greatness and to ask to be written in to the book of life,

---

[44] 1 Samuel 1:26–28.

[45] R. Yishai Chasidah, *Encyclopedia of Biblical Personalities,* 197. See also Pesikta Rabbati 44:1.

[46] R. Yishai Chasidah, *Encyclopedia of Biblical Personalities,* 197. See also Berachot 29a.

as apparently were the souls of Isaac (Yitzchak), Samuel (Shmuel), and Benjamin (Binyamin).

Chanah's Enduring Prayer

Then Chanah prayed and said:

My heart exults in God; my pride has been raised through
    God;

My mouth is opened wide against my antagonists,

For I rejoice in Your Salvation.

There is none as holy as God, for there is none besides
    You,

And there is no Rock like our God."

1 SAMUEL 2:1–10[47]

Chanah's prayers to God mark a transition to a deeper understanding of prayer and purpose in the social structure of B'nai Yisrael. Moving from the era of judges, who were chosen by the Creator, Chanah's son Samuel inaugurates the period of the dynastic monarchy of kings, which becomes a birthright. The Chronicle of Kings shows that with the inheritance of the birthright, leadership fails and the moral leadership is placed with the prophets, who are holy seers and Israel's guides.

Studying the Torah

In terms of the reciprocity of vessel and emanator, prayers elevate the stature of Shiloh itself, for it is said that every day the Creator weeps three tears. "My eyes will drip tears, for the flock of God will have been captured."[48] We learn further that God weeps for the person who has the ability to study the Torah but does not, for a person who is not able to study the Torah but does (and professes to be a rabbi), and for a leader who intimidates his community.

Chanah studies the Torah and performs her rituals enthusiastically. She is an example to her community. Her presence is an addition

---

[47] Read the entire Song of Chanah in appendix 1.

[48] Jeremiah 13:17.

to the sanctuary at Shiloh, referred to in Baraita as the resting place of the Creator, while Jerusalem is "the heritage that God your Lord is giving you."[49] The Shechinah is clearly "resting" in Shiloh, the place of the Tabernacle prior to the building of the First Temple in Jerusalem, and the person who consecrates the Creator there is illuminated by the Divine Immanence of the Creator. But Shiloh did not last. Why not?

Shiloh's Destruction

We learn a great deal about the inner nature of Netzach by examining the destruction of Shiloh. Considered the "resting place" of the Creator, it is said that Shiloh is destroyed because of two evils "that prevailed there: immorality and treating holy things with contempt. Where does it say that they were guilty of immorality? For it says 'now Eli was very old. When he heard [w]hat his sons [Chofni and Pinchas] were doing to all Israel, and about the acts of adultery that they engaged in with women who gathered in great numbers at the entrance of the Tent of Meeting,'"[50] he became brokenhearted. "And even though R. Shmuel B. Nachmani said in the name of R. Yochanan: 'Those who say that the sons of Eli are sinners are mistaken; [he says that the verse should not be taken literally; what is meant is] since Chofni and Pinchas, delayed the bringing of the sacrifices (bird offerings) that the women who gave birth were required to bring, Scripture considers their act of delaying as if they had committed adultery. [The other sin was] Treating holy things with contempt. (How do we know that?) Because it says (about Eli's sons)'" that they demanded meat to cook for the priest before the fat offering on the altar was made.[51]

The notion that preventing the women who had recently given birth from bringing their offering was adultery clarifies the bird offering at Shiloh as an elevation and thanks-giving offering for the partnership with the Creator in giving birth. It is the quintessential teaching of Chanah's life that for a woman, the womb is the holy Beit Hamikdash (Temple)

---

[49] Deuteronomy 12:9.
[50] 1 Samuel 2:22.
[51] Yoma 9b.

of the Creator. The external Temple where a woman offers thanksgiving for life inside the Holy of Holies of her body is her reciprocal action, her thanksgiving to the one who gives life.

The Years of the Tabernacle

Because Shiloh is the resting place of the Holy Tabernacle, the indwelling presence of the Shechinah, much as Mt. Moriah is pivotal in Sarah's life, the Temple at Shiloh is pivotal in Chanah's life and the progressive development of the People of the Book.[52]

The Temple at Shiloh: The Creator's Resting Place

The Temple of Shiloh is itself important and draws our attention to what Moses said: "[N]ow you have not yet come to the resting place and the heritage that God your Lord is giving you."[53] Jerusalem is referred to as "heritage" in Jeremiah. While Jerusalem is mentioned in some of our blessings and prayers as the resting place of our God, Rashi (R. Shlomo

---

[52] R. Yaakov Ibn Chaviv, *Ein Yaakov,* Zevachim, 756, 757, footnote. "From the Exodus until the building of the first Beit Hamikdash was 480 years. The years of the Tabernacle add up to 39 + 14 + 57 = 110. Thus the Tabernacle in Shiloh stood 480–110 = 370 less part of one year. We learned in Baraita, The Tabernacle in the wilderness lasted thirty-nine years: the Tabernacle at Gilgal lasted fourteen years, namely the seven years of conquest (of Eretz Yisrael) and the seven years of apportioning the land (to the tribes.) The Tabernacle of Nob and that of Gideon lasted fifty-seven years. Thus for Shiloh there are left three hundred and seventy years less (part of) one year. . . . When Eli the priest died after hearing that the Ark had been captured, he fell back in his chair and died. Now we learned in Baraita: When Eli the priest died, Shiloh was destroyed, and they moved the Tabernacle to Nob. When Samuel died, Nob was destroyed and they went to Gibeon. And it says, 'A long time elapsed from the day that the Ark was housed in Kiriath-Jearim, twenty years in all: and the entire House of Israel was drawn to God.' The Ark was placed in Kiriath–Jearim when it was brought back from the land of the Philistines where it had been for four months."

[53] Deuteronomy 12:9. One opinion is that the "resting place," alludes to Jerusalem and "heritage" alludes to Shiloh, for it says, "[T]his is My resting place forever and ever, here I will dwell, I have desired it." It also says, "For God has chosen Zion, He has desired it for His habitation." Moses tells us that this is not a statement of chronological order, for Shiloh precedes Jerusalem as the site of the Mishkan, but rather "not only have you not reached the resting place [Jerusalem], you have not even reached the heritage [Shiloh]." The more common interpretation, however, is that Shiloh is the resting place and Jerusalem the heritage.

ben Yitzchak) says, "[I]n Deuteronomy, Chapter 12:9 states that Menucha (rest) is Shilo and Nachala (heritage) is Jerusalem."[54]

The Importance of Three

As with the other species associated with each prophetess, Chanah's fig has its own song, drawn from Proverbs 28:18: "The protector of a fig tree will eat its fruit."

During the first three years of growth after planting, all are forbidden to take any produce from the fruit trees of Israel. Similarly, the number 3 finds meaning in Netzach and the nature of faith itself, to which prayer is attached. In Netzach we see the embodiment of doing the mitzvah, of carrying out the will of the Creator. This is reflected in how the 613 Commandments (mitzvot) have been condensed by prophets and kings over the centuries into underlying principles for life.

The prophet Micah set forth the mitzvot as three fundamental principles of decorum: "He has told you, O man, what is good! What does God require of you but [1] to do justice, [2] to love kindness, and [3] to walk humbly with your God?"[55]

In tractate Makkot we learn that Isaiah "condensed them to one principle, as it says, 'For thus said God to the House of Israel: Seek Me and live.'"[56] "But it is Habakkuk, who came and boiled down the [613 Mitzvot] to one fundamental underlying principle, as it says, 'The righteous person shall live through his faith.'"[57]

King David's Eleven Principles and Isaiah's Six

Both King David and the prophet Isaiah have left us their versions of what God intends for us and how we can fulfill His will. See Psalm 15 for David's version.

---

[54] Private correspondence with Rav Avraham Brandwein.

[55] Micah 6:8.

[56] Amos 5:4.

[57] Makkot (after 23a). See also Habbakuk 2:4. Refer also to R. Yaakov Ibn Chaviv *Ein Yaakov,* Maharsha, 715–16.: ". . . which means that all the Mitzvot are included in the mitzvah of emunah [faith], the first of the Ten Commandments."

A psalm of David. God, who may sojourn in your tent? Who may dwell on Your holy mountain? (1) One who walks in perfect innocence and (2) does what is right, and (3) speaks the truth from his heart; (4) who has no slander on his tongue, (5) who has done his fellow no evil, (6) nor casts disgrace on his close one; (7) in whose eyes a contemptible person is repulsive, (8) but who honors those who fear God; (9) who stands by his oath ever to his detriment; (10) who does not lend his money on interest, and (11) takes not a bride against the innocent. The doer of these shall not falter forever. (Psalms 15)[58]

Isaiah came and condensed [the 613 Mitzvot] to six fundamental principles as it says, "(1) He walks with righteousness, and (2) speaks with truthfulness; (3) spurns extortionists profits, (4) and shakes off his hands from holding a bribe, (5) he seals his ears from hearing of bloodshed, (6) and he shuts his eyes from seeing evil. He shall dwell in lofty security."[59]

The beauty of each of these summaries teaches us a basic principle about Torah study and Torah-based living. We all have our own lens through which we see and act in the world. At the root, however, we are the same.

The Shemoneh Esrei (Eighteen Benedictions), or Amidah

Chanah devised the formula of the Shemoneh Esrei (literally, eighteen blessings), or Amidah. While the sages composed the explicit prayer after the long Babylonian exile of the Jewish people, it was from Chanah's life that they drew inspiration for the prayer's structure. When the rabbis use the word prayer (tefillah), they are referring to these benedictions. Said two or three times a day, the prayer takes the place of daily offerings in the Temple. First, supplicants praise the Creator, then they ask for what they need, and in closing, they take their leave by bowing in three direc-

---

[58] R. Yaakov Ibn Chaviv, *Ein Yaakov,* Makkot, 714.
[59] Ibid., 715; Isaiah 33:15–16.

tions. This is the internal structure of the Shemoneh Esrei (Amidah). The prayer teaches us how to rendezvous with God through the service of the heart.

Prayer below creates a vessel for God to fill reciprocally. Chanah's gift to us is not only that she birthed of one of the greatest prophets (Samuel), but also that she showed us that God is accessible to us when we pray with our heart (Binah) and mouth (Malchut), the first and last Hay of Yod Hay Vav Hay, God's holy name. Teshuvah creates the vessel for God to fill and self-nullification empowers the prayer's ascension.

The nineteen years of desire Chanah endured during which she did not yet have a child has an interesting correspondence to the prayer called the Amidah or standing prayer, which she is credited with expressing. It is said that by "standing in prayer," we emulate the patriarchs, who, it is said, were able to rouse the angels and chant eighteen benedictions to the Creator: "Our prayer is made up of 18 praises to the Creator."[60] According to the Talmud, these in turn reflect our eighteen vertebrae, symbolizing the Creator's oneness. We have learned that 18 is the number for the word that means "life" in Hebrew. We can see why the eighteen years of barrenness during which Chanah prayed may have resulted in life in the nineteenth year. Additionally, the Talmud teaches "that the number eighteen corresponds with the eighteen times God's Name is found in Psalm 29; the eighteen times it is found in the recitation of the Shema . . ."[61]

GEMATRIA

499: *Tzvaot*

Tzvaot צבאות (Host): צ Tzadee (90) ב Bet (2) א Alef (1) ו Vav (6) ת Tav (400) = 499

Until Abraham, no one had called God Adonai, which is the merciful and loving name of our Creator. Chanah was the first to call the Creator by the name Host of Hosts. To better understand the significance of Tzvaot (in this case, the Host of Hosts, Master of Legions) as

---

[60] Berachot 28b.

[61] R. Feuer, *Shemoneh Esrei,* 22.

it applies to Chanah and Netzach, let us examine some of the words and expressions that equal its numeric value, 499.

We first encounter a reference to God's legions in a reference to Israel itself. "It was at the end of the 430 years, and it was on that very day that all the legions of God left the land of Egypt. It is a night of anticipation for God to take them out of the land of Egypt, this was the night for God; a protection for all the children of Israel for their generation."[62] This suggests that the legions below, B'nai Yisrael, are comparable to the legions above.

when he departed out of בצאתו (left, Genesis 12:1): ב Bet (2) צ Tzadee (90) א Alef (1) ת Tav (400) ו Vav (6) = 499

This phrase first appears when God calls to Abraham and tells him to leave his land, relatives, and father's house for "a land that I will show you. . . . So Abram went as God had spoken to him and Lot went with him; Abram was seventy-five years old when he left [when he departed out of] Haran."

Here is the beginning of the creation of the People of the Book; all separate from the familiar when they leave what is known and place their faith in the Creator. This suggests that when we leave what we know, we can make contact with the power that emanates from God as Host of Hosts. Just as Samuel is the seed of Chanah, whose womb is the resting place of God's mercy (Chesed, seed of life), so too B'nai Yisrael, the People of the Book, are characterized as God's seed of love in the world. Just as Abraham must have faith in God to go out to an unknown place promised him by God, so too must we each go out from our imprisonment to be victorious over our lower inclinations, despite our doubt of the presence and power of the Creator to help us. Faith (*emunah*) leads to victory.

So accustomed is Chanah to making the Temple a part of her life that it is only natural for her to turn to the Creator through Temple worship and sacrifices. Just as Sarah and Abraham sacrifice Isaac, so Chanah,

---

[62] Exodus 12:41–42.

as a member of the right-hand pillar (Chesed overall), pays loving tribute to the Creator, devoting as a sacrifice her son, should he be conceived by her, to serve in the priesthood: "Give your handmaid seed of men,"[63] "a man (distinguished) among men [Samuel] . . . A son who will anoint two men: [David and Saul], [Our sages say: A son] who will be average among men, neither tall nor short . . . [so that people should not speak about him, and place an evil eye on him.][64]

The Amidah: The Standing Prayer

prayer תפילה (tefillah): ת Tav (400) פ Pey (80) י Yod (10) ל Lamed (30) ה Hay (5) = 525

Chanah's total devotion in prayer is the progenitor of the formula expressed in what is called the Amidah or standing prayer (or Shemoneh Esrei). It is recited at least twice a day, in the morning and evening, as is the holy Shema prayer, the last words on a Jewish person's lips at death: "Hear oh Israel, the Lord our God, the Lord is one . . . praised be His glorious name and His kingdom, for ever and ever."

The Positive Commandments

God gave the Jewish people 613 commandments: 248 positive commandments and 365 of them, standing for the days of the year, negative things that we should not do. It is interesting to note that the 365 negatives are associated with the solar year (the masculine aspect), the days of the year being our physical mortality, while the positive mitzvot are inseparable from the woman and the lunar cycle. Though the moon may be smaller than the sun, its tides make possible procreation on earth. The tides are the Creator's divine breath that makes the holy waters in all life-forms—whether the sea or the womb of the woman—capable of supporting life.

womb רחם (rechem): ר Reish (200) ח Chet (8) מ Mem (40) = 248

It is noteworthy that this has the same numeric value as the number of positive commandments. Chanah may have understood intuitively that

---

[63] 1 Samuel 1:11.
[64] Berachot 31b.

by conceiving and giving birth to a child, a woman spiritually fulfills all of the positive commandments.

370: The Number of Years the Tabernacle Stands at Shiloh

A brief examination of clues about the number of years (370) the Tabernacle is at Shiloh reveals these words or phrases in Hebrew.

dwelt שכן (dwell, Genesis 14:13): ש Shin (300) כ Caf (20) ן Nun (50) = 370

This refers to Lot, Abraham's nephew, who is taken captive while Abraham dwells in Mamre.

complete שלם (full, Genesis 33:18): ש Shin (300) ל Lamed (30) ם Mem (40) = 370

This refers to Jacob's arrival in Shechem intact, complete, whole.

green tree רענן (Deuteronomy 12:2): ר Reish (200) ע Ayin (70) נ Nun (50) ן Nun (50) = 370

These words appear when Israel is told by God to destroy the fields and property—including every "leafy green tree"—of the places where idol worship has taken place.

and your heavens שמיכ (Deuteronomy 28:16, 28:23): ש Shin (300) מ Mem (40) י Yod (1) כ Caf (20) = 370

This phrase appears when HaShem warns the Israelites that if they do not hearken to His voice, "accursed will you be . . ."[65] and your heavens over your head will be copper and land beneathe you will be iron."[66]

Many other words suggest the ruination that was to befall Shiloh for failing to uphold the Torah. These elements show us that before God withdraws His protection, we are warned. Shiloh's history teaches us not to debase the holy in ourselves and in the world. When we attend to His

---

[65] Deuteronomy 28:16.
[66] Deuteronomy 28:23.

Word, the Shechinah, His indwelling presence, is with us and prophecy is made possible.[67]

Shiloh stands for the prayer of every person, for it is where Chanah's prayers are answered. Prayer at Shiloh enables the heart to its song (Jerusalem). B'nai Yisrael moves from God's resting place in Shiloh to Hebron and then to its final heritage in Jerusalem.

346: Shiloh

Shiloh שׁילֹו: שׁ Shin (300) י Yod (10) ל Lamed (30) ו Vav (6) = 346

The place Shiloh embodies important blessings.[68] A number of words and phrases share the numeric value of Shiloh.

and the name וׁשם (shem, Genesis 2:13): ו Vav (6) שׁ Shin (300) ם Mem (40) = 346

This refers to the naming of the second river that flows out of Eden. "The name of the second river in Gan Eden is Gichon, the one that encircles the whole land of Cush."

His [its] name שמו (Genesis 2:19): שׁ Shin (300) מ Mem (40) ו Vav (6) = 346

This refers to the name that Adam gives to every living thing. We

---

[67] Readers are encouraged to examine this number—370—more fully on their own. The number embodies an aspect of both Chanah and High Priest Eli at Shiloh, showing us that the Tabernacle itself is the indwelling presence of the heaven of God. It is the location in which the Shechinah rests, and this is Chanah's teaching about God's resting place (Shiloh) and heritage (Jerusalem). Chanah's own son Samuel the prophet anoints and crowns the first kings of Israel and blesses the Creator's resting place (Shiloh).

[68] R. Yaakov Ibn Chaviv, *Ein Yaakov*, Taanit, 306: "R. Nachman b. Isaac teaches that 'we have learned: R. Yose says: it is not the place that honors the person, it is the person that honors the place.' We find an example of this with regard to Mount Sinai. As long as the Shechinah rested on it, Torah says, 'Even the cattle and sheep may not graze near the mountain' (for the Shechinah honored the mountain), but as soon as the Shechinah departed from the mountain, it says, 'But when the trumpet is sounded with a long blast (as a sign that Shechinah has withdrawn).' As long as it remained pitched, the Torah commanded, 'to send out of the camp everyone who had a leprous mark or a male discharge, but once the curtain (of the Tabernacle) was rolled up (to be transported to a new site), both those with male discharge and a leprous mark were permitted to enter the place.'"

also learn that the penalty for man and woman staying together during the woman's **menses** מקור (her source, the fountain, Leviticus 20:18) מ Mem ק Kof ו Vav ר Reish means that they shall be cut off from the people. It is interesting that *niddah,* family purity, the precedent to proper childbirth, is accentuated by the word *source* being the same numeric value as Shiloh, which was destroyed in part because Eli's sons prevented the women who had recently given birth from going up to make their personal sacrifices in a timely manner, instead requiring that they stay away from their husbands overnight at Shiloh. This is considered adultery of the heart, if not the body. Family purity and childbirth are connected. Here we see an example of the reasons for Shiloh's destruction, which is concealed within its name.

favor רצון (Deuteronomy 33:23): ר Reish (200) צ Tzadee (90) ו Vav (6) ן Nun (50) = 346

"Naphtali satiated with favor and filled with God's blessings; go and possess the sea and its South shore."[69] In at least two instances, the waters of life, procreation, and the nourishment that comes from the land are equal to Shiloh. We must conclude then that prayer and devotion to God and His Word lead to the blessing of rain in its proper time and the conception of children in their proper time.

Knead לושי (Genesis 18:6): ל Lamed (30) ו Vav (6) ש Shin (300) י Yod (10) = 346

This word appears when the three angels come to Abraham, who then goes to Sarah's tent and instructs her to "Knead and make cakes." We are reminded of what is referred to as the avodah of the heart, the work or tilling of the heart that every person is required to do.

Returning for a moment to the theme of the right pillar on which Chanah resides, kneading is the action that prepares the dough for shaping, an activity associated with Chesed, the Sefirah above her on the right pillar. Kneading our characters suggests the self-refinement we must

---

[69] Recall that it was ten thousand men from the tribe of Naphtali—Zevulun and others—who waged a successful war with Devorah and Barak against the Canaanites.

engage through self-nullification in order to make ourselves vessels for the word of God and for His blessings to flow to us.

guilt offering הֿאֿשֿם (Leviticus 5:16): ה Hay (5) א Alef (1) שׁ Shin (300) ם Mem (40) = 346

This tells us that with the ram, the Kohen Gadol can provide atonement and the guilt offering for the people, examined earlier in Sarah's life as the sacrifice of Isaac and commemorated in the guilt offering of a ram. (In this we see the fact that what is above flows down to each Sefirah below.) Sarah occupies Chesed on the right pillar above Chanah in Netzach below her. We see then the act of sacrifice being presented first in Chesed through the sacrifice of Isaac and then institutionally in Netzach with the priests, reminding us that everything each of us does is connected.

Thus, Eli the High Priest, though his sons fall from the way, is himself able to intercede on the people's behalf. By rearing Samuel and preparing him for prophecy, Eli makes Samuel his son in a spiritual sense. Despite the failing of Eli's own bloodline, his student goes on to judge all of Israel, as does the prophetess Devorah before him, and anoint two kings, Saul and David. Netzach prepares us for the royal lineage in the material world of the House of King David and Moshiach, as well as the inheritance of Jerusalem as the holy heritage of Israel. Chanah and Netzach promote all this as the next step of the People of the Book toward ultimate revelation.

The Fig and Tu B'shevat

fig תֿאֿנֿה (taynah, as the symbol of Netzach, nourishment): ת Tav (400) א Alef (1) נ Nun (50) ה Hay (5) = 456

The fig symbolizes the blessings and the bounty of the land, the theme of Tu B'Shevat, and is acknowledged in the blessings after the meals. The fig blooms in June and in August each summer.

The holiday of Tu B'Shevat, in keeping with the theme of renewal and sacrifice and the fact that the fig, the species associated with Netzach, is used during the holiday of the blessing of the trees, shows us that the

Figure 6.1. Early fig, Jaffa, Israel.

renewal of life occurs through faith and enduring commitment. Like the fig tree, which produces figs that are sweet and full of seeds, we see that prayer bears much fruit—a fruit of conjugality in Song of Songs. In the Bible the fig is the first fruit mentioned.[70] It is also included in the list of the seven species that are the bounty of Israel.[71]

When eaten on Tu B'Shevat, the fig is part of the celebration for the reawakening of agricultural life, a new year of the trees. Considered a minor holiday that is not mentioned in the Bible, after the destruction of the Second Temple, Tu B'Shevat was observed in the middle of the month of Shevat. (Passover—Pesach—and Shavuot—Tabernacle of the Booths—are also observed in the middle of the month.) Some commentators have suggested that the fig (Netzach) may have been the tree in the Garden of Eden from which Adam and Eve were forbidden to eat. Others

[70] Genesis 3:7.
[71] Deuteronomy 8:8.

suggest that the forbidden tree was a wheat staff (Chesed) or perhaps, as the chapter here on Chuldah suggests, an olive tree (Yesod).

63: The Numeric Value of Chanah's Name

Chanah חנה (Hannah): ח Chet (8) נ Nun (50) ה Hay (5) = 63

As we conclude our journey with Chanah and Netzach, let us look at the story concealed in the fourth prophetess's name. Just as we discovered a particular pattern in the names of each of the other prophetesses, and we learned the significance of related words of equal numeric value, so too can we find in Chanah's name the nature of Netzach and its purpose in our lives.

Chanah's life reveals our relationship to God, the community, and our children. She also demonstrates that we each have a place to be. We are to hold that place with all our faith and humility, in partnership with the Creator. We learn from Chanah and Shiloh that it is the person whose presence elevates the place. In the following Parshiot with words and expressions that are equal to the numeric value of Chanah's name, we find examples that focus on relationships and place.

one אחדים (common, Genesis 11:1): א Alef (1) ח Chet (8) ד Dalet (4) י Yod (10) ם Mem (40) = 63

"The whole earth was of one language and a common purpose." This verse occurs just prior to building the Tower of Babel. All humanity is aware of its singular purpose, which is to serve the Creator and each other.

sinning against מחטו (Genesis 20:6): מ Mem (40) ח Chet (8) ט Tet (9) ו Vav (6) = 63

God keeps King Avimelech from consorting with Sarah and thus sinning against the Creator: "sinning against Me."

Prophet נביא (Genesis 20:7): נ Nun (50) ב Bet (2) י Yod (10) א Alef (1) = 63

"But now return the man's wife, for he is a Prophet, and he will pray for you and you will live, but if you do not return her, be aware that you shall surely die; you and all that is yours." Here, God is telling Avimelech to do as he instructs, to return Sarah to Abraham or know that he and all that is his will perish.

and you shall eat ואכלו (Genesis 45:18): ו Vav (6) א Alef (1) כ Caf (20) ל Lamed (30) ו Vav (6) = 63

"Bring your Father and your households and come to me. I will give you the best of the land of Egypt and you shall eat the fat of the land." In this passage, we encounter the phaorah telling Joseph to say this to the people.

and the beast והבהמה (Exodus 9:19): ו Vav (6) ה Hay (5) ב Bet (2) ה Hay (5) מ Mem (40) ה Hay (5) = 63

Instructions are given by HaShem to Moses to "gather in your livestock and everything you have in the field; all the people and the animals [beasts] that are found in the field that are not gathered into the house— the hail shall ascend upon them and they shall die."

he [was] encamped חנה (Exodus 18:5): ח Chet (8) נ Nun (50) ה Hay (5) = 63

"Jethro, the father-in-law of Moses, came to Moses with his sons and wife, to the wilderness where he was encamped, by the Mountain of God." Jethro then instructs them in how to adjudicate disputes through the elders.

their slaughter מזבחו (sacrifice, Exodus 34:15): מ Mem (40) ז Zayin (7) ב Bet (2) ח Chet (8) ו Vav (6) = 63

God reveals His thirteen attributes of mercy (Exodus 34:5–7) and then tells Moses and the people not to "seal a covenant with the inhabitants of the land and stray after their Gods, slaughter [sacrifice] to their Gods, and he invites you and you [to] eat from his slaughter."

offers as a sin offering המחטא (Leviticus 6:19): ה Hay (5) מ Mem (40) ח Chet (8) ט Tet (9) א Alef (1) = 63

"The Kohen who performs its sin offerings service shall eat it; it shall be eaten in a holy place; in the Courtyard of the Tent of Meeting." Here God tells Moses to speak to Aaron and his sons regarding the laws of the sin offering.

a free will offering בנדבה (Numbers 15:3): ב Bet (2) נ Nun (50) ד Dalet (4) ב Bet (2) ה Hay (5) = 63

God speaks to Moses of the libations, telling him that they will come to a land he designates, and there they are to perform "a fire offering to God—a burnt offering or a feast offering because of an articulated vow or as a free will offering, or on your festivals to produce a satisfying aroma to God . . ."

shall bring them in יביאם (Numbers 27:17): י Yod (10) ב Bet (2) י Yod (10) א Alef (1) ם Mem (40) = 63

Moses speaks to God and asks for a successor: "May God, God of the spirits of all flesh, appoint a man over the assembly who shall go out before them and come in before them, who shall take them out and bring them in; and let the assembly of God not be like sheep that have no Shepherd."

and he destroyed them ויאבדם (caused them to perish, Deuteronomy 11:4): ו Vav (6) י Yod (10) א Alef (1) ב Bet (2) ד Dalet (4) ם Mem (40) = 63

Moses reminds the people that they witnessed the miracles of God, including when He destroyed the army of Egypt, horses and riders: "And God caused them to perish until this day."

and he shall separate him והבדילו (set him aside, Deuteronomy 29:20): ו Vav (6) ה Hay (5) ב Bet (2) ד Dalet (4) י Yod (10) ל Lamed (30) ו Vav (6) = 63

"God will set him aside for evil from among all the tribes of Israel. . . ." This warns the congregation of Israel against idolatry. God tells them that those who take part in idolatry will be separated from B'nai Yisrael if their hearts turn away from being with Him.

SUMMARIZING THE IMPORTANCE
OF CHANAH

Each of these Parshiot related to the numeric value of Chanah's name shows God's role in life. In each there is action and a relationship between God and B'nai Yisrael or between the people and their leaders. In each of them we witness the merciful guidance the Creator provides and the clarity with which He makes His will known. The mitzvot are clarified as obligatory, and we are girded by our faith in God and His teachings.

In Sarah's name, we find the vessels of holiness. In Miriam's, we discover an issue of sinning or not sinning. Purification and atonement are revealed. In Devorah's name, we see the extremes of elements in life: day and night, life and death, the scales of justice. Now, in Netzach, where we are challenged to endure, to take action from the right side, we see clearly instances of significant community events and relationships. Numeric equivalents include the time prior to the building of the Tower of Babel; when Avimelech kidnaps Sarah; when Joseph is able to give to his people land from which they can eat; when Jethro encamps and gives over the ways of adjudication with the elders; the moment when the people are told not to eat from idolaters' sacrifices; that we have sin offerings and free-will offerings; that Moses wants his flock to have a shepherd to bring them in after he is gone; that all is God's and we have a covenant to keep.

In these Parshiot, Chanah's name reveals the way in which God is among us and how in her case her son becomes a shepherd of Israel. In asking God "am I of the earth, or am I not?" Chanah makes clear that we must ask this of ourselves: Who are we, what are we here for, what are we each to do? In addition, in her prayers and sacrifices every year at Shiloh, we learn that self-nullification is a vital component of prayer from the heart. Asking what our place is, what we are here for, and what we are to do is a form of supplication before the Creator.

It is said that Chanah's co-wife, Peninah, taunts Chanah to bring her to beseeching God. Like B'nai Yisrael's Egyptian enslavement and the miracles it makes possible when the community calls out to God, Netzach as victory and eternity shows us that our victories are due to God's presence, which is eternal. The fig's bounty, as our prayers teach us, is due to God's blessings. Victory, like defeat, can be swift and clear, and the covenant of B'nai Yisrael requires ongoing vigilance and right action. In the simplest of terms, in calling God Host of Hosts (Host of Legions) for the first time in humankind's history, Chanah shows that there is only one ruler, one Creator of all life.

The Royal Bloodline

The body is for the purpose of concealment; the soul is for the purpose of revelation. Though we are taught that the soul is a radiant nature of oneness, the body is made of particular parts. By drawing the body into holy deeds—mitzvah, prayer, song, and Torah study—we elevate the body to a more holy stature, making it luminous because the soul is emanating the supreme eternal model from which all of humanity is drawn. The relationship between prayer and song is proved by Chanah's revelation in song. Her declaration of the Creator as Host of Hosts is a moment of revelation. This is her prophecy in addition to what she knows beforehand of Samuel's life and purpose and her own as his mother. Devorah says of herself: until she "arose a mother in Israel." We might also say of Chanah that the prophet Samuel would not have been born until she "arose a mother of Israel."

As the Shechinah descends, we witness the preparation for the royal bloodline. Through self-nullification and enduring effort, Chanah prepares the nation for the royal bloodline, inaugurating through her son Samuel the age of kings. This means that once we supplicate ourselves entirely to the Creator for the gift of eternity (descendants), we are able to participate in the royal lineage of the People of the Book. The individual is anointed as ruler over his or her own body or kingdom, and we learn through prayer and right action to elevate our lives, making them fit for receiving the downflow of love (the seed, Chesed) from the Creator.

It is interesting that after we travel with Chanah to Shiloh, we travel with Avigail to Hebron and Jerusalem, where the kingdom of David is formed, where the nation and the individual reinvigorate the promise of the shine of Moshiach. The Temple is built and the people are brought back to God.

Avigail Continues Where Chanah Leaves Off

Just as we see how Chanah elevates B'nai Yisrael to a new and deeper level of awareness of the Creator, tradition teaches that we cannot really understand Netzach (Chanah) without studying Hod (Avigail). "The Zohar refers to them as 'two halves of one body, like Twins.'"[72] The reader may find it of interest that Chanah's story is told in the first book of Samuel. When Samuel dies, which is essentially the end of Chanah's story, the prophetess Avigail arrives in world history, as told in the Torah. Thus we find that the stories of these prophetesses who represent the "two halves" of Netzach and Hod are located in the same book of the Torah.

The Collective Narrative of the Prophetesses: From Ohel to Shiloh to Jerusalem

Each prophetess's symbols contribute elements to a larger story narrative. With Sarah, we reside within the ohel, the tent of learning, and find that the root of Shabbat meals are a source of loving-kindness. Miriam then brings us the well, song, dance, and deliverance as the ongoing process of judgment and Teshuvah. Devorah illuminates the high hills of Mt. Ephraim under her palm tree, teaching us moral order, the proper relationship to one another, and the importance of a civil society based on sacred Law. Chanah then takes us to the long-standing Temple in Shiloh for prayer and sacrifice, the way of life of our communal and private nullification before the Creator.

We have moved from the holy lamp of our temporary dwellings to the necessity of water, the attribute of mercy and discernment for all life to flourish, then to the importance of natural harmony and moral order, then to the place of religious communal and personal devotion and worship. Each stage of the Shechinah's descent is an elevation of our progress. In this way, we can see that as the spiritual light takes root in the world, the physical world becomes more attached to the spiritual, and by this design, matter is eventually elevated through our awareness to its essential spiritual nature. In addition, the vessels for holding God's light become more permanent in B'nai Yisrael's story.

---

[72] R. Moshe Cordovero (the Ramak), *The Palm Tree of Devorah*, x.

In *Daat Tevunot* (The Knowing Heart), R. Moshe Chayim Luzzatto teaches that the Creator designed the physical body for concealment of His light and the soul for a revelation of the one eternal source. In the world, the greater the presence of the Shechinah, the more vital becomes the vessel in facilitating its luminosity.

Just as a person can endow the body with the light of the soul through proper eating, prayers, and acts of kindness, so the community elevates the entire fabric of its society when its holy vessels—the place of prayer, the house of worship, the hall of study, the home on Shabbat, the heart during prayer—become capable of holding the emanation of the one God. When humans fail to live in a refined and Godly manner, it is only natural that the holy vessels of communal worship will themselves fall into ruin. The community is weakened by immorality, and destructive influences can take hold. The community becomes a place where the light cannot shine, where the Shechinah cannot rest.

By the time the collective story of the prophetesses is told, we will discover that the more we align ourselves with the will of the Creator, the greater the insight, revelation, and prophecy we or our community receives. The more developed our spiritual will, the more capable we are of surrendering the ego's will.

The Growth and Advancement of the People

We have followed the Israelites from their history as wanderers whose holy gathering place was a tent, to the time when they have a portable Tabernacle, to when they have moral judgment, to when they have a place of worship before the building of the First Temple in Jerusalem. As the development of the People of the Book progresses through incarnations of the prophetesses, we also see a progression in their place for magnifying and worshipping divinity, the Creator, the Father in heaven. Gradually, through the Torah story, the People of the Book find a place for personal and communal ritual, witnessing the gradual descent of the Shechinah into physicality and into structures that grow in scale and become more stationary. Simultaneously, there is an ascent of the Creator's role in the community's life and living. There is an inner and an outer testament to the relationship with God. The Temple around which the community revolves is built both internally and externally.

Chanah teaches us about endurance, staying the course, and attachment to the divine in faith. In her story we discover the miracle of conception, childbirth, and the surrender of her child to the service of God and the Torah. Following the descent of the light as a literal process as well as a symbolic one, we find in Chanah's life qualities associated with each Sefirah prior to Netzach and with each prophetess who exists prior to her.

We discover a narrative built entirely around supplication to the divine, arguing with the divine, and ultimately cherished praise of God's miracles. Netzach brings from Chesed the love of the Creator, the need to give, and the need to procreate. From Gevurah it brings the notion that the heart is bitter, repentant, rebellious. From Tiferet, Chanah makes her prayer beautiful, her praise exceptional. In Netzach and through Chanah's life itself, from her own shine, we learn how to remain faithful to our goal, to do everything in our power to succeed as she did. Netzach is called eternity and victory, for in the eternal nature of human endeavor, we find the quest for fulfillment of our purpose. Devorah is the first to give us moral order, and Chanah teaches us individual and community supplication as a spiritual order.

The Etz Chayim elevates our individual incarnations to holy, spiritual vessels for the Creator to illuminate and inhabit. Each prophetess teaches us a particular aspect of our holy anatomy, as souls inside a body. In addition, each of their lives depicts the progress made by the holy nation it represents and the world we all inhabit. In this way, we once again see that the repair of one human is vital to the overall repair of humanity. We are each connected to each other and to the entire world. The *tikkun olam* (repair of the world) of which each of us is part, when done with deliberateness and with each of us in our own place, is a good and important addition to the world.

Netzach endows us with the spiritual will and ability to move in all directions. Prayer is the body of our intention, and our intention is the soul of prayer. An idea we hold in our minds and hearts is given ability to emanate from the spoken word of prayer. Chanah shows us that to elevate the world and ourselves, we must use prayer and praise of the Creator. Our prayers elevate the sparks, which are transformed by the spoken word when we praise and give thanks to the Creator, the Host of Hosts, in whom everything is reunited. When we do this together, we become fitting members of the royal family of humanity, as is revealed by our next prophetess, Avigail.

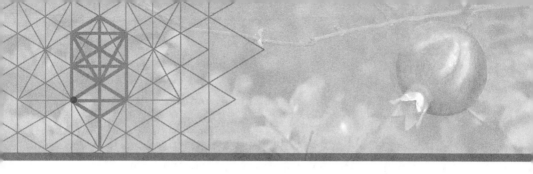

7

Avigail

Hod · Humility and the Royal Bloodline

. . . the humble shall inherit the earth, and delight in an
abundant peace.

PSALMS 37:11

Avigail אביגיל (Abigail)

א Alef (1) ב Bet (2) י Yod (10) ג Gimel (3) י Yod (10) ל Lamed (30) = 56

Sefirah Correspondence: Hod

Titles: Prophetess, Peacemaker

Family: Wife of Naval, wife of King David, mother of Chileab

Time Period	Jewish Calendar	Gregorian Calendar
Life (birth–death)[1]	2854–2924	906–836 BCE
David's rule	2884–2924	876–836 BCE

Developmental Stage: Royal bloodline

Day: Thursday

Sacred Species: Pomegranate

Body Correspondence: Left leg

Ritual: Peacemaking

---

[1] Based on known dates of David's life

Holidays: Lag B'Omer, Shavuot

Symbols: Wedding chuppah, king's palace in Hebron and Jerusalem

Prayer: Modeh Ani (prayer of Thanksgiving)

Shine of Avigail–Hod: Restoration of shine of the royal household in Jerusalem, peace for Israel in the world

Prophecy Source: 1 Samuel 25:23–44, "Let my Lord not set his heart against this base man . . ."

SEFIRAH: HOD

As partner to Netzach, Hod endows us with the splendor of humility. Here, we experience complete self-nullification in the love of God and preparation for union with the Creator.

Phase of Development: Avigail shows that to serve God, we must discern with good intention and Halacha (the Law) what benefits others. Hod, like Tiferet, has the ability to elevate every situation to its highest quality, with special attention given to the contribution of peace through humility. Humility, a lowering of ego, is an elevation of the soul. Avigail's life contributes to the majestic bloodline of the royal household of David: She becomes one of King David's wives and gives birth to their son, Chileab, David's second of six sons.

Life Principle: We are all asked to sacrifice our own needs in life. Avigail believes in the sanctity of life over the safety of her own life, showing that when we preserve one life, we save the whole world. In keeping David from sin, she preserves the entire bloodline for the Jewish people. We learn of our obligation to help others avoid bad choices.

World Action: In the world, Hod allows for the reconciliation of parts. From Tiferet it gains beauty, from Gevurah an eye for justice, from Netzach the will to do. From Yesod, the next Sefirah after Hod, it acquires a lifelong commitment to the covenant of law and order under God.

Spiritual Action: Hod facilitates surrender of the ego and application of will to peacemaking, looking for the glory of God in each situation.

Meaningful Work: Hod's meaningful work amounts to organizational efforts that balance many needs. It is important for religious work, counseling, and negotiation.

Day Focus: Thursday is a good time to examine attachments that prevent us from growing. Hod is a time to evaluate our sense of humility.

Species: The pomegranate represents Israel's bountiful land. It is one of the fruits of Israel with which the Israelite spies return when first entering the Holy Land. It is the symbol that, combined with bells, decorates the hem of priestly robes. As a symbol of fertility, it is said that the fruit's 613 seeds stand for the 613 mitzvot (the deeds we are to do and those deeds we are to refrain from doing).

AVIGAIL'S STORY

Avigail was married to **Naval** (Nabal), **the rebel,** a man who was less refined than she. We are told that she was intelligent as well as beautiful. While her husband was a man of great wealth, because of his rebelliousness he refused to pay his fair share of the territorial defense by offering to the soldiers the customary gift of rations. Aware of Naval's blunder, and having been told by a soldier that David planned to come and kill her husband for his refusal, Avigail prepared **gifts** and supplies and went out to meet David in order to prevent bloodshed in her household. When **Avigail and David met,** she pleaded for his forgiveness, trying to prevent David—who was not yet king—from blood libel and attempting to protect her household.

During the course of their first meeting, she prophesied King Saul's desire to kill David, for which David thanked her before departing. Avigail thus contributed to the **peace** of the kingdom. When she returned home, she did not tell Naval of her deeds because he was in a drunken temper. Ten days later, he was struck by God and died. **David then sought out Avigail,** a result of what some commentators say can be construed as Avigail's arrogance: At their first meeting, she told David, "[R]emember thy maidservant." Indeed David did remember, and wanted to wed Avigail, giving her **the crown of royalty. Avigail's beauty** was renowned, and once wed, she and David conceived a child, contributing to **the royal bloodline.**

SYMBOLISM OF AVIGAIL

Wife of Naval, the Rebel

We learn that the fifth prophetess is "Avigail, wife of Naval."[2] As the text says, "The woman was intelligent and beautiful, but the man [Naval] was difficult and an evil doer; (he was a descendant of Calev [Caleb]."[3] "Avigail is included in the list that answers the question, "who were the seven Prophetesses? Sarah, Miriam, Deborah [Devorah], Hannah [Chanah], Avigail, Chuldah, and Esther."[4]

Naval is a man of great wealth, a sheep and landowner of whom David has heard while traveling through Carmel. He feeds and takes care of Naval's herders when they rest with David's men, so David sends ten of his soldiers to Naval to ask for a donation of goods. (It was customary for landowners to pay for the military defense of the territory with rations and other supplies for the troops.)

Yet Naval asks David's emissaries, "Who is David, who is this son of Jesse, and who are you?" (At the time of this incident, Saul is still alive and is known as king, so perhaps Naval really does not know who David and his men are and therefore feels that they deserve nothing.) He tells David's men, "[T]hese days the rebellious servants have increased, each against his master! Should I take from my bread and my water and my meat that I have slaughtered for my shearers and give them to men about whose origin I do not know?"[5] While it is easy to sympathize with Naval's reasonable questions, the Torah makes a point of telling us that

---

[2] 1 Samuel 25:3.
[3] 1 Samuel 25:3.
[4] Megillah 14a.
[5] 1 Samuel 25:10–11.

he is arrogant and evil, suggesting that his ruse is an effort to avoid paying his equal share of the military defense from which he benefits.

The troops return to tell David what happened with Naval, whereupon David calls for four hundred men to go with him to kill Naval and destroy all that is his, while two hundred others are to stay behind and guard the camp.

One of Naval's attendants (herders) runs to tell Avigail that David "sent messengers from the wilderness to greet our master and he drove them off. These men were very good to us; we were not shamed nor were we lacking anything all the days that we traveled with them in the field. They were a protective wall over us, both by night and by day all the days we were with them tending the sheep."[6]

Avigail's Gifts: A Story of the Sefirot Preceding Her

Aware of the calamity about to befall her husband and household, Avigail decides to intervene secretly. "So Avigail took two hundred breads, two containers of wine, five cooked sheep, five se'ahs of grain, a hundred raisin-clusters, and two-hundred cakes of pressed figs."[7] She gathers these abundant gifts, loads them on donkeys, and sends them ahead with her attendants, shortly following to meet David. She is able to hide her peacemaking journey from Naval because he is drunk.

From a perspective of the Sefirotic elements involved in Avigail's peacemaking efforts, she takes with her the attributes of all the other prophetesses and the Sefirot preceding her. This tells us the secret to humility: first acquiring what it is we are to surrender in service to the Creator. In going out to meet David, Avigail acquires and emanates the attributes of the prior prophetesses. She takes with her wheat (Chesed), cooked sheep (sacrificial offerings of Gevurah), wine and raisins (products made from grapes, Tiferet), and pressed figs (Netzach). When she encounters David and bows at his feet, she expresses the emanation of Hod, humility. In this way her gifts are symbolic of the qualities she humbly offers in service to David, who will become king. As a stage in

---

[6] 1 Samuel 25:14–17.
[7] 1 Samuel 25:18.

the descent of the Shechinah in Israel's life, Avigail's humility suggests a mature partnership between the community and God, where the seed of the Creator's love (Chesed) has become a reciprocal love based on humility. Avigail or any of us is shown that if we surrender to the service of the Divine Planner all that is ours materially and spiritually, we become members of the royal household, the children (vessels) of His light. We become royal emanators.

Avigail and David Meet

Avigail does not tell her husband of her plans to take gifts to David and his army, and while she is "clandestinely descending the mountain, behold—David and his men were descending [the other mountain] toward her, and she met them."[8] David then claims that all the efforts of his guard to have protected Naval were "for naught and that he [Naval] has repaid my kindliness with evil."[9] When Avigail sees David, she dismounts the donkey she is riding and she falls on her face at his feet and says, "With me myself, my lord, lies the sin. Let your maidservant please speak in your ears, and hear out the words of your maidservant. Let not my lord set his heart against this based man—against Naval—for he is as his name implies—Naval is his name and revulsion is his trait: and I your maidservant did not see my lord's attendants whom you sent."[10]

The two go on to discuss the situation: ". . . Please forgive the sin of your maidservant," Avigail continues, "for my God shall certainly make for my lord an enduring house, for my lord fights the wars of God; and no blame has been found in you in your days."[11]

Of Avigail, it is said her wisdom was apparent during her first meeting with David when, despite her own concern for her husband's fate and David's rage, she calmly put a ritual question to him. "She said to [David], 'Does one judge cases involving capital punishment at night?' He said to her, 'Since Naval is rebelling against the King, it is not necessary to

---

[8] 1 Samuel 25:20.
[9] 1 Samuel 25:21.
[10] 1 Samuel 25:23–25.
[11] 1 Samuel 25:25–28.

formally try him.' She replied, 'Saul is still alive, and the world does not yet know that you were anointed King.' He answered, 'Blessed is your discretion and blessed are you who have kept me from incurring blood guilt.'"[12]

Avigail then prophesies Saul's pursuit of David:

> A man has risen up to pursue you and to seek your life! May my lord's soul be bound up in the bond of life, with God, your God, and may He hurl away the soul of your enemies as one shoots a stone from a slingshot. And may it be that when God performs for my lord, all the beneficence of which He has spoken and done regarding you, and appoints you as leader over Israel, that this not be for you a stumbling block and a moral hindrance for my lord, to have shed innocent blood for my lord to have avenged himself.[13]

Avigail concludes her remarks, "And may God act beneficently towards my lord and may you [then] remember your maidservant."[14]

Avigail and Hod's Contribution to Peace

David responds to Avigail, "Blessed is God, God of Israel, who sent you this day to meet me. And blessed your advice and blessed are you, who have restrained me from coming to bloodshed and avenging myself by my own hand." After accepting the gifts she has brought, David tells the prophetess Avigail to "go up in peace to your house. See, I have heeded your advice, and I shall show you grace."[15]

The gift of peace in our house is a metaphor for Moshiach's arrival. The vineyard of peace is humanity's divine inheritance. Shalom habayit, peace in the house, is the foundation of a society at peace. Shalom is treasured as the reward of a God- and Torah-centered life and is the vessel of blessing over Israel. While the traditional Kabbalah of the Arizal con-

---

[12] R. Yishai Chasidah, *Encyclopedia of Biblical Personalities,* 13. See also 1 Samuel 25:33, Megillah 14.

[13] 1 Samuel 25:29–31.

[14] 1 Samuel 25:31.

[15] 1 Samuel 25:35.

siders peace as residing in Malchut, the Kingdom, we can say that the peace cultivated in humility in Hod is the peace that eventually resides in Malchut, or the world.

When Avigail returns home, she does not tell Naval what has occurred—he is drunk from the feast he is holding: He is "pleased about himself."[16] So Avigail waits until the following morning to tell him what has occurred. We are told that when he hears, it is as though his heart dies within him and he is stunned. Ten days later, "God struck Naval and he died."[17]

David acknowledges that it is God who has done this to prevent David's sin, and he sends his men to get Avigail in "Carmel and spoke to her saying: David has sent us to you, to take you for himself as a wife. . . . She arose and prostrated herself to the ground and said, '. . . your maidservant is merely a handmaid to wash the feet of the servants of my lord.'"[18] She follows David's messengers and becomes David's wife. Later we learn that David's six sons include "his second son [who] was Chileab [born] to Avigail."[19]

Looking at Avigail's actions and words, we discover additional clues about the nature of Hod. Avigail believes King David's claim is just but perhaps unnecessary. She goes out to meet him with food and wine. The oral tradition teaches that Avigail, knowing the law, asks a question meant to postpone any action: When (meaning "what time of day") could an individual be put to death? David replies that he cannot investigate it until the next morning. Avigail suggests that the death sentence on her husband also be postponed. David accuses Naval of being a rebel, to which she replies, "You are not yet king." This reveals her powers of prophecy; she sees that he has not yet been anointed. In addition, the Ruach HaKodesh is upon her when she tells King David, "[T]he soul of my Lord shall be bound in the bundle of life."[20]

After Naval dies, just ten days after their first encounter, David sends

---

[16] 1 Samuel 25:36.
[17] 1 Samuel 25:38.
[18] 1 Samuel 25:41.
[19] 1 Samuel 3:3.
[20] Lamentations 21:1.

for Avigail. After ninety days pass, to be sure she is not pregnant with Naval's child, David marries her.[21] She accompanies him throughout his wanderings, "and to Hebron where he became king." Avigail bears David a son, Chileab, who is also known as Daniel,[22] but he is not a contender for the throne. The crown goes to Daniel's stepbrother Solomon. We do not hear of Avigail's son, Daniel, again in the Torah.

We learn in Hod that humility is loving regard for God's supreme authority over us and can lead to seeing the future. We can also delay a moment of anger in ourselves or in others, and thereby transform the energy into something of merit. In Avigail's case, a prevented death results in a cherished birth.

Additionally, the thesis of the Sefirotic descent is supported by a small fact in the Torah: When Avigail leaves her home in Carmel in order to join David in Hebron as his wife, the Torah says, "Abigail then hurried, arose and mounted the donkey, with her five maids traveling with her, and she followed David's messengers and became his wife."[23] Her five maids can represent the five prophetesses through which the Shechinah has descended up to this point—or Avigail plus her five maids leads us to the sixth prophetess, Chuldah, and the next stage in our development highlighted by the Sefirot Yesod.

The Importance of Doing Good Deeds

From the oral tradition we learn information that is implied but not explicit in the Torah. When Avigail first encounters David, she is credited with saying,

> My Lord the King, [if the following each comes before you, what will you do?] If a poor man comes and says to the master of the house, "be Kind to me and give me a loaf of bread," and the master of the house does not help him, and then the poor man attacks the master of the house and kills him, and the case is brought before you to judge—what

---

[21] 1 Samuel 25.

[22] 1 Samuel 3:3.

[23] 1 Samuel 25:42.

will you do? You won't be able to speak and pronounce a verdict, for people will say, "Did he not do that to Nabal?" Do not say that because you are king nobody will rebuke you. Rebuke yourself, and remember your maidservant.[24]

She then says, "Remember the person who prevented you from incurring blood guilt." He responds, "It is not your doing, God has sent you to me."[25]

Avigail as Hod reveals the importance of doing good deeds, highlighting humility as the root of prophecy. The first letter in the words *prophet, prophecy,* and *prophetess*—Nun—shows us that humility is the foundation of Torah. Bowing properly, an attribute ascribed to the letter Nun, is the foundation in prayer, as discussed in our study of Netzach and Chanah. Our spiritual discipline cultivates humility. When we bow, we make ourselves flexible to God's will, surrendering our will to His.

David Seeks Out Avigail

Avigail is sometimes faulted by commentators for telling David to "remember your maidservant"—some say it is unbecoming for a woman to say this when she first encounters David and offers him a reason not to kill Naval. Yet it is David who seeks her out after Naval's death. Based on the negative commentary Avigail has received, we might assume that it is she who goes to find David after her husband dies.

We learn in Niddah, one of the tractates of the Talmud, that a man searches for a wife. Why? An answer can be found in Song of Songs 2:14:

He who lost the thing goes in search of what he lost. . . . Adam searches for his rib from which Eve was fashioned, and why is a man easily appeased and woman is not easily appeased? He derives his nature from the place from which he was created (from the earth, which is pliable), and she derives hers from the place from which she

---

[24] 1 Samuel 25:31.
[25] Shocher Tov 53:1.

was created (the rigid bone of a rib). Why is woman's voice sweet and man's voice is not sweet? He derives his voice from the place from which he was created (one strikes the earth and it produces a dull sound), and she derives hers from the place from which she was created (when you strike the hollow bone it produces a resonant sound). And so it says, "Let me hear your voice, for your voice is sweet and your face comely."[26]

Avigail prophesies to David before he is crowned king.[27] Her prophecies include foretelling his sin with Batsheva: "This shall not be grief unto thee [the issue of Naval], [but another matter will.]"[28]

The Crown upon David's Head

In the Aggadah, the Midrash ("exposition," or Rabbinic commentary on the Bible) is generous "in praise of Avigail's beauty, wisdom and power of prophecy. She is counted among four other women of surpassing beauty in the world; Sarah, Rachel, Rahav[29] and Esther. It is reported that "even memory of Avigail inspired lust."[30]

As the bride of David (Israel), Avigail is the bride queen, much like Yocheved when she remarries Amram. The Shechinah rests in a person's home or in a community when there is peace (shalom) producing joy (simcha).[31]

In keeping David from blemishing his character and from any poten-

---

[26] R. Yaakov Ibn Chaviv, *Ein Yaakov*, Niddah, "A Man Searches for a Wife," 800.

[27] R. Yishai Chasidah, *Encyclopedia of Biblical Personalities,* 13.

[28] 1 Samuel 25:31. The People of the Book are told that we—including a king—must not take many wives. According to Bava Metzia (115a), "He (i.e., a Jewish king) shall not take many wives (Deuteronomy 17:17)—even if they are like [as righteous as] Avigail."

[29] Rahav is a harlot who hides Caleb, Miriam's second husband, and the Israelite spies among the flax. At the age of fifty, after the forty years of wandering, she converts from her Egyptian heritage (she left Egypt at the age of ten) and asks that she be forgiven in the merit of the rope, the window, and the flax, all the elements with which she saves the spies, the Israelites sent by Moses to gain their entry into Israel.

[30] Megillah 15a.

[31] A further study of the word **shalom** שלום is illuminating: ש Shin (300) ל Lamed (30) ו Vav (6) ם Mem (40) = 376.

tial ruination of the royal lineage he is to represent, Avigail elevates him, and for this she is rewarded. Even though they are not yet married, Avigail is the crown upon the head of her future husband. After Naval dies, David "delayed three months before marrying her to ascertain whether or not she was pregnant."[32]

Avigail, the prophetess representing the crown of royalty, initiates through prophecy the heralding of David's kingship and hence the potential for Moshiach. In Judaism there are three crowns: that of priesthood, that of the Torah, and that of royalty. Because Chanah and her son Samuel are expressions of the crown of priesthood, it is Avigail and David who first represent the crown of royalty. We see again the partnership of Netzach (Chanah, priesthood) and Hod (Avigail, crown of royalty). Enduring devotion to the Torah and prayer (Netzach) imparts the aptitude and station for priesthood, but it is through humility that we inherit the crown of kingship over our nature and the world.

> R. Yochanan said: There were three crowns (on the vessels of the sanctuary); that of the Altar, that of the Ark, and that of the Table. (They symbolize the three crowns of Israel: the crown of Priesthood, Torah and Royalty respectively.) The Crown of the Altar (priesthood) Aaron deserved and took it (for himself and his descendants). The Crown of the Table (Royalty) David deserved and took it (for himself and his descendants). However, the Crown of the Ark (the Torah) is still lying there, and whoever wants to take it, may come and take it. (The priesthood and Royalty are hereditary; not so the Torah—it can be acquired by each person.) Perhaps you will say that the Crown of Torah is inferior, (and that that is why there are few takers) therefore it says, "[The Torah says] 'Through me Kings reign' (Proverbs 8:15), consequently, the Torah is greater than Royalty."[33]

---

[32] R. Yishai Chasidah, *Encyclopedia of Biblical Personalities,* 14. See also Tanchumah, Toldot 6.
[33] Yoma 72b.

Further, "There are three keys the Holy One, blessed be He, has kept under his control and not delegated to an agent, namely: the key of rain, the key of child birth, and the key of the revival of the dead."[34]

Hebron

Avigail is important in Hebron, Jerusalem, and King David's household. Looking at the pathway in the Tree of Life between Hod and Chesed, we see the story of the light of Hod (Avigail) returning to Chesed (Sarah) through Tiferet (Devorah) or their mutual beauty. Sarah is buried in Hebron. From Chesed until we arrive at Hod, we refine ourselves for the elevation in Chuldah, where we inherit the World to Come by embodying all the other five Sefirot. After the death of King Saul, David is anointed there, and Hebron becomes his royal city.[35]

The Shechinah's continuing descent into the life of Israel is evidenced in greater and greater physical artifices. Hebron becomes a spiritual center after Shiloh. It's soil is rich,[36] and after Saul's death, David chooses Hebron as his place of residence. It is there that the Cave of Machpelah (the burial place of the matriarchs and patriarchs) is located. Only later does he move to Jerusalem.[37]

Hebron sits between the lifestyle of the shepherd of flocks or the farmer of pastureland and the lifestyle of the Bedouin trader of the desert. It has always been a center of commerce, and its rule has changed many times. As one of Avigail's symbols—it is fertile for the grazing of sheep, symbolizing the lamb of sacrifices—Hebron reflects the essential nature of having performed the *avodah* (work) in our heart and tilled the soil of our life. Hod enjoys the bounty of harvest; hence Hebron is fitting as a commercial and spiritual nexus.

---

[34] R. Yaakov Ibn Chaviv, *Ein Yaakov,* Taanit, 287.

[35] 2 Samuel 2:1–4.

[36] Hebron is also called Kiriath-Arba; its name is derived from the three-letter root HBR, meaning "friend." Biblical Hebron was south of today's location, a strategic hill (Jebel al-Rumayda) that was the site of later Israelite settlements.

[37] After the destruction of the Second Temple, in 68–70CE, the Jewish Hebronites were exiled.

Avigail's Sacrifice Leads to Glory

In general, Avigail's actions teach us about self-nullification: We are not here for ourselves alone but for the benefit of the community and world. The self-sacrifice she exhibits leads to the experience we call glory, when we are endowed with the presence of the Shechinah, which gives us the insight to bring harmony and resolution to issues of conflict. In traditional Sefirotic correspondence, High Priest Aaron, brother of Miriam and Moses, is given this attribute. Aaron is remembered for his desire to keep peace among the various communities of the tribes of Israel and the mixed multitudes. Likewise, the fifth prophetess of Israel keeps peace for David before he is anointed king. The manner in which she does this highlights the Sefirah of Hod and why it represents the glory of God. To experience the glory of God, the indwelling presence of His Immanence, we must each come to total self-nullification, bending, symbolically, our left knee to Him. Hod is characterized by performing selfless acts of loving-kindness and the pursuit of justice and mercy, all that we have been learning prior to arriving at this Sefirah.

The Holy Fire of Lag B'Omer

The epitome of Hod can be experienced on the holiday called Lag B'Omer. Hod of Hod, the thirty-third day of the Counting of the Omer, is when we celebrate Lag B'Omer, a fire holiday during which we burn away the dross of our egos.[38] During the seven-Sabbath-long (hence seven-week) ritual process of Sefirat HaOmer (Counting of the Omer), counting enters the Sefirah of Hod in the fifth week. This is when the supplicant has close contact with the inner essence of Hod, the fifth of the Sefirotic middot, and hence Avigail's purpose in the descent of the Shechinah in our lives and in the life of B'nai Yisrael.

It is said that from the second night of Pesach until Lag B'Omer in the second century CE, R. Akiva's (one of the greatest Kabbalah and

---

[38] According to Yoma, 191: "Our Rabbis taught: There are six different kinds of fire: Fire that eats but does not drink; fire that drinks but does not eat; fire that eats and drinks; fire that burns dry as well as moist things; fire that pushes away fire; and fire that eats fire . . ."

Torah masters of all ages) twelve thousand pairs of students (twenty-four thousand) died. Others teach that R. Akiva's students died between Pesach and Shavuot.[39] To honor their memory, during Sefirat HaOmer until after Lag B'Omer, on the thirty-third day of Sefirat HaOmer, we do not hold weddings or receive haircuts or do things customarily prohibited during a time of mourning. The Counting of the Omer is a period of purification for the observant prior to receiving Torah on Shavuot, the fiftieth day after the second Pesach meal.

R. Akiva thought of his students in pairs, emulated in the last century by R. Yehudah Leib Ashlag's Kol Yehudah Yeshivat in Jerusalem, which today is presided over by R. Avraham Brandwein. R. Yehudah Ashlag would have two men pair up for both study and life learning. Whatever one needed the other was to provide, thinking of each man's basic material and deeper spiritual needs. "Rabbi Akiva, the exemplar of love for others, wanted his students to think of themselves as partners, rather than as individuals. This attitude was necessary in order for the Jewish people to acquire the Torah."[40] It is said that R. Akiva's students loved each other, but not in the proper way. Some have said that they showed a false love, Chesed without Gevurah. It is said that they failed to critique each other's arguments properly out of love for truth that went beyond courtesy or false regard for others' feelings. Holding opposites in harmony, as we learned in Tiferet and Devorah, brings us to truth. Another interpretation of their failure is that they competed with each other regarding interpretations of the Torah, rather than attending solely to the development and needs of one another. This may give us a clue as to why Netzach and Hod are considered inseparable partners, just as our legs are when they are in ideal health.

Eighteenth of Iyar

Why, though, we might wonder, is this day, the thirty-third night of the Counting of the Omer, the barley offering, so important and relevant to our study of Avigail and the Sefirot of Hod? The Torah teaches that

---

[39] Yevamot 62b.
[40] R. Shimon Finkelman and R. Nosson Scherman, eds., *Lag Ba' Omer, Its Observance, Laws and Significance*, 13.

on this same day in biblical history, manna was bestowed on the exiled People of the Book. On the seventeenth of Iyar[41] God tells Moses that on the following day, the eighteenth day, manna would begin to fall from heaven. As we discovered in chapters 3 and 4, manna represents the spiritual downflow of Chesed and Gevurah and comes as a result of supplication, teshuvah (a return to a path of God), and humility on the part of the recipient. It is said that only those who eat manna can receive Torah, meaning that only those who humble themselves to God's commandments—to the "yoke of Torah"—are capable of performing and hearing Torah. Because manna fell on the eighteenth of Iyar, we are once again reminded of the symbolic meaning of the word for "life" in Hebrew 'ח—ח Chet (8) ' Yod (10)—whose numeric value is also 18. Torah gives us life as well as spiritual sustenance.

Humility, Secrets, and the Zohar

Hod and Avigail teach us about humility and devotion to God and His Torah, which are required for us to receive all four levels of Torah's meaning, including the deepest, the sod (secrets) of Torah revealed to the world as they were on the date of the first public teaching of the Zohar. On the thirty-third day of Sefirat HaOmer (Counting of the Omer) on Lag B'Omer (Hod of Hod, representing the glory within glory as its essence), death ceased and life returned to the remnants of Akiva's academy.[42]

After the deaths of his academy students, R. Akiva traveled south to begin teaching again. Until then ". . . the world was desolate [for lack of Torah learning], until R. Akiva came to the Rabbis in the south and taught them the Torah [and created a new chain in the transmission of the Torah]. They were R. Meir, R. Yehudah, R. Yose, R. Shimon, and R. Elazar B Shamua, and they were the ones who restored the Torah at that [critical] time."[43] It is also interesting to see the connection among

---

[41] Iyar is the second month of the ecclesiastical year on the Hebrew calendar. It corresponds to April/May on the Gregorian calendar.

[42] When we are sick or a community is besieged by plague, we are to repent for our sins. Any physical ailment reflects a spiritual root above in disrepair.

[43] Yevamot 62b.

Hod, Lag B'Omer, and this chain of descent of the secret teaching of the Torah, the Zohar of Kabbalah, around which revolves the secret oral tradition. Historically, it is of note that the author of the Zohar, R. Shimon bar Yochai, received the tradition of Kabbalah directly from R. Akiva.

R. Simon bar Yochai had been taught many of the glories of the Torah by R. Akiva on the day Akiva ascended to the heaven worlds. He learned even greater secrets while he and his son, Elazar, lived in a cave during their thirteen years of hiding from the Romans. During this time, God revealed to R. Simon bar Yochai and his son the secrets of the Torah. It was on Lag B'Omer, some suggest, that they emerged.[44]

On the *yahrzeit* (anniversary) of a tzaddik's death, the illumination from the soul's effluence is preciously near to us. On the "day of his death, [Lag B'Omer], R. Shimon bar Yochai declared, 'all the days that I was bound to this world, I was [in fact] bound only to the holy one, Blessed is He.' When he studied Zohar, it is said the angels would become silent in order to hear the wisdom flowing from his lips."[45] When R. Akiva died, his home was surrounded by a spiritual fire, suggesting that those on the outside could not come in and those on the inside could not go out. He is said to have instructed each of his disciples privately on that day, with the final word on his lips being the first line of the Shema, "The Lord is our God, the Lord is One."

The Zoharic Lineage

R. Akiva said to R. Shimon bar Yochai: "It is sufficient that I and your Creator recognize your strength [your spiritual qualities.]"[46] Today, on Lag B'Omer, bonfires are lit on hills and in backyards to signify the spiritual fire of our love for the Creator. So, too, humility is our own ritual fire for burning away our pride and attachments, the glory of the Creator residing in making peace among others, which is accomplished by sur-

---

[44] R. Shimon Finkelman and R. Nosson Scherman, eds., *Lag Ba' Omer, Its Observance, Laws and Significance*, 48.

[45] Ibid., 64. See also Zohar, Parshat Shemot.

[46] Bereshit Rabbah 35:2.

rendering our desire for anything but peace. This is the environment in which the light of the Shechinah can be fully present. This immanent presence of the Creator in shalom is a sign of Moshiach himself, who can bring peace to the countless many. This highlights why it is said that only the vessel of shalom (peace) could hold the Creator's blessings for Israel, or what could be called the Vineyard of Peace.

Summary of Historic Dates of Lag B'Omer, Eighteenth Iyar

- Manna falls
- R. Simon bar Yochai emerges from a cave after thirteen years of seclusion with his son to give over the Zohar
- R. Shimon bar Yochai dies, giving over secrets of the Zohar, and is buried in a cave in Meron

It is significant that all of these events occurred on Lag B'Omer, Hod of Hod, showing us ultimately the response of loving-kindness from the Creator when we are humble[47] and attached to Him in our lives. It reiterates all that we have learned thus far. What we each do has an effect in both the material and the spiritual worlds. The more we align ourselves with God and refine our characters, the better able we are to be divine vessels.

Prophecy, as we know, is when an individual is selected by God to speak to the people on His behalf. We do not reach this state of emissary by occasional acts of devotion and good deeds. A prophet or prophetess is always present to the way of the middle path. Our very alignment of meaning and purpose is based on our relationship to God. All else grows from that.

In itself, Hod is the glory we receive from God, the grace of His loving presence as we begin our final turn in descent of the Tree of Life from the

---

[47] "... [T]here you aquired your glory and your strength," declares the song of bar Yochai, authored by Kabbalist R. Shimon Labia, who died in 1584 CE. The song's lyrics reflect Hod (glory) and the Sefirah above it (Gevurah, strength), and the song is sung on Lag B'Omer in Meron, Israel, where R. Simon bar Yochai is buried.

left pillar to the middle pillar. The garment of the Shechinah covers us as we enter the Sefirah of Yesod. In Yesod, another level of commitment is revealed as requisite to our redemption and ultimate resurrection.

Humility Is the Foundation of Greatness

We learn from the Aggadah that humility is not just a simple addition to our character, but rather the underpinning of greatness. In Chullin, we learn that

> R. Elazar b. R. Yose Hagelili said: it says, "It was not because you had greater numbers than all the other nations that God embraced you and chose you" (Deuteronomy 7:7). The Holy One, blessed be He, said to Israel: I love you because even when I bestow greatness on you, you humble yourselves before Me, "I am mere dust and ashes" (Genesis 18:27). I did the same to Moses and Aaron, but they said, "We are nothing" (Exodus 16:8). I bestowed greatness on David, yet he said, "But I am a worm and not a man" (Psalms 22:7).

We learn further in this Aggadic teaching that "R. Illa'a said: The world continues to exist only in the merit of a person who restrains himself in a fight. For he says, 'He suspends the world on belimah (from the verb balam, to restrain [oneself]. To close one's mouth).'"[48] Avigail's accomplishment stands as testimony to this quality of personal restraint.[49] It is said that Avigail is righteous.

Hod Elevates the Sparks

Hod instructs us that the sacrifices we must make include the sacrifice of ourselves and of what we love. What is more precious to a teacher than his students? What is more precious to a wife than her husband and children? And to God, what is more precious than our love and attachment to His teachings? Hod teaches us that God shows us how to sacrifice

---

[48] R. Yaakov Ibn Chaviv, *Ein Yaakov,* Chullin, 773.

[49] Admonition against marrying more than one woman, even if she is as righteous as Avigail.

our own desires for communal development. In this way, the royalty of which we each possess a spark is emblazoned in us and made part of B'nai Yisrael, the field in which Moshiach of the House of David will be born. It is said of the Zohar's progenitor, R. Shimon bar Yochai, that his soul possessed a spark of Moses. On Hod of Hod we can experience this holy spark of the light of the Zohar and the wisdom that Moses received in the Commandments. Ultimately, this suggests that humility combined with action in the world elevates the sparks of holiness, which, when they are all elevated, will bring into being the prophesied thousand years of peace.

Energy and the Tree of Life

Returning to the prophetess's story, we note that Avigail does not try to convince David that he is wrong to consider her husband a rebel. She herself calls him "churlish." She says that his crudeness is his trait, but that she is wise enough to realize that we can subdue other people's bad decisions, sometimes by being generous, so that they will possibly have a change of heart. This demonstrates the character of a merciful heart and how spirit moves through the life of the individual or the community. When each individual is elevated, all are affected.

When we demonstrate that acts of loving-kindness stand on the foundation of personal humility, when we make ourselves hollow, when we make ourselves empty of arrogance and self-centeredness, we create the flow from below to above and vice versa that is restorative to the very environment in which we live. Humility is an energetic uplifter and leads to the experience of joy (simcha). Like the caduceus (which the medical community uses as its symbol) or the double helix of DNA, the zigzag path of the light that descends and ascends in the Etz Chayim represents the energetic flow that humility enables and through which God energizes a person or vessel with His living glory.

As we descend the Tree of Life from left to right, then from right to left, at each change of direction there occurs energetically a slingshot effect. In order to flow through the next channel, the turns in each vessel are what propel the action forward. We can see a similar effect in the children's game called the whip. In it, children form a line by holding hands, then one at the front of the line runs faster and faster in an ever tightening spiral until the momentum of the children at the end of the line "whips" everyone to a speed that leads most to stumble. The momentum is so great that it seems as though all the children on the line are shot from a slingshot, propelled forward at an accelerated pace.

This is the property of energy as we ascend and descend the Tree of Life. This is why each Sefirah carries some of the qualities above and below it but is itself a distinct vessel with its own unique qualities, which in turn affect the way we experience the other Sefirot or personal traits. Prophecy, like the Sefirot, is an energetic elevator of the community, a heavenly propeller. The souls of the prophets and prophetesses propel the community into a state of awareness that is not the customary place of daily focus or insight.

Prophecy can be viewed as an energetic transformation operating at a subatomic level, at the level of Beriyah (creation). The holy teachings of the prophetesses engender an energetic or etheric template that changes the pattern through which matter will flow in order to manifest as events. This is why it is said that our prayers can annul decrees set in motion by prior behavior and that humility surrenders our imagination and the will of our desires, deferring to those of Almighty God. This is a rectification of the sparks within us, a systematic discipline that burns off the dross of the ego, opening the gates of prayer in our heart. Effective prayer is made in humility and praise of God. Prayer and good deeds propel us into another, more refined state of being.

Royalty of Heart

This refinement of the heart benefits not only us as individuals but also the community. As we will see in the Parshiot containing words equal to the numeric value of Avigail's name, it is this very lesson—not hating your brother in your heart—that her name's secret (sod) and literal (peshat) life story represents. As the prophetess succeeding Chanah, who showed us right spiritual conduct, Avigail shows us that a royal bloodline is conceived in self-control. Halacha (the Law) must always be considered, meaning that our relationship to God takes precedence in action, in knowing and deciding what we do. Participation in royalty is the result of keeping the mitzvot and having love for others.

Kindness Is Greater Than Charity

According to Psalms 33:5:

> We learn in Baraita: In three respects acts of kindness are greater than charity: Charity you can give only with your possessions, but acts of kindness you can do both with your person . . . and with your possessions. . . . [C]harity you can give only to the needy; acts of kindness you can perform both to the rich and to the poor. Charity you can give only to the living; acts of kindness you can perform for both the living and the dead. . . . R. Elazar said furthermore: If a person does charity and justice, it is as if he had filled the whole world with kindness, for it says, "if a person loves righteousness and justice, then the kindness of God fills the earth."[50]

Avigail's Beauty

The fact that Avigail's beauty is renowned, like that of the prophetesses Sarah in Chesed and Esther in Malchut, suggests that in all three women there is a strong radiance of Tiferet (Devorah)—beauty. In fact, we see that Tiferet is in direct contact with both Sarah and Avigail, but not with Esther (Malchut). Esther is reached only through the intermediary of Chuldah (Yesod), which is hidden.

Avigail Embodies Preceding Sefirotic Strengths

In the story of each prophetess we have traced remnants of elements from each woman's preceding guardians. In Avigail, the fifth prophetess, we also see the shine of those prophetesses who have come before her.

In Avigail and Hod there is the kindness of Chesed (when she goes out with food to meet King David on the road as he approaches with the

---

[50] Sukkah 49b.

army) and the wisdom of Gevurah (when she asks about the Halacha, or Law, with respect to the death penalty). We witness the physical beauty of Tiferet, which knows how to use all elements to bring justice, and we see the spiritual wisdom of Chanah in Avigail's knowledge that our relationship to God and the world is through action from the heart and that, as a woman, she can incubate and give birth to the next generation of tzaddikim. For men and women, right spiritual action produces holy vessels and holy children.

In Hod we reach a level of prophecy and personal decorum that allows us to diminish our own needs in exchange for the consideration of the welfare of others. We become God's partners, we become each other's collaborators in a holy path of peace. We can say that just as the other Sefirot have their particular shine, the shine we receive from Hod is one of righteousness and humility. In Hod we gain the promise of Moshiach as the royal representative of God. Humility is the foundation of Moshiach and the royal bloodline just as righteousness is the foundation of redemption and resurrection.

The Meaning of the Royal Bloodline

Associating the royal bloodline of the Davidic kingdom with the Sefirah of Hod suggests that B'nai Yisrael and all of us must go through all the stages represented individually and collectively by each prophetess and the Sefirah or middot (emotions) she reflects. When we go up (aliyah) to read from the Torah, we are contributing to this holy bloodline of Moshiach—both to His eventual appearance and to our own experience of this oneness with God and the world. Once again, we all become Adam and Eve rectified, and we are differentiated by the subtly unique DNA "names" in our blood.

During Avigail's time as a wife of King David, she first settles in Hebron, building a sanctuary there. Then she and King David move to Jerusalem, where they build a kingdom and initiate the plans for the building of the holy Temple. Hod, as a place of revelation, unites the material and spiritual worlds in community. Its overarching accomplishment is the glory of God, which is ultimately the shine of peace and royalty.

Figure 7.1. The author at the edge of David's city, outside the Temple walls. Photo by Mare A. Hieronimus.

Peace is the vessel for the blessings God gives Israel and hence the world. When this is manifest in the community, we see the building of other vessels to facilitate the presence of the Divine Immanence of the Creator. A society builds communal halls of worship; cities flourish, invigorated in biblical times by alignment with sacred practices. King David's royal bloodline, assisted by Avigail's intervention, reveals that humility is the vessel of royalty.

Royalty can be inherited by birth in Malchut, but spiritual royalty in Hod is inherited through individual effort. The Parshiot of Avigail add another level of understanding to the development of the royal bloodline and what it means for each person and nation on earth. We will see that the Parshiot concerning the descendants of Adam—of all humankind— are connected to those related to God favoring those who are pure in intent; that what is impure must be called impure; that all relationships offer the opportunity for holiness and royalty.

In fact, the Aggadah says of Avigail, "[S]he was better for David than all the sacrifices in the world. For had he [David] done to Nabal what he had planned, all the sacrifices in the world would not have atoned for him. But she came to him and saved him."[51]

Marriage and Moshiach

Avigail's very purpose is defined by both of her marriages. In the first, she prevents her husband, Naval, from being put to death. In the second, when she marries King David, she is betrothed to him because of her righteousness, which makes her a suitable vessel to help bring offspring into the royal household, as she does.

Additionally, the People of the Book believe that marriage and the birth of children more than fulfill the mitzvah of procreation and that spiritually, the redemption of the people of Israel rests upon them.

> R. Assi said: Mashiach will not come before all the souls are removed from the Guf [the place in Heaven that holds the souls of the unborn people], for it says, "the souls will keep Mashiach from coming, and the souls that I have made, are a prerequisite for the coming of Mashiach."[52]

> Our Rabbis taught: if a person loves his wife as he loves himself, and honors her more than he honors himself, and raises his sons and daughters on the right path and marries them off close to the age of maturity, about such a person Scripture says, "You will know that your tent is at peace."[53]

> R. Chelbo said: You should always be careful to give your wife the honor due to her, because your home is blessed only because of your wife, for it says, "He [metaphorically referring to God] treated Abram well because of her."[54]

---

[51] Shocher Tov 53:1; R. Yishai Chasidah, *Encyclopedia of Biblical Personalities,* 13.
[52] Isaiah 57:16; R. Yaakov Ibn Chaviv, *Ein Yakkov,* Yevamot, 362
[53] Job 5:24; R. Yaakov Ibn Chaviv, *Ein Yaakov,* Yevamot (after 62b), 359.
[54] Genesis 12:16; R. Yaakov Ibn Chaviv, *Ein Yaakov,* Baba Metzia, 529.

Shavuot: The Wedding Day of Israel and God

Shavuot is one of the three pilgrimage festivals. It is known in English as the Feast of Weeks or Pentecost, the festival of the giving of the Law. The seven weeks between the second night of Pesach and Shavuot, the receiving of the Torah, is referred to as Sefirat HaOmer (the Counting of the Omer), described earlier. The Torah was given on Mt. Sinai on the Hebrew date Sivan 6 (in the month of June, celebrated during the holiday of Shavuot) at the start of the summer harvest, which delineates the barley harvest that precedes it.

In more modern times, Shavuot is celebrated with foods made from dairy products to symbolize the bounty of the land in Eretz Yisrael. Created in ancient days with processions of the first fruits of the Temple as offerings, today the festival is marked by sharing the first of many kinds of fruits. By the time Shavuot arrives, seventeen days after Lag B'Omer, we have proceeded with the Counting of the Omer, traversing through each and every Sefirah and its mixed qualities. We purify ourselves just as we do by descending and ascending the seven steps in the Mikvah in order to keep family purity or prepare for a holiday or to receive the holy Torah, the word of God on Sabbath. The night before Shavuot, on the forty-ninth day of Sefirat HaOmer, men stay up studying the Torah through the night in order to prepare themselves for the Bride, the Shechinah vested in the Torah. On the fiftieth day after the forty-nine days of the Counting of the Omer, the holiday of Shavuot occurs. It is the culmination of seven Sabbaths (seven weeks) of self-refinement each of us undertakes. On the holy day of Shavuot, fitting for Avigail and Hod, King David is born and later dies.

Because it is the wedding day between Israel and God, Shavuot reflects the culmination of Israel's ritual immersion in the Torah. Like the holiday of Shavuot, which culminates after seven weeks of ritual purification, the Mikvah itself enables us to experience this ritual completion every week of the year before Shabbat, when some people keep the mitzvah of Mikvah: "The Mikvah of Israel is God."[55]

---

[55] Jeremiah 17:13; R. Yaakov Ibn Chaviv, *Ein Yaakov*, Yoma, 213.

Sevens in the Torah

In numerous instances, we find "seven" in the Torah, showing us the number's purpose in completion and totality.

The Sabbath is the seventh day of the week. There are seven weeks in the Counting of the Omer before Shavuot, as we have just learned.[56] In Israel there are seven days of Passover and of Sukkot.[57] Every seventh year, the land lies fallow during *shmita* (the sabbatical year).[58] After seven cycles of shmita, there occurs the jubilee year (*yovel*).[59] When a close relative dies, the Jewish people sit in mourning (*shiva*) for seven days. On Sukkot we shake seven species—one lulav, one etrog, two willows, and three myrtles. Jethro, the first real convert to Judaism, has seven different names and seven daughters, including Tzipporah, who marries Moses. Moses is born and dies on the same day: the seventh of Adar. Our sukkahs are "visited" by seven guests (Ushpizin): Abraham, Isaac, Jacob, Moses, Aaron, Joseph, and David. The menorah in the Temple has seven branches. Achashvarosh, king of Persia during the miracle of Purim, holds a party for seven days (Esther 1:5). There are seven primary holidays in the Jewish year: Rosh Hashanah, Yom Kippur, Sukkot, Chanukah, Purim, Passover, and Shavuot. In addition to the 613 Commandments, the sages add seven more. There are seven Noachide Laws pertaining to all humanity.[60] There are seven prophetesses of Israel.

> Our Rabbis taught: There were seven people who together encompass the existence of the world (their combined ages extend from Creation until the end of days. Each one learned from the other and carried

---

[56] Leviticus 23:15.

[57] Leviticus 23:6, 34.

[58] Leviticus 25:4.

[59] Leviticus 25:8.

[60] R. Yaakov Salomon, ed. and author of the Artscroll series (New York: Mesorah Publications). Sanhedrin, 56. See also Genesis 9:1–17. The seven Noachide Laws are laws given to all of humankind by God after the Deluge (the flood) ends. They comprise prohibition of idolatry, prohibition of murder, prohibition of theft, prohibition of sexual promiscuity, prohibition of blasphemy, prohibition of cruelty to animals, and the requirement to have just laws.

on the tradition.) For Methuselah saw Adam, Shem saw Methuselah, Jacob saw Shem, Amram saw Jacob, Achiyah HaShiloni (the prophet, teacher of Elijah) saw Amram, Elijah saw Achiyah HaShiloni, and Elijah is still alive.[61]

The seven prophetesses of Israel express this sequential development in B'nai Yisrael's history.

Blessings of Bride and Groom

Another element of seven relative to marriage is reflected in the Sheva Brachot, the seven blessings recited under the chuppah, the bridal canopy, and at special celebrations in honor of the *chatan* (bridegroom) and *kallah* (bride). The couple are considered king and queen during the seven days of celebration following their wedding.

There are many sayings regarding what we sing to the bride when we dance with her. Beit Shammai (17a) says: "We describe her as she is without embellishments or overstating her qualities." Beit Hillel says: "[We sing], What a beautiful and charming bride she is!" . . . "When R. Dimi came [from Eretz Yisrael] he said: This is what they sing to the bride in Eretz Yisrael, 'She needs no eye makeup, no cosmetics, and no braiding [of the hair], and still she is a graceful gazelle.'"[62]

Simchat Torah: A Wedding Dance

On another holiday, Simchat Torah, which can be likened to dancing with the bride, all of the scrolls are taken out of the Ark and are honored. Through this, we gain additional insights into the glory of Hod and the intimate relationship between the People of the Book and their holy tradition.

In ancient days, the girls of Jerusalem would come out into the vineyards wearing borrowed white dresses (so that none would feel ashamed by her poverty in comparison to the wealth of others). The single men in the community would come out to choose a wife from among these girls.

---

[61] Bava Batra; R. Yaakov Ibn Chaviv, *Ein Yaakov,* "From Adam to Eternity," 585.
[62] Ketubot 16b.

Ulla Bira'ah said in the name of R. Elazar: In days to come, the Holy one, blessed be he, will make a circle for the righteous, and he will sit among them in Gan Eden. Every one of them will point with his finger toward Him, as it says, "And they will say on that day, 'Behold, this is our God: we hoped to Him that He would save us; this is to God Whom we hoped, let us exult and rejoice in His deliverance.'"[63]

On Simchat Torah, each of the scrolls of the Ark is carried by the congregants in a circuit of seven rounds around the sanctuary, *bimah* (an elevated platform where Torah scrolls are placed during their use in a service), or synagogue interior. This same ritual is performed in some wedding ceremonies by the bride, who makes seven circuits around the groom. On Simchat Torah, congregants dance and sing with the Torah scrolls in their arms, and celebrants rejoice as the annual reading of the Torah concludes and a new cycle begins.

A Torah reading for the children under the age of Bar and Bat Mitzvah are blessed with the same blessing Jacob gave to his grandchildren in Genesis 48:16. The ceremony is called Kol Ha-Ne-Arim (All of the Youngsters). Another portion of the ceremony on Simchat Torah is called Chatan Bereshit: Bridegroom of the Beginning. Here, a male member of the community is honored with the privilege of initiating the new Torah reading cycle for the year. He is called the Chatan Torah, Bridegroom of the Law.

Hod Preparation for Consumation

Shavuot and Simchat Torah reflect the nature of Hod as the last of the Sefirah in a descent of the Etz Chayim before the middle path is the only path. We have crisscrossed the Tree of Life from our beginning in Keter to Chochmah, Binah, Daat, Chesed, Gevurah, Tiferet, Netzach, and Hod. The rapid movement of light has been a method of understanding the descent into matter that each soul takes in being born and living.

---

[63] Isaiah 25:9; R. Yaakov Ibn Chaviv, *Ein Yaakov,* Taanit, "They All Danced in Borrowed Dresses," 318.

In Yesod and Chuldah, our next Sefirah and prophetess, there is summation, a holding of all that has been accomplished thus far, all that has been experienced prior to our reaching Yesod, where a transfer is made for the completion of the Son (Zeir Anpin) being joined with the Daughter or Bride (Malchut), the vessel of the queen's chamber itself. Through total nullification of the self in the divine love of the Creator, the marriage is consummated under the chuppah of total devotion. In Song of Songs, the beloved two become one, as the Shema prayer induces us to be with God: "Hear O Israel, the Lord our God, the Lord is One." The erotic imagery in Song of Songs teaches us of the ultimate balance in the world offered by the marriage of a man and woman. Their union, like that between Yesod and Malchut, as we will explore, is a reflection of spiritual components within each one of us that can be brought into holy union for the expression of the Creator's love for humanity and our expression of divine right order. Avigail and King David teach us about this marriage, which is ultimately the story of the body and the soul, the mortal and the immortal, the spiritual and the material, the Creator and the created in perfect union.

Ten, Seven, and Three

From a Sefirotic perspective, while this study focuses on the seven lower Sefirot, the Etz Chayim is a model of a ten-dimensional universe. In part because the descriptions of letters and numbers themselves have value, no matter what number we choose to learn from, the beautiful teachings of the Jewish sages give us an opportunity to reflect on our own lives and the life of the People of the Book. The rabbis teach that

> [t]en things were created during the twilight of the first Shabbat eve. They are: the well, manna, the rainbow, writing, writing instrument, the Tablets, the grave of Moses, the cave in which Moses and Elijah stood, the opening of the donkey's mouth, and the opening of the earth's mouth to swallow up the wicked [Korach and his party]. Some say also the staff of Aaron with its almonds and its blossoms. Others

say, also the demons: still others say, also Adam's garment [the leather garments that God made for Adam and his wife].[64]

Our Rabbis taught: Seven things are hidden from man, They are: the day of death; the day of consolation [when he will be relived of his worries] (Rashi); his final Divine judgment; no one knows what his neighbor thinks; and no one knows where he is going to earn money; and when the kingdom of David will be restored; and when the wicked Kingdom [the Roman empire] will come to an end.[65]

Our Rabbis taught: there are three things that God intended to create, and if it had not occurred to Him to create them, it would be essential that He Should create them. They are: that the dead body should decay (otherwise the family would keep it unburied, and they would constantly be reminded of their sorrow); that the dead should be forgotten (otherwise people would mourn them all their lives); and that produce eventually should rot (otherwise farmers would hoard their produce, create a food shortage, and drive up the prices (Rashi). Some say that coins should be used as currency [and replace the ancient barter system].[66]

"In Baraita we learned that seven things were created before the world was created. They are the Torah, Repentance, the Garden of Eden, Gehinom, the Throne of Glory, the Beit Hamikdash [Temple], and the name of Moshiach."[67]

Hod holds the shine of the throne of glory on which rests the Shechinah's presence and that informs us in our farther descent into the world of matter.

---

[64] R. Yaakov Ibn Chaviv, *Ein Yaakov,* Pesachim, 163.
[65] Ibid., "Ten Things, Three Things, and Seven Things," 163.
[66] Ibid., 54b, 163.
[67] Ibid., 54a, "When Was Fire Created?" 162.

GEMATRIA

296: Perek Shira and the Pomegranate

pomegranate רמון‬ :ר Reish (200) מ Mem (40) ו Vav (6) ן Nun (50) = 296

In keeping with our inclusion of the texts of the Perek Shira (Song of the Universe) assigned to each of the sacred species of Israel (with the exclusion of the olive), the pomegranate is described thus: "As many as the pomegranate's seeds are the merits of your unworthiest, within your modest veil" (Song of Songs 4:3). This tells us that we never know the worthiness of the humblest of people, that "history is replete with unexpected courage and self-sacrifice from the least likely people."[68] As we have already seen, these qualities are apparent in Avigail's actions and nature.

As one of the seven species of the land of Irael, the pomegranate conceals thousands of seeds within a hard red skin. It is used to represent Israel's agricultural fertility: It was one of the fruits that the twelve spies brought back to Moses as proof of the land's fertility.

Other words and texts equal to 296, the numeric value of the Hebrew word for "pomegranate," include the following.

the earth הארץ (Genesis 1:1): ה Hay (5) א Alef (1) ר Reish (200) ץ Tzadee (90) = 296

"In the beginning of God's creating the heavens and the earth . . ." This, the very first sentence in the Torah, is linked to the pomegranate.

to the land ארצה (Genesis 11:31): א Alef (1) ר Reish (200) צ Tzadee (90) ה Hay (5) = 296

"Terah took his son Abram, and Lot the son of Haran, his Grandson, and his daughter-in-law Sarai, the wife of Abram his son, and they departed with them from Ur Kasdim to go to the land of Canaan; they arrived at Haran and they settled there." This excerpt reveals that the very beginning of the sojourn of the People of the Book is connected to

---

[68] R. Nosson Scherman, *Perek Shira,* 51.

the species pomegranate through its numerical value and the context in which **to the land** first occurs. It is fitting that it it is a sign for Israel's bounty when the People of the Book first come to the land later after the Exodus.

and a pomegranate ורמן (Exodus 39:26): ו Vav (6) ר Reish (200) מ Mem (40) ן Nun (50) = 296

"A bell and a pomegranate, a bell and a pomegranate on the hem of the robe all around, to minister, as God commanded Moses." The Kohen Gadol's robe uses the two elements to dispel the kelipot, the influence of evil. Again, we see that the pomegrante, like an individual's humility, is linked to the priestly elevation of the people.

and Miriam ומרים (Numbers 12:5–13): ו Vav (6) מ Mem (40) ר Reish (200) י Yod (10) ם Mem (40) = 296

"God descended in a pillar of cloud and stood at the entrance to the Tent, and he summoned Aaron and Miriam, the two of them went out." He said,

> "Hear now My words. If there shall be Prophets among you, in a vision shall I, God make myself known to him; in a dream shall I speak with him. Not so is my servant Moses; in my entire house he is the trusted one. Mouth to mouth do I speak to him, in a clear vision and not in riddles, at the image of God does he gaze. Why did you not fear to speak against my servant Moses?" The wrath of God flared up against them, and He left. The cloud had departed from atop the tent, and behold Miriam was afflicted with Tzaraas [tzarat], like snow! Aaron turned to Miriam and behold, she was afflicted with Tzaraas [tzarat] . . . Moses cried out to God, saying "please God, heal her now."

It is interesting that Miriam as Gevurah is on the left column, above Hod of Avigail. This portion of the Torah shows their deep connection.

The Pomegranate in Song of Songs

In Song of Songs the pomegranate represents love and sensuality; its red color is often associated with passion and fire. According to the Midrash, there are 613 seeds in a pomegranate, corresponding to the mitzvot described in the Torah. The fruit's crown lends itself to the kingship theme, in keeping with Avigail's relationship to King David. To this day the decorative metal ornaments crowning the Torah are called pomegranates or, in Hebrew, *rimonim.* To these, bells are often attached, making the procession with the Torah scrolls in the synagogue reminiscent of the High Priest's robe during the holy ritual services. In keeping with the lineage of the Zohar, which has a special connection to Hod, R. Akiva, whom we credit with bringing the secrets of Torah from concealment for our current generations to enjoy, claims that Song of Songs is the most beautiful portion of the Torah. It is a love song between the Creator and the created and it expresses the heart that is wide open and in love with God, as God is with humankind.

The Chuppah

As we progress down the Tree of Life, which is actually a spiritual ascension with a deeper immersion into the world of commitment and obligation to the welfare of others and love of God, we see that, like the Mikvah (ritual bath), we descend or ascend seven steps before we are fully immersed in the healing waters of God. It is said that the Torah is the Mikvah of Israel. The night before their wedding day, a bride and groom each proceed to the Mikvah for their ritual cleansing and preparation before God. The holiday that follows Lag B'Omer is Shavuot, considered the betrothal between Israel and God. In some Sephardi communities, a marriage contract, or *ketuba,* is read before the Ark, commemorating Israel's receiving of the Torah, a betrothal between God and the People of the Book. All this tells us that humility is the foundation of love and good relations. We see clearly that all of life is relational—among us and between us and God. When Avigail and David wed, it is likely they did so with the ceremony of chuppah.

chuppah חפה: ח Chet (8) פ Pey (80) ה Hay (5) = 93

In ancient Israel, at the end of a betrothal period, the bride was escorted by a lavish procession to her husband's room or tent, where their marriage was consummated. The term **chuppah** refers to the bridal chamber, the bridal canopy, and the ceremony of marriage itself. In Talmudic times (200 BCE–500 CE), the father of the bride erected the chuppah using trees planted at the birth of each child, making the marriage the fulfillment of the parents' hopes for their children's lives. Tradition also holds that the chuppah represents the couple's first home, which is fragile because it is young—but it is built upon their faith in God, Torah, and the Tree of Life, and the love of each other, upon which depends Shalom habayit (peace in the home).

56: The Numeric Value of Avigail's Name

Avigail אבגיל: א Alef (1) ב Bet (2) י Yod (10) ג Gimel (3) י Yod (10) ל Lamed (30) = 56

Following our practice of looking at the hidden or inner story of each prophetess and the hidden story of the Torah presence of each woman, we look at the numeric value of Avigail's name and the story it conceals. By examining other places in the Torah where words of the same numeric value occur, we can see, as we have in the stories of the other prophetesses, a reconfirming of the Sefirotic role for the individual, B'nai Yisrael, and the world.

day יום (Genesis 1:5): י Yod (10) ו Vav (6) ם Mem (40) = 56

"God called to the light: 'Day,' and to the darkness He Called 'Night.' And there was evening and there was morning, one day." The first day of creation reflects the world's order and the relationship among parts.

and every וכל (and all, Genesis 2:1): ו Vav (6) כ Caf (20) ל Lamed (30) = 56

"Thus the heaven and the earth were finished, and all their array . . . God blessed the seventh day and sanctified it, because on it he abstained from all his work which God created to make." This relates to the Sabbath and to the relationship of days to the week.

to the Lord ליהוה (to God, Genesis 4:3): ל Lamed (30) י Yod (10) ה Hay (5) ו Vav (6) ה Hay (5) = 56

"After a period of time, Cain brought an offering to God of the fruit of the ground; and as for Abel, he also brought the firstlings of his flock from their choicest. God turned to Abel and to his offering but to Cain and to his offering He did not turn. This annoyed Cain exceedingly and his countenance fell." God then tells Cain to repent, that sin follows him, but that he can conquer it. Cain does not repent, however, and then he kills Abel in the field. When God asks him where his brother is, Cain asks, "[A]m I my brother's keeper?" Given an opportunity to repent and confess, he does neither and is "cursed more than the ground" (Genesis 4:11). This example shows the relationship of God to people and that those who are favored by God are pure in their intent.

he begot ויולד (Genesis 5:3): ו Vav (6) י Yod (10) ו Vav (6) ל Lamed (30) ד Dalet (4) = 56

"When Adam had lived one hundred and thirty years, he begot in his likeness and image and he named him Seth, and the days of Adam after begetting Seth were eight hundred years and thirty years; and he died." (Note that Chanah was 130 before bearing Shmuel HaNavi, or Samuel.) This passage shows the relationship of Adam to humanity, birth lineages, and the genealogy of humankind.

and go ולכ (Genesis 27:13): ו Vav (6) ל Lamed (30) כ Caf (20) = 56

"But his Mother said to him, 'your curse be on me, my son; only heed my voice and go fetch them for me.'" This is from the story of Rebecca, who facilitates Isaac's conferring the blessing of the first son (who is Esau) on the younger son, Jacob. Jacob tells his mother, Rebecca, that he is concerned his father, Isaac, will know it is him and he will be known as "a mocker in his (Father's) eyes; I will bring upon myself a curse rather than a blessing." This speaks to the relationships between father and son and mother and son and husband and wife, and to the blessing of future generations that will come from Jacob, rather than Esau.

they are delivered וילדו (they have given birth, Exodus 1:19): ו Vav (6) י Yod (10) ל Lamed (30) ד Dalet (4) ו Vav (6) = 56

The midwives said to the pharaoh, "[B]ecause the Hebrew women are unlike the Egyptian women, for they are experts; before the midwife comes to them, they have given birth. . . . God benefited the midwives—and the people increased and became very strong." Miriam and her mother, Yocheved, confound the pharaoh's plot of infanticide, meriting the well. This text is related to the relationship of midwives—Miriam and Yocheved—to the pharaoh and the people. The generation of B'nai Yisrael is born.

complete כלו (fulfill, Exodus 5:13): כ Caf (20) ל Lamed (30) ו Vav (6) = 56

"The task masters pressed, saying, 'complete your work, the daily matter each day, as when there was straw.'" The suffering of the Jewish people is increased, as is their population, as if they were doomed to live out the toiling of Cain—the tikkun of Cain—the first son. This occurs just prior to Moses asking God, "[W]hy have you sent me? If this is what you do, increase my people's suffering." God then promises Moses, "Now you will see what I shall do to Pharaoh . . ." This text reveals the relationship between the people and the pharaoh.

thyself alone לבדך (Exodus 18:14): ל Lamed (30) ב Bet (2) ד Dalet (4) כ Caf (20) = 56

"The father-in-law of Moses saw everything that he was doing to the people, and said, 'what is this thing that you do to the people? Why do you sit [thyself] alone with the people standing by you from morning to evening?'" Jethro advises Moses to appoint men of accomplishment as leaders to help adjudicate, while Moses remains the representative of God. Jethro then departs; it is the last time Moses and Jethro see each other. In this text, we see the relationship between Moses and B'nai Yisrael and the birth of the justice system.

he shall divide יבדיל (he shall separate, he shall split, Leviticus 1:17):
י Yod (10) ב Bet (2) ד Dalet (4) י Yod (10) ל Lamed (30) = 56

"He shall split—with its feathers—he need not sever it; the Kohen cause it to go up in smoke on the Altar, on the wood that is on the fire—it is a burnt offering, a fire offering, a satisfying aroma to God." "Offering" (*karban*) comes from the root for "coming near," Kof Reish Bet. We are instructed that even an offering of fowl can bring us near to God if that is our clear intention. Shown is the relationship between people and the Kohen Gadol as facilitator who brings us near to God through the burned offering of fowl.

contaminated וטמא (Leviticus 13:3): ו Vav (6) ט Tet (9) מ Mem (40) א Alef (1) = 56

"The Kohen shall look at the affliction in the skin of the flesh; If hair in the affliction has changed to white, and the affliction's appearance is deeper than the skin of the flesh—it is a tzaraas [tzarat] affliction; the Kohen shall look at it and declare him contaminated." This text shows the relationship between the Kohen Gadol and the people and the Kohen Gadol's obligation to determine what is or is not clean.

in your heart בלבבכ (Leviticus 19:17): ב Bet (2) ל Lamed (30) ב Bet (2) ב Bet (2) כ Caf (20) = 56

"You shall not hate your brother in your heart; you shall reprove your fellow and do not bear a sin because of him. You shall not take revenge and you shall not bear a grudge against the members of your people; you shall love your fellow as your self—I am God." Relative to the story of Avigail and her husband and her mediating to prevent King David from killing him, this section of the Torah is a direct expression of this warning. Avigail helps King David to fulfill this, and this, in part, is why King David calls for her to be his wife. Illustrated is our relationship to all of B'nai Yisrael.

in your heart בלבבכ (Deuteronomy 7:17): ב Bet (2) ל Lamed (30) ב Bet (2) ב Bet (2) כ Caf (20) = 56

". . . and you may say in your heart, 'My strength and the might of my hand made me all this wealth.'" Moses tells the People of the Book that it is God who has brought them through the wilderness, provided manna, and provided water. Moses tells the people to know in their hearts their dependency on God's mercy, kindness, and all that He provides or withdrawals, that B'nai Yisrael is subservient to the Creator. We can reflect in our hearts on the bounty that God, the Creator, provides in every instant of life in the world. While appearing to be in Tiferet, the heart is in Binah, the place of woman and understanding, suggesting that women are naturally closer in heart to God and that Tiferet, where the torso houses the heart, is a place of beauty in which we seek balance in all things. Through beauty this understanding is exemplified in the world. Our prayer, our conduct, our life must be beautiful.

that are born יולדו (who are born to them, Deuteronomy 23:9): י Yod (10) ו Vav (6) ל Lamed (30) ד Dalet (4) ו Vav (6) = 56

"Children who are born to them [Edomites and Egyptians] in the third generation may enter the Congregation of God." This shows the relationship of the generations of converts to the holy lineage of God's people.

SUMMARIZING THE IMPORTANCE OF AVIGAIL

If we look at the following list of themes in the Parshiot containing the words numerically equivalent to Avigail's name, we see a specific pattern. There is the entire story of the royal descendants of Adam and Eve—potentially all of us. Hod, then, is an expression of relationship, and in each word or phrase we learn about a type of glory that resides in humility.

- The first day of creation: the world's order and the making of the Sabbath and the relationship among the days of the week
- The relationship of God to the people and that those favored by God are those of pure intent

- The relationship of Adam to humanity, birth lineages, and the genealogy of humankind
- The relationship between father and son, mother and son, and husband and wife for the blessing of future generations
- The relationship of midwives—Miriam and Yocheved—to the pharaoh and the people; the birth of the generation of B'nai Yisrael
- The relationship between the people and the pharaoh
- The relationship between Moses and B'nai Yisrael and the beginning of the justice system
- The relationship between the people and the Kohen Gadol as a facilitator for bringing them near to God
- The relationship between the Kohen Gadol and the people and the Kohen Gadol's obligation to determine what is or is not clean

All of these relationships revolve around the individual's and humanity's relationship to God, and the individual's ability to choose good over evil freely. As we can see, Avigail's name paints a portrait of personal and communal relationships. This tells us that Hod or Avigail's role in our development and the development of Israel is one of taking our spiritual talents into the world. While the right leg of Netzach (Chanah) gets us to the place, the left leg and our humility elevate the sparks. Relationships have everything to do with living, as the Torah shows us. Everything is interconnected. When we can give up our selfishness and give ourselves over to what we know in our souls to be right action, we experience the glory of peace. Peace is the reflected consciousness of unity, *echad,* as R. Akiva, the progenitor of our current Zoharic and Kabbalistic wisdom, showed us with his last dying word.

Hod is an expression of relationship, and in each instance of the Parshiot, we learn about a type of majesty that resides in these relationships. Further, we see that each person or group of people has its place. In the instance of Avigail, it is her wisdom that enables King David to change his mind about doing harm to her husband, which would have impaired the generation of David HaMelech (the king). It is through her righteous intervention that she is later betrothed to King David and contributes spiritually and physically to the lineage of Moshiach. Thus Hod as majesty teaches us that when we keep to our proper place, there is a type of glory, a radiance of humility, that is the root of harmony, the World to Come, and redemption.

Glory or Hod has an attribute of beauty that is radiant (Tiferet), a hidden quality of spiritual right conduct (Chanah, Netzach), the ability to limit its expansive state of surrender through Gevurah (Miriam), and the ability to lead us to the World to Come, Olam HaBa, in Yesod (Chuldah). Avigail's is the story not just of her life, but also of our royal descent prior to entering Olam Haba.

What we see in Avigail is the summation of all that has preceded her and is embodied in the majestic royal bloodline from which Moshiach will come. This is shown to us in the articles she takes with her when she first meets David. These are descriptive of what each of us takes into any situation when we engage life with humility.

Avigail and Hod show us the kindness of Chesed (carrying food to meet King David as he approaches with his army) and the wisdom of Gevurah (asking about the Halacha concerning the death penalty). In Avigail's story we witness the physical beauty of Tiferet, which knows how to use all elements to bring justice; and we see the spiritual wisdom of Chanah in knowing that we can have a strong relationship to God and the world through action from the heart and in understanding that a woman can incubate and give birth to the next generation of tzaddikim. For men and women, right spiritual action produces holy vessels. In Hod we reach a level of prophecy and personal decorum that allows us to forget ourselves and our own needs in exchange for the consideration and welfare of others. This produces a state of majesty and splendor. All of these attributes reflect an observance of the Torah's 613 mitzvot, which, when practiced, can lead to prophecy.

Avigail's symbol of the pomegranate reminds us of the union between the Creator and His created. Prophecy is the method He uses to make His will known. The righteous serve as vessels for the Shechinah to inhabit. Once we know that the 613 seeds of the pomegranate compare to the 613 mitzvot, we can close our journey with Avigail by reviewing some of the sages' teachings regarding these holy mitzvot that the people of Israel accept when they receive the Torah during Shavuot, an activity of Hod.

> . . . Isaiah condensed the 613 Mitzvot to two fundamental principles, as it says, "Thus says God: 1) Observe justice and 2) perform righteousness" (Isaiah 56:1). Amos came and condensed them to one principle, as it says, "For thus said God to the House of Israel: Seek me and live" (Amos 5:4). R. Nachman b. Yitzchak challenged this: "Perhaps the passage means: Seek Me by observing the entire Torah and live? But it is Habakkuk who came and boiled down [the 613 Mitzvot] to one fundamental underlying principle, as it says, 'The righteous person shall live through his faith'" (Habakuk 2:4).[69]

Hod and the prophetess Avigail ultimately reveal the qualities for which righteousness is known. In Hod we accept that it is our humility and faith in the Creator that is the foundation of our oneness in His glory and splendor.

Humility is not only the prerequiste to receiving prophecy on any level, but it is also the foundation upon which the covenant is built between the Creator and the People of the Book, as is revealed by the next prophetess, Chuldah, and the Sefirah she occupies, Yesod.

---

[69] This means that all of the mitzvot are included in the mitzvah of *emuna,* faith, the first of the Ten Commandments. See R. Yaakov Ibn Chaviv, *Ein Yaakov,* Makkot, "Emunah/ Faith," 716.

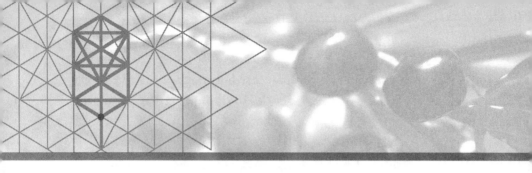

8

Chuldah

Yesod · The Covenant and Promise of the World to Come

Hide the Holy Ark in the House that Solomon, Son of David, King of Israel Built.

2 CHRONICLES 35:3

Chuldah חלדה

ח Chet (8) ל Lamed (30) ד Dalet (4) ה Hay (5) = 47

Sefirah Correspondence: Yesod

Titles: Prophetess, Teacher, Librarian, Adviser (to King Josiah)

Family: Wife of Shallum

Time Period	Jewish Calendar	Gregorian Calendar
Chuldah's prophecy	3303	457 BCE

Developmental Stage: Foundation

Day: Friday

Sacred Species: Olive oil

Body Correspondence: Reproductive organs

Rituals: Reading of the Torah, Brit Milah

Holidays: Yom Kippur, Chanukah

Symbols: Torah scroll, Huldah's Gate (House of Study)

Prayers: Kaddish, Brit Milah, Kabbalat-Shabbat

Shine of Chuldah–Yesod: Promise of the Redeemer's presence on the Mount of Olives, herald of Moshiach: revelation of the Ark for the Third Temple

Prophecy Source: 2 Kings 22:15–20, "She said to them, Thus said HaShem, God of Israel: Say to the man who sent you to me, Thus said HaShem: Behold, I am bringing evil upon this place and upon its inhabitants—[*namely*] all the words of the Scroll that the King of Judah read—because they have forsaken Me and burned offerings to the gods of others . . ."

SEFIRAH: YESOD

As the Sefirah that connects the rest of the Etz Chayim to Malchut (Kingdom), the final vessel, Yesod, often represents the coupling organs of sexuality. For the male, Yesod is the phallus, which undergoes the circumcision (brit). For the woman, Yesod is the womb. Hence, the ritual of the brit for men suggests a sacrifice of the body to the royal lineage of Moshiach and as testimony to a love and awe of God.

Phase of Development: In this stage of individual, collective, and global experience, we are conscious of how life in the world is a preparation for our spiritual life in the World to Come, Olam HaBa. Connecting the material and spiritual in our devotion to God is the literal brit (removal of foreskin or covering) of the generative organ and the spiritual brit of the heart. As we witness in the jubilee, when all returns to the Creator and to owners of origin—the slave to its family, the land to its former holder, the land to its silence—in Yesod one experiences how everything belongs to God, the Creator.

Life Principle: We are immortal souls in a mortal body. Awareness of the soul's purpose on earth prepares the soul for experience in the

World to Come. Everything is eternal through the covenant with the Creator.

World Action: Yesod shows us that each of us is part of humanity, whose task is to elevate the material to the spiritual, the life now to life after life. Those whose vision is fixed on the afterlife as part of the cycle of birth, death, and rebirth understand the purpose of committing our life to Torah, moral principles, and God's truth. This commitment is for this world and the World to Come.

Spiritual Action: In Yesod we learn detachment from our material possessions and attachment to spiritual values. We also learn that the physical world and our possessions are for our service to the Creator.

Meaningful Work: The work of Yesod is work in hospice and psychological transformation; work in teaching spiritual traditions that help refine material life; and work with emotional and physical fertility issues, career planning, and city planning. Yesod is important for the long-term view of things.

Day Focus: Friday is the time to put to rest qualities, ideas, activities, and relationships that no longer serve a spiritual commitment. Refine what you are committed to spiritually and make it a life goal to accomplish this. Meditation, prayer, and song are tools to use.

Species: The eternal light comes from the oil made when we press olives. So too the light of the eternal soul comes from refining the personality. Our lives become an eternal light to the world when we reflect the holiness of the source from which it comes: God. The olive stands for beauty, immortality, and longevity. (The olive tree can live for a thousand years.) It is said that around our table, our children flourish like olives.

CHULDAH'S STORY

Chuldah was the wife of Shallum, the wardrobe keeper for the king. She was a renowned educator in Jerusalem, running a women's yeshiva. Some say she was also a librarian. The south side of the Temple Mount in Jerusalem bears Chuldah's name. Living at the end of the time period of the Second Temple, prior to its destruction, Chuldah became a pivotal prophetess through a **scroll and King Josiah**: The king was given a scroll found in the Temple, and the scroll was open to a passage in Deuteronomy. He needed an intepreter to translate to him what it meant, and the **king chose Chuldah.** Chuldah's prophecy inspired the **king's teshuvah** (repentance). Not only did he reinstitute the rituals in the Temple, beginning with the Passover meal, but also Chuldah gave the Jewish people a deeper understanding of their covenant with God.

SYMBOLISM OF CHULDAH

Chuldah's Lineage

We know that Chuldah is the wife of Shallum, son of Tikvah, the wardrobe keeper of the king. Some say that Ruach HaKodesh (the Holy Spirit) rests upon Chuldah in merit of her husband's piety and generosity. Born of nobility, he is a practitioner of generosity: "Shalom, son of Tikvah, one of the great men of the generation, did acts of kindness every day. He would fill a pouch with water and sit at the entrance to the city, and whoever would come from the road, he would refresh by giving a drink. In the merit of this kindness, Divine Inspiration rested on his wife Huldah."[1] Chuldah is "one of the descendants of Joshua and Rahab."[2]

Chuldah as Educator

Chuldah is far more than a librarian, which some sources suggest is her occupation. She runs an academy (yeshiva) in Jerusalem.[3] The current Huldah's Gate (Chuldah's Gate) in Jerusalem has a corner leading to her school. Like Sarah and Miriam, she is known for teaching women and prophesying to the people.

---

[1] Pirkei d'Rabbi Eliezer 33; R. Yishai Chasidah, *Encyclopedia of Biblical Personalities,* 188.
[2] Megillah 14b.
[3] 2 Kings 22:14 (Rashi).

Is Chuldah Arrogant?

Some say that Chuldah means "weasel," while others say it refers to "mole." Either way, the mole and weasel are clever, concealed, and ubiquitous, accomplishing what they need with certainty, a reason why some of the commentators over the centuries have said that Chuldah's nature is arrogant. She shares this with her predecessor on the middle pillar, Devorah in Tiferet: The two have engendered the same criticism. "Two women who were assuming had unpleasant names, Devorah (bee) and Huldah (mole)."[4]

The criticism of Chuldah stems from the fact that she does not address the king using his royal name, but rather refers to him in her prophecy as "the man."[5] We know, too, that the Rabbinic scholars criticize each of the other prophetesses for arrogance: Sarah is criticized for questioning whether she could conceive a child at the age of eighty-nine, noting also her husband's advanced age. Miriam is criticized for challenging Moses' sole prerogative to speak on God's behalf. Devorah is criticized for calling Barak to her before their war campaign. Avigail is criticized for telling David to remember her. In each of these instances, there are other ways to interpret the actions of the prophetesses. For certain, we know that the most essential spiritual story of each prophetess is concealed in the composition of her name. In looking at Chuldah's name through gematria (see later in this chapter), we find the promise of redemption, procreation, and sovereignty for B'nai Yisrael and those living a holy life according to Torah's teachings.

Yesod: The Eternal Flame of Love and the Covenant

Yesod is, in many respects, a concealed Sefirah just as olive oil is concealed first in the olive itself and then in the flame of the eternal lamp. In Yesod the covenant we have with God is concealed within us, but the light it produces is apparent in our countenance and actions in the world.

For the People of the Book, a Torah-based life reflects the covenant

---

[4] Megillah 14b.
[5] 2 Kings 22:15.

and produces the zohar (splendorous light) in the same way that olive oil reveals itself as light when ignited by fire. When we are ignited by our love and awe of God, the light of our own Holy of Holies is lit. Thus we are able to illuminate the hearts of others. All of Yesod is defined by the masculine Son (Zeir Anpin), culminating in the ascension of the feminine Daughter (Malchut), who then is elevated to Binah (Mother, understanding), while the Son is elevated to Chochmah (Father, wisdom). The revealed (Chochmah) is hidden in Yesod, only to be revealed again in its ascent from Malchut (Daughter). Yesod facilitates the descent and ascent of the Shechinah.

Yesod also brings everything that comes before it to the final Sefirah, Malchut. Yesod performs the function of both completing the descent and ensuring an ascent. This makes Yesod pivotal. Teshuvah (repentance) is a daily return to the Creator and His Word and is the foundation of the covenant embodied by Yesod. Reflecting the light of the Holy One—having on and within us the Ruach HaKodesh and the higher levels of the Shechinah's inhabiting shine—is the foundation on which the world stands. It is the Jewish people's foundation stone, and it adds value to the fact that the Creator is called Our Rock and Redeemer. Our *kedusha* (holiness) elevates all and turns the descent of matter into ascent, taking matter and spiritualizing it. We are the conscious vessels through which matter is refined. This constitutes the raising of the sparks.

The light that is hidden in every living thing comes from the same source. All things are eternal when we look at them in this way, and everything returns to its source. Chuldah's prophecy performs this function for the Jewish people of her time and in our lives today, pointing the Jewish nation and the king to the World to Come, Olam HaBa. Her presence and teachings reveal the promised redemption for humankind, a grace that follows personal and communal repentance (teshuvah), just as it does for King Josiah. "And now, if you hearken well to me and observe My covenant, you shall be a people to me, a Kingdom of ministers and a holy nation."[6]

---

[6] Exodus 19:5–6. See also Deuteronomy 7:6.

The Brit Milah

The ritual of Yesod revolves around the brit (circumcision) of the male phallus on the eighth day of life. This is the circumcision that all Jewish families conduct when their sons are born. Another brit is equally incumbent upon women: the brit of the heart. In the same way that the phallus's covering is removed, we must remove the covering of our heart, which is made of pride, conceit, and self-centeredness. It is this spiritual transformation that can occur in the life of each of us.

> R. Nechemiah said, "[The mitzvah of] milah [brit] is so great that, if not for the brit [milah], the holy one, blessed be He, would not have created His world, for it says, 'Thus said God, If not for My covenant (brit) day and night (a reference to brit milah), I would not have set up the laws of heaven and earth (Jeremiah 33:25).'" Rebbi said, [The mitzvah of] milah is so great that it equals all other Mitzvot in the Torah put together, for it says, "This is the blood of the covenant (brit) that God is making with you regarding all these words" (Exodus 24:8).[7]

It was the patriarch Abraham whom God first requested the mitzvah of circumcision from, and after performing the mitzvah, Abraham was called "perfect": "Walk before me and become perfect." The next verse states, "I will set my covenant between me and you."[8] Yesod then enables us to commit our very being to the service of the divine plan, the seminal idea of a repaired world accomplished.

In procreation, the seed of the male who has undergone the brit has made the covenant with God and is able to seed holy souls who are concealed for nine months in the womb of the mother. Only after the proper incubation time is the outcome of the union among mother, father, and God made visible. In the same way, the spiritual reality of B'nai Yisrael's long incubation in exile heralds Elijah's return, which in turn heralds the coming of Moshiach.

---

[7] R. Yaakov Ibn Chaviv, *Ein Yaakov,* Nedarim, "Importance of Mitzvah of Milah" (31b), 401.
[8] Genesis 17:1–2.

The two brits or circumcisions of Yesod—of the male organ of pro-creation and of our hearts—make clear that though one is revealed (the phallus is on the outside of the body), the other is hidden (the heart remains hidden) and is known only through our presence and decorum. Some say that these two stages of concealment and revelation correspond to the two phases of Moshiach.

The Two Redeemers

In the Chassidic tradition it is taught that there will be two redeemers, each a portion of the other, in the same way that Netzach and Hod, like our two legs, are partners or that Chesed and Gevurah, like our two arms, are partners. The warrior redeemer will be from the lineage of Joseph, the youngest son of Jacob and the grandson of Abraham. Therefore, a descendant from the first line of Abramic expression of the covenant will lead the world to seeing that even through war, God is supreme and Israel is protected.

The second redeemer, ushering in a thousand years of peace, is Moshiach Ben David, who will be of the Davidic bloodline, the line of kings who designed and built the Temples, signified by Malchut.[9] In Yesod, the blood of the nation is committed to God through circumcision of body and heart (soul). Peace will come to the world when God—with oversight from all that is, was, or will be—is acknowledged by all of humanity. Then Israel will shine as the nation of priests, a living example of Yesod and Malchut lighting up the entire Tree of Life with the fulfillment of purpose. This, too, is the royal lineage of all humanity and every person potentially. This fulfillment of the world's development is the journey on which each person progresses during his or her many consecutive lives.

When Will Moshiach Come?

Though the two-stage redemption is represented by people from royal lineages, the time of Moshiach also represents a stage of communal enlightenment that will come after the world is in the darkest, most immoral,

---

[9] David's son Solomon is given the right to build the Temple, for David "had blood on his hands" from the wars he has waged and won.

and Godless state of faith: "R. Nehorai said: In the generation when the son of David will come, young people will humiliate the elderly, yet old people will rise [respectfully] before the young. Daughters will rebel against their mothers; daughters-in-law against their mothers-in-law. The leaders of the generation will act in the way dogs act, and a son will not be ashamed before his father."[10] Perhaps it is this form of spiritual anarchy that explains why the predecessor to Moshiach Ben David will be a warrior and why it is said the war of Gog and Magog will herald redemption. The first Moshiach will be Moshiach Ben Joseph. We are told that he will appear as a warrior king and represent Yesod, the brit of the covenant since the time of Abraham. Following him will be Moshiach Ben David, the redeemer of Israel from the royal House of David. How will we know the Moshiach is about to arrive? The holy messenger Elijah the prophet will precede him.

According to Malachi (3:23): ". . . The Sages said: He [Elijah] will come neither to remove people nor to bring near, but to make peace in the world, as it says, 'Behold, I send you Elijah the prophet before the coming of the great and awesome day of God. He will turn back [to God] the hearts of fathers with their sons, and the hearts of sons with their fathers.'"[11] This tells us that together Elijah and David HaMelech (the king) will herald in the thousand years of peace in the Kingdom (Malchut.)

Now that we understand that there is some hidden connection between the brit and the World to Come, the covenant of the seed and the return of the people to God, let us examine Chuldah's role in Yesod and the purpose she serves for the king and for the people of her time.

A Scroll and King Josiah

Chuldah's primary importance as a prophetess occurs in the biblical setting at the end of the time period of the Second Temple, prior to its destruction. Josiah, King David's grandson and successor (Solomon's son), is given a scroll from High Priest Chilkiah through the king's scribe,

---

[10] R. Yaakov Ibn Chaviv, *Ein Yaakov,* Sanhedrin, "The Advent of Mashiach," 661.
[11] Ibid., Eduyot, "When Will Elijah come?" (10a) Mishnah 5:7, 726.

Shaphan, who retells this story: "'I have found a scroll of the Torah in the Temple of God,' said the Kohen Gadol." Though some of the oral commentaries state that the king himself finds the scroll, the Torah tells us that it is brought to him by his scribe, and upon hearing the words his scribe reads to him, the words revealed when the High Priest found the scroll open, the king rends his clothes.[12]

It is important to appreciate the scroll's importance, not only for its revelatory contents, but also for the fact that it is found at all. Sixty-seven years has passed since the beginning of Manasseh's reign. During that time, Manasseh destroys all of the Torah scrolls and alienates the People of the Book from the Torah so completely that few are familiar with anything in it. The portion of the Torah to which the scroll is open when Chilkiah finds it, according to one Talmudic teaching, is Deuteronomy, chapter 28:36:[13] "God will lead you and your King whom you will set up over yourself to a nation you never knew—neither you nor your forefathers—and there you will work for the gods of others—of wood and stone."

The Prophet Samuel's Prediction Comes True

The prophet Samuel (son of Chanah) argues with God prior to anointing the first king, Saul, in hopes of preventing the appointment of kings and even warning the people that, like other nations, once there was a king, they would lose their way and forget the Torah. They have been warned by the Creator, through the prophet Samuel, that they would worship the idols of others and that even when they called for their king to help them, he would be unable to do so. Here, in the life of Chuldah, we witness the outcome that Samuel prophesies.

Another Version of Josiah's Lesson

In another teaching, we are told that when the priest gives the Torah to the scribe, who in turn reads it to the king, the king weeps and rends

---

[12] 2 Kings 22:8.

[13] R. Nosson Scherman, ed., *Tanach: The Torah, Prophets, Writings—The Twenty-Four Books of the Bible*, 939.

his clothes due to the judgment upon himself and upon the nation, as the Torah describes. "When Chilkiah had found the scroll in the Temple courtyard, it was rolled to the verse 'Cursed is he who will not uphold the words of his Torah'" [Deuteronomy 27:26]. It is over this that the king rends his clothes and says, "We must uphold it."[14]

When the king sees the verse—Deuteronomy 28:36, "God will lead you and your King into a nation which you have not known . . ." ["God will bring you and your elected King to a nation unknown to you and your forefathers"]—he stands up and hides these holy things (the Ark and its implements) somewhere under the Beit Hamikdash (Temple).[15] "He said to the Levities [the lineage of priests], consecrated to God, the teachers of all Israel, 'Hide the Holy Ark in the House that Solomon, Son of David, King of Israel Built, you will no longer carry it on your shoulders, now serve the Lord your God and His people Israel.'"[16]

It is interesting to note that Yom Kippur provides atonement through a focus not on sins between humans and their Creator, but on sins between each of us and our community, "because on this day you shall have all your sins atoned."[17]

It is said that on Yom Kippur, a penitent supplicant has an opportunity to reach the level of divine inspiration (Ruach HaKodesh). Through this inspiration, the supplicant "can understand things with a knowledge completely different than anything that he ever experienced previously. He may also gain information about lofty mysteries not accessible to logic alone. He can reach a level where he is clearly aware of otherwise imperceptible spiritual entities and structures."[18]

---

[14] Midrash HaGadol, Deuteronomy 27:26: "Accursed is one who will not uphold the words of the Torah, to perform them, and the entire people shall say 'Amen.'"

[15] Yoma 53a.

[16] Chronicles 35:3.

[17] Leviticus 6:30. See also R. Yaakov Ibn Chaviv, *Ein Yaakov,* Yoma (86a), "The Four Kinds of Atonement," 213.

[18] R. Aryeh Kaplan, *Handbook of Jewish Thought,* vol. 1, 91. See also R. Moses Ben Maimon (Maimonides; the Rambam), *Yesodei HaTorah,* 7:1.

The Greatness of Repentance

Rabbi Levi said: great is repentance, for it reaches up to the throne of Glory, as it says, "Return, O Israel, to God your Lord" (Hosea 14:2). R. Yonatan said: Repentance is so great that it brings about redemption [before the preordained time], for it says, "A redeemer shall come to Zion, and to those of Jacob who repent of willful sin" (Isaiah 59:20). He expounds: "How is it that a redeemer shall come to Zion [prematurely]?" Because of "those of Jacob who will repent willful sin. . . . We learned in a Baraita: R. Meir used to say: "great is repentance, for on account of a single individual who repented, the sins of the whole world are forgiven, for it says, I will heal their rebelliousness, I will love them freely, for My anger is turned away from him" (Hosea 14:4). It does not say, "from them," but "from him."[19]

The King and Chuldah

After we learn of the king's dramatic return to the Torah, we are told that for its interpretation, King Josiah's priestly and other servants take the scroll to Chuldah, rather than to Jeremiah, the male prophet best known at that time: "So [C]hilkiah the Kohen, Achikam, Achbor, Shaphan and Asaiah went to Chuldah the Prophetess, the wife of Shallum son of Tikvah son of Harhas, the keeper of the [royal] garments, who dwelled in Jerusalem, in the study house, and they spoke to her."[20]

Here, we learn that Chuldah dwells in Jerusalem, in the study house. This attests to her stature as a great teacher during the time when the Temple still stood. The southern wall of the Temple Mount shows us the location of the entry to her academy. The three-arched entry to the Temple is sealed today, as is the corner entrance thought to be the one to her school. Like these sealed entryways that hide the entrances, the Torah does not reveal that the king tells the High Priest and others to go to Chuldah, but we are to assume they take concealed orders. The king chooses Chuldah for a scholarly and prophetic interpretation of the

---

[19] R. Yaakov Ibn Chaviv, *Ein Yaakov,* Yoma (86b), "The Greatness of Repentance," 214.
[20] 2 Kings 22:14.

Figure 8.1. Corner entry to Chuldah's academy.

scroll. Through oral teachings, we are assured that "Huldah was a rela-tive of Jeremiah, who did not mind that she prophesied in his place even on a topic which he had prophesied."[21] We are to assume that the king's decision to choose a prophetess rather than a prophet is an unusual one.

Traditionally, we are given two reasons for the king's concealed order and choice of Chuldah, a female prophet. Some say that Jeremiah is not in Jerusalem at the time,[22] but this is a minority point of view. More often, other reasons are cited: In the king's selection of Chuldah, we are shown the intimate connection between Jeremiah and Chuldah. Jeremiah is related to Chuldah, which we are to see as an affirmation of the prophetic talent in the bloodline, in the same way that this talent is represented by Miriam and her brothers, Moses and Aaron. Jeremiah and Chuldah are both descendants of Joshua and

---

[21] Maharsha, Megillah 14b.
[22] Megillah 14b.

Figure 8.2. Huldah's Gate and the southern wall of the Temple.

Rahab.[23] Joshua is the successor of Moses, and Rahab is the convert who saves Joshua and Caleb by hiding them. Joshua and Rahab are themselves part of holy events connected to a holy lineage. (In the same way that Yesod fulfills the manifestation of the royal bloodline in the person of king who is redeemed, here Chuldah's predecessors Joshua and Rahab are themselves part of the royal lineage of the People of the Book.)

Additionally, we are told that the king reasons that Jeremiah will not resent Josiah's preference for Chuldah. Yet Jeremiah is known for admonishing the people and preaching repentance to the men, and Chuldah performs the same kind of prophetic oration for the women. Why, then, does the king select her?

Josiah's preference is not due to any inherent prophetic lack on Jeremiah's part. Rather, the king believes a woman is naturally more

---

[23] Also known as Rahav, a convert to Judaism who hid Jewish spies when B'nai Yisrael first prepared to enter Israel and Moses sent his spies to assess the situation.

Figure 8.3. The author at the three-arched Huldah's Gate.
Photo by Avinoam Glick.

merciful than a man; that her interpretation will be endowed with deeper understanding; that her Chesed, Gevurah, Tiferet, Netzach, Hod, Yesod, and Malchut will produce greater benefit. The Torah tells us only that he asks his servants to speak to God for him: "Go and inquire of God on my behalf, and on behalf of the people and on behalf of all Judah, concerning the words of this Scroll that was found . . ."[24] Yet the oral tradition reveals that King Josiah believes a woman will be more compassionate in her interpretation. Given that the people have already seen the ominous passage in the Torah, mercy—which is the root of Binah, the mother—suggests that as a woman, Chuldah will be compassionate and ask God to intercede on their behalf. God will answer His prophetess. This is evidenced in the lives of each of the other holy prophetesses discussed here: Abraham has faith in Sarah's word; Miriam has the ability to lead and provide water for her people; Devorah shows justice and mili-

---

[24] 2 Kings 22:13.

tary leadership; Chanah shows devotion to God and His Temple; Avigail evidences peacemaking; and Chuldah interprets the holy scroll found in the Temple.

The Number of Prophetesses and the Abundance of Torah Interpretations

Perhaps this capacity of every woman to possess extra Binah answers in part why there are only seven prophetesses of Israel, though there are forty-eight prophets (forty-nine, including Moses).

Just as the Daughter (Malchut) is one, the Son, Zeir Anpin, is composed of six elements (Chesed through Yesod) but has less Malchut of his own and must unite with the female in order to be made complete. He must find a Malchut, have a wife, to be made whole. This shows us that the energetic pattern of creation is revealed in the patterns of our physical lives: "as above, so below." The Torah is the activator of our holy anatomy (Adam Kadmon) or the primordial man in each of us, now and in the World to Come.

We can also ask why the words of the Torah have been interpreted so often over the centuries, with additions to the biblical personalities not detailed in the Torah. It is said that divine inspiration and prophecy rest on others who are given additional information suitable to the age in which they deliver their teachings, and we are to respect all teachings as additions. No one, however, is permitted to alter even a single letter or punctuation point of the Torah itself.

Chuldah's Prophecy

It is interesting that Chuldah's prophecy in 2 Kings, like those of the other prophetesses in the Torah, is relatively short.

> She said to them, "Thus said God, God of Israel: Say to the man who sent you to me, 'Thus said God: behold, I am bringing evil upon this place and upon its inhabitants—[namely] all the words of the Scroll that the King of Judah read—because they have forsaken Me and burned offerings to the gods of others, in order to anger Me with all

their handiwork; My wrath has been incited against this place, and it will not be extinguished,' And concerning the king of Judah who sent you to inquire of God, thus should you say to him: 'Thus said God, God of Israel [regarding] the word that you have just heard—because your heart is soft and you humbled yourself before God when you heard that which I have spoken about this place and its inhabitants, that they would become a desolation and a curse; and you rent your garments and cried before Me, and I, too, have heard—the word of God. Therefore, behold, I will gather you in to your forefathers—and you will be gathered to your grave in peace—and your eyes will not see all the evil that I am bringing upon this place.'" They brought this report back to the king.[25]

As concise as Chuldah's prophetic words of record are, the oral tradition has added to our knowledge of her.

The King's Teshuvah

The king's repentance is said to postpone the destruction of the Temple and the exile of his people until after his death. Chuldah's intervention through prayer on Israel's behalf was instrumental as well. The king's repentance and the destruction of all idols and graves of those who had led the Israelites to worship foreign gods accompany a national observance of the Pesach offering for the first time since the reign of kings. In addition, the king's acts of loving-kindness suspend God's judgment, leading to the final destruction of the Temple in 70 CE.[26]

> R. Shmuel b. Nachmani said in R. Yochanan's name: "he did what was pleasing to God, and he followed all the ways of his ancestor David" (2 Kings 22:2). . . . If so, how do you interpret, "There was no king like him before who returned to God with all his heart and soul and resources" (Ibid 23:25), [which implies he sinned before he repented.]

---

[25] 2 Kings 22:15–20.

[26] In Josiah's merit, the destruction occurs after Pharaoh Neco kills him in battle, when Josiah is thirty-nine.

[The Gemara answers:] This teaches you that he corrected every judgment he made from the time he was eight years old until he reached the age of eighteen (he became King and acted as a judge when he was eight years old) (Ibid 22:1). When he reached the age of eighteen, a Torah scroll was found (Ibid 22:8). He began to study its written and oral laws and realized that all his verdicts had been wrong (Rashi). He then refunded to the owners the amounts they had paid as result of his incorrect verdicts [and this is the meaning of Shav, he returned] . . . Now, R. Shmuel b. Nachmani disagrees with Rav. For Rav said: There was no greater Baal Teshuvah than Yoshiyahu (Josiah) in his generation and a certain person in our generation; and who is that? Abba the father of R. Yirmiya b. Abba . . .[27]

"Before him there had never been a king like him who returned to God with all his heart, with all his soul, and with all resources, in accordance with the entire Torah of Moses, and after him no one arose like him."[28]

The Sabbath before Yom Kippur is considered a time for total teshuvah, the reuniting of the final letter Hay and the first Hay in the Creator's name: ׳ Yod (10) ה Hay (5) ו Vav (6) ה Hay (5). This requires nullification of any personal need other than to serve the Creator and His Word as Chuldah did. As the earthly representative of the Creator's will, the king leads the flock of his nation to water—to the Torah—through the example of himself. As Abraham is an example in the first brit of the People of the Book, King Josiah elevates his nation by bringing them closer to God and the Torah through his own soft heart, referring to the brit of the heart. Chuldah, his spiritual guide through whom the king is given God's Word, represents the final stage, the gateway to the Holy of Holies. Like the Ark itself, Chuldah illuminates the nation by reminding individuals of their covenant with the Creator.

Redemption is the prerequisite to resurrection, in which our soul becomes the master of our kingdom (body) and suffuses the body with

---

[27] R. Yaakov Ibn Chaviv, *Ein Yaakov*, Shabbat, "King Yoshiyahu [Josiah]," 95.
[28] 2 Kings 23:25.

light, making it immortal. Immortality is the outcome of our thought, speech, and action and lives on in the soul as its garment after the body is buried.

In Yesod, the Individual Merges with the Group

Here, we have the direct and explicit link among Netzach (Chanah), Hod (Avigail), and Yesod (Chuldah). Hod and Yesod are the repositories of all that has come before them and are the last link in the chain of descent of both B'nai Yisrael and the individual toward total fulfillment of destiny. In Yesod (Yom Kippur), the nation is called to total teshuvah as one people. Our attendance to God's Word is not only for our own development, as Chanah (Netzach) teaches. Spiritual endurance is the act of willing attachment to the Creator. This quality possessed by Chuldah and King Josiah shows how Yesod, Hod, and Netzach are fully cognized and used for the elevation of the Kingdom—the material world. Yesod shows us that redemption, prophecy, and the promise of a world redeemer are as dependent on each person as they are on the group.

The Importance of Return to the Torah

It is said therefore that before birth, all Jewish souls are instructed in all of the Torah. Then at birth an angel comes and puts a finger to their lips, leaving the indentation on the upper lip and making us forget all that we learned beforehand. Through gradual accomplishment, we secure knowledge of the law and its performance, peace, and immortality.

During life, we are preparing for our experience in the World to Come (Olam HaBa). Our proper actions are the remembering of all the parts (sparks) of the Torah (letters) that exist and permeate all creation. Just as in Hod we elevate the sparks by humility, in Yesod we gather all the sparks of all realms and worlds, depositing them in Malchut. It is in Malchut that the light is assimilated completely and returned upward ("the returning light," as the Kabbalah terms it). This returning light becomes ascending light only after Yesod has purified us, releasing the last vestiges of ego. Just as the soul surrenders its body at death, in Yesod we cast off our earthly ego in exchange for its living eternal soul. For all of B'nai Yisrael, this suggests that in Israel there will be no peace, which comes from the Hebrew word for wholeness or completeness, until every Jewish person returns to the way of the Torah. The Kabbalistic masters show us that this is God's plan, not an interpretation of religious ideas. As we have been learning through the lives and symbols of each prophetess, the Tree of Life shows us the progression of development in which all of us participate.

Chuldah as Teacher

It is through Yesod that all of the upper branches of the Tree of Life (Etz Chayim) connect to Malchut, the Queen. In some respects, Yesod is the King and Malchut the Queen. Thus we must ask what relationship Chuldah has to Queen Esther or to King Josiah, her male counterpart.

Chuldah teaches the people the importance of repentance and obedience as a way to prevent harsh judgment (Gevurah) and that we, as leaders of our household and as the kings of our own decorum, are equally responsible for the fate of the nation. No station in life, whether that of commoner or king, exempts us from the obligation of repentance. The fact that Chuldah has her own academy shows her stature as a Torah scholar and her dedication to the word of God.

Teachers such as Chuldah are considered to have many children. By opening their students' hearts, they bring to students a spiritual circumcision of emotional life, and this is the foundation of a righteous life (Yesod). Coming into self-mastery makes us sovereign human beings (Malchut):

> Moses called the evil impulse the Yetzer Hara, the uncircumcised. For it says, "Circumcise the foreskin of your heart" (Deuteronomy 10:16). David called it unclean, for it says, "Create a pure heart for me, O God" (Psalms 51:2), which implies that there is an unclean one. Solomon called it the Enemy, for it says, "If your enemy is hungry, give him bread to eat [engross yourself in Torah study]; if he is thirsty, give him water [Torah] to drink . . . Ezekiel called it Stone, for it says, "I will remove the heart of stone from your body and give you a heart of Flesh"(Ezekiel 36:26). Joel called it the Hidden One, because the

Yetzer Hara is hidden inside a person's heart, as it says, "I will drive the hidden one far from you" (Joel 2:20).[29]

Hidden Vessels

Chuldah's connection to King Josiah is pivotal, for he hid the Ark, the container of manna, the flask of anointing oil, the staff of Aaron with its almonds and flowers, the box that the Philistines had sent as a gift to the God of Israel—the very same implements of the Temple to be revealed at the arrival of Moshiach. In this we see the connection between the prophesied two Moshiachs: Moshiach Ben Joseph (Yesod) and Moshiach Ben David (Malchut).

The Importance of the Olive

Olive oil as an element representing Yesod is the source of the anointing oil for priest and kings. The oil is also the miracle of the lamp in Sarah's tent (Chesed) and symbolically in every synagogue in the world, representing God's loving-kindness as the eternal emanator and sustainer of our spiritual life as well as our physical life and light. Olive oil is the central miracle of Chanukah, which, along with Purim,[30] is said to be the holiday that will remain after Moshiach arrives. Why?

The holiday of Chanukah, though traditionally associated with Malchut, is aligned in this study with Yesod. It is a Rabbinic holiday that serves to remind us of the Maccabeans' faith in God during their resistance of the Roman military, who outnumbered them. The story of Chanukah reveals that when the holy lamp in the Temple had only a day of oil remaining, by some miracle it stayed lit for eight days. During the menorah celebration of Chanukah, we add a candle every night to honor

---

[29] R. Yaakov Ibn Chaviv, *Ein Yaakov,* Sukkah, "The Seven Names of the Evil Impulse," 228.

[30] Purim is a holiday often associated with Yesod, but in this study it is more appropriately aligned with Malchut and Queen Esther, given that the holiday itself is a celebration of Esther's life. Like Chanukah, the holiday of Purim grew from life circumstances and sacrifices made by Queen Esther and her people.

Figure 8.4. Valley of Jehoshaphat, above which Chuldah is buried on the Mount of Olives.

Israel's redemption from its enemies. Likewise, we each earn redemption from our own personal limitations (or any adversary). The olive oil is central to Yesod and Chuldah, just as olive oil is central to the miracle commemorated by Chanukah.

It is also interesting that of all the biblical figures in the Torah, only King David and Chuldah are buried in Jerusalem. Chuldah is buried on the Mount of Olives in a cave overlooking Jerusalem, where she taught and prophesied, highlighting the source of her Sefirah's holy olive oil.[31] In addition, it is an olive branch that the white dove brings to Noah in the Ark when the floodwaters subside—a branch taken from the Mount of Olives in Jerusalem, which was untouched by the Flood. This shows us God's desire for humanity's survival and that this continuity and survival are deeply connected to the Mount of Olives in the Holy Land. These facts make it possible to suggest that the Redeemer may come to the Mount of Olives as a prerequisite to peace for the world. Perhaps the olive tree is our eternal inheritance as a sign from Gan Eden.

---

[31] Is Jerusalem the holy anointing oil of the world? Will Jerusalem be the site of the world's redemption, as prophesied by the People of the Book?

Synthesis of the Middot Leads to Foundation

In Yesod we inherit the loving-kindness of Chesed and the wise judgment of Gevurah. We have learned to harmonize all parts to their greatest potential (Tiferet); to stay on the path of our spiritual attachment to the Creator in love and awe (Netzach); and to nullify ourselves in order to support the blueprint of earthly perfection (Hod), His majesty. Now we are asked to mark ourselves, as men cut off the hood of the phallus and its inner covering, as proof of our attachment to His Word. All of us are to cut off the encasing layer around the heart—selfishness and ego—in order to make ourselves entirely available to the Shechinah, to God's presence.

The King's Garment

Inside the Tabernacle of the Temple are housed all the sacred ritual implements. It is King Josiah who orders their concealment (Yesod) so that they can be revealed at the time of Moshiach. The shine of the promise of Moshiach is concealed in the Holy of Holies, which is visited only once a year by the High Priest, on Yom Kippur. It is then that God brings His full glory and majesty (Hod) to rest upon the High Priest so that his ritual prayers, his song on the evening of Yom Kippur, the Kol Nidre, will highlight all of our good endings and beginnings.

Yesod's promise is the end in Malchut to come and a return to a new life, the resurrected life of the spirit. Yom Kippur, then, is the hallmark of Yesod, for Yesod is the last place of standing before we enter the Holy of Holies, Malchut. Likewise, in the World to Come we prepare for the next incarnation by redeeming the life we just passed. By marking our every day with proper thought, speech, and action, we enhance the garment the king has lent us. We are taught that God wants us to return this garment (body) to Him in clean and perfect order, in the same way we return in good condition those clothes we borrow from a lender.

The parable of the king's garment as a teaching about our soul and body, about the world now and the World to Come, is a fitting parable for Chuldah and Yesod, wherein things are concealed. It is also appropriate given that Chuldah is married to Shallum, the son of Tikvah, the king's wardrobe keeper.

The World's Foundation

Chuldah's story—as an expression of Yesod, meaning "foundation"—has within the time period it represents historically the teachings on the concealment of the Ark and its relationship to the foundation stone of the world. *Shetiyah* is "the foundation of the world."[32]

The Mishnah says:

[O]nce the Ark had been taken away, [at the destruction of the first Beit Hamikdash], there was a stone [where the Ark formerly stood] that had been there since the days of the early prophets [Samuel and David] (Rashi), which was called Shetiyah [Foundation of the world], with a height of three fingers above the ground, on which the Kohen Gadol would place the shovel of burning coals [and burn the incense].

R. Yechidah, however, differs with others about the Ark's location and says, "The Ark was hidden in its original place, for it says 'The poles of the Ark projected so that the ends of the poles were visible in the Sanctuary, but they could not be seen on the outside, and there they remain to this day'" (1 Kings 8:8).[33]

While there are a variety of opinions about whether the Ark was hidden or went into Babylonian exile and then was returned, the Aggadah tells us about the Ark and the shetiyah, the foundation of the world. In Baraita we learn why it was called *shetiyah*, "foundation stone": "Because it was from this central point that the entire world was founded [this was the nucleus around which the world was formed]."[34] In Job (38:38), we are shown that "[t]he earth runs into a main mass and its sides are stuck around it." Does this suggest that the very root of creation is the Holy of Holies at the center of the world, the center

---

[32] R. Yaakov Ibn Chaviv, *Ein Yaakov,* Yoma (53b), "Where Was the Holy Ark Hidden?" 203.

[33] Ibid.

[34] Ibid., Yoma (54b), 203, "Shetiyah, The Foundation of the World?" 204.

Figure 8.5. The author above the hills of Jericho, where some say the Ark is hidden. Elul 5766 (August 2005). Photo by R. Avraham Sutton.

of our bodies, the heart? Is this why the heart is often called the seat of the soul?

When the Ark was hidden:

> . . . there was hidden along with it the jar containing manna, and a bottle containing the anointing oil (with which the Kohen Gadol was installed), the staff of Aaron with its almonds and blossoms, and the chest that the Philistines had sent as gifts to glorify to the God of Israel; as it says "Take the Ark of God and place it on a cart, and put next to it in a chest the gold objects you are paying Him as a sign of guilt. Send it off, and let it go its own way" (1 Samuel 6:8), (proof that the chest was next to the Ark, and when the Ark was hidden the chest was hidden along with it).[35]

---

[35] R. Yaakov Ibn Chaviv, *Ein Yaakov,* Yoma (54b), "The Hidden Ark of the Covenant," 202.

Who Hid the Holy Ark in the Time of Chuldah

As for who hid the Ark, the Gemara tells us that it is King Josiah (Yoshiahu) himself, he whom Chuldah serves as prophetess: "He said to the Levites, consecrated to God, the teachers of all Israel, 'Hide the Holy Ark in the House that Solomon son of David, King of Israel, built. You no longer will carry it on your shoulders. Now serve the Lord your God and his people.'"[36] We are told that Josiah hides the Ark somewhere under the Beit Hamikdash (Holy Temple). The king understands that an exile is approaching and the Temple's destruction is imminent; it occurred after his death.

Just as the identity of Esther, who represents the Sefirah of Malchut, is concealed, it is through Esther–Malchut–Moshiach Ben David that the Ark will be revealed at the coming of Moshiach and the age of sovereign enlightenment brought to fruition. The symbols coordinated together in a pattern suggest the Ark may be hidden inside the Mount of Olives (Yesod) and may be connected to the Temple through a tunnel (concealed) system, likewise connecting Moshiach Ben Joseph (Yesod) and Moshiach Ben David (Jerusalem) in Malchut.

The Hidden in Yesod and the World to Come

Because Yesod is the place of activity regarding the concealed becoming revealed, it is fitting that we find Chuldah there. She teaches B'nai Yisrael about the World to Come, the concealed afterlife, and King Josiah's hiding of the Ark is part of her story. Her prophecy causes this to occur. Together, the king and Chuldah are appropriately positioned in Yesod. It is also interesting to learn that Chuldah, whose species is olive oil, is buried on the Mount of Olives. As we have learned, Perek Shira has songs for the six other species of the land of Israel, which, according to the Holy Arizal, correspond to the Sefirot, but there is no song for the olive or olive oil. Is it hidden, like the Ark, until our *geulah* (redemption)?

King Josiah hides the Ark and Chuldah speaks of the concealed World to Come, Olam HaBa. The beginning and end of creation is

---

[36] 2 Chronicles 35:3. See also R. Yaakov Ibn Chaviv, *Ein Yaakov,* Yoma (52b), "The Hidden Ark of the Covenant," 202.

expressed in the partnership between the Ark and the World to Come, for we are told that this holy vessel, which holds the teachings of God, will be the Ark for all of humankind. In keeping with the teaching that blessings fall only on that which is hidden and which goes uncounted, "R. Yitzchak also said: Blessing is bestowed only on things hidden from sight (i.e. things that have not been counted, weighed or measured)."[37]

The World to Come or the afterlife has several meanings in the tradition of the People of the Book. One is that Olam HaBa is the abode of the soul after the body is deceased and we complete our lifetimes of refinement. Having no need to reincarnate, we remain in the eternal abode of the Creator. The World to Come also represents an eternal physical existence in which the body and soul are united, each a fitting balance for the other. Some say only the righteous will inherit the World to Come, where body and soul are both immortal; others say everyone will inherit some portion of the World to Come as the place in which the soul receives homage. But the reward for the righteous is identified, much as the Children of Israel and the brit of Yesod are identified, securing a special inheritance.

There are numerous teachings about who has a share in the World to Come. The Mishnah says:

> All Israel [even sinners] have a share in the World to Come, for it says, "your people [Israel] are all righteous, they shall inherit the land [i.e., a share in the hereafter] for all time, They are the shoot that I planted, My handiwork in which I glory" (Isaiah 60:21). However, the following do not have a share in the World to Come [if they do not repent]: A person who says that the resurrection of the dead is not alluded to in the Torah, or that the Torah is not given by God, or an apikoros [i.e., someone who belittles a Torah scholar].[38]

---

[37] R. Yaakov Ibn Chaviv, *Ein Yaakov*, Taanit, "Blessing on Things Hidden from Sight," 296.

[38] Ibid., Sanhedrin, 640.

Who Will See Moshiach?

The mystery of Moshiach is bound up in the secret of redemption (geulah), which is the outcome of God's covenant with humanity.

> . . . Ulla said, "Let Moshiach come but let me not see him!" [Ulla would rather not be present during the intense suffering that precedes his coming.] Rabbah, too, said: "Let Mashiach come, but let me not see him!" But R. Joseph said: "Let him come, and may I be worthy to sit in the shadow of his donkey's dung." Abbaye asked Rabbah, "Why don't you want to see the Mashiach coming? Is it because you are afraid of the pangs associated with his coming? But we learned in Baraita, Elazar was asked by his students: What can a person do to escape the birth pangs of Moshiach? And he replied: Let him get involved in the study of Torah and in acts of Kindness. And you Rabbah practice both Torah study and kindness [to perfection, so what are you afraid of]!" Rabbah replied, "I am afraid that a sin will erase whatever merits I have earned."[39]

Yesod: Friday

Yesod stands for Friday and preparation for Shabbat. Just as Chuldah helps the community understand that life is preparation for the World to Come, her day of the week is preparation for a taste of that world. It is a time for immersing ourselves in the tasks necessary to welcome the Shechinah, the holy Sabbath. In the same fashion, our lives are vessels for preparing a place for the Shechinah at our tables, at the royal banquet to be held when the messianic age arrives.

The Kabbalists say that Friday expresses the age of our current modern era of Yesod, the stage before our redemption and the promised thousand years of peace:

> R. Katina said, the world will exist for six thousand years, and for one thousand years [i.e., the seventh millennium] it will be desolate,

---

[39] R. Yaakov Ibn Chaviv, *Ein Yaakov,* Sanhedrin, "The Birth Pangs of Mashiach," 665.

as it says, "God alone will be exalted on that day" (Isaiah 2:11). . . . In the Yeshiva of Eliyahu it was taught: The world will exist for six thousand years: In the first two thousand years there was the desolation [the world was without Torah]. The second two thousand years the Torah prospered. The third two thousand years is the messianic era [Moshiach will come at some point during those two thousand years]. But because of our many sins, all those years have elapsed [and Mashiach did not come at the end of the fourth millennium].[40]

At the time of this publication, the Jewish calendar marks the year 5768–69. "Since we are awaiting Mashiach, and God is awaiting him, what delays his coming? The divine attribute of justice delays his coming [because of our sins]. But since the attribute of Justice delays his coming, why do we await him? To receive the reward [for yearning for him]. For it says, 'happy are all who wait for him' (Isaiah 30:18)."[41] There are numerous other opinions about redemption and the arrival of the messianic era, yet one perspective unites them all: "R. Eliezer said if the people repent they will be redeemed; if not, they will not."[42]

Chuldah and King Josiah: A Holy Partnership

Continuing the theme of the prophetesses' male counterparts, Chuldah's husband is a generous man: He makes sure the people have water to drink while Chuldah gives them spiritual water—the Torah. Nevertheless, her spiritual partner is King Josiah, much like Avigail's male collaborator is King David. Indeed, the place and spiritual station of the male collaborator seems to magnify the presence and purpose of each prophetess.[43]

In each Sefirah there occurs activity between polarities. This inter-

---

[40] R. Yaakov Ibn Chaviv, *Ein Yaakov,* Sanhedrin, 662.

[41] Ibid., "Calculating the Time of the Redemption," 662.

[42] Ibid., "If All the Jews Repent, Mashiach Will Come," 663.

[43] Where would Miriam's story and prophecy be without Moses and her brother Aaron? Where would Sarah's be without Abraham or Devorah's without Barak or Chanah's without High Priest Eli or her son Shmuel HaNavi (Samuel the prophet)? As we will learn, Purim would have no miracle without a Mordechai for Queen Esther.

weaving of masculine and feminine is a Kabbalistic and universal principle of balance. Kedusha (holiness) resides in a balance of two polarities showing us that all of our relations are important and that we would do well to examine them within the template of their devotion to God. Exemplifying the middle path, Yesod integrates the purpose of the entire body in service to the divine Creator.

Yesod, the Ark, and the World to Come

Through Yesod, the holy oil, and the Ark of the Tabernacle we are shown that the light of the Or En Sof, the limitless light of the realm of Atzilut (emanation), resides in a vessel—that in our hearts the Holy of Holies is concealed. When the light of our soul in that Holy of Holies is devoted and consecrated to God, the heart becomes the hidden Ark. The Ark within our heart and the Ark of the Temple are revealed in the World to Come and during the age of Moshiach, when everything will be returned (teshuvah) and elevated (aliyah) to the Holy of Holies of Malchut, the physical Third Temple on Mt. Moriah and the temple in living people. The purpose of the material body will move to its fulfillment. The Shechinah will reinhabit the world.

In this way, we begin to see that the light, which descends, also has its ascent, just as the soul at the end of its life in a body reascends without its physical shell. In Yesod we see the ability to both conceal and reveal: What is hidden on earth is revealed in heaven; what is revealed in heaven is concealed on earth. Even without the Temple, the Ark, or the holy anointing oil and other Temple instruments—and regardless of our exile (gelut), our separation from Jerusalem (the holy heritage of God's presence)—we are all to serve the Creator and the world. The removal of that which covers a physical and spiritual disposition or organ (as in the brit) is the ritual reflecting this eternal covenant. This covenant of body, heart, and soul is the foundation on which stands redemption.

Yom Kippur and Olam HaBa

In the afterlife we review our sins. We relive our sins until we can ask for forgiveness properly before the King, and Yom Kippur, like Yesod, allows us to return fully to our Maker every day and every year. On Yom Kippur, the sins we have committed against others are rectified when we ask each person's forgiveness. Like Yesod, which secures our future in the redeemed World to Come and the time of Moshiach, it is through teshuvah and repentance that this shine of our soul is secured. "God arranged Creation so that even while in the physical world, man would be able to open the door to the spiritual and experience the Divine. This would constitute the highest perfection that a mortal can attain."[44]

It is taught that it is in heaven that partners of like shine are chosen. "Didn't Rav Yehudah say in the name of the Rav: Forty days before the creation of a child a Heavenly voice comes forth and proclaims: The daughter of so-and-so shall marry so-and-so, the house of so-and-so, the field of so-and-so is for so-and so!"[45]

The Talmud and Forgiveness

There are 527 chapters in the Talmud, broken down into tractates under general headings: Zera'im (seeds), Moed (season), Nashim (women), Nezkin (damages), Kedoshim (sacred things), and Tohoroth (purities). The headings alone instruct us about the regard Jewish Law has for planting our seeds (actions) in the world, keeping with the season (time and place), differentiation between things that are holy and unholy, and the obligations we each have to any damage we have caused. This is one of the reasons that on Yom Kippur, the holiday associated with Chuldah, we ask for forgiveness from our fellow community members if we have done them any wrong. We are obliged to return any borrowed items to their rightful owners. We learn that God can forgive the sinner here and in the hereafter, but human beings can forgive each other primarily during life. The rectification we must undertake comes not just from things we have done, but also from things we have promised but have not done.

There are two ways in which we can obligate ourselves by our word: through an oath and through a vow. An oath obligates us to keep our

---

[44] R. Aryeh Kaplan, *Handbook of Jewish Thought,* vol. 1, 83. See also R. Moses Ben Maimon (Maimonides; the Rambam), *Derech HaShem,* 3:2–3.
[45] Sotah 2a.

word. To do otherwise is considered lying. A vow, however, gives us a new obligation, one of the reasons we are told not to make vows without serious consideration of our ability to keep them. He who makes "a vow to God, or makes an oath to make something forbidden to himself, he must not break his word; he must do all that he expresses."[46]

GEMATRIA

47: The Numeric Value of Chuldah's Name

Chuldah חלדה :ח Chet (8) ל Lamed (30) ד Dalet (4) ה Hay (5) = 47

Completing our study of Chuldah, let us turn to the Parshiot hidden in Chuldah's name. Using mispar hechrachi to find other words and phrases in the Torah with the same numeric value as Chuldah's name, we uncover another inner story. As you will see, most of these words or phrases reflect our redemption and the redemption of B'nai Yisrael. Also noted in each example is the Sefirotic influence in each element of the hidden parts of Chuldah's essence, to demonstrate how our stories are composed of the entire Etz Chayim (Tree of Life.). In this way, we can see that the Sefirot are present in everything in the created world and are formative forces derived from the spiritual kingdoms.

his Mother אמו (Genesis 2:24, Sefirotic influence = Chesed): א Alef (1) מ Mem (40) ו Vav (6) = 47

"Therefore a man shall leave his Father and his Mother and cling to his wife and they shall become one flesh." The creation of Eve from Adam's rib is the foundation for the teachings regarding the purpose of man and woman as one flesh, as one vessel of unity, though created separately. Maturity means leaving our parents in order to create our own family. Yesod as the organ of regeneration and the womb as the place of incubation show us that only together as one flesh in conjugation, male and female, do we have the capacity to populate the earth. This suggests Chesed (love) of the Mother (Binah) as the primary quality of the words **his Mother.**

---

[46] Numbers 30:3. See also R. Aryeh Kaplan, *Handbook of Jewish Thought*, vol. 1, 264.

to him אליו (Genesis 8:9, Sefirotic influence = Gevurah): א Alef (1)
ל Lamed (30) י Yod (10) ו Vav (6) = 47

> But the dove could not find a resting place for the sole of its foot,
> and it returned him to the Ark, for the water was upon the surface of
> all the earth. So he put forth his hand, and took it, and brought it to
> him to the Ark. . . . He waited again another seven days, and again
> sent to the dove from the Ark. . . . The Dove came back to him in
> the evening—and behold! An olive leaf! It had plucked with its bill!
> And Noah knew that the waters had subsided from upon the earth.

Gevurah as deliverance (geulah) is apparent here—deliverance for
both the survivors of the Deluge, who have been delivered from annihilation (a theme that reappears in the promise of redemption from Egypt)
and humanity in general from its own evil inclinations. Also mentioned
is the olive branch that the dove took from the Mount of Olives and
brought to Noah.

was born בהולד (Genesis 21:5, Sefirotic influence = Yesod): ב Bet (2)
ה Hay (5) ו Vav (6) ל Lamed (30) ד Dalet (4) = 47

"And Abraham was a hundred years old when his son Isaac was born to
him." It is through Abraham's family that B'nai Yisrael is granted protection
and eternal love of the Creator. The number 100 suggests a holy nature in
the patriarch Abraham; the letter Kof, equal in value to 100, is the first letter in the word for **holy** קדש: ק Kof (100) ד Dalet (4) ש Shin (300). In
this sense, we see the actuality of the promised nation and the prophesied
redemption of humanity through the particular story of the People of the
Book and through Yesod. It reconfirms the brit of the people as the special
mark of this covenant, first undertaken at God's command by Abraham
himself. In Chuldah, in the place of Yesod we see reflected the holy patriarch
with whom the covenant and brit is initiated.

ram ואיל (rams, Genesis 15:9, Sefirotic influence = Gevurah, Tiferet,
Hod, Malchut): ו Vav (6) א Alef (1) י Yod (10) ל Lamed (30) = 47

God speaks to Abraham: "Take to me three heifers, three goats, three rams, a turtledove, and a young dove." The animals—save the birds—are cut up, and Abraham falls into a deep sleep and is shown "that all of your offspring shall be aliens in a land not their own—and they will serve them, and they will oppress them—four hundred years. . . . But also the nation that they will serve, I shall judge, and afterwards they will leave with great wealth."

Just as King Josiah intuits the coming exile, considered to be the energy of Gevurah, and the destruction of the Temple prior to the events occurring, the revelation of exile and redemption is shown to Abraham, because it is the future redemption (Malchut) of the Jews from Egypt. The covenant (Yesod), as the Torah (Tiferet) given on Mt. Sinai (Malchut), is like a wedding document (Hod) between God and Yisrael. Just as Chuldah is able to inspire the king to teshuvah by her prophecy, so too the Israelites are instructed how to make amends for their behavior.

in them בהם (upon them, Genesis 48:16, Sefirotic influence = Yesod, Malchut): ב Bet (2) ה Hay (5) ם Mem (40) = 47

"May the angel who redeems me from all the evil bless the lads and may my name be declared upon them, and the names of my forefathers, Abraham and Isaac, and may they proliferate abundantly like fish within the land." As we have learned, blessings rest on what is uncounted, just as the fish in the sea cannot be counted but are blessed. Here, Jacob blesses the tribes who are the progeny (Yesod) of the patriarchs and matriarchs before them, the seeds of fruition.

to sacrifice לזבח (bring offering, Exodus 8:25, Sefirotic influence = Hod): ל Lamed (30) ז Zayin (7) ח Chet (8) ב Bet (2) = 47

Moses says, "Behold! I leave you and I shall entreat God—and the swarm will depart from Pharaoh, from his servants and from his people—tomorrow. Only let Pharaoh not continue to mock, by not sending out the people to bring offering to God."

Just like the sacrifices of the foreskin of the phallus and heart, here sacrifice is confirmed as the obligation of God's Israelites. This tells us that redemption comes from fulfillment of the mitzvot and self-refinement.

and the Tent וְהָאֹהֶל (Numbers 3:25, Sefirotic influence = Chesed, Malchut): ו Vav (6) ה Hay (5) א Alef (1) ה Hay (5) ל Lamed (30) = 47

"The Charge of the sons of Gershon in the Tent of Meeting was the Tabernacle, [and] the Tent, its Cover, its screen of the entrance of the Tent of Meeting; . . . the curtains of the Courtyard, the Screen of the entrance of the Courtyard that surrounded the Tabernacle and the Altar, and its ropes—for all its labor."

Gershon is a son of Levi. It is the Levites who replaced the firstborn in service to the Kohen Gadol. The tent is the holy meeting place of the people and the Creator. The ohel, which is for the living and the dead, is where the Shechinah manifests herself. We are told how to conduct ourselves here, to prepare the right environment for communion with God and in the World to Come.

separate yourselves הִבָּדְלוּ (Numbers 16:21, Sefirotic influence = Gevurah, Netzach): ה Hay (5) ב Bet (2) ד Dalet (4) ל Lamed (30) ו Vav (6) = 47

". . . separate yourselves from amid this assembly, and I shall destroy them in an instant." Moses and Aaron fell on their faces and said, "O God, God of the spirits of all flesh, shall one man sin, and you be angry with the entire assembly? . . . God spoke to Moses saying: Speak to the assembly, saying Get yourselves up from all around the dwelling places of Korach, and Datan, and Avriam [the wicked men]."

The earth then opens its mouth and swallows Korach and his party. This capacity of the earth to open its mouth for this moment is one of the ten things we are told are created in the first day of creation. God destroys the evil ones. As with the Deluge, He uses nature to annihilate the foes of His holy order. While the circumcision of the phallus separates B'nai Yisrael's men from the men of the seventy nations, the brit of the heart separates the righteous from the wicked.

to good לטוב (our good, Deuteronomy 6:24, Sefirotic influence = Tiferet): ל Lamed (30) ט Tet (9) ו Vav (6) ב Bet (2) = 47

"God commanded us to perform all these decrees, to fear God, our God, for our good; all the days, to give us life, as this very day." This follows the Shema prayer: Moses instructs the Children of Israel in the tradition of the People of the Book. Here Moses tells B'nai Yisrael the prerequisite for goodness all the days of their lives and in the World to Come. Our thought, speech, and action in this world determine our experience of the afterlife and when we will be counted among the righteous, who are given eternal life.

your sacrifices זבחיכ (your burnt offerings, Deuteronomy 12:27, Sefirotic influence = Gevurah): ז Zayin (7) ב Bet (2) ח Chet (8) י Yod (10) כ Caf (20) = 47

"You shall perform your burnt offerings, the flesh and the blood, upon the Altar of God, your God; and the blood of your feast offerings shall be poured upon the Altar of God, your God and you shall eat the flesh." We are told how to prepare our sacrifices and what we are to eat. One sustains the soul, the other the body. Both are dedicated to serving the Creator as are our body and soul in this life and in the afterlife.

and dip וטבל (Deuteronomy 33:24, Sefirotic influence = Hod): ו Vav (6) ט Tet (9) ב Bet (2) ל Lamed (30) = 47

"Of Asher he said: the most Blessed of Children is Asher; he shall be pleasing to his brothers, and dip his feet in oil." Asher is Isaac's second son by Zilpah (Leah's handmaid), and no son is more righteous, thus it is his feet, not his head, that are dipped in anointing oil. His lowest extremity, like Malchut in Etz Chayim, is anointed. Here we see the olive oil of the Mount of Olives (Yesod) consecrating B'nai Yisrael through Asher's feet (Malchut). This can be seen as a portent of the two Moshiachs: perhaps that one (Moshiach Ben Joseph) will anoint the feet of the other (Moshiach Ben David) in oil.

SUMMARIZING THE IMPORTANCE
OF CHULDAH

In Chuldah's spiritual essence as revealed by the letters and numeric value of her name and in her role as the sixth prophetess of Israel, we find the full composition of Yesod. The meaning of this stage of development—referred to here as redemption and Olam HaBa, the World to Come—clearly requires our complete and total devotion in body and soul.

Summarizing some of the Parshiot related to her name, we encounter the creation of woman (Eve), the redemption of humanity, the capacity of God to save humanity after the Deluge, the promise of the redemption of B'nai Yisrael, and the actuality of the promised nation. (Isaac blesses his sons, who will bring the nation to fullness.) We also encounter the eve of redemption, for the Torah is the wedding document and the promise of the covenant revealed. The Torah is the guidebook to this life and the afterlife, the World to Come. The tent of our hearts is the holy meeting place of the people and the Creator, who destroys the evil ones (our selfish inclinations). As in the Deluge, God uses nature to annihilate the foes of His holy order. Moses tells B'nai Yisrael the prerequisite for goodness all the days of their lives. For sustenance of both the soul and the body, we are told how to prepare our sacrifices and what we are to eat. Both our soul and our body are in service of the Creator. To anoint our feet is to put the lamp in Malchut. In the Holy of Holies, in Malchut b'Malchut (Malchut of Malchut), there is the shine of the promise of Moshiach Ben David, the Ark in the Temple. The shine of resurrection animating the material world shows us, in Yesod, the World to Come and guides us, in Malchut, to immortality and resurrection, the complete refinement of the material world and our lives.

Yesod as revealed through Chuldah's name integrates all of the preceding Sefirot: Chesed (the seed of creation), Gevurah (destruction of evil and deliverance of the people), Tiferet (the blessings on the people with a code of moral law), Netzach (the making of holy life through spiritual attendance) and Hod (our sacrifices). Yesod takes all of these qualities and adds to them the importance of the World to Come, the resting place of the immortal soul, teaching us that this life is preparation for our eternal experience, even though while we are alive on earth, it seems that the World to Come is only the footnote to living. In fact, this life and the life to come are inseparable aspects of the journey each created life endures and celebrates. Therefore, Zeir Anpin, the Son or Sons of Israel (B'nai Yisrael) represented by all six Sefirot as a unit, are joined in Yesod, where they deposit all these qualities into the last and final Sefirah of the ten Sefirot of the Tree of Life: Malchut.

As R. Avraham Brandwein, of Jerusalem, has made clear, the denser the vessel, the finer the light. Malchut as the kingdom, the realm of action (Asiyah), the place in which we live, is the densest of vessels, yet it holds the most refined light. Esther, as the representative of Malchut and the seventh prophetess of the land of Israel, shows us the fulfillment of prophecy, as we will learn in the next chapter.

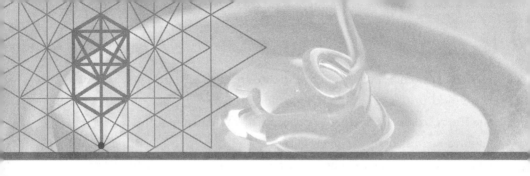

9

Esther

Malchut · The Redemption and Resurrection of Life

The Shechinah and the Moshiach both stand together and do not separate from each other.

> R. MOSHE CHAIM LUZZATTO,
> SECRETS OF REDEMPTION, 3:95, 158

Whoever repeats something in the name of one who said it, Brings redemption to the world.

> PIRKEI AVOT 6:6, MEGILLAH 15A

Esther אסתר

א Alef (1) ס Samech (60) ת Tav (400) ר Reish (200) = 661

Sefirah Correspondence: Malchut

Titles: Prophetess, Queen of Persia

Family: Niece of Mordechai[1] and wife of King Achashverosh

Time Period	Jewish Calendar	Gregorian Calendar
Feast of Achashverosh	3395	365 BCE
Esther crowned queen	3398	362 BCE
Purim	3405	355 BCE

---

[1] Some are of the opinion that Esther also became Mordechai's wife.

Developmental Stage: Redemption and resurrection

Day: Sabbath (Saturday)

Sacred Species: Date honey

Body Correspondence: Feet and mouth

Rituals: Keeping Sabbath, keeping Kashrut, prayer, and fasting

Holidays: Sabbath, Purim, Simchat Torah

Symbols: Robe of royalty, royal kingdom, the Earth

Prayers: Shema, blessings on Torah, blessings at a wedding

Shine of Esther–Malchut: The shine of the messianic age, the third Temple built, Moshiach and resurrection

Prophecy Source: Megillat Esther 4:16, "Assemble all the Jews . . . and fast for me . . . then I will go in to the king."

SEFIRAH: MALCHUT

Malchut is the last of the ten Sefirot and represents the day of Sabbath in the week and the feet and mouth in the body. It is analogous to the moon, to the Shechinah fully embodied. It is the kingdom of God and humanity from whence the light returns. Malchut is the repository of everything preceding it, bringing to fruition all the elements of the Etz Chayim. Standing as it does for Asiyah, the physical world referred to in Kabbalah as kingdom and sovereignty, it is here that all things can be brought together in a harmoniously manifest way. Here, Atzilut, the highest source of light, emanates into the lowest vessel and is reflected in Asiyah.

Phase of Development: In the seventh stage of the Shechinah's descent, like the sixth millennium we will experience on earth, when there will be a thousand years of peace, here we and nations are fully awakened to our covenant and role in the world as the Creator's partners in perfection. In Malchut we experience union, redemption, and the promise of resurrection as we rededicate ourselves to serving God and His Word, using for this purpose everything we are given: our wealth, our intelligence, our labor, our place and station. Here, we stand fully aware of our interdependent part in the whole.

Spiritual Work: Malchut requires a surrender that is not simply emotional or even spiritual, but is also physical. Here, the mitzvot are anchored in the world; here, the soul's garment in speech is perfected in word and action. Because Malchut is analogous to the mouth, we perfect our speech as the Chazal suggest, rectifying the Shechinah and bringing world redemption.

World Action: Malchut asks us to repair the physical world, to build, to create. Malchut elevates and reflects all that is good in humanity, inspiring the community to holiness and righteousness.

Spiritual Action: In Malchut, the righteous are refined and illuminated. Committing ourselves entirely to God's Word, the world and body are made holy and the Shechinah, the Divine Immanence of the Creator, illuminates all life. Here, the body and soul unite in total surrender to serving God and His world of manifestation.

Meaningful Work: Malchut activities serve for the delivery of any direct services and for careers that elevate the earth, such as environmentalism, animal stewardship, farming, the sciences, and Torah study.

Day Focus: Saturday, or Sabbath, is the day of rest, commemorating God's act of creation. Because during it, we give over our entire focus to study and service of God's Word in personal and communal worship, Sabbath illuminates the rest of the days of the week with peace and truth.

Species: Our redemption is sweet, like date honey, the seventh on the list of the sacred species of Eretz Yisrael. Coming from the date palm tree, date honey is a symbol for the flourishing of the Jewish people, and the date palm itself is a symbol for the righteous, as we learned in the chapter on the prophetess Devorah.

ESTHER'S STORY

Queen Esther was the final of the seven prophetesses to lead B'nai Yisrael and to change world history. Of all the prophetesses, our knowledge of Esther's life is by far the most detailed and complete. Other than Miriam, Esther is the only prophetess about whose childhood we know something. **Esther's story,** recounted in Megillat Esther (the Book of Esther), reveals how she **saved the Jews from annihilation in Persia.** Both of her parents died—her father after her **conception** and her mother after her **birth.** As an **orphan,** Esther was taken into her uncle Mordechai's house, and with his aid, she was guided and protected throughout her life, and given the name Hadassah. **The king, searching for a queen,** eventually **married Esther,** who changed her name from Hadassah to conceal her Jewish identity. Through her **seven maidens,** she kept kosher and kept **the Sabbath** in the royal household.

Esther's story is one of the **prophetess as heroine,** revealing **the evil designs of Haman,** the king's viceroy, who planned to kill all the Jewish people, including Esther's uncle Mordechai, whom Haman planned to hang. Through her bravery and fasting and prayer, the Shechinah came to Esther, who was able to win the king's favor and his response to her petitions, showing us that the prayers of the righteous are answered. The holiday of Purim commemorates Queen Esther and Mordechai's wisdom—a story of redemption for the Jewish people. Esther's story is the last entry of the Torah, a story less focused on God's miracles than on prayer and action, teaching us how to use everything we have in the service of the Creator.

SYMBOLISM OF ESTHER

Malchut: The Shine of Resurrection

We find in the life of Esther, the seventh prophetess, and in the Sefirah of Malchut, an addition to the progression of qualities of the six prophetesses who precede her. In her story are elements of Sarah (Chesed and loving-kindness), Miriam (Gevurah and disciplined deliverance), Devorah (Tiferet and moral order), Chanah (Netzach and enduring commitment to God), Avigail (Hod and the quality of extreme humility), and Chuldah (Yesod and a commitment and willingness to risk our life for the covenant with the Creator). Esther and Malchut exemplify finding redemption through committing all of our resources to God. Esther embodies and represents the fulfillment of the Torah's teachings and the promise of Moshiach. Esther shows us the shine of redemption and eventual resurrection for all of humanity.

Esther's Story

The seventh prophetess to appear on the world stage in the age of prophecy is the heroine Esther. Her story, Megillat Esther, "preceded the building of the Second Temple by two years."[2] It is said, "[T]here is a hint" of Esther in Deuteronomy 31:18, where it is written, "I will surely hide my face on that day."[3] As the last of the seven prophetesses and as redeemer of her people, Esther is at first concealed. Like the Shechinah, which appears gradually in stages, the divine presence of the Creator is at first concealed in Esther, being revealed only later. The three-letter root of Esther's name comes from the word meaning "concealing" or "hiding" as well as "protecting"—ס Samech (60) ת Tav (400) ר Reish (200) = 660.[4]

Esther Saves the Jews from Annihilation in Persia

The biblical Book of Esther (Megillat Esther) describes the Jewish queen of Persia as the heroine of the People of the Book. On Purim, her story is read and her life is honored in synagogues worldwide.

Esther, raised by Mordechai, who is either her mother's brother or her cousin, was called first by her Hebrew name, Hadassah, but she later assumes the name Esther. When the king of Persia, Achashverosh, has his wife, Vashti, executed for disobeying him, he chooses Esther as his new wife. Without revealing her Jewish identity, Esther becomes queen of Persia.

Haman, the king's viceroy, decides to kill all Jews because he is

---

[2] Lekach Tov, Esther 1.
[3] Chullin 139b.
[4] Matityahu Clark, *Etymological Dictionary of Biblical Hebrew*, 177.

angered when Mordechai, Esther's spiritual guardian, refuses to bow down to him. Haman manages to get the king to agree to his plan of genocide by telling him that there are a people scattered in the land who refuse to obey the king's laws.

Haman casts lots (Purim stands for "lots" in Hebrew) to decide in which month the Jews will be murdered. He then distributes orders to slay all Jews on the thirteenth day of the Hebrew month of Adar.[5] Mordechai asks Esther to appeal to the king, even though he knows that by doing so, she risks having her own life taken. To prepare for this dangerous mission, the Jews fast for three days at Esther's urging and example. Esther subsequently risks her life by going to the king without first being summoned, which is against Persian law. The king accepts Esther's presence and asks what she wants. She requests the presence of the king and Haman at a banquet she will make. This first banquet is followed by a second one held on the day after the first, at which time the queen asks the king to end Haman's plan. The king is angered by Haman's murderous schemes and has Haman hanged by the gallows that the viceroy had erected to hang Mordechai. Mordechai is promoted to Haman's job as the king's viceroy, and the Jews are saved. Mordechai then declares the fourteenth and fifteenth days of the Hebrew month of Adar as days of rejoicing, as the feast of Purim.

This is an abbreviated telling of the background for the holiday Purim, which, the sages tell us, along with Chanukah (Yesod), will be the only holiday celebrated after the arrival of Moshiach. In this sense, Purim is the culmination of the process of refinement afforded the observant by the Jewish holidays.

---

[5] The Jewish calendar is a lunar calendar adjusted to the solar year. The first known calendar, calculated with the day of creation in 3761 BCE as year 1, was created in the second century BCE by R. Yose Ben Halafta. Each cycle is a month, and there are twelve months in a year. The lunar year has about 354 days. Because it is eleven days shorter than the solar calendar, a thirteenth month is sometimes added to the Jewish calendar, and these years of thirteen months are leap years. The names of the Jewish months are Babylonian in origin. Adar falls sometime in our months of February and March. Nissan, or March/April, is the first month of the Jewish calendar year, the astrological sign of Aries. See Geoffrey Wigoder, *The Student's Encyclopedia of Judaism*, 65–66.

The Conception and Birth of Esther

"When Esther was conceived, her Father died; when she was born, her Mother died."[6] From the very beginning, Esther's life is a dramatic story of a child born into the world without parents. The fact that each parent dies is important. The Father as Chochmah or wisdom, whose seed of Yesod is implanted in the womb of the Mother (Imma and Binah), dies after performing the sacred function as impregnator. In this way, we are taught something about the act of insemination: Our egos must die, our self-interest must die, for we are for the world and the Creator. The fact that the Mother dies—an extinguishing of the vessel that holds the incubating light of the upper Sefirah of Binah, the partner to Chochmah—suggests the downward flow of the light into Malchut from Binah, from Mother to Daughter. Yesod (Son or Zeir Anpin) is the seed of the male, which enters the womb of the female, giving birth to the child, who in Kabbalah is called the Daughter, or Queen, which is expressed in Esther's life. Here, we see a secret about resurrection and eternal life: The entire Etz Chayim is rectified in one individual as well as by the nation or world.

The Entire Tree of Life in the Story of Esther

The death of the physical body must occur before we can birth the body that is made of the highest raiment of light. Esther's birth shows us a three-stage process that, in some ways, finds its expression in the three pillars of Kabbalah, referred to as the right column (Chesed, comprising Chochmah, Chesed, and Netzach), the left column (Gevurah, comprising Binah, Gevurah, and Hod), and the middle column (comprising Keter or the Crown, Daat, Tiferet, Yesod, and Malchut). In Esther's story we see not only all seven prophetesses, but also the entire Tree of Life. She shows us that each of our births is in effect the birth of an entire Tree of Life. The death of Esther's parents adds a deeper mystery to the concealment of her glory. Esther's life also shows us why God treasures the orphan and that one of our mitzvot—commanded good deeds—is to care for the parentless child. Let us look a little deeper at Esther's birth story.[7]

---

[6] Megillah 13a.

[7] Taking care of the orphan is considered a mitzvah, a good deed, an obligation.

Malchut: Two Deaths, Eternal Life

Esther's father dies at insemination, and her mother dies after giving birth to Esther. We could interpret this to mean that first the will of the "I" and then the vessel of its desire (ego) are extinguished. When we leave this world, all that we have accomplished emanates to the world. Esther is the direct recipient of Chochmah (wisdom), symbolized by the life of her father, who deposits all of his raiment and glory into her conception as he passes away into the spiritual realms. Her mother, who exemplifies Binah, also flows directly into Malchut, the Daughter, by dying when Esther is born. This reveals that Esther's conception and birth are the outcome of a marriage compelled by the holy process of a spiritual teshuvah, a total return to God in body and soul. We can say that both of Esther's parents live for the purpose of giving birth to the Shechinah, the Queen of Israel, the Bride of the Jewish people, the herald of the redeemer.

Esther is a descendant of King Saul. As such, his soul benefits by her merit as the ultimate redeemer and embodiment of the Shechinah, showing us that the living bring blessings to the deceased. Samuel the prophet anoints Saul, showing us Esther's connection to Netzach and Chanah (recalling that Samuel is the son of Chanah), who teaches us about spiritual will and endurance.

Classical Kabbalah

The Chassidic tradition reveals that the hidden relationship between the Mother (Imma and Binah) and the Daughter (Malchut) reflects the mystery of the Creator's name. In numerous teachings on the subject, we learn that the return of the final letter Hay (Malchut) to the first Hay (Binah) of God's name, Havaya (Yod Hay Vav Hay), represents the act of return, the teshuvah of the individual and the nation as on Yom Kippur (Yesod). Esther's conception and birth tell us that she is endowed with Chochmah and Binah, and that the Or En Sof, the limitless light, has been hidden within her. This makes it easier to see what is meant by the description that she is "donned in royalty" and why she is destined to become queen.

The Mother (Imma) Lends Her Clothes to the Daughter (Malchut)

Imma, as the Mother or Binah, the Sefirah of understanding, brings down to Malchut the name Elokim, which stands for the "Ark of the Covenant." Elokim represents the name of God associated with Gevurah, discipline and judgment, which comes from the left pillar of the Etz Chayim. In the Zohar, this describes the Daughter (Malchut) who dresses up in clothes of the Son (vessels of the Son or Zeir Anpin) and adornments from the Mother (Binah). We see this esoteric teaching in Esther's story.

The six preceding prophetesses—middot (the Son or Zeir Anpin)—provide the light that is deposited into Malchut or Esther. Just as Esther's seven maidens help her to keep track of the days of the week so that she can honor Shabbat—and just as Shabbat brings redemption in the week—Esther herself brings the light of redemption to the world. Esther is the summary reflection of the preceding nine Sefirot (which include the upper triad of Keter, Chochmah, and Binah) or the preceding six Sefirot (which include only the middot, or emotions, represented by the six prophetesses who precede Esther). These stages of development also show us the stages of exile and the eventual completion of creation in resurrection.

Sons and Daughters

As we have already learned, the six Sefirot occupied by the six prophetesses preceding Esther are referred to collectively as Zeir Anpin, or the Son. The last Sefirah, Malchut, is referred to as the Daughter, woman (Nukvah), or Queen. In Esther's case, the Father and Mother are extinguished in order for the Daughter to arise. Called Nukvah herself, she is the addition to Zeir Anpin that makes this Son whole, the crown upon her husband's head. Here, we are shown that the nation's egoist sense of self, its nationalism, must be replaced by a spiritual betrothal to the Creator and His holy teachings. For the Daughter to rise, for the Queen as Israel to elevate the community, the People of the Book must strive for righteousness. As we will discover, this righteousness is represented by Malchut and is a quality for which Esther is well known.

Esther Shows Us the Meaning of Rectification

In our individual lives, Esther shows us that our emotions, once refined, give birth to our Malchut, our body of light. This body is the result of having removed all evil shells (kelipot) from our nature. As we descend the Tree of Life, we are actually ascending the spiritual worlds' potentials and actual emanations, refining the body as well as the soul. When we are born, the light becomes concealed progressively in our lives. Eventually, the greatest possible light is revealed, even greater than before our birth. This seems to occur at the death of the body. When we die, the entire shine of our soul illuminates the world. In Esther's case, the shine of wisdom and understanding are foundations upon which are built her life and body, which is an inheritance from her parents. She is of superior intellect and is connected to the higher realms of the Crown or Keter in Atzilut (emanation), from which comes the Torah.

Esther's conception and birth tell a story in the realms of Beriyah (creation) of Chesed (Sarah) and conception and of Gevurah (Miriam) in Yetzirah (formation). Here we see birth and deliverance, represented in the Etz Chayim by Sarah and Miriam, respectively. Already, we see in Esther's life some aspects of both Chochmah and Chesed on the right pillar (Father and Sarah) and Binah and Gevurah (Mother and Miriam) on the left.

The Luminous Body

On a person's yahrzeit, the annual anniversary of his or her death, this shine of the soul is accessed. This is what also occurs on every Jewish holiday. The illumination of the original events being commemorated shine on the world. Both a person's yahrzeit and the holidays offer us the shine of its original emanation (Atzilut), its creation (Beriyah), its formation (Yetzirah), and its manifestation (Asiyah) from the root of God's will. In this way, we see some of the meanings of resurrection and eternity. Resurrection is both a spiritual continuity and a physical redemption from the shells of evil. Resurrection is the natural outcome of a material life when it has been elevated even beyond its original perfection prior to manifesting in the world of matter.

Resurrection: An Elevation

Resurrection is an elevation of each human soul. Being born and dying are for the purpose of being born to eternal life. This tells us that resurrection for the body and soul is akin to prophecy for the mouth, Malchut. The resurrected body not only suggests a perfecting of Gan Eden, the Garden of Eden, as earth, but also it tells us that this resurrected body of light is even greater than its original form. The effort exerted in this process by each of us and by humanity in general becomes an addition to the quality of the shine of the body with which God endows us at birth. Esther's origins and life story show us this reality. Just as prophecy is the outcome of the Torah, resurrection is the outcome of being born. Diminishing precedes elevating.

The Union of the Material and the Spiritual

Esther's birth, then, is a description of the process by which the upper and lower worlds, the world of the spiritual and the world of the material—hence their waters—are united in Malchut. The birth of the holy one, Moshiach, comes from the collective death of self-interest, from the mother and father sacrificing their self-interests for their children; our wisdom (Chochmah), understanding (Binah), and knowledge (Daat) being used for the refinement of our emotions and body, our sons and daughters (Zeir Anpin and Nukvah).

Esther's Name

We are told that Esther's uncle Mordechai adopts her and raises her as his own daughter. "Mordechai's wife nursed Esther, and Mordechai reared her."[8] "She behaves modestly in the house of Mordechai for seventy-five years, and did not look at the face of any man except Mordechai."[9] Esther is also called Estahar (Ishtar or Ishatar) by "the nations of the world," who "called her this, a name which means 'as beautiful as the Moon.'" Others interpret her name Estahar as meaning "star of light."[10]

---

[8] Shocher Tov, 22.

[9] Targum Esther 2:7; R. Yishai Chasidah, *Encyclopedia of Biblical Personalities*, 99.

[10] Yalkut Shimoni, Esther 1053; R. Yishai Chasidah, *Encyclopedia of Biblical Personalities*, 99.

Elevation of Women Marks the Ascent of the World

It is interesting to note that after the righteous, which is most often associated with Yesod and the tzaddikim, comes the resurrected, the perfected Adam and Eve, the elevated man and woman who come into eternal form. This takes place in Malchut. This same gradual elevation of the world is described in one of the traditional writings about the sun and the moon, represented by Esther's promotion to partner of the king.

While we know that the Creator made "two great lights . . . [t]he greater light . . . and the smaller light" (Genesis 1:16), showing us that the sun is greater than the moon, the Chazal teach us that

R. Shimon b. Pazzi pointed out . . . originally the Sun and the moon were the same size. The moon then said to the Holy one, Blessed be He, "Master of the universe! Is it possible for two kings to wear the same crown? [I should be larger than the sun.]" God answered, "Go make yourself smaller." "Master of the universe!" pleaded the moon, "why should I make myself smaller just because I made a legitimate suggestion!" God replied, "Go and rule [shine] by day and by night." "But what good will my light be [during the day]!" moaned the moon. "For what good is a lamp in broad daylight?" God consoled the moon, "Go [and be satisfied], for Israel will count the days of the months and the years according to you." "But it is impossible," said the moon, "to calculate the Jewish calendar without taking into account the solar year, for it says, 'They shall serve as signs [and define] festivals, days and years.'" God appeased the moon, saying, "Go [and be satisfied] for the righteous will be named [the small] after you, as we find, Jacob the Small, Shmuel the Small, David the Small." Seeing that the moon was not placated, the Holy One, blessed be He, said "Bring an atonement for Me because I made the moon smaller." This is what R. Shimon b. Lakish had in mind when he said: "Why is the male goat that is offered on the new moon singled out in that it is described as a sin-offering to God?" (Numbers 28:15). (The words to God are not mentioned in connection with sacrifices on other festivals.) Because the

Holy one, blessed be He, said, "Let this male goat be an atonement for Me for making the moon smaller."[11]

We learn from this story that the diminishing of the moon is for the purpose of the eventual elevation of humanity and a union between humanity and the Shechinah. Prophecy, as the speech of the Shechinah, becomes the breath of the Creator realized through our intelligence. The prophetesses become the created vessels for the divine manifestation of His Word. They show us the spiritual body of the Shechinah. They show us how to refine ourselves step by step in order to become collective vessels that God, divinity, and the Shechinah can inhabit.

The story of the sun and moon represents the progressive story of male and female in our civilization and the inner part of ourselves that is distinctly male and female. From it we learn a great deal about Esther's ordeal. Occupying Malchut, Esther represents the Shechinah embodied as the moon. Her renowned humility makes greater sense. Her righteousness is what makes her humble, and this "smallness" or humility is what leads to worldly greatness, "largeness." In the same way, one day there will be two great lights in the sky: The sun and the moon will stand side by side. Likewise, we are shown that though Eve is made from Adam's rib—made from a small part of him—she is the crown on her husband's head. The woman is not just equal to the man, but is also able to elevate him spiritually. Just as the moon will one day be observed during the day, so will women be respected as much as men in the world.

Esther as Hadassah

Esther is originally called Hadassah, "myrtle," one of the four species used during the holiday of Sukkot (see chapter 5). Hadassah also refers to the righteous. She is called Esther by the time she is selected by the king to be his bride, "because she hid her origins, as it is written, 'Esther still told nothing of her kindred or her people.'"[12] Myrtle is the species that

---

[11] R. Yaakov Ibn Chaviv, *Ein Yaakov,* Chullin (60b), "Why Is the Moon Smaller than the Sun?" 772.

[12] Megillat Esther 2:20, Megillah 13a.

stands for eyes and vision, which is suggestive of Queen Esther's spiritual vision, connecting her to the matriarch Sarah (Chesed) and the prophetess Avigail (Hod). According to the Torah, Esther—like Avigail, Sarah, and Rahab—is one of the four most beautiful women in the world.[13] All who gaze upon her believe she is of their ancestry.

With her vision, Esther demonstrates the nature of the Sefirah Malchut, which she represents. Malchut acts as a mirror. Like the moon, which is said to have no light of its own and reflects the light of the sun, it is this reflecting capacity that Esther possesses, making it possible for all to see themselves in her. As Esther 2:15 recounts, "Esther would find grace in the eyes of all who saw her. . . . She looked to each person like a member of his own nation."[14]

The King Searches for a Queen

Esther is living in Persia when King Achashverosh eliminates his wife, Vashti, for her refusal to come to him and his guests when she is called. After she is put to death, he begins searching for a new queen. For a period of four years, "Esther [is] hidden in the capital of Shushan" by Mordechai while women from all over the kingdom, perfumed and adorned with jewelry, are brought to the royal palace, prepared to audition before the king.[15] Nevertheless, when King Achashverosh learns that there is "one young girl more beautiful and gracious than all the maidens" who have been brought before him, he issues a decree "that every young girl who evaded the King's messengers [is] to be killed. Upon hearing the decree, Mordechai [brings] Esther his niece to the marketplace, and she [is] taken by the King's messengers."[16]

Upon being brought into the royal palace, Esther refuses to use any of the means of beautification employed by the other women. Hagai, who is responsible for preparing the women for their auditions for the king, asks Esther, "[W]hy do you not adorn yourself like all the women? If the

---

[13] Megillah 15a.
[14] Megillah 13a.
[15] Seder Olam Rabba 29.
[16] Targum Sheini 2:8.

King finds out, he will kill me, for you are more beautiful than them all." Esther replies, "I do not require anything."[17]

Her beauty is greater than that of all other women. This tells us that her adornment is from within—she is adorned by the grace and presence of the Creator's effluence. According to Esther 5:1, "Esther donned royalty, Divine inspiration clothed her."[18]

The King Marries Esther

"Achashverosh did not give a marriage contract or a dowry to any of the women he wed. Only to Esther, who was of a fine, distinguished family, did he give a marriage contract and dowry."[19] Here we learn explicitly that Esther comes from a distinguished Jewish lineage, connected as she is to the former king Saul of Israel, predecessor to King David, though at the time she weds the king, no one knows of her holy lineage.

Shabbat Reflects the Light of Olam HaBa

As the seventh and last prophetess to lead the People of the Book during the age of prophecy, Esther also represents the practice and purpose of Shabbat, the seventh day of the week. The outcome of God's Creation, Sabbath is Israel's partner, the bride of Israel. R. Chanina says, "Come, let us go forward to greet the bride, the queen!"[20] As we learned in chapter 3 on Sarah and Chesed, Shabbat includes the making of challah, the sacramental bread, and the lighting the two holy Shabbat candles. One candle bears witness to our obligation to remember (zachor) Shabbat and the other to guarding (shomer) Shabbat. Esther did both of these, even though she lived in the Persian royal palace.

The Seven Maidens (Seven Middot)

Queen Esther has seven maidens, and by their regulated rotation as her daily attendants, she is able to keep track of the days of the week and

---

[17] Aggadat Esther 2:15.
[18] Megillah 13b.
[19] Pesikta Rabbati 15:111; R.Yishai Chasidah, *Encyclopedia of Biblical Personalities,* 100.
[20] Baba Kamma 32b.

keep Shabbat without either the maidens or the king realizing she does so throughout her royal place as Queen of Persia. Others suggest that Esther converts all her maidens secretly.[21]

These seven maidens and the days upon which they serve the queen are: "Chulsa (the first of the weekday servants) served her on Sunday; Rukisa (skies), Monday; Genunisa (gardener), Tuesday; Nehorisa (light), Wednesday; Ruchshisa (animal), Thursday; Churphisa (quick), Friday; Reguisa (rest), the Sabbath. All of them were righteous and fit to prepare food for her."[22] We can see in this statement that the seven prophetesses are fit to embody and serve the Shechinah in the same way all seven maidens are fit to emanate to (serve) Esther, the final prophetess of the People of the Book.

The King of the Kelipot

The king in Esther's story is not the king of Israel, but the king who represents the kelipot, the dark side of creation. He, like other oppressors in the world, prevents peace and freedom for others. He represents the ability of our own evil inclinations to deprive us of inner peace and inner freedom. Through Haman, whom she defeats, Esther shows us how the animal nature, the *yetzer hara*, destroys life.[23]

Esther's Double

King Achashverosh marries Esther, but we are told that she does not have to suffer being forced to have conjugality with an uncircumcised man. The Midrash suggests she does not consummate her marriage with the

---

[21] Midrash Megillah, Otzar HaMidrashim. R. Yishai Chasidah, *Encyclopedia of Biblical Personalities,* 100.

[22] Targum Esther 2:9. R. Yishai Chasidah, *Encyclopedia of Biblical Personalities,* 100.

[23] The king's marriage to the Jewish lineage of King Saul (Esther is from this family tree) is also the result of Saul's own failure to eliminate another former murderous king, the Amalekite king Agog. As we learned earlier, through Samuel the prophet as a messenger of God, Saul is told to kill King Agog, the Amalekite people, and their animals. Saul fails to do so. The king impregnates a woman who gives birth before the prophet Samuel carries out God's command of eliminating the source of evil, Agog himself. Esther must accomplish in her generation what Saul fails to do in his: She must eradicate Haman, who, we are to understand, is the reincarnation of the Amalekite lineage.

king sexually, but that a type of demoness, her double, does so while she herself leaves the royal household and returns to her uncle Mordechai. We are also told that in Esther's ordeal, Mordechai sees a much greater story. He wonders, "How could such a righteous woman [be forced] to marry an uncircumcised [gentile? It must be that] a great calamity is to befall the Jews and they are to be saved through her."[24] Here we see that Mordechai, too, is capable of prophetic insight.

The Prophetess as Heroine

We are also told that while Esther lives in the royal household as queen, Mordechai takes up his station outside the gate but near enough so that Esther can ask him her Halachic (Jewish Law) questions about menses and other issues, and so he can be sure that Esther is well cared for. In a sense, then, Esther is the Jewish people's spy. This shows us that we are to "spy" on our evil inclination—keep an eye on it—and manage ourselves accordingly. This arrangement—Mordechai stationed by the gate—is made possible because Esther tells the king that other kings have had their advisers. For example, Nebuchadnezzar had Daniel the prophet. She convinced the king that he too needed an Israelite seer in his entourage.

In addition to keeping niddah (family purity) through using a double for consummation with the king, Esther keeps a kosher and observant life. As already mentioned, for example, she keeps track of the days of the week through her seven maidens, and even converts them secretly to Judaism.[25]

As in the stories of Miriam and Devorah, then, we see in Esther's story a conspiracy of women whose purpose in the life of Israel is to redeem the People of the Book from oppression. In Miriam's story it is to free the people from their Egyptian enslavement. Devorah leads the revolution against the Canaanites. Queen Esther delivers the people from their Persian oppressors.

---

[24] Esther Rabbah 6:5.
[25] Megillah 13a, Targum Esther 2:9.

The Evil Designs of Haman

The basic dynamic of Esther's story is that of holiness overcoming evil. The story shows us that redemption comes as a result of the refinement of humanity. Redemption is the designed outcome of humanity's ages, and the creation of the immortal body a consequence of that journey. The war between what are sometimes called the sons of light and the sons of darkness is played out in Esther's life and in the realm of Asiyah in which we all live. The particular characters that perform the various functions of this dynamic include Queen Esther; her uncle Mordechai; the king; and the king's viceroy, Haman, who wants to annihilate the Jewish people, just as the Amalekite king and Hitler attempt in their respective ages. Haman begins with a campaign to have Mordechai hanged. Through a series of banquets Esther convenes for the women and on the behalf of the king and Haman, she is able to interfere with Haman's plans.

Esther rectifies the light within the evil by turning it in favor of the Jewish people with the help of God. In this way, Esther elevates the sparks in Haman's evil plans. She allows his own pride to destroy him. Ultimately, Haman and his sons die in the manner designed for use against Mordechai: death by hanging from the gallows.

Dancing with the Bride

It is fitting that Esther's story, like that of Devorah, reflects two partnerships: one (with Mordechai) held in holiness, signifying life, and the other, to King Achashverosh, the kelipot, signifying death. Esther's very life—much like our own lives—reflects two worlds simultaneously. In Malchut we become aware of our dual nature and our ability to integrate both halves into a holy vessel, to elevate to good even the evil to which we are inclined. In Malchut, the realm of action, we learn about Esther's modesty as the Bride of Israel. As we discovered in our study of prophecy in chapter 1, humility is the foundation for receiving the holy spirit or higher levels of prophecy.

Malchut, the kingdom over which Moshiach has sovereignty, is the realm in which Israel is wed to the Creator. In the ritual of dancing with the bride (Malchut), Queen Esther is commemorated. The bride,

Moshiach, and Israel all express the elevation of life to holiness, the climax of the light's descent, being its return. When our rabbis ask, "What do we sing to the bride when we dance for her?" we have already learned. "When R. Dimi came [from Eretz Yisrael] he said: This is what they sing to a bride in Eretz Yisrael, 'She needs no eye makeup, no cosmetics, and no braiding [of the hair], and still she is a graceful gazelle.'"[26]

All rituals have numerous levels and hidden meanings, which are reflected in the various Jewish holidays. Each represents some configuration of Sefirot and their proper combinations, and each has an order and purpose.

The Sefirot and Holidays

We can see many other instances in the Torah where the People of the Book are themselves called the Groom or Bride of Israel. During the celebration of the Torah on Simchat Torah, we make seven circuits around the synagogue with the scrolls of the Ark, as the bride circles the groom during their wedding ceremony. We dance with the Torah scrolls as we dance with the bride at her wedding. Also, a prominent Torah-observant man is given the opportunity to end and begin the Torah reading for the year. Called the Chatan of the Torah—the Groom of the Torah—an open covering usually made from men's tallit (prayer shawls) is held over the worshipper, just as the open-sided chuppah, the bridal canopy, stands over the bride and groom during their wedding ceremony.

Esther and the Celebration of Purim

Modesty is the precursor to prophecy, which is itself a brilliant radiance (zohar). Modesty is a concealment of our own desire and a bonding to the Creator. In her modesty, Esther becomes even more radiant, making her the woman desired most by the king of Persia.

The Chazal teach us that along with Chanukah, Purim, the holiday that celebrates Esther's life and the miracles God did for the Jewish people as a result of their repentance, will be the only holiday that the Jewish people will celebrate after Moshiach comes. Purim represents the culmi-

---

[26] R. Yaakov Ibn Chaviv, *Ein Yaakov,* Ketubot, "Dancing for the Bride," 377.

nation of all Jewish observance, and Malchut represents the culmination of creation. Esther, then, as a heroine, is the queen of redemption, the final repository for all of humankind. Each of us has a part to play in the redemption of the world and humanity.

Esther means "hidden" and Megillah means "revealed." Purim is primarily about the future: God's radiance will be revealed in its completeness. After wiping out human egoism (Amalek or Haman), the holy Temple will be built for the indwelling of the Shechinah, the final resting place of God's glory, and the arrival of Moshiach.

Shechinah and Esther

The holiday of Purim honors the queen's victory with the help of God's mercy. The story of Esther's victory comes with the rigor of a three-day fast and prayer period so that when she is ready to go to the king with her petition, she is endowed with the presence of God, the Shechinah.

> Now it came to pass on the third day [of the fast] Esther donned royalty and stood in the inner court of the king's palace facing the king's house while the king was sitting on his throne in the throne room facing the chamber's entrance. When the king noticed Queen Esther standing in the court, she won his favor. The king extended the gold scepter that was in his hand, and Esther approached and touched the tip of the scepter.[27]

Though the law forbids entering the king's chamber without being summoned, Esther does so after preparing herself through fasting and prayer. We learn that she has been so weakened by three days of abstinence from food and by her vigorous petition and praise of the Creator that the king notices her changed appearance. We are also told that God sends an angel to extend the king's hand and his scepter, a sign of acceptance by him and an indication that all of these events occur through divine intervention. The king then asks Esther what her petition is; even if she wants half the kingdom, her request will be granted. Instead, she

---

[27] Megillat Esther 5: 1–2.

asks that the king and Haman come to a banquet that she will prepare and "tomorrow I will do the king's bidding."

During the banquet, the king again asks Esther what she desires. She replies that she wants them to come to yet another banquet on the following day. That night the king is unable to sleep and reads his own journal, a record of his rule. In it he discovers that Mordechai prevented the king's assassination, even though the official record, which Haman controls, removed Mordechai's name and inserted Haman's. Realizing that Mordechai had saved his life, the king asks his page, "[W]hat honor or dignity has been conferred on Mordechai for this?"[28] Learning that nothing has been done, the king asks, "[W]ho is in the court?" Haman has just arrived and is planning to come to speak to the king about hanging Mordechai on the gallows that he had his men erect during the night. The king then instructs the page to let Haman enter, whereupon the king asks Haman, "What should be done for the man whom the king especially wants to honor?" Of course, Haman in his arrogance thinks that the king is referring to himself and replies,

> For the man the king especially wants to honor, have them bring a royal robe that the king has worn and a horse that the king has ridden, one with a royal crown on his head. Then let the robe and the horse be entrusted to one of the king's most noble officers, and then attire the man whom the king especially wants to honor, and parade him on horseback through the city square proclaiming before him, "This is what is done for the man whom the king especially wants to honor."[29]

Later, the king's chamberlains arrive at Haman's home, where he has gone, to bring him to the second banquet Esther has arranged. At this second banquet, King Achashverosh asks Esther, "[W]hat is your petition, even if it be up to half the kingdom, it shall be fulfilled."[30]

Esther then asks for her life and that of her people, telling the king

---

[28] Megillat Esther 6:3.
[29] Megillat Esther 6:7–9.
[30] Megillat Esther 7:2.

that this wicked Haman has decreed that all of her people will be slain. At this point in the story, Haman trembles in terror before the king and queen. It is the first time the royal couple is discussed as a unit. The king retreats to the palace garden for a moment while Haman remains to beg Queen Esther for his life, prostrating himself "on the couch upon which Esther was; so the king exclaimed upon finding Haman there, 'would he actually assault the Queen while I am in the house?'"[31]

As a result of what the king learns and sees, Haman and his ten sons are hanged on the gallows made for Mordechai. This suggests that all ten Sefirot of the kelipot—recalling that for everything that is good, there is an evil counterpart—were eliminated. King Saul had failed to eliminate this root in King Agog's descendants. Esther's request of King Achashverosh completes this rectification. Haman and his ten descendants, his Tree of Life, are eradicated. This suggests that in Malchut, in the kingdom of life, we have the capacity to elevate the sparks to goodness and peace. We can elevate the light concealed in everything. It is in the material world that spiritual rectification reaches its apex.

The king then distributes Haman's estate to Queen Esther. Esther puts Mordechai in charge of the inheritance, with one-third going to Mordechai and Esther, one-third going to those who toil in the Torah, and one-third going to the construction of the Temple.[32] The queen then begs the king to cancel Haman's decree of genocide of the Jews. Achashverosh tells Esther to "write whatever you desire, in the king's name, and seal it with the Royal signet, for an edict," because such an edict is irrevocable.

The dispatchers carry Mordechai's handwritten decree saying, "[T]he king had permitted the Jews of every single city to organize and defend themselves; to destroy, slay, and exterminate every armed force of any people or province that threaten them, all with their children and women, and to plunder their possessions, on a single day, in all the provinces of King Achashverosh . . . upon the thirteenth day of the twelfth month, that is the month of Adar."[33]

---

[31] Megillat Esther 7:8.
[32] Shocker Tov 22:32.
[33] Megillat Esther 8:10–12.

We are taught that Haman and the holiday that celebrates the triumph of good over evil serve as a remembrance that God will save the Jewish people, just as he saved them from Haman's decree.

Mordechai Is Esther's Male Spiritual Counterpart

As we saw with the previous six prophetesses, Queen Esther has a male spiritual counterpart: Sarah has Abraham; Miriam has her brothers, Moses and Aaron; Devorah has Barak; Chanah has Eli, the High Priest; Avigail has King David; Chuldah has King Josiah; and Queen Esther has Mordechai.

Esther is instructed by Mordechai to risk her life for the sake of the people. If she does not take this risk, he says that another redeemer will come, but, he asks, what will become of Esther's own lineage and the House of Saul? Esther speaks to him "improperly" and says: "Now I have been summoned to come to the king . . ." (Megillat Esther 4:11). He is angry with her and replies, "If you persist in keeping silence . . . you and your father's house will perish" (Megillat Esther 4:14). Esther then replies to him properly—"Assemble all the Jews . . . and fast for me . . . then I will go in to the king" (Megillat Esther 4:16) and Mordechai acknowledges that what Esther says is right: "and he did exactly as Esther commanded him" (Megillat Esther 4:17).[34] As Esther's male counterpart, Mordechai himself is later elevated to the position of the king's right-hand man after he is almost put to death by Haman.

How to Achieve God's Mercy

The facts in Esther's story, particularly her fasting and determination to risk her life, show us that God's mercy follows our devotion and sacrifice. The eradication of Amalek is the eradication of the evil nations, meaning the bad attributes of each of our middot. Using Haman's arrogance, Esther lets him assume that the banquets she is preparing are in his honor, that he alone is invited to the celebrations. Yet Esther knows from her righteous upbringing that "pride goes before

---

[34] Tanna d'Bei Eliyahu Rabbah, R. Yishai Chasidah, *Encyclopedia of Biblical Personalities*, 100.

ruin."[35] She teaches us two things by this wisdom: Our own arrogance will be our downfall, stemming as it does from concentrated selfishness. In addition, when we are confronted by the evil in a situation (the kelipot), in order not to succumb to its power, we need only appear to be unaware of this evil, all the while turning our hearts and minds to God for guidance.

King Saul and Amalek, Queen Esther and Haman

Esther shows us in another way how we may sometimes find ourselves in situations whose root we cannot see but are to remedy. Rather than feeling powerless as victims, for guidance we need to recall Esther's wisdom and courage. During Saul's lifetime, Samuel the prophet tells him that God has ordered Saul to kill Amalek. Yet Saul fails to do so, thinking he knows best. The task falls instead to Samuel. Esther, King Saul's descendant, has a responsibility to complete what her lineage in Saul did not. Amalek (referring to King Agog and the Amalekite people) as well as Haman represent the same dark forces of evil attempting to eliminate the light. Without having a sword of iron, but instead having only prayer and fasting at her disposal, Esther brings down the evil of Amalek as Haman with her faith in God. Esther rectifies the flaw of King Saul.

Here, in Esther's story, we see the Chassidic teaching that the living person can add blessings to the deceased and the lesson that we can perform loving acts of kindness even for those who no longer live. We can each rectify the sins of our ancestors through our own right actions. In this way, we are also given confirmation that all of humanity and each link in the chain of incarnations we experience are interconnected.

It is said that when Saul becomes king, prophecy is removed from him, but divine inspiration remains with him so that he can judge correctly the cases brought before him,[36] yet we see that Esther as queen is elevated spiritually and is endowed with the presence of the Shechinah.

---

[35] Proverbs 16:18.
[36] Zohar 2:15a.

The Freedom of the Soul

R. Avraham Brandwein teaches that Amalek is the root of doubt. The Chazal say that "there is no joy so great as the elimination of doubt."[37] In the Purim celebration, we are obligated to drink wine until we see only the good in everything. This is an experience of the light of Chochmah, wisdom, which comes from the drinking of wine (moral order, Devorah, Tiferet). Dressed in masks and disguises of all sorts, the celebrants in Purim come to a state of having conquered Amalek within and without. We experience the eradication of division between the animal soul and the divine soul. As on the day of Purim, we acknowledge that we are cursed be Amalek and rejoice in the soul's freedom. The phrase "blessed is Mordechai" is said in order to experience the shine of the holiday that infuses each of us with the same divine light of the Torah that infuses Queen Esther. God's hiddenness in nature (current events) shows us that we and all of nature are subservient to the one Creator. The chronicle of Esther takes place over nine years, and God's name is never mentioned in the story, to accentuate further the hiddenness of the miracle of redemption.

Megillat Esther and the Role of Women

Megillat Esther, one of the five Megilot[38] the Jewish people read each year, and the most popular read from a scroll today, exists because of Esther's insistence that it become part of the sacred writ of the People of the Book. Because she has already been entered into the records of Persia, she reminds the sages that she is already known throughout the world. She then asks them forthrightly, "[S]hould not our people know of the miracles God did for us?" Esther points out that after three days of vigilance and a daily fast broken by an evening meal, the miracle of Purim includes an uncustomary fast on Pesach. Pesach's two-day ceremonies include a communal meal and ritual reading of the story of deliverance from Egypt. Pesach is a holiday on which the People of the Book do not fast. So she says to the assembly of elders that without the Jewish people,

[37] R. Avraham Brandwein, *Classical Kabbalah*, 97.
[38] The other four Megilot are Song of Songs, Ruth, Eichah (Lamentations), and Koheles (Ecclesiastes).

there would be no Pesach; without Esther, there would be no Purim. She is making clear that Pesach, an etsbalished holiday, is hidden within Purim, another story of redemption.

Purim is a holiday in which women are required to take part, in particular to hear Megillat Esther read, for it is because of Esther and women's faith and righteousness that the redemption of the Persian Jews occurs. We are told that the conclusion of the Exodus is in the merit of the women, and we are told as well that the coming redemption and the arrival of Moshiach will be due to the righteousness of the women of the world. The seven prophetesses act as guides for this time period.

We might say, then, that the honoring of women represented by the Sefirah of Malchut can redeem Israel and the entire world. Each woman is a wife or mother and a natural vessel for the Shechinah. The seeds each woman bears in thought, speech, and action and in her children, students, or deeds in the world are the offspring of King David, the royal lineage of which we are all part. Esther is the resurrection of God's promise as made to us with Sarah and Abraham. The cycle is completed as we emanate from within all that has been poured into us from without. The upper and lower waters meet.

The Importance of Prayer of the Righteous

According to the teachings of the People of the Book, God yearns for the prayer of the righteous, withholding rain until Adam prays for it. Likewise, when Esther fasts and asks the people to fast and pray with her, God rains down mercy upon the people, thereby seeing to the eradication of Haman, the personification of evil. We are to pursue the eradication of Amalek, the eradicatation of arrogance in ourselves and in the world. Prayer brings illumination that comes from Malchut and returns to Keter. Prayer, the proper and holy use of speech, is the returning light.

From Watchfulness to Resurrection

In the chapter of the Aggadah called Sotah, we learn of a sequence of qualities that each give birth to the next and that, when added together, lead to resurrection.

R. Pinchas b. Yair used to say: Watchfulness leads to zeal, zeal to cleanliness, cleanliness to restraint, restraint to purity, purity to holiness, holiness to humility, humility to fear of sin, fear of sin to saintliness, saintliness to the possession of the holy spirit, the holy spirit to the revival of the dead; and the revival of the dead comes through Elijah of blessed memory. May the Almighty make us worthy to witness his coming speedily in our days. Amen.[39]

Chanukah and Purim

Just as there will be two Moshiachs, Moshiach Ben Joseph (Yesod, Chanukah) and Moshiach Ben David (Malchut, Purim), it is interesting that under Chuldah the implements of the Temple were hidden and they will be concealed under Moshiach Ben Joseph, who, like Chuldah, is associated with Yesod. Likewise, the lineage and royalty of Esther are revealed under Esther just as B'nai Yisrael's true identity will be revealed to the world through Moshiach Ben David.

Though we associate Purim with Esther, her *chag* (holiday) is, according to one tradition, in Yesod rather than Malchut—and Chanukah, which we associate with King David, is in Malchut. In this book, we place Chanukah in Yesod. Esther and Purim reflect the light of Yesod (Chuldah and Chanukah) and begin the process of the ascent of the Etz Chayim. In this way they are one—Malchut, like the moon, being the reflector. Thus we might expect from Purim, when disguise is used to learn about concealment, that Moshiach Ben Joseph could be in disguise and present himself from Shiloh, the resting place of the Shechinah; Moshiach Ben David will be known by the heritage of the rebuilding of the holy Temple in Jerusalem.

Chuldah and Esther, Yesod and Malchut, show us the deep interconnection between these two and the Sefirot they occupy. As to whether Chanukah is best placed in Yesod and Purim in Malchut or vice versa is not as important as seeing the interrelatedness of the two Sephirot and their holidays, just as Shiloh and Jerusalem or the two Moshiachs are

---

[39] Megillah 14b.

connected. They represent the conjugality of man and woman, Creator and the created.

The Chazal teach us that these two Rabbinically ordained holidays will remain after Moshiach comes, because both are the revelation of God above nature. Each holiday celebrates the triumph of the Jewish people over the normal course of history and over the nations that sought to destroy them. We are told that those who bless Israel shall be blessed and that those who curse Israel will be cursed.

Origin of Chanukah and the Eternal Flame

"God spoke to Moses, Saying 'command the Children of Israel that they shall take for you pure olive oil, pressed for illumination, to kindle a continual lamp. Outside the partition of the Testimony in the Tent of Meeting, Aaron shall arrange it, from evening to morning, before God, continually; an eternal decree for you. On the pure Menorah shall he arrange the Lamps, before God continually.'"[40]

Hillel the Elder taught that each day of Chanukah, we increase the light of the emanation from God. Beit Shammai taught that we begin with eight lighted lamps and reduce one each night, thus showing a diminishing light. The Arizal, however, taught that every day is an increase, that creation is always an addition. Furthermore, the seven nights of Chanukah correspond to the seven middot of refinement and the arrival of the Queen, the holy Malchut dressed in the raiment of her glory—just as the lamps of Aaron and the Kohen Gadol (High Priest) find their place in Malchut with Queen Esther. On the eighth day of Chanukah, the entire assembly is elevated above nature. The progressive ascent of the light makes possible the return of the light in Malchut. The Daughter is returned to the Mother, Shechinah is returned to Zion, and Zion is returned to God. (Eight lights conceal the miracle of Yesod—the promise and the covenant of the circumcision of the male baby, which takes place on the eighth day of life.) Chanukah (Yesod) shows us that Chuldah's teachings about the World

---

[40] Exodus 27:20.

Figure 9.1. Eastern Gate of Mercy, through which tradition teaches that Moshiach Ben David will enter Jerusalem.

to Come facilitate Esther's teaching on redemption and resurrection.

The Temple was rededicated on Chanukah, and the restoration of the Jewish people's heritage passed from Shiloh to Jerusalem, as it will in Moshiach's time. First will come Moshiach Ben Joseph on the Mount of Olives as Yesod, from where the olive oil for the menorah was derived, and then Moshiach Ben David will be revealed. Might there be date trees where he stands, given that the species associated with Esther is date honey?

Purim

Purim, the holiday of redemption, teaches us that we can elevate the sparks in everything, that even in evil there is concealed some holy light. By hiding her Jewish identity while queen of Persia, Esther tells us that our soul is concealed inside our body or our nation. Our identity is concealed. It is also the metaphor of the humble. Those living with humility can be great (as we learned, with great light) and yet conceal their true identity as a mighty presence. Esther shows us that this humility has a radiance all its own. It is the glory of God, the adornment of the Shechinah showing us that humility and dedication to the mitzvot and to the Torah enable us to attract the adornment of royalty in the deepest sense of the word. It is Hod at the spiritual pinnacle of perfection in Asiyah, the material world of action (Malchut).

Esther has all the riches of the land available to her as well as all the adornments of costume and makeup. She chooses to use none of them. Why, then, does Purim accentuate the act of dressing up, adorning ourselves in robes and masks and other accoutrements to conceal our identity? It does so in order that we might experience what it is to be hidden on the outside so that the inside can be revealed. We learn that no matter what dress we put on, what mask we use, that which is inside is still the same, regardless of external circumstance. The Neshamah (soul's pneuma, or breath) remains concealed, and only our conduct—what we do with our royalty, our possession of the holy body—determines the merit we earn in the World to Come.

It is said that what is hidden receives blessings; what is not counted receives the protection of God. The capacity to hide our light or true standing as members of royal lineage is concealment for the benefit of blessings. This is precisely what Esther does, as the soul is hidden in the body. From this we learn that just as Moses veiled his face, there are times for concealment both of our own person and of God's presence. From this concealment, which is the combination of all seven middot, a pure light—a light like the refined, sweet date honey (redemption is sweet) and the oil (Yesod) that is on the altar and in the menorah—completes the journey from Sarah, where the first lamp is lit.

Esther's story revolves around concealment until we have overcome our own ego and fear of personal death and are able to cloak ourselves in the royal robes of the Holy Spirit, as Esther herself does after three days of fasting: "Divine inspiration clothed her."[41]

The entire purpose of prophecy and liberation is expressed by her risking her life for the benefit of the Jewish people. She does so for Israel and the world.

Esther, Malchut, and Shabbat

> [Shabbat] is a sign between Me and the children of Israel.
> EXODUS 31:17

As the seventh day of the week, Malchut stands for Shabbat. As the day of the week when the observant withdraw from worldly activities and focus on prayer and study of the Torah, Shabbat is the source of illumination for all the other days of the week. Rather than thinking we work all week in order to rest on Shabbat, we are told that we rest on Shabbat in order to work the rest of the week. This tells us that our behavior in our relationship to God determines the quality of the rest of our lives.

"For R. Shimon b. Lakish said: On the eve of Shabbat, the Holy One, Blessed be He, gives a Jew a Neshamah Yeteirah [an additional soul] and the conclusion of Shabbat He takes it away from him, for it says 'on the seventh day he rested and was refreshed'" (Exodus 31:17).[42]

Shalom Shalom

You should know that the Shechinah radiates with all its great rectifications, through a certain spiritual luminary, that takes first place. No other spiritual light is comparable to it, due to its abundant intensity and glory. This spiritual luminary is called Shalom. When this spiritual luminary is strengthened, in it every creation is attached from the smallest to the largest. When it will irradiate into them. Then will all be in great peacefulness. . . . You should know from where this spiri-

---

[41] Megillah 14b.
[42] Beitzah 16A.

tual luminary emerges, it is from a certain spiritual level. At the very beginning of creation, it was then, that this spiritual luminary became very strong. Why did it become so strong? Since, it became connected to the higher spiritual level that is also called Shalom. Then the lower spiritual luminary was also named Shalom, just like the higher one that illuminates it. When the upper Shalom, connects with the lower Shalom it says "I created the utterance of lips of, Shalom Shalom to the far and the close by" (Isaiah 57: 19). Then the spiritual sustenance is complete, and peace spreads out to all.[43]

The Ramchal teaches us that the purpose for the soul coming to the world is the rectification and illumination of the body, and that this will be ultimately corrected in the days of Moshiach.

It is regarding the soul that it says—"you are my son." However, regarding the body, which is already rectified it says—"and he said to me you are my servant." Regarding Israel who likewise have already been rectified it says: "Israel, in you I will be glorified" (Isaiah 49:3). The Truth is that the beauty of the holiness will intensify in the body more than in the soul, since this is the very reason why the soul is sent into the world, in order to rectify the body that starts at the lowest level—as is known. When the body is rectified it is said: "And, all flesh together will see" (Isaiah 40.5), and it will itself glow, just as—"the skin of Moses' face has become radiant" (Exodus 34:29).[44]

Esther is adorned with garments of light reflecting the nature of the Shechinah for Israel and Moshiach, and the Shechinah has various garments of light.

The Queen and the Inner Chamber
Esther's entry into the inner chamber of the king represents our ability to resurrect the body into a body of light, the throne upon which the

---

[43] R. Moshe Chayim Luzzatto (the Ramchal), *The Secrets of Redemption*, 132.
[44] Ibid., 3:95, 161.

Shechinah and God can rest, both Zion and Jerusalem, both body and soul. It is the same process represented by the High Priests' annual entry into the Holy of Holies on Yom Kippur (Yesod). In this instance we are given guidance about our preparation through fasting and prayer before seeking an audience with our God. In this way we are shown that minor and major fasts are preparatory for the body and soul in their ascent.

Redemption and Resurrection

The Ramchal's understanding of redemption and resurrection—a gift he has given us all—closes our study of prophecy and the prophetesses. In *Secrets of Redemption* he writes:

> In Isaiah (61:10) we are told that "I will sure be glad in God, my soul will rejoice in my lord, when the prophets see the great happiness that Israel will experience at the time."
>
> . . . In this verse you will see a very hidden secret. You should know that there are two types of spiritual sustenance for the Shechinah. One is part of her, in order to rectify her various levels of spiritual light. Regarding this it says, "I will surely be glad in God." Gladness Shin (300) Vav (6) Nun (50) refers, we are shown "to the constant flow of spiritual sustenance, blessing after blessing." There is another type of spiritual sustenance that is for all her extended-forces especially Israel who are the children of God blessed be He and the Shechinah. Regarding this it says "my soul will rejoice in my Lord." "Rejoicing"— concerns the righteous one as well, but (it is used in this context) of a father "to" Israel who are righteous, because from them they were formed and we emerged, the hint to this is: "the father of the righteous one will surely rejoice" (Proverbs 23, 24). Therefore it says: "My soul will rejoice in my Lord." "He says: 'For He has dressed me in the garments of salvation'" (Isaiah ibid). The secret is the garments that cover the body. Every garment is external. And is from the judgment, since loving kindness is hidden within. During the exile the garments were gloomy and darkened; the secret of the shell that surrounds the inside. Therefore, because of this, the light is obscured and does not shine.

However at the time of redemption, then the garments will be, "garments of salvation. The judgments are called so, since it is on the left side, and the truth is that these garments come from there."

Surrounding all [it says]: "A cloak of righteousness He has wrapped me with, this is the precious and honorable cloak that is given to her from the King. It is given at the time of the connection it is called righteousness, because righteousness is the higher [spiritual] connection."

All these garments are expressions of how the higher levels radiate the Shechinah, and thus are revealed by the Shechinah during the redemption period.[45]

GEMATRIA

Malchut the Moon

moon לבנה/ ל: Lamed (30) ב Bet (2) נ Nun (50) ה Hay (5) = 87

Interestingly, Malchut is the Sefirah referred to traditionally as the moon. As the symbol for the Shechinah, it is helpful to understand what the sages have taught over the centuries about blessing the New Moon, a tradition in Judaism for which women in particular should be mindful.[46] "R. Acha b. Chanina said in the name of R. Yochanan: Whoever blesses the New Moon in its proper time is regarded like one who greets the Shechinah. For one verse says, 'This month' (Exodus 12:2), [referring to the New Moon]: and elsewhere, when the Israelites witnessed God's majesty at the parting of the Sea, it says, 'this is my God and I will glorify him.'"[47]

661: The Numeric Value of Esther's Name

Esther אסתר: א Alef (1) ס Samech (60) ת Tav (400) ר Reish (200) = 661

Completing our examination of Esther and the Sefirah of Malchut, as we did with the prophetesses preceding her, let us see what her name reveals.

---

[45] R. Moshe Chayim Luzzatto (the Ramchal), *The Secrets of Redemption*, 3:91, 151.
[46] Here we see Chesed (Sarah) and Rosh Chodesh in Malchut (Esther).
[47] Sanhedrin 42a.

As with the six prophetesses who precede her, we see in all of these Parshiot qualities that Esther embodies in her life and story. As we have learned, our names instruct the body and soul about our purpose.

shall I be hidden אסתר (Genesis 4:14): א Alef (1) ס Samech (60) ת Tav (400) ר Reish (200) = 661

Cain speaks to God: "Behold, you have banished me this day from the face of the earth—shall I be hidden from Your presence? I must become a vagrant and a wanderer on earth; whoever meets me will kill [me]!" God then says that whoever kills Cain before seven generations have passed will be punished. "And God placed a mark upon Cain, so that none that meet him might kill him. Cain left the presence of God and settled in the land of Nod, east of Eden."

Here we witness once again the important rectifications of the holy sparks out of the kelipot (shells of evil) that take place over a period of seven days, seven years, or seven millennia. In this sense, concealed in Esther is the reflection of this cycle of seven: in the seven maidens who serve her and by whom she identifies the days of the week. In a certain sense, she has the protection of the seven Sefirot, each serving her purpose as the seven years serve the rectification of Cain's sin of killing Abel. Here we find the subject of being hidden.

you will bring down והורדתם (you will have brought down, Genesis 42:38): ו Vav (6) ה Hay (5) ו Vav (6) ר Reish (200) ד Dalet (4) ת Tav (400) ם Mem (40) = 661

Jacob speaks to his sons, who are preparing to return to Egypt to prove their trustworthiness to Joseph as viceroy. Reuben argues for taking the youngest brother, Benjamin, with him. Jacob answers: "My son shall not go down with you, for his brother is dead and he alone is left. Should disaster befall him on the journey which you shall take, then you will have brought down my hoariness in sorrow to the grave."

The descent into the kelipot (Egypt) to rescue the sparks is a dangerous enterprise. **My Son** is Zeir Anpin, the six middot that precede Malchut. Taking the youngest son, Yesod, into Egypt, is tantamount to the Akeidah, a sacrifice of an heir. Jacob is concerned for the fate of B'nai Yisrael. This is a similar situation to that of Esther approaching the king when doing so is customarily a reason for being put to death. Nevertheless, she descends into the king's chamber, the king of evil, hence elevating the sparks that are there through the accompanying presence of the Shechinah.

and that which remains והנתר (that is left, Exodus 12:10): ו Vav (6) ה Hay (5) נ Nun (50) ת Tav (400) ר Reish (200) = 661

"You shall not leave any of it until morning; any of it that is left, morning you shall burn in the fire. . . . So shall you eat it; your loins girded, your shoes on your feet, and your staff in your hand; you shall eat it in haste—it is a Pesach offering to God." Here we see once again the accentuation of Malchut as the moon (collecting manna under the moonlight)—the role of Malchut in determining the holidays and Rosh Chodesh (the New Moon). What is not eaten under the moon's presence must be destroyed. What is not endowed by the divine Shechinah should be burned. The Pesach offering is also the finding of *chometz* (leavened wheat) the night before Pesach, and what is found is burned the following day before the Pesach Seder. (This symbolizes burning away the ego and pride.) It is said that the evening prior to the morning on which Haman's evil decree is to have been carried out is Pesach eve, when there occur open searches for the leftover chometz. It is said that Esther herself is involved in such a ritual and that this prevents her from knowing the scale of evil planned against her and the People of the Book.

The first Pesach offering and the ritual of chometz are united in our ritual experience to this day showing us the divine Shechinah and the service we do in her honor by marking the end of the Egyptian exile. That this falls in words related to Esther suggests that she signifies the ending of our exile—the ending of the divine Shechinah's exile and the return of Israel's Bride. In addition, as we have learned, the Chazal teach that in messianic times, the moon will once again be as visibly bright as the sun.

and their bones וְעַצְמֹתֵיהֶם (Numbers 24:8): ו Vav (6) ע Ayin (70)
צ Tzadee (90) מ Mem (40) ת Tav (400) י Yod (10) ה Hay (5) ם Mem
(40) = 661

Balaam's third blessing: "It is God who brought him out of Egypt according to the power of His Loftiness, he will consume the nations that oppress him and crush their bones, and his arrows shall pierce them. He crouched and lay down like a lion cub—which can stand him up? Those who bless you are blessed and those who curse you are accursed."

It is a great calamity to have our bones crushed into dust, for then, we are told in the Chassidic writings, we cannot be resurrected. It is said that a bone residing at the base of the skull may be the source from which the resurrected body is informed, while other teachings say it is the bone memory itself in the afterlife that is restored to form, with all previous bodily deformities corrected.

Your word אִמְרָתְךָ (Deuteronomy 33:9): א Alef (1) מ Mem (40)
ר Reish (200) ת Tav (400) כ Caf (20) = 661

This is Moses' blessing upon the Children of Israel before his death: "The one who said of his father and mother, 'I have not favored him'; his brothers he did not give recognition and his children he did not know; for they [the Levites] have observed Your word and Your covenant they preserved. They shall teach Your ordinances to Jacob and Your Torah to Israel; they shall place incense before Your presence. and burnt offerings on Your Altar. Bless, O God, his resources, and favor the work of his hands; smash the loins of his foes and his enemies, that they may not rise."

In this passage we are shown the destruction of arrogance and desire for power. Moses praises the steadfast loyalty and "bravery of the Levites in the wilderness and blessed them as the teachers of the nation." Esther's own courage and keeping of Shabbat and the Kosher diet make her the minister to God and teacher to B'nai Yisrael. Esther keeps the word of the Torah and helps to preserve the covenant just as the Levites do during their time.

SUMMARIZING THE IMPORTANCE
OF ESTHER

We see that Esther's story is ultimately a parable for the journey of the Shechinah and the rectification of the shells that encase the light of the Creator on earth, preventing the ultimate revelation of its shine. King Achashverosh desires the light that he himself cannot receive. Esther's own status in his kingdom is spiritually greater than his own, for he represents the shells of evil (kelipot) themselves.

Similarly, just as the people stand with Esther and undertake fasting and prayer for three days, "the Shechinah and the Moshiach both stand together and do not separate from each other. . . ."[48] Thus we see that the Shechinah, the light of the Creator contained in all life forms, is revealed through our awareness. Redemption and resurrection are therefore states of awareness that ultimately herald, like the great sounding of the shofar, the thousand years of peace, when Shalom Shalom (peace peace) shall be heard and seen throughout the world. This is the precedent to eternal resurrection of the holy human, the Adam Kadmon from whom each of us is created. The miracle of Esther is the last of all miracles recorded in scripture.[49] What she stands for is not only the last stage of humanity's development but also the beginning of a new world for all, a time of world peace, shalom.

The very last section of the oral tradition's record is a tractate called Uktzin. It is the final Mishnah of the Talmud. In it we are told the reason for shalom. "R. Shimon b. Chalafta said: the Holy One, blessed be He, found no vessel that could hold the blessing for Israel except peace, as it says: God will give might to His nation, God will bless His nation with peace" (Psalms 29:11).[50]

We have seen in our journey through the seven Sefirot and the lives of the seven holy women of Israel their connection to the *sechol* (intellect)

---

[48] R. Moshe Chayim Luzzatto (the Ramchal), *The Secrets of Redemption,* 3:95, 158.
[49] Yoma 29a.
[50] R. Ibn Yaakov Chaviv, *Ein Yaakov,* Uktzin, 803.

and how all ten Sefirot function as a totality designed by the Creator for our own access to His glory, eternity, and peace. The seven prophetesses contribute successfully the qualities inherent in this holy template. Progressing as we have together from Chesed to Gevurah to Tiferet to Netzach to Hod to Yesod and, finally, to Malchut, we learn that we all have the same capacity as the prophetesses to make our kingdom holy.

Each of the seven prophetesses represents a stage in the progressive descent into matter of the holy immanence of the Creator, the Shechinah. In Sarah we begin our journey in life or in conceiving an idea or plan with loving-kindness. Miriam shows how to manifest or deliver an idea. We must use our strength in judgment to discriminate between what is good and what is not, what is useful and what is superfluous. Devorah establishes the method for harmonizing all of the parts into a beautiful whole, elevating all to its highest potential, making the whole moral and beautiful. Chanah reminds us that everything we do is for the Creator and that our attendance to God's will through action, prayer, and meditation leads to victory and eternity. What we do has lasting effect within and without. Avigail shows us that when we use all that we have in the world to serve the royal bloodline of which we are part, we give birth to holy children or ideas. When we sacrifice our egos for the benefit of the world, we experience the glory and splendor of God's divinity. Chuldah reminds us that how we do what we do on earth determines the outcome of our lives in the afterlife, or World to Come. Our lives are the covenant between the Creator and the created, and this is the foundation of living a meaningful and holy life.

Finally, Esther reveals that when we are aware of all of these stages of development that we must perfect, we complete our assignment of being God-like in both our personal and our global kingdoms. We redeem the sovereign human made in the image of God as eternal beings. We inherit an eternal body as a companion to our eternal soul. This is the true meaning of the sovereign kingdom, which Malchut and Esther reflect.

10

The Shechinah
The Divine Immanence of the Creator

*Come, let us go up to the mountain of the Lord, to the
Temple of the God of Jacob, and He will teach us of His
ways and we will walk in His paths. For from Zion
will the Torah come forth, and the word of God from
Jerusalem.*

ISAIAH 2:3

To assimilate all that we have learned about the prophetesses and the
seven-stage descent of the Shechinah, the Divine Immanence of the
Creator, we conclude our journey with the seven holy guides through a
deeper exploration of what is meant by the Shechinah and the relationship of this presence of God to prophecy, the prophetesses, and our world
and lives.

PROPHECY: NAVIAH

Prophecy (the three-letter root) נבא: נ Nun (50) ב Bet (2) א Alef (1)

Stage 1: Humility. Prophecy, as we learned, depends on the merit of
the generation as well as the individual prophets. At all levels it is built
on the foundation of an individual's or community's humility and thus
the self-nullification of the individual and group. This humility—as

suggested by the first letter (Nun) of the root of the Hebrew word for "prophecy," "prophet," and "prophetess"—can be compared to the hollowing out of a vessel. Nun itself has been compared to a man bending forward in humility and prayer. Once we have as an objective of mind this goal of self-nullification—to overcome the animal nature, to make of our person a holy Temple in which the soul is given its kingdom and the heart is given its Tabernacle—then we are able to do the work (avodah) required to receive the Shechinah, which is sometimes called the Word of God.

Stage 2: Purification. The second letter of *prophecy* in Hebrew, Bet, is called the house or container, and its place in the middle of the word suggests that the ongoing process of separating the holy from the unholy—a process of perpetual self-improvement and ongoing balancing of the *yetzer tov* (good inclination) and the *yetzer hara* (evil inclination) or the selfless and selfish inclinations—is the way in which we are prepared for prophecy. How we live in our "house" (body) is important. The Shechinah, as an effluence of a particular vibration and quality, can rest only where a suitable vessel can hold the light without breaking.

Stage 3: Receiving the Creator's Word. The final letter, Alef, suggests the influx of the divine emanation, for the entire Alef-Bet is concealed in Alef. Equal to the number 1, Alef, as the last letter in the three-letter root of the Hebrew word for "prophecy," suggests that a prophetess must first cultivate humility and then ongoing self-purification, and finally, she must unite with the Creator and His Word, the Shechinah, to become one as receiver with the emanator. This is the sacred holy marriage: The individual or nation becomes one with God.

Or En Sof (Limitless Light) and Malchut (Female Vessel)

The vital energy that, like the prophetesses, each of us receives is from the holy light of the Creator as it descends gradually from the Or En Sof—the limitless light from the realm of emanation (Atzilut), the highest of the four worlds—into the material world (Asiyah), the lowest of the realms, where we exist. Once infused with this descending light, the soul is given information that flows from the Crown (Keter) into the mind of the prophet, who then becomes the mouthpiece of the Creator. The *peh* (mouth or Malchut) of Atzilut (emanation) is made visible in the peh (Malchut) of Asiyah (the physical world). In this way we see that the speaking human is the vessel through which the Creator is seen (Chochmah), heard (Binah), and known (Daat). In a sense, we are the garment the Shechinah wears in order to be known.

Speaking Words Creates Vessels for the Word of God

When prophecy is spoken, this effluence of supernal wisdom (Chochmah Illah—the Chochmah of Atzilut, or source of God's supernal radiance) coming from the word of God (Shechinah) fills the vessel made by those who speak. In addition, the testimonies of the prophetesses are in part mentioned and recorded in the Torah. These "vessels" have been kept alive and vivid through our repetition, attention, and understanding of them. All of Jewish ritual and celebration is based on this awareness. Each moment described in the Torah opens a window at the same time each year or time of month or day of the week or even hour of the day, in all realms simultaneously, for they are all interconnected. As long as there are people observing their faith, pronouncing the prayers, performing the mitzvot, these vessels in the world remain radiant, each doing its part in holding the light of the Creator. Just as the moon reflects the light of the sun today but in the future will have a light of its own, each of us will reach revelation and be illuminated, like the prophets and prophetesses of Judaism.

    R. Yehudah Leib Ashlag teaches that "[t]he Holy Zohar says: 'He is Shochen (lit. Dweller), and She is Shechina [sic] (lit. Divinity).'"[1]

---

[1] R. Yehudah Leib Ashlag (the Baal Ha'Sulam, 1882–1995), *Shamati* (What I Heard), edited by R. Avraham Mordechai Gottleib (Bnei Brak, Israel: Or Baruch Shalom, 2003), 27. "We should interpret its words: It is known with regard to the upper light, that they say that there is no change, as it is written, 'I the Lord change not.' All the names and appellations are only with respect to the Kelim [vessels] which is the will to receive contained in Malchut, being the root of creation, and from there it hangs down to this world, to the creatures."

The Prophetesses and the Seven Stages of Descent of the Shechinah

It is important to appreciate the meaning of Sarah and Chanah being on the right pillar; Miriam and Avigail being on the left; and Devorah, Chuldah, and Esther being in the middle. They are the embodiment of the Creator's mind and thus manifestations of the process by which the Shechinah descends into life. The descent of the Creator's light is literally described by the sequential lives of the seven prophetesses. Recalling that each Sefirah has an analogous body part and an inherent attribute of behavior, the prophetesses become the holy guides in our own perfection. They are examples of each Sefirah in its utmost purity. It is also vital to recall that there are elements of every Sefirah in each one of them in the same way that each of us has the genetic makeup of our parents and grandparents and great-grandparents. In other words, the vessels, or kelim, are the Shechinah that holds the upper light. All of creation has its root in Malchut, holding as it does the light of all preceding Sefirot. This book has focused especially on the descent of light through seven stages.

Seven Cycles of Seven

We experience the seven-stage descent in our emotional makeup. Recall that the upper three Sefirot of the Etz Chayim are called the intellect, sechel; the lower seven are called the emotions, middot; and the eternal grouping of seven is epitomized by the forty-eight prophets (with Moses being the forty-ninth) and the seven prophetesses, and is replete in the worship cycles for the People of the Book.

The seven prophetesses—representing the world of Asiyah, the physical world in which we live—reflect the seven cycles of seven, the same number of weeks and days in Sefirat HaOmer, the Counting of the Omer, between the second night of Pesach and Shavuot. As we have learned, Sefirat HaOmer is an annual process by which B'nai Yisrael prepare and purify themselves to receive the holy Torah. These forty-nine days are a Kabbalistic process by which each of the seven Sefirot are experienced, one each week for seven weeks, with the qualities of each Sefirah depositing some of its light into every other vessel. For instance, the first week of the Counting of the Omer is made up of Chesed of Chesed, Gevurah of Chesed, Tiferet of Chesed, and so on until Malchut of Chesed. The second week is Chesed of Gevurah, Gevurah of Gevurah, Tiferet of Gevurah, and so on until arriving in Malchut of Malchut (Malchut B'Malchut) on the forty-ninth day, the night before Shavuot, the holiday in which we celebrate the receiving of the Torah. On Shavuot, it is said we become the Groom who weds the Shechinah, or the Bride of Israel, before she unites with God. Shavuot, like prophecy, is the culmination of the self-purification process and devotion to God in total faith and love. The descent of the Shechinah through the lives of the prophetesses reflects this very reality in the life of B'nai Yisrael.

This shows us that the seven Sefirot are the vessels by which we are brought into rapport with the holy emanations of the Creator. As women upon whom the Shechinah rests and who have played prominent roles in the development of B'nai Yisrael, the prophetesses represent the development of the Shechinah in each phase of God's descent. It was for this reason that the sage R. Moshe Cordovero (the Ramak) shows that the prophetesses represent the seven Sefirot of the middot (emotions), and the holy Arizal says the seven middot have correspondence with the seven holy species of the land of Israel. The prophetess stands for the physical manifestation of spiritual fruit and the vessel projected from the highest realm of the Creator's mind into the physical world. The prophetesses thus help sustain us even to this day with their holy guidance and presence historically seated in particular Sefirot in the realm of Asiyah, the material world.

The Descent of Seven as a Ritual Process
This descent of Or En Sof in a process of seven stages is expressed in many rituals involving cycles of seven. As we learned earlier, there are seven complete steps we take to descend into the Mikvah (ritual bath for purification) and thus seven ascending steps we take to leave. The bride makes seven circuits around the groom at the chuppah. On Simchat Torah, the congregation makes seven circuits around the inside

of the sanctuary, carrying the Torah scrolls. Seven cycles of seven years occur before the fiftieth year, the jubilee or Shemitta, when everything and everyone is free from ownership. We can say that as a progressive development and as a template for personal and global evolution, we all seek union with the beloved Shechinah. There are seven stages through which we must progress, individually and collectively, to accomplish this goal, just as there are six days of creation followed by a seventh day, the Sabbath.

Union with Shechinah as Love Story

The Shechinah and the prophetesses are inseparable, for one is made of the vessels that receive prophecy and the others are the source of prophecy. The story of prophecy, both scientific and spiritual, is the essential divine love story. Prophecy reflects an eternal bond the Creator has made with the created. It is the way humankind and God speak to one another in an intimate fashion.

This love story, energized by prayer, is also reflected in our own lifetime. In marriage, two people can be close and tender, committed and selfless. Yet the contrary experience of partners feeling separate, disconnected, and distant from one another is also descriptive of marriage and can also portray our separation from the beloved Creator and His Shechinah—what is most often referred to as exile.

Thus, the seven stages of descent are also seven stages of ascent, which Kabbalah describes in particular. This may explain a popular observation that there are seven-year stages or phases in our lives and marriages in terms of emotions and development.

Song of Songs is a beautiful telling of this love story between the Creator and the created, the male and female expression of the one divine source, the one God. In Judaism, it is the love story between God and Israel. A successful marriage blends both partners' talents into one united whole, which acts as a repair in the world, bringing greater harmony to the world and family. Therefore, the union of male and female is not just the story of the prophet and prophetess and God, but also the love story that describes the union of each of our souls and God.

ADAM KADMON: OUR SPIRITUAL DNA

We are each composed of both masculine and feminine energies, with a woman being more female than male and a man being more male than female. Our inherent design is the story of the descent of the light—the seven days of creation, with six active days and the seventh day of rest. When we use this pattern as a guide and model our lives on it, as the Torah and observant Judaism describe, we allow the divine form, Adam Kadmon (heavenly or primordial man), to express itself through us. We turn on all the circuits to the divine immortal blueprint enlivening us and underlying every nerve and synapse that occurs in our bodies and in everything we think, say, or do.

Five Parts of the Soul

Likkutei Amarim Tanya by R. Shneur Zalman of Liadi, Russia, is one of the most revered Kabbalistic classics on the theology and science of Chassidut, whose foundation rests in the Torah and the Zohar. *Likkutei Amarim Tanya* teaches us that the soul has five distinct levels of being. During life, each of these soul parts is inseparable from the others but identifiable. To understand Adam Kadmon and the light that emanates from that perfected design for all of humanity, we must briefly turn our attention to the human soul, which, in Judaism, is said to be composed of five different elements, each with a root in a particular spiritual realm attached to a particular physical organ in the body. This will help to explain the various experiences in prophecy, from the lesser degree of Ruach HaKodesh to Sarah's direct communication with God.

The first three of the five aspects of soul in ascending order, beginning with the Nefesh as the densest of the soul vehicles or the one closest to the physical world, are contained within the body, while the last two are outside the body.

The **Nefesh (soul)** is located in the medium of the blood, liver, and skin. It relates to the world called Asiyah, the realm of action.

The **Ruach (spirit)** is located in the medium of the breath. It acts primarily through the nose and the sense of smell and is a function of the world of Yetzirah, or formation.

The **Neshamah (pneuma, or breath)** is exhibited through the ears and hearing and is connected to the realm of Beriyah, or creation.

The **Chayah (life force)**, as an aspect of the soul that resides outside of the body, is experienced and facilitated through the eyes. Seeing is a function from the realm of Atzilut, the world of emanation.

The **Yechidah (spark of God)** is identified as the skull in toto, the En Sof, the limitless light where Adam Kadmon, the perfected human, remains potentized as the root of our inevitable perfection and resurrection.

In Yechidah, the level of knowing with all our mind, heart, and soul is comprehensive without words, a type of whole knowing that is Chochmah (wisdom) combined with Binah (understanding), which together create the conditions for prophecy, an aspect of divine revelation.

The upper two realms, Yechidah and Chayah, are spiritual umbilical cords to the more refined and less material realms of existence considered the realms of emanation (Atzilut) and En Sof, the limitless light. The three components of the soul that reside within the body—the Nefesh, the Ruach, and the Neshamah—are responsive to communicating through images and are capable of a knowing beyond intellectual reasoning. They are vessels for receiving prophecy, enabling our reception of

World	Sefirah	Aspect of Soul	Sense
Adam Kadmon	Keter	Yechidah (spark of God)	Will
Atzilut (emanation)	Chochmah	Chayah (life force)	Seeing, thought
Beriyah (creation)	Binah	Neshamah (pneuma, or breath)	Hearing
Yetzirah (formation)	Chesed through Yesod	Ruach (spirit)	Smell
Asiyah (action)	Malchut	Nefesh (soul)	Speaking

divine wisdom through speaking, smelling, hearing, seeing, and feeling. These soul components give voice to the higher realms of emanation and creation, of which the physical world—the world of Asiyah, the realm in which we reside during life—is the final outcome.

The Soul Is Rooted in Heaven

We can say that if creation is a beginning, the physical world is an ending. If two parts of the soul remain inhabitants of the spiritual realms, their endings are in the physical realm. In this way, the soul is literally rooted to heaven while on earth, and while in heaven it is connected to earth through its good deeds and descendants. The soul's desire is performed by its ministers: the body and its harmoniously organized parts. We have learned that the garments of the soul are our thoughts, speech, and actions. While on earth, we are given the opportunity to embody the heavenly balance implanted in our makeup. We, like our forefathers, are given challenges to overcome. We wrestle between our divine soul—our good inclination, the yetzer tov—and our animal soul, or the selfish and therefore evil inclination of the yetzer hara. All of life is a product of this ongoing struggle between these two aspects of ourselves. Prophecy is one method the Creator has for increasing the desire for good, but it can come only to those who are themselves in greater self-possession through a devotion to God and His precepts as recorded in the Torah and other holy teachings.

Because the aspects of the soul that closely attend the body during life are also faculties or organs of life—the mouth, ears, eyes, and brain, all faculties that reside in the head—we can surmise that the soul is visible in the world through our experiences, including those of the body. The body, then, is a sort of actualizer, a capacitor for a certain type of information. Prophecy is the ultimate use by the Creator of the created human, with both the Creator and the created in total rapport and in conversation with one another.

The five levels of the soul—three of them residing in the body during its life and expressing themselves in our sensory organs—help explain why a prophet will sometimes hear, see, or even smell the hint of the divine.

The use of incense in ritual is better understood from this vantage point, showing us how it engages the Ruach aspect of the soul. In prophecy, one or more of these senses can be engaged. These are the organs of the soul, while our thought, speech, and action are its garments both in the physical world and in the World to Come.

DNA and the Etz Chayim

In our blood, the medium of the Nefesh of the soul, we see the polarity of male and female, positive and negative, which is the makeup of electromagnetism and the working of vital energy. All manifestation is based on this polarization and duality. We are dominated by this law. Just as the flow of our blood embodies our will and the Nefesh (the seat of the animal soul), the Neshamah (the seat of the divine soul) is reflected in our minds. This combining of male and female, the Creator and the Shechinah, is the process by which prophecy occurs and revelation and redemption for the entire world are made possible. Kabbalah's Etz Chayim is like the double helix of DNA. Each turn from one chamber (Sefirah) to another, connected by pathways, provides a type of energetic momentum that accounts for its ever-moving flow. The Sefirot also depict our nature and the way in which our masculine and feminine attributes (the masculine right pillar and the feminine left) are intermingled up and down, left and right, expanding and contracting, spiraling and returning, descending and ascending.

The indwelling presence of the Creator as the Shechinah and the King who is the one emanator show us the universal lovers whose whole being is built on truth (Keter), wisdom (Chochmah), and understanding (Binah) of the harmonious combination of opposites as well as of the visible and the invisible. It is through this refinement of harmonizing opposites that we experience divine knowledge (Daat) or ChaBaD (Chochmah, Binah, Daat).

Male and Female Union in Kabbalah

Experiencing the Shechinah is ultimately based on the harmonious union of male and female, the intuitive and rational capacities in the world and within ourselves. All human beings are the sons and daughters of the Creator. This balance in creation and manifestation is central to Judaic cosmology and human activity. In addition, it is the underpinning of much of Kabbalah and Jewish mysticism in general. In Kabbalah, the Shechinah is the Creator's Divine Immanence. In most instances, we encounter the Shechinah as a distinctly female quality of life, representing illumination, protection, and nurturance and acting as an accompaniment to prophecy.

Because the Shechinah is the facilitator of prophecy itself, it is important to examine what tradition teaches us about it. Yet it is vital to appreciate that for the People of the Book, God's Divine Immanence, though called the Queen or Bride, is not separate from God, as we find in many other world traditions. This Queen is not a separate deity, but rather a mode of God's divine presence. Simply put, when God is close to us as individuals or as a community, we can experience Him in His Immanence that we experience as female. This is why R. Ashlag cites the Zohar's explanation: "He is Shochen (lit. Dweller), and She is Shechina [sic] (lit. Divinity). The dweller is known by His presence which is called divinity."[2]

THE EXILE OF THE SHECHINAH

It is said that the Shechinah went into exile with the Jewish people after the destruction of the Second Temple in 70 CE, which is why the tradition claims that prophecy of the highest kind left the Jewish people at that time. Maimonides suggests that this exile was not the result of the general explanation given—the failure of the elders and the diminishing of the Sanhedrin (the court of seventy sages), which was ultimately abolished by the Romans—but instead the result of a diminishing of the imagination among all of Israel. According to the Rambam, imagination and courage are the two primary attributes necessary for the prophetic talent. Maimonides also teaches that with Moshiach's arrival, the imagination will be restored.

---

[2] Ashlag, *Shamati*, 27.

In *Tzava'at Harivash, The Testament of Israel Baal Shem Tov*, this Holy Sage of Chassidut, R. Israel Baal Shem Tov, writes that "[t]he Shechinah (the Immanence of the Creator) is in exile because all words of speech derive from Her and ought to be for the service of the Creator, but . . . our primary usage of words is for material matters, idle talk and falsehoods."[3]

The Aggadah tells us:

Come and see how much the Holy one, blessed be He, loves the Jewish people. For wherever they were exiled, the Shechinah went with them. When they were exiled from Egypt, the Shechinah was there, as it says, "Did I not appear to your ancestors' family when they were in the Egypt?" (1 Samuel 2:227). When they were exiled to Babylon, the Shechinah was with them, as it says, "because of you I was sent to Babylon" (Isaiah 43:14). When they were exiled to Edom [Rome] the Shechinah was with them, for it says "Who is this redeemer—[i.e., the Shechinah] that comes from Edom, with sullied garments from Botzarah" (Isaiah 63:11). And also in the future when they will be redeemed, the Shechinah will be with them, as it says, "God will then return with your returning exiles" (Deuteronomy 30:3).[4]

R. Baal Shem Tov also teaches that in the Zohar we learn that the Shechinah is the very root and source of all souls.[5] We are similarly taught that because of this connection between our souls and God, any ailment—physical, emotional, or spiritual—experienced by any of us is felt as well by the Shechinah, the embodiment of His presence in the world. In this way, we learn that the personal *tikkun* (repair) and *avodah* (work) we must do to correct flaws in our own natures—in our thoughts, words, and deeds—is a collective repair, not just an individual restoration. Throughout the world, we are all interdependent.

---

[3] R. Israel Baal Shem Tov, *Tzava'at Harivash, The Testament of Israel Baal Shem Tov*, 78.

[4] R. Yaakov Ibn Chaviv, *Ein Yaakov*, Megillah 29a, "The Shechinah Is with Us in Exile," 283.

[5] Every soul is a spark or "limb" of the Shechinah (Zohar 1:25a, Tikunei Zohar 3b).

The Shechinah in the Material World

Though the Shechinah seems to be separate from God, it is in fact one of the vehicles by which His presence is made known to the material world. In other words, as suggested here, the Shechinah is the Divine Immanence of the Creator when it is held inside a vessel and the light is given boundary. In the case of the prophetesses, it is in the realm of Asiyah and the Sefirah of Malchut as Nukvah, Daughter, in her totality. (See map 4 in chapter 2.) With regard to these seven prophetesses originating from the Or En Sof and hence Malchut of Atzilut, the highest realm of Malchut, their lives, like our own, are the result of the gradual descent of the Creator's emanation from the Or En Sof, the descent of the limitless light of the Crown to the material world in which we live and in which their lives take place.

Deeper study of Kabbalah reveals the intriguing depth of this statement, but for the sake of our brief exploration of how God manifests in ways we experience as a divine female quality in Judaism and how the Shechinah relates to the prophetesses and the process of personal and collective development, it is important to appreciate that this very subject dominates much of the Judaic mystical tradition. Ending the *galut* (exile) of the Shechinah, who is called by various names—Bride, Israel, Sabbath, and Beloved—is the primary objective of prayer, meditation, and Torah observance. These and other names are expressions of the Creator in relationship to the material world and our souls. In this sense, we can even use Shechinah to name the world, meaning that our collective soul is an integral part of the Shechinah's soul—all are created by the word of God.

The Shechinah Manifests in Judaism

Unlike other faiths, which may view the divine feminine as separate from the Creator, as a separate being in exile, in Kabbalah this dynamic partnership of male and female attributes is a unity reflected by humanity's refinement and by the Jewish people's role of becoming a Torah-observant community. In our collective refinement, we become vessels for holding the higher light of emanation from the Creator. The more refined we become, the greater our desire for closeness to the Creator, the more refined the light, and the higher we ascend in the spiritual worlds. The reason for this becomes clearer as we review what others have taught for centuries about this feminine form of the elusive yet fundamental immanence of God. It would take volumes to portray accurately the many points of view regarding the Shechinah and how to describe God's being as both masculine and feminine, with each aspect having a different purpose—yet this notion remains central to Jewish mysticism and comprises a unity rather than any inherent separation.

Here are a few examples of the many different ways in which the Shechinah is approached as a subject and how the male–female balance reveals itself in the way the Creator of the universe participates in the constant creation of the world—which is much as we participate in both the procreation of humanity and the ongoing refinement of the world and ourselves through our words, thoughts, and deeds.

The weekdays and Shabbat. R. Aryeh Kaplan points out that even in the structure of the week, we encounter this mysterious Kabbalistic balance of male and female: "The six weekdays are masculine, while the Sabbath is feminine. During the six weekdays, the world is renewed through the original momentum of creation, and therefore they pertain to the past (masculine). But on the Sabbath we partake of the World to Come—the ultimate future—the world when all will be Sabbath."[6] Here Kaplan is referring to the fact that Chesed through Yesod is called the Son, Zeir Anpin. These six Sefirot are related integrally, for it is in Zeir Anpin that we learn to integrate polarities of our emotional life: Chesed (mercy) and Gevurah (judgment), Netzach (enduring effort) and Hod (total humility). We are taught in Chassidut that in the spiritual realms, opposites do not combine—that only on earth, through human beings, can these opposites be integrated thoroughly.

The holy family of life. In the Tree of Life there are a right, middle, and left pillar, and the human is sometimes called the middle pillar. This tells us that Tiferet—itself a vessel but also the name used when we speak

---

[6] R. Aryeh Kaplan, *Immortality, Resurrection, and the Age of the Universe,* 58.

of the entire Partzufim of Zeir Anpin (the Son), containing all six Sefirot (Chesed, Gevurah, Tiferet, Netzach, Hod, and Yesod)—unites with the Daughter or the Daughter of the King when joined with Malchut or Nukvah. This partnership of the royal Son (Zeir Anpin) and royal Daughter (Nukvah) is augmented by a partnership above them, that of the King (Keter) and the Father (Abba) and Mother (Imma). This is one reason why it is said that during impregnation, the mother and father form a partnership with the Creator. What we also learn is that the very esoteric tradition of Kabbalah is based on spiritual patterns and relationships reflected in our lives.

From a hidden perspective, then, this reveals why the mitzvah (commandment) is to have at least one son and one daughter: This adds to the repair and balance of these aspects in the spiritual realms. Kabbalistic patterns act as a map for global and familial relations as well as describing personal development, which leads to closeness to the Creator. The family unit becomes a form by which the entire community can be elevated and the exile of divine prophecy ended. In Judaism, the family and communal observance are the core of the survival of the Jewish people. Individual retreat and isolation from family living, which many of the world's traditions practice, is prohibited as a way of life in the Jewish tradition. We can now see that there are profoundly rich spiritual reasons for having a family—that it is pursued not simply for the obvious benefit of repopulating a people who for centuries have been massacred and whose population worldwide today is 0.2 percent of the entire global population.

The Torah is both masculine and feminine. Referring to the differentiation between the six workdays and the holy day of Sabbath, R. Kaplan tells us the main difference between men and women in the Torah: "Man's obligations are directed to the past, while woman's [are] directed towards the future." Kaplan writes that when the Torah was given, "[I]t was taught to the women first (Exodus 19:3): 'Thus shall you say to the house of Jacob [the women]—and tell the sons of Israel.'"[7]

Impregnation: masculine emanator–feminine receiver. In procreation, we can see easily how the father's seminal role is played out in a

---

[7] R. Aryeh Kaplan, *Immortality, Resurrection, and the Age of the Universe*, 59.

singular event of impregnation, which quickly becomes the "past," responsible for joining in partnership with his wife and the Creator, while the mother incubates the child in her womb for the next nine months.

Rosh Chodesh: the New Moon. One of Judaism's distinctly female traditions is the ongoing celebration of the New Moon, Rosh Chodesh, which women were said to merit due to their refusal to participate in building the golden calf. Each New Moon (Rosh Chodesh) is a day when women are to cease working in order to honor God and to pray properly for the blessings of the new month, which signals the beginning of a new development cycle of the Shechinah as the moon. The Hebrew word *chodesh* literally means "something new." The moon is what determines the Jewish holidays, most of which fall on a full moon. Operating with a lunar calendar inside a solar year, "the lunar month is based in the phases of the moon, going through a complete cycle of birth, growth, and death, and constantly anticipating the future," writes Kaplan, while the Sun "is responsible for the measure of years, which is a simple repeating cycle. The very word year, "shanah" [in Hebrew], means "repetition." The sun is therefore the masculine element, repeating the past."[8]

In this way, we are shown that male and female, sun and moon, day and night have a distinct yet interdependent role. What does it tell us, though, about the divine feminine in Judaism and the Shechinah?

Judaism and the Shechinah. Through a study of the Torah, Kabbalah, and the oral traditions accompanying the written holy books, we discover that the Shechinah makes manifestation possible. It is the light of the Creator filling the created, or the seed planted in the vessel. Where there is a vessel that desires to be filled, there is the possibility of the Shechinah. The Shechinah is the outcome of an effluence or emanation from the masculine aspect of the Creator that, once emanated, is received because of the desire inherent in the vessel, whereupon the Creator's effluence becomes feminine, nurturing, embracing, and protective as it fills a place, a receiver that desires to be filled. Thus the divine feminine in Judaism is dependent on place and time—physicality in the material world as well as boundary in the spiritual worlds.

---

[8] R. Aryeh Kaplan, *Immortality, Resurrection, and the Age of the Universe,* 61.

"It is from the Shechinah which is clothed in the shrine of the Holy of Holies of each and every general or particular world that light and vitality are extended and diffused to the whole world and the creatures contained therein, the souls, angels, and so forth, for all of them were created by the ten fiats in the act of creation, these being the 'word' of G-d which is termed 'Shechinah.'"[9]

Adam Kadmon and the Tree of Life

In *Likkutei Amarim Tanya* we learn that all the organs of the body receive their vitality or life force from the brain and that

> . . . figuratively speaking . . . the world of manifestation itself is clothed in "His blessed will, wisdom, understanding and knowledge which are called the 'intelligence' (ChaBaD) [Chochmah, Binah, Daat], and these are those which are clothed in the Torah and its commandments. The manifestations of this general flow of life are the source of the vitality which the worlds receive, each one in particular. Only a glow is diffused and shines forth from this source in a similar manner as the light radiates from the sun, by way of example, or as the powers of the organs of the body derive from the brain, as discussed above."
>
> . . . It is the source called the "world of manifestation" or "matron" or "nether Matriarch" or "Shechinah." The Baal Ha Tanya [R. Schneur Zalman of Liadi], author of Tanya, says this comes "from the scriptural phrase 'That I may dwell among them' (Exodus 25:8). For this source is the beginning of the revelation of the light of the En Sof, which extends to and illumines the worlds in a 'revealed' manner." It is this source "which extends to each individual thing, the particular light and vitality suitable for it, and it [the light] dwells and is clothed in them, thereby animating them. Therefore it is figuratively called 'mother of the children,' and 'community of Israel,' for from this source have emanated the souls of Atzilut (emanation) and have been created the souls of Beriyah (creation), and so forth . . ." What is important to appreciate is that all of them are "derived only from the extension

[9] R. Schneur Zalman of Liadi, *Likkutei Amarim Tanya*, 277.

of the vitality and light from this source, which is called 'Shechinah' resembling the radiation of light from the sun."[10]

The Shechinah Reveals the Presence of the Creator

"But as for the Shechinah itself," R. Schneur Zalman writes,

> . . . namely, the origin and core of the manifestation whereby the blessed En Sof illumines the world's in a "revealed" form which is the source of all streams of vitality in all the worlds . . . the worlds cannot endure or receive the light of this Shechinah, that it might actually dwell and clothe itself in them without a garment. The receiver needs a garment to conceal the vitality of the light so that the vessel is not nullified by the radiance of this light . . . The garment that clothes and conceals the light, (the Shechinah) is His blessed will and wisdom, and so forth, which are clothed in the Torah and his commandments that are revealed to us and to our children, for "The Torah issues from Wisdom which is Chochmah Ilaah (Supernal wisdom) that is immeasurably higher than the world of manifestation . . ."[11]

Wisdom and the Shechinah Descend

This wisdom, we are told, came down into the world through "obscuring gradations, from grade to grade. The wisdom (an emanation from Chochmah) descended until it clothed itself in matter, namely the 613 commandments of the Torah." The Shechinah also descended in this fashion, and clothed itself in each world. "This is the shrine of the 'Holy of Holies,' which is contained in each world."[12] This is where each Sefirah and prophetess gain their shine.

---

[10] R. Schneur Zalman of Liadi, *Likkutei Amarim Tanya*, chapter 52, 271–72.

[11] Ibid., 271–73.

[12] Ibid.: "So it has been stated in Zohar and Etz Chayim, that the Shechinah, which is Malchut d'Atzilut [Malchut of Atzilut] (being the light manifestation of the light and vitality of the blessed En Sof, which illumines the worlds, [wherefore] it is called the 'word of God' and the 'breath of his mouth' as it were, is in the case of human beings, by way of example, speech reveals to the hearers, the speakers secret and hidden thought, clothes itself the shrine of the Holy of holies of Beriyah namely the Chabad of Beriyah . . ." The Baal HaTanya is showing us that all things come down to the physical world in

The Shechinah Rests in the Ten Commandments

When the First Temple stood, it is said that the Shechinah rested in the Holy of Holies through the presence of the Ten Commandments, the Decalogue, the writings of God. They did not descend in a gradual way, but were the perfect union of the Shechinah (Malchut of Atzilut), the aspect of the revealed light of the blessed En Sof, which dwelled there and was clothed in the Ten Commandments, far higher and stronger, and with a greater and mightier revelation, than its revelation in the shrines on the Holy of Holies above in the upper worlds. The Ten Commandments are the . . .

> . . . "all embracing principles of the whole Torah," which comes from the Higher Wisdom that is far higher than the world of manifestation. . . . The "Shechinah" which rested in the Holy of Holies of the First Temple, [did so] through its clothing itself in the Ten Commandments.[13]

From this we are to appreciate that the Ten Commandments, like the ten utterances[14] that created the world or the ten digits of the hands and feet, the ministers we utilize in each of our own "worlds," are a spiritual dynamic reflecting the Creator's design. As is illustrated by the ten Sefirot of the Tree of Life, our lives are a ten-dimensional reality, which modern physics has confirmed.

These Ten Commandments reflect the highest realm of God's emanation, and through our attendance to them, we engage the Shechinah and prophecy.

---

stages, through the various worlds and their own Etz Chayim's, each within its own world (i.e., Atzilut, Beriyah, and so on each has a Chochmah, a Binah, a Tiferet within them). This is true for each Sefirah as well, in that each contains all ten Sefirot within themselves.

[13] R. Schneur Zalman of Liadi, *Likkutei Amarim Tanya,* chapter 53, 277.

[14] R. Yaakov Ibn Chaviv, *Ein Yaakov,* Chagigah, "Ten Creations on the First Day," 341–42: "Rav Yeudah also said in the name of Rav: Ten things were created on the first day, and they are: heaven and earth, Tohu (chaos) and Bohu (desolation), light and darkness, wind and water, the twenty-four hours of day and night. Heaven and Earth . . . ('The Ten Instruments of Creation'). R. Zutra b. Tuvyah said in Rav's name: With ten things the world was created: With wisdom, understanding, knowledge, strength, rebuke, might, righteousness and judgment, kindness and compassion."

THE TEN COMMANDMENTS[15]

Chapter and Verse	Commandment
20:1	And God spake all these words, saying,
20:2	I am the LORD thy God, which have brought thee out of the land of Egypt, out of the house of bondage.
20:3	Thou shalt have none other Gods before me.
20:4	Thou shalt not make unto thee any graven image, or any likeness of any thing that is in heaven above, or that is in the earth beneath, or that is in the water under the earth:
20:5	Thou shalt not bow down thyself to them, nor serve them: for I the LORD thy God am a jealous God, visiting the iniquity of the fathers upon the children unto the third and fourth generation of them that hate me;
20:6	And showing mercy unto thousands of them that love me, and keep my commandments.
20:7	Thou shalt not take the name of the LORD thy God in vain; for the LORD will not hold him guiltless that taketh His name in vain.
20:8	Remember the Sabbath day, to keep it holy.
20:9	Six days shalt thou labor, and do all thy work
20:10	But the seventh day is the Sabbath of the LORD thy God: in it thou shalt not do any work, thou, nor thy son, nor thy daughter, thy manservant, nor thy maidservant, nor thy cattle, nor thy stranger that is within thy gates:
20:11	For in six days the LORD made heaven and earth, the sea, and all that in them is, and rested the seventh day: wherefore the LORD blessed the Sabbath day, and hallowed it.
20:12	Honor thy father and thy mother: that thy days may be long upon the land which the LORD thy God giveth thee.
20:13	Thou shalt not kill.
20:14	Thou shalt not commit adultery.
20:15	Thou shalt not steal.
20:16	Thou shalt not bear false witness against thy neighbor.
20:17	Thou shalt not covet thy neighbor's house, thou shalt not covet thy neighbor's wife, nor his manservant, nor his maidservant, nor his ox, nor his ass, nor any thing that is thy neighbor's.

[15] From Exodus 20:1–17. The Ten Commandments are also listed in Deuteronomy 5:5–21 with slight variations from how they appear in Exodus.

The Shechinah Remains with Us

We are told that in the Second Temple the Shechinah rests only by means of a gradual descent: "in it rested the Shechinah i.e. Malchut d'Yetzirah [Malchut of Yetzirah] which was clothed in the Holy of Holies of Asiyah. . . . Therefore, no man was permitted to enter there, except the High Priest on the Day of Atonement."[16] This, then, is an emanation from a world beneath that of the First Temple, coming not from Atzilut, the world of emanation, but from the realm of Beriyah, creation, and its resting in Asiyah, the world of action, which is the final descent into matter. We are told that in the time since the destruction of the Second Temple, "each individual who sits by himself and occupies himself in the Torah, the Shechinah is with him . . ."[17] We are similarly instructed that where ten gather to pray, she is present; where three gather to judge, she is present; and where two gather to study, she is there.[18]

Summarizing, then, *Likkutei Amarim Tanya* teaches us that the Shechinah is the outcome of the supernal emanator's effluence in its descent through the Sefirot, creating a Holy of Holies in each world.[19] The deepest descent of her embodiment, and therefore the finest light, would be in our lives, epitomized by the story of Queen Esther, the last of the seven prophetesses, and by the collective story told by the lives of all seven prophetesses of Israel.

Esther, by analogy to the descent of the Shechinah through the Sefirot and the worlds, is comparable to the place of the Holy of Holies of Malchut B'Malchut (Malchut of Malchut) of Asiyah, Queen of the Kingdom. Esther's story is the repository of our future and our world, the vessel of the most refined emanation, albeit the one that is farthest from the source. Thus in Esther we find the way in which the return of the light and its ascent proceed after the Etz Chayim is repaired in the material realm through our own elevation, accomplished with God's help. Now we can see why we say that from the shine of Purim the future

---

[16] R. Schneur Zalman of Liadi, *Likkutei Amarim Tanya,* chapter 53, 277.

[17] Ibid.

[18] R. Yaakov Ibn Chaviv, *Ein Yaakov,* Berachot, 9.

[19] Malchut of Atzilut, Malchut of Beriyah, Malchut of Yetzirah, Malchut of Malchut.

comes to us and from the shine of Moshiach we are called to the Torah and mitzvot now.

THE RIGHTEOUS ARE THE FACE
OF THE SHECHINAH

Rabbi Yosi, Rabbi Yehudah and Rabbi Chiya were traveling on the road and Rabbi Elazar met them. As soon as they saw him, they all got off their donkeys. Rabbi Elazar said: For certain I see the face of the Shechinah. When one sees the righteous or the pious of the generation and meets them, certainly they represent the face of Shechinah. Why are they called "the face of Shechinah?" It is because the Shechinah hides within them, the Shechinah is concealed in them, but they are visible. Therefore, those who are closest [to] Her are called "her Face." Who are those that are close to her? They are those with whom She prepares to appear before the supernal King, Zeir Anpin, meaning who elevate Mayin Nukvin (Female waters) to unite the Holy One, Blessed be He, with his Shechinah . . .[20]

Torah and Prayer as Procreation

In Judaism's esoteric traditions, the Creator is both an emanator (masculine) and a receiver (feminine), and this is the natural role of these two parts in both our lives and the realms of science. Likewise, in Proverbs 1, we are told that there is a distinctly masculine and feminine Torah: "Hear, my son, the teaching of your father, and do not abandon the Torah of your Mother." On one level, we can say that the written Torah received on Mt. Sinai is the Torah of the fathers, and that the oral Torah (the Mishnah)—representing speech and the Sefirah of Malchut, the woman as Nukvah—is the Torah of the mother and customs that will be innovated in all generations. In this way we see the unity of male and female, written and spoken Torahs, reason and intuition, law and interpretation as a totality.

---

[20] Zohar Terumah.

Prayer Is an Emanation

We can refer back to the opinion of R. Baal Shem Tov that it is our misuse of words that causes the ongoing exile of the Shechinah and note the fact that the oral Torah is feminine. Both of these traditional teachings are based on the representation of Malchut and the mouth as the place of the Shechinah. As we saw earlier, in the world of the Creator's words (Atzilut, the realm of emanation) and in our own lives, speech is an emanation. Yet what does this mean in relationship to everything we have already learned?

Spoken prayer, as service of the heart, becomes the way in which the soul communicates to the Creator, because prayer is a form of attending divinity. During prayer, we are counseled to speak every word out loud but quietly enough not to disturb the prayers of others. It is this act of speaking that creates the vessels filled by our intention and emotion. In this way, we become more like the Creator. Speaking is an emanation, and the words become the vessels filled by our intentions as the soul of the words. Our breath, invested in each pronounced word, is like the breath the Creator places in Adam or the Neshamah of our soul. We sustain the lives of the letters of the Torah through prayer and study, invigorating the "limbs" of the Shechinah. The actions of the mitzvot and the angels involved in each one of them are called to attendance by our efforts. All of us engaged in prayer and devotion to God are part of the long line of humanity whose individuals have sustained, as partners with the Creator, the coming return of the light, the messianic age we so dearly await.

The Importance of Articulating Prayer

We are taught further by R. Baal Shem Tov why our words of prayer must be articulated.[21] The words are the body of prayer, "its essence or soul is kavanah, the mental involvement and concentration. Prayer is 'deep calling unto deep,' the depth of man's heart and soul seeking union with, and absorption in, its ultimate root and source, i.e. Shechinah. Prayer thus expresses the soul's longing for Divinity ('My soul thirsts for You,

---

[21] Zohar 3: 294b, Berachot 31a.

my flesh longs for You.' Psalms 63:3), being bonded to the love of God, continuously enraptured by it like the love-sick whose mind is never free from his passion . . . as Solomon expressed it allegorically (Song of Songs 2:5) 'I am sick with love.'"[22]

In addition, Baal Shem Tov teaches that "[p]rayer is the zivug (coupling) with the Shechinah. Just as there is motion at the beginning of coupling, so too, one must move (sway) at the beginning of prayer. Thereafter one can stand still, without motion, attached to the Shechinah with great deveikut. [And can ascend from katnut (smallness) to Gadlut (greatness).]"[23]

The Shechinah and Place

In the realm of a life, place is both a location and an intention invested in an action. The intention (kavanah) that we put into our prayers, our daily tasks, our hopes and deeds, is actually what describes them spiritually. *Small* (*katnut*) and *great* (*gadlut*) are terms often used to denote not physical size, but spiritual light—much as *close* and *distant* in Kabbalah are not descriptions of physical space, but refer instead to likeness and dissimilarity. We are said to be close to the Creator when we emulate the Creator's attributes. We are said to be far when we deviate from holy decorum. Who among us has not experienced how close we can feel to God or someone far away physically, yet how distant we can feel from a person standing next to us? We learn, then, that closeness or distance is a question of affinity and similarity, not a condition of space.

In addition, each of the seven prophetesses reigns over a certain element in the community's life. In summarizing the places represented by each prophetess where the Shechinah rests, we discover a beautiful story that progresses from one element to the next. Beginning with a singular dwelling in Sarah's life, we conclude in the sovereign world of the kingdom in Esther's. The tent (Sarah), the well (Miriam), the court (Devorah), the temple (Chanah), the royal house (Avigail), the academy

---

[22] Maimonides, *Halachot Teshuvah*, 10:3.

[23] R. Israel Baal Shem Tov, *Tzava'at Harivash* (The Testament of R. Israel Baal Shem Tov), 54–55b, 68. See also Maimonides, *Halachot Teshuvah*, 10:3.

(Chuldah), and the kingdom (Esther) describe the progressive descent of the Shechinah in the life of the People of the Book.

Because place and intention are two aspects of receiving the Divine Immanence of the Creator, the Schechinah, our emotions and thoughts have the capacity to receive this emanation. Thoughts and emotions condition our inner environment. When the emanation of God embodies itself in place (location or vessel), it is a mating of another type, a spiritual relationship. We become the royal bride and queen and the Creator becomes our partner as king, or Shabbat becomes our queen and we become her groom. In this way, relationships and the love story are defined by the descending and the ascending lights. Metaphorically, we reach up to meet what is coming down toward us. It is this flux of ascent and descent that sustains the world and each living thing as much as the breath in our bodies or the tide in the sea sustains all life. This flux is the breath of the universe; each created thing comes from and returns to its source.

The Kabbalat Shabbat

Many of the great Chazal reveal that Shabbat is the light at the head (*rosh*) of the week. It is the source from which the days of the week receive their influx of energy, just as the organs of the body receive energy from the vitality of the brain. We are given the opportunity on Shabbat to have the Shechinah rest in our homes and hearts. This is one reason the Kabbalists created the Kabbalat Shabbat, a Friday-evening prayer welcoming the Bride. The light of Shabbat illuminates all the following days of the week.

If we consider the six days of the work week as masculine, concerned with present, everyday concerns, and the Shabbat as feminine, a source of the future, we can say that it is the light of the future that illuminates our daily lives. In this sense, we see the wisdom in the Sefer Yetzirah's teaching that the end is embedded in the beginning. The end is the source from which the preceding moments receive their sustenance. We can see, then, why we say that prophecy is the end or final outcome of creation and that redemption is the shine of the future that illuminates our lives today, for we are told that in the future, all will be Shabbat. When we keep Shabbat, we come into rapport with that shine, as the holy sage Baal Ha Tanya called the Shechinah, and with what can be best thought of as the shine from the future—the Holy of Holies of Creation from its beginning to end, the same light Adam saw at the beginning of creation, a light that is still in the repository of the messianic deliverance to come.

Shabbat: Greeting the Bride

The Talmud (Shabbas 119a) teaches us that as the Shabbas drew near, the Talmudic sage "Chanina" would don his finest clothing and invite others to join him in going out to greet "the bride," the (Shabbas) Queen. A thousand years later, the Kabbalists of Safed embellished this custom by actually walking out to the fields to welcome the Shabbas. It was there, in Safed, that the Kabbalat (Kof Beit Lamed Tav) Shabbat (Shin Beit Tav), welcoming the Shabbas, service was first formulated, and from there it spread to the entire world.[24]

JOY INVITES THE SHECHINAH AND PROPHECY

The quality of the emotional joy we bring to prayer is said to be precious in making prayers that fulfill their function in either praise or supplication. The emotion in our prayers is like the emotion of love with which we invest a kiss with the beloved. In the world, place is location; in the spiritual realm, place is the boundary of the limitless light. Thus, we read in the Torah that the Shechinah rests in Sarah's tent, in the Tent of Meeting, between the cherubim of the Ark of the Tabernacle, in the tents of the Israelites after the tenth plague in Egypt, at the Kotel (the Western Wall of the Beit Hamikdash—Temple—in Jerusalem), in our sukkahs during Sukkot, under the chuppah of the bride and groom, in the Mikvah (the ritual bath of purification), and even in the faces of the righteous. Each is a place where we are devoted to the Creator and engaged in the performance of mitzvot (commandments). As the Rambam teaches,

---

[24] R. Nosson Scherman and R. Meir Zlotowitz, eds., *The Complete Artscroll Siddur*, 44.

prophecy, in addition to all that we have already learned, can rest upon a person who performs a mitzvah with spontaneous and utter joy. This expansive and inclusive emotion, called *simcha* (joy) in Hebrew, is powerful indeed.[25]

Women and Mitzvot

In Judaism women are not obligated to participate in most time-structured mitzvot (commandments)—those mitzvot whose times are determined by the solar day, by the sun coming up and going down, which has already been established Kabbalistically as a masculine force that establishes at what time we should pray. Other than making challah, lighting the candles at Shabbat, keeping family purity (niddah) based on the menstrual cycle, hearing the Megillah of Esther read on Purim, and participating in Pesach (Passover), for women there are few time-based observances required by Jewish Law. This is not to say that observant Jewish women don't participate in every holiday, pray daily, or honor the entire Shabbat, beginning with sundown, but they have greater leeway in designation—when and what they should occupy themselves with in prayer.

In Kabbalah we are taught that women have extra Binah (understanding). In the Partzufim of the divine family, Binah is called the Mother, Imma, and is partnered with Chochmah (wisdom)—Abba, or Father. This endowment of extra intuition or understanding, which is wisdom applied, makes women more able to communicate directly with God on their own. This additional portion of understanding allows a woman to care for the home, raise children, teach and study with others, work in the world, and do tzedekah (acts of charity)—all based on her own daily structure. As vessels of God's light, women are designed to elevate everything with which they come in contact. As counterparts to the Shechinah spiritually, women spiritualize matter, so to speak. In the Torah it is taught that a "woman is the crown upon her husband's head." Her spiritual status also explains the tradition in Chassidic Judaism that

---

[25] Learn about the importance of simcha in more detail by reading the Rambam's *Hilchot Yesodei HaTorah*.

a man without a wife is considered to be only half a person, a home without a Shabbat, a home devoid of the Shechinah.

The Sun and the Moon

In Kabbalah, in the Sefer Yetzirah we learn more about the dynamic between the sun and the moon. Isaiah 30:26 says: "The light of the moon will be like the light of the sun," referring to a time when the inequality between man and woman will be eliminated.

The story of the sun and the moon forms the basis of a great deal of literature in Kabbalah. Yehudah Leib Ashlag (Baal HaSulam) points to our ultimate redemption in the classical story told about the sun, the moon, and the Creator. Ultimately, it is the story of the elevation of the divine feminine within each one of us, male and female alike—an elevation of intuition, loving-kindness, and holy stewardship of the earth. It is an elevation, however, hallmarked first by a diminishment.

This elevation implies the eventual rededication of the Temple of the world and each of us as servants to the Creator, a restoration on earth of Eden, the Holy of Holies, Malchut of Malchut. It is a story whose essential plot is an initial diminishing for an eventual elevation, and from this we can gather hope for the future redemption and safekeeping of our world and planet.

The sanctity of the location of the Beit Hamikdash is an eternal promise that the Shechinah will never leave it. "And God said to him: . . . I have sanctified this house which you built, to put My Name there forever. My eyes and My heart shall be there perpetually."[26]

Today, any person who visits Jerusalem and prays at the Kotel can experience this divine emanation, the Shechinah.

> Anyone can appreciate that there is a Divine Presence at the Wall even though the Beit Hamikdash no longer stands. . . . Anyone who has prayed at the Kotel and has been overwhelmed by a sense of religious exaltation and fervor, can readily perceive—as did Ya'akov Avinu—

---

[26] Meir Simcha Sokolovosky, *Prophecy and Providence*, 180.

Figure 10.1. The Kotel—the Western Wall of the Beit Hamikdash—in Jerusalem.

"How awesome is this place" (Bereshit 28:17), even in its ruins, for it is truly "the house of God and the gate of Heaven"—the site of the Divine Presence in Israel. The Wall reinforces our hope and faith that we will speedily merit the revelation of the Shechinah upon the "mountain of God" and the rebuilding of the Beit Hamikdash, as the Prophet Yeshayahu prophesied.[27]

The remnant of the Temple, in which resided the various degrees of God's presence, acts as reflector of all that will come in the future. We are taught that the People of the Book do not cremate the body at death, for from the remnants of the body comes the body of resurrection—and likewise, in modern-day Israel, the Jewish people have the remnant of the Temple to provide the shine of redemption and eternal resurrection of the righteous.

---

[27] Meir Simcha Sokolovsky, *Prophecy and Providence,* 2:2.

We have seen that from the age of prophecy we are given the tools of redemption and the ending of the exile of the Shechinah—the end of our separation from God. We are each charged with the task of refining our nature in order to receive the Creator's effluence on earth. The tikkun olam (repair of the world) is an obligation to both the world we live in and the inner world of our individual incarnations. Together, we represent the Temple of the world. Doing good deeds enlivens the Creator's presence (Shechinah) among us, and prayer invigorates the soul's attachment to God. We are each part of this partnership between the created and the Creator. The prophetesses show us that all people have the capacity to participate in this spiritual accomplishment of elevating humanity to the holy lineage of God's created humanity. All of us and all that we accomplish in our spiritual, emotional, and intellectual development contribute to the eventual redemption of all humankind. As midwives for the birth of the messianic age, we are blessed. May each one of us, man, woman, and child, delight in the holy humanity we are becoming, and may each one of us pray that we may merit to see Moshiach in our days.

The seven prophetesses, each providing a different shine from the Holy of Holies of Atzilut reflected in the realm of Asiyah, guide all of us in the rebuilding of our personal and our communal Temple, the world itself, and the promised Third Temple of Jerusalem.

Knowing now that the Etz Chayim is a divine treasure map for rebuilding three temples—with the sanctuary being the holy earth itself and the physical Third Temple being in Jerusalem—and that it is the Temple that each of our lives represents, we can summarize all that we have learned.

- The purpose of self-refinement is for the capacity of prophecy: being able to speak with and on behalf of the Creator, our beloved HaShem, or God.
- Each prophetess reflects some element of the sixth millennium, when Moshiach consciousness will be shared by all. Together, they contribute a "measured flow" (middot) of the nature of the Creator in

whose image we are made to our own nature, and they show us how to use each Sefirah for our own rebuilding of the temple of our body and soul and our residence on earth and in the World to Come.

- From Sarah and Chesed we inherit the shine of the promise of Moshiach's conception and Mt. Moriah as the site of the Third Temple. We learn that our bodies are the holy temple we are to rebuild, that the earth is a sacred sanctuary where God's presence is revealed, and that loving-kindness is the mortar that holds together all of the worlds and our own.

- From Miriam and Gevurah we inherit the shine of the promise of the Redeemer's eventual birth. We are each capable of rebirth through teshuvah and humility. Day by day, stone by stone, we rebuild our lives and the earth and, eventually, the Temple in Jerusalem, the cornerstone of all of them being our humility, our discernment between what is good and what is not, and a dedication to each other and the love of God.

- From Devorah and Tiferet we inherit the shine of the reconstructed Sanhedrin, composed of wise men and women. We are all destined to be wise judges over our own decorum and in our communities. Being able to elevate all to its rightful purpose leads to truth and beauty.

- From Chanah and Netzach we inherit the shine of the reenactment of the holy rituals and prayers at the Temple and the arrival of a new age of prophecy. We have the opportunity to fashion a life based on divinity in our daily conduct and works and in our rituals and prayers, sources for closeness to God. Devotion that is constant and accomplished with will and zeal, living our lives with an attachment to the Creator, leads to eternity and victory over the darkness within and without. The age of prophecy (a new enlightenment) is made possible.

- From Avigail and Hod we inherit the shine of the royal bloodline, the DNA of glory. We each become anointed as members of God's holy family, a holy humanity. The promise of the Redeemer's physical birth and the age of redemption is confirmed, giving rise to world peace and total splendor on earth. The Beit Hamikdash, the Temple itself, is rebuilt on earth and in Jerusalem, making our lives a holy implement to the Temple of God's created earth.

- From Chuldah and Yesod we inherit the shine of our eternal immortality. Knowing that our thought, speech, and action craft the garment for our soul, we learn that all that we have and do is for the sake of the oneness of all. The Holy of Holies in the physical Temple in Jerusalem and the hearts of all human beings are dedicated to God's divine will on earth and in heaven. Humans become holy humans and the innermost part of the Temple of the world, human hearts, is made perfect in their covenant with God.

- From Esther and Malchut we inherit the shine of peace and wholeness. The Temple is rebuilt, and the ritual of living is made holy. We speak with and for the Creator. With HaShem's help, we redeem earth from all evil and redeem our body and soul from imperfection. We fulfill the purpose of having been created. We become the immortal humanity, demonstrating perfect free will in alignment with divinity (the Shechinah). The earth and each person become the Temple and its implements restored in the kingdom of God. As prophecy is the outcome of the created human, resurrection is the final outcome of being born. Moshiach and messianic consciousness are this prophesied completion.

The Etz Chayim of Kabbalah and the Torah from which it springs are the holy maps to the inner secrets of the People of the Book, blessings from God we can use in our lives to complete our purpose as God's chosen humanity.

With Sarah and Chesed we discover how acts of loving-kindness are the seeds of the Creator's love. We see in Gevurah and Miriam's life how our deliverance comes from forbearance and boundary-making, that things have their time and place. In Devorah and Tiferet we learn how beauty is a moral order, an ability to distinguish between right and wrong and good and evil and to combine discipline with mercy and compassion. Chanah and Netzach show us how our spiritual will enables us to endure and succeed in our life's purpose. Avigail in Hod reveals the nature of humility as the underpinning of material and spiritual royalty. Chuldah and Yesod show us that our commitment to the Creator must be in body, mind, and soul, that the brit of the heart for all people and the circumcision of all males' generative organs are the binding links for the People of the Book throughout all generations—a foundation upon which redemption and resurrection depend. Finally, in Malchut, we see that here, in our physical world, we elevate all the fallen sparks to their original place of holiness. Here, in Malchut, we are able as individuals and collectively as humanity to come together in our honoring of the glory of God. Here in our material, embodied lives we create the body of redemption for the World to Come.

The seven prophetesses of Israel teach us how to become vessels fit for prophecy, how to become a humanity of divine conduits, how to become a world redeemed, fulfilling the purpose of creation, which is eternal life for all. Our life is an opportunity to refine our nature, to create the garments of right thought, speech, and action. Our lifetime is part of the process by which we elevate the body to becoming an eternal partner of the eternal soul. We are a creation reflecting our lifetime of effort, which will culminate in the world's thousand years of prophesied peace.

The shine of each Sefirah contributes to the composition of our mortal and eternal raiments. United as the Sefirot are in each person and in the world, we become the fruit of God's Tree of Life. We become the Creator's partners in a royal marriage. We fulfill our destiny of becoming God-like. Ultimately, the women of prophecy, the seven holy prophetesses, are divinely chosen guides for humanity's self-refinement and the experience of prophecy, the purpose and outcome of creation. Sarah, Miriam, Devorah, Chanah, Avigail, Chuldah, and Esther show us how to behave every day of the week, how to elevate our secular actions to sacred involvements. When we listen to them, we are given the secret tools leading to our personal and collective completion and repair (tikkun) of life on earth and in the World to Come.

As we have learned, the Shechinah and Moshiach stand together and do not separate from each other. May we merit His coming speedily in our days. Amen. Selah!

Flee, my Beloved from your common Exile and be like
a gazelle or a young hart in Your swiftness to redeem
and rest your Presence among us on the fragrant Mount
Moriah, site of Your Temple.

SONG OF SONGS 8:14

The Songs of Miriam, Devorah, and Chanah

MIRIAM'S SONG
Exodus 15:20–26

Miriam the Prophetess, sister of Aaron, took the drum in
her hand and all
the women went forth after her with drums and with
dances. Miriam spoke up
to them, "Sing to HaShem for He is exalted above the
arrogant, having hurled
horse with its rider into the sea."
Moses caused Israel to journey from the Sea of Reeds and
then went out to
the Wilderness of Shur; they went for a three-day period
in the Wilderness, but
they did not find water. They came to Marah, but they
could not drink the
waters of Marah because they were bitter; therefore they
named it Marah. The
people complained against Moses saying, "what shall we
drink?"

He cried out to HaShem, and HaShem showed him a tree;
he threw it into the

water and the water became sweet. There he established
for [the nation] a

decree and an ordinance and there He tested it. He said,
"If you hearken

diligently to the voice of HaShem, your God, and do what
is just in His eyes,

give ear to His commandments and observe His decrees,
then any of the

diseases that I placed in Egypt, I will not bring upon you,
I am HaShem, your

Healer."

SONG OF DEVORAH
Judges 5:1–31

Devorah Sang—as well as Barak Son of Abinoam—on
that day saying:

When vengeances are inflicted upon Israel and the people
dedicates itself to God—Bless HaShem.

Hear, O Kings; give ear, O Princes! I, to HaShem shall I
sing; I shall sing praise to Hashem God of Israel!

HaShem, as You left Seir, as You strode from the fields
of Edom, the earth quaked and even the heavens
trickled; even the clouds dripped water.

Mountains melted before HaShem—as did Sinai—before
HaShem, the God

of Israel.

In the days of Shamgar, son of Anath, in the days of Jael,
highway travel

ceased, and those who traveled on paths went by circuitous
roads.

They stopped living in unwalled towns in Israel, they
stopped; until I,

Devorah, arose; I arose a mother in Israel.

When it chose new gods, war came to its gates; was even a
shield or a spear

Seen among forty thousand in Israel?

My heart is with the lawgivers in Israel who are devoted to
the people,

[saying] "Bless HaShem."

O riders of white donkeys, [you] who sit in judgment, and
you who walk

the roads, speak up!

Rather than the sound of arrows [aimed] at the water-
drawers, there they

will recount the righteous deeds of HaShem, the righteous
deeds for His open

cities in Israel. Then the people of HaShem descended
[again] to the [open] cities.

Give praise, give praise, O Devorah! Give praise, give
praise, utter a song!

Arise, O Barak, and capture your prisoners, O son of
Abinoam!

Now the survivor dominates the mightiest of the people;
HaShem has given

me dominion over the strong ones.

From Ephraim, who root [fought] against Amelek; after
you came Benjamin with your people. From Machir
descended lawgivers; and from

Zebulun, those who ply the scribal quill.

The leaders of Issachar were with Devorah, and so was
[the rest of] Issachar

with Barak; into the valley he was sent on his feet. But in
the indecision of

Reuben there was great deceit.

Why did you remain sitting at the borders to hear the
bleatings of the flocks?

The indecision of Reuben demands great investigation.

Gilead dwelled across the Jordan; and Dan—why did he gather [his

valuables] onto ships? But Asher lived by the shores of seas and remained [to

protect] his open [borders].

Zebulun is a people that risked its life to the death, so did Naphtali, on

the heights of the battlefield.

Kings came and fought—then the kings of Canaan fought, from Taanach

to the waters of Megiddo, without accepting monetary reward.

From heaven they fought, the very stars from their orbits did battle with

Sisera.

Kishon Brook swept them away—the ancient brook, Kishon Brook—but

I myself trod it vigorously.

Then the horses' heels were pounded by the gallopings, the gallopings of

their mighty riders.

"Curse Meroz," said the angel of HaShem, "Curse! Cursed are its inhabitants, for

they failed to come to aid [the nation of] HaShem, to aid [the nation of] HaShem against the mighty."

Blessed by women is Jael, wife of Heber the Kenite; by women in the tent

will she be blessed.

He asked for water, she gave him milk; in a stately saucer she presented

Cream.

She stretched her hand to the peg and her right hand to the laborers' hammer.

She hammered Sisera, severed his head, smashed and
    pierced his temple.
At her feet he knelt, he fell, he lay. At her feet he knelt, he
    fell; where he knelt there he fell, vanquished.
Through the window she gazed; Sisera's mother peered
    through the window.
"Why is his chariot delayed in coming? Why the
    hoofbeats of his
carriages so late?"
The wisest of her ladies answer her, and she, too, offers
    herself responses.
"Are they not finding [and] dividing loot? A comely
    [captive]. Two comely
[captives], for every man; booty of colored garments for
    Sisera, booty of colored embroidery, colored, doubly
    embroidered garments for the necks of the looters."
"So may all Your enemies be destroyed, O HaShem! And
    let those who love
Him be like the powerfully rising sun.
And the land was tranquil for forty years."

CHANAH'S SONG OF PRAYER
1 Samuel 2:1–10

Then Chanah prayed and said:
"My heart exults in HaShem; my pride has been raised
    through HaShem;
my mouth is opened wide against my antagonists,
for I rejoice in Your Salvation.
There is none as holy as HaShem, for there is none besides
    you,
and there is no Rock like our God.
Do not abound in speaking with arrogance,
let not haughtiness come from your mouth;

for HaShem is the God of thoughts, and (men's) deeds are accounted by Him.

The bow of the mighty is broken,

while the foundering are girded with strength.

The sated ones are hired out for bread,

while the hungry ones cease to be so;

while the barren woman bears seven,

the one with many children becomes bereft.

HaShem brings death and gives life; He lowers to the grave and rises up.

HaShem impoverishes and makes rich, He humbles and He elevates.

He raises the needy from the dirt, from the trash heaps He lifts the destitute,

to seat (them) with nobles and to endow them with a seat of honor—

for HaShem's are the pillars of the earth, and upon them He set the world.

He guards the steps of his devout ones, but the wicked are stilled in darkness; for not through strength does man prevail.

HaShem—may those that contend with him be shattered,

let the heavens thunder against them.

May HaShem judge to the ends of the earth.

May He give power to his kind and raise the pride of His anointed one."

APPENDIX 2

Stones and Houses

A Kabbalistic Method for Deciphering Words

This method is referred to in chapter 5, the chapter on Devorah, as a method for studying the words **judge, judging,** and **judgment.**

In the Sefer Yetzirah, or the Book of Formation, attributed to Abraham, there are instructions for using the letters of words in a way that's different from the method of gematria practiced in this book to understand their deeper and concealed meanings. This method is referred to as Stones and Houses.

Chapter 3, section 16, of the Sefer Yetzirah states: "Two stones build two houses, three stones build six houses, four build twenty-four houses, five build one hundred and twenty houses, six build seven hundred and twenty houses and seven build five hundred and forty houses. From thence further go and reckon what the mouth cannot express and the ear cannot hear."

Using the three-letter root in the words that make up **judge, judging,** and **judgment**—the elements of justice being wrought: שׁ Shin (300) פ Pey (80) ט Tet (9)—we see the meaning of this guidance. As we have already learned, letters are cosmic units of particular energy. Depending on their placement, their order in a word affects their character and purpose. In Kabbalah, letters are considered souls and words are bodies. If we consider three letters, as in the following example, we see easily how from three stones (letters) make six houses, or words.

First we will complete the exercise using numbers so that the pattern is clear. Reading from right to left, as we do for Hebrew, we can see how three numbers (stones) make six combinations (houses).

321

231

312

132

213

123

Now substituting the three letters that make up the word **judge**, we see how this method can be used in the search for meaning. As with the numbers, read this example from right to left, as Hebrew is read.

Letters (3 Stones)	Houses	Other Words Derived from Root
Tet Pey Shin	I	judge
Pey Tet Shin	2	wash away, flood
Tet Shin Pey	3	plain meaning
Shin Tet Pey	4	NA
Shin Pey Tet	5	NA
Pey Shin Tet	6	NA

This shows us that sometimes a word contains other words within it when the letters are rearranged. In this case, the additional words and their meanings tell us about the nature of judging: They include **clarity,** the plain meaning of things, "the letter of the law," which is the foundation of Torah study as presented in chapter 2, in the section on the four ways to study the Torah (*peshat* is the literal meaning of Torah). The word for **flood** or **wash away** in Hebrew suggests the importance of proper judgment as a means to prevent the flooding of emotions that can pervert justice, or, positively, it suggests flooding as a means for washing away sin or, conversely, being flooded by sin.

We can use this method with any word. I often use it with three-letter root words for their simplicity (six houses) and representation of the three paths in the Etz Chayim: the right, left, and middle pillars. In this case, Tiferet itself integrates six parts, creating the Partzufim of Zeir Anpin, or the Son. Not all words, however, have other words hidden within after the letters are rearranged. For example, **echad—א** Alef (1), ח Chet (8), ד Dalet (4)—meaning "one" or "oneness" in Hebrew, has no other words concealed within it. This suggests a unity, a singularity, a oneness in its nature. It is a clear demonstration of what is meant when the People of the Book say that the Creator is one in the sacred Shema prayer: "Hear O Israel, the Lord [Adonai/Chesed] our God [Elokhanu/Gevurah], the Lord [Adonai] is One [Echad]." One is one and not more. The Sefer Yetzirah asks, "Before one what do you count? regarding the eternal connection between the beginning and end: 'just as the flame is wedded to the live coal; because the Lord is One and there is not a second one, and before one what wilt thou count?'"[1]

---

[1] Sefer Yezirah, 1:6.

The Counting of the Omer

The Omer is counted at night, while we are standing, immediately following the evening prayer. We begin with this blessing: "Blessed are You, L-rd our G-d, king of the universe, who has sanctified us with His commandments, and commanded us concerning the counting of the Omer."

Following this blessing, we count the specific day of the Omer and then recite the following prayer.

May the Merciful One restore the Holy Temple to its place, speedily in our days; Amen.

For the Choirmaster; a song with instrumental music; a Psalm. May G-d be gracious to us and bless us; may He make His countenance shine upon us forever; that Your way be known on earth, Your salvation among all nations. The nations will extol You, O G-d; all the nations will extol You. The nations will rejoice and sing for joy, for You will judge the peoples justly and guide the nations on earth forever. The peoples will extol You, O G-d; all the peoples will extol You, for the earth will have yielded its produce and G-d; our G-d, will bless us. G-d will bless us; and all, from the farthest corners of the earth, shall fear Him.

We implore you, by the great power of Your right hand, release the captive. Accept the prayer of Your people; strengthen us, purify us, Awesome One. Mighty One, we beseech You, guard as the apple of the eye those who seek Your Oneness. Bless them, cleanse them; bestow upon them forever Your merciful righteousness. Powerful, Holy One, in Your abounding goodness, guide Your congregation. Only and Exalted One, turn to Your people who are mindful of Your holiness. Accept our supplication and hear our cry, You who knows secret thoughts. Blessed be the name of the glory of His kingdom forever and ever.

Master of the universe, You have commanded us through Moses Your servant to count Sefirat Ha-Omer, in order to purify us from our evil and uncleanness. As You have written in Your Torah, "You shall count for yourselves from the day following the day of rest, from the day on which you bring the Omer as a wave-offering; shall be for seven full weeks. Until the day following the seventh week shall you count fifty days," so that the souls of Your people Israel may be cleansed from their defilement. Therefore, may it be Your will, L-rd our G-d and G-d of our fathers, that in the merit of the Sefirat Ha-Omer which I counted today, the blemish that I have caused in the Sefirah be rectified and I may be purified and sanctified with supernal holiness. May abundant bounty thereby be bestowed upon all the worlds. May it rectify our nefesh, ruach and neshamah from every baseness and defect, and may it purify and sanctify us with Your supernal holiness. Amen, selah.[1]

---

[1] From R. Simon Jacobson, *The Spiritual Guide to Counting the Omer,* www.meaningfullife.com.

Letters of Commendation

I am coming in this letter of mine to advocate for Zohara Meyerhoff Hieronimus of Baltimore, MD (USA), since I am already acquainted with her for many years for her support and assistance for those who study Torah and for her great contribution to funds for charity and kindness.

Since she returned to the sources of Judaism, she desires to spread the wisdom of Israel and specifically to draw Jewish women close to Judaism. She is presently ready to publish a book in English about the prophetesses of Israel from the Bible, with an explanation of the unique significance of each prophetess and the hope that women will thereby learn and recognize the great wisdom of the prophetesses and they will draw close to the Torah of Israel. Since, in this generation, our specific role is to draw close our distant brothers, therefore, I hope that this book will also fulfill its goal.

Signed with blessing,
R. Avraham Brandwein
Dean, Kol Yehuda Yeshivat
Old City, Jerusalem

In this remarkable volume, Zohara has skillfully woven a multifaceted tapestry from traditional exoteric and esoteric sources combined with her intuitive insights and passion for the truth. From a detailed description of prophecy and the Divine worlds of the Sefirot, to fascinating correspondences between the seven Prophetesses and the seven species of the Land of Israel, Zohara has provided the reader with specific goals for personal refinement and a road map for the journey of the world.

Based on the unbroken chain of Kabbalistic teachings from Adam to Moses to our times, found in the Bible, Mishnah, Talmud, Midrash, Zohar, Maimonides, Arizal, and Chassidic Masters, a ladder of ascending rungs is built on a secure foundation, as described in the letter of Nachmanides and in the works of the Ramchal. As prophets, the children of prophets, we all have the potential for Divine Inspiration, the Holy Spirit.

By following the pure Kabbalistic tradition, Zohara has unveiled some of the mysteries, yet has left far more hidden, waiting to be revealed by those who put forth the effort and are blessed with Divine grace.

May the Almighty bless Zohara and guide and support her in her life's passion to spread forth the wisdom of truth and the inner teachings of Torah.

Rabbi Noah Shavrick

Baltimore, Maryland

12 Tammuz 5767 (June 28, 2007)

This is indeed a unique book to see the light in "these times" of our spiritual quest journey, a dark/bright moment in our human evolution, rediscovering once more, the power of prophecy among the women of ancient Israel, which is very relevant to our actual world situation.

Zohara lovingly offers us a magnificent book, an eloquently written document, to help us intimately encounter a fresh new look at our Hebrew tradition, with the ancient and new practical wisdom of the sacred Kabbalah.

This book is an impeccable portal to the state of sanity, which our humanity urgently needs at this perplexed and confused time. Study this book closely, so we may help increase light within us and participate on the completion of "Tikkun Olam."

Samuel Ben-Or Avital

Samuel Ben-Or Avital is a mime performer, teacher, creator, and practitioner of Body-Speak, "trickster extraordinaire." He is the founder and director of Le Centre du Silence Mime School in Boulder, Colorado, and author of several books, including *The Invisible Stairway: Kabbalistic Meditations on the Hebrew Letters* and *The BodySpeak Manual*.

Glossary

Alef-Bet: The Hebrew alphabet, composed of twenty-two letters.

Ark: The traveling container (box) that held the Ten Commandments or the place where the Torah scrolls are housed in the synagogue are housed.

Asiyah: Realm of action, lowest of four realms, the material world in which we live.

Atzilut: Realm of emanation, highest of the four worlds.

Bat Kol: Daughter of the Voice, a level of prophecy in which a voice is heard.

Binah: Sefirah of understanding.

Beriyah: Realm of creation—next to the highest realm of four worlds.

B'nai Yisrael: Children of Israel, refers to the People of the Book.

chag: Holiday

Chanukah: Holiday commemorating the miracle of the one day of holy oil that lasted for eight days.

Chesed: Sefirah of loving-kindness.

Chochmah: Sefirah of wisdom.

Daat: Sefirah of knowledge.

Eretz Yisrael: Land of Israel.

Etz Chayim: Tree of Life.

galut: Exile or captivity.

gematria (gematriyah): "Numerology" systems of converting words into number values.

geulah: Redemption.

Gevurah: Sefirah of judgment and strength.

HaVaYa: Four-letter name of God (Yod Hay Vav Hay).

HaShem: Literally, "the name"; refers to the Creator's ineffable name.

Hod: Sefirah of glory and majesty.

Holy of Holies: Most inner chamber of the Temple, reserved only for the High Priest.

Kabbalah: Received tradition of correspondences.

kedusha: Holiness.

kelim: Vessels (referring to the Sefirot).

kelipah (singular), kelipot (plural): Shells of evil encasing the fallen sparks.

Keter: Crown, the highest Sefirah in Etz Chayim.

kohanim: Priests.

Kohen Gadol: High priest.

Lag B'Omer: Thirty-third day of the Counting of the Omer, the day manna fell from heaven.

LaShon HaKodesh: The holy language (referring to Hebrew).

Malchut: Sefirah of kingdom and sovereignty; the lowest of the Sefirot in Etz Chayim.

middot: "Measured flows," representing our emotions in Etz Chayim; the six Sefirot of Chesed through Yesod.

Mikvah: "Collection" or "gathering" of water for ritual immersion.

milah (brit): Circumcision.

minyan: "Number," refers to the traditional requirement for ten men over the age of thirteen to pray in assembly in order to bring the Shechinah's presence.

Mishkan: Tabernacle, tent of congregation.

Mishnah: Literally, "teaching" or "instruction"; the first written collection of oral law (20–200 CE).

mitzvah (singular), mitzvot (plural): commandment.

Modeh Ani: "I give thanks"; the prayer said upon rising in the morning.

Moshiach: "Anointed one"; the prophesied Redeemer of Israel and the world whose arrival is imminent.

Moshiach Ben David: Messiah, Son of David.

Moshiach Ben Joseph: Messiah, Son of Yosef.

Netzach: Sefirah of victory and eternity.

ohel: Tent of gathering.

Olam HaBa: The World to Come.

Olam HaZot: This world.

Or En Sof: Limitless light.

Parshat (singular), **Parshiot** (plural): Referring to one of the Pentateuch's fifty-four portions.

Partzufim: Family personas in the Tree of Life (Etz Chayim) that have correspondences to the Sefirot.

Pentateuch: The Five Books of Moses.

Perek Shira: A text with the translated title "The Song of the Universe."

Pirkei Avot: Chapters of the Fathers, from the ninth book in the Mishnah.

Pesach: Passover, the celebration commemorating the Exodus from Egypt.

Purim: Holiday commemorating Queen Esther's life and victory over evil.

Ruach HaKodesh: The Holy Spirit, the level of prophecy any righteous person can attain.

Rosh Chodesh: The New Moon.

Rosh Hashanah: Holiday of the Jewish New Year.

Sanhedrin: Sitting council of seventy elders.

Sefer Yetzirah: The Book of Formation, a Kabbalistic text attributed to Abraham.

Sefirah (singular), **Sefirot** (plural): Ten vessels in Etz Chayim that hold the light of God.

Sefirat HaOmer: Forty-nine-day period (from the second night of Pesach until the night before Shavuot) of the Counting of the Omer, the barley offering, which is a Kabbalistic ritual of self-refinement.

Shabbat: Sabbath.

shalom: Peace.

Shavuot: Holiday of receiving of Torah at Mt.Sinai; one of three pilgrimage holidays.

Shechinah: The Divine Immanence of the Creator or the word of God.

Shevirat HaKelim: Breaking of the vessels, an event that resulted in creation of the kelipot.

Shema: Prayer said twice a day and prayer that is to be the last words on a Jewish person's lips at death: Hear O Israel, the Lord our God, the Lord is One . . .

Simchat Torah: Holiday of "rejoicing of the Law," the end of the annual reading cycle.

Sukkot: Holiday of the Booths, celebrating God's pillar of glory during Israel's Exodus from Egypt.

sukkah: Booth used on Sukkot.

Talmud: Central body of Jewish Law and folklore, accumulated between 200 and 500 BCE.

teshuvah: Repentance, return.

tikkun olam: Repair of the world.

Tiferet: Sefirah of truth and beauty.

Torah: Literally, "to teach"; teaching, instruction, all of Judaism's teachings, more commonly referring to the Five Books of Moses, or the Pentateuch.

Tu B'Shevat: New Year of the Trees.

yahrzeit: Anniversary of a person's death.

Yesod: Sefirah of foundation and covenant.

Yetzirah: Realm of formation, next-to-last realm of the four worlds.

Yom Kippur: Holy day of repentance.

Zohar: Book of Splendor, the major Kabbalistic work, transmitted orally and then written down from 1200 to 1500 CE. In the twentieth century, it was translated from Aramaic into Hebrew by R. Yehudah Leib Ashag (Baal HaSulam).

Bibliography

Abohav, R. Yitzchak. *Menoras Hamaor, The Ten Days of Teshuvah.* Lake Wood, N.J.: Torah Script Publications, 1983.

Ashlag, R. Yehudah Leib. *Shamati.* Edited by R. Avraham Mordechai Gottleib. Bnei Brak, Israel: Or Baruch Shalom, 2003.

Avital, Samuel Ben-Or. *The Invisible Stairway: Kabbalistic Meditations on the Hebrew Letters.* Boulder, Colo.: Kol-Emeth Publishers, 2003.

Baal Shem Tov, R. Israel. *The Testament of Rabbi Israel Baal Shem Tov.* Translated by R. Jacob Immanuel Schochet. New York: Kehot Publication Society, 1998.

Basser, R. Tuvia. *Pirkei Avos, Maharal of Prague: A Commentary Based on Selections from Maharal's Derech Chaim.* New York: Mesorah Publications, 1997.

Birnbaum, R. Mayer. *Pathway to Prayer: A Translation and Explanation of the Shemoneh Esray.* New York: Feldheim Publishers, 1997.

Blumberg, Raphael, trans. *The Blueprint of Creation: The Chofetz Chaim on Torah Study.* Jerusalem: Bais Yechiel Publishers, 1990.

———. *The Chofetz Chaim Looks at Eternity.* Jerusalem: Bais Yechiel Publishers, 1989.

Bokser, Ben Zion. *The Maharal (1512–1609): The Mystical Philosophy of Judah Loew of Prague.* Northvale, N.Y.: Jason Aronson, 1954.

Brandwein, R. Avraham. *Classical Kabbalah: The Hidden Teachings of Torah and the Zohar.* Translated by R. Noah Shavrick. Owings Mills, Md.: Zohar Press, 2005.

Buxbaum, Yitzhak. *Jewish Spiritual Practices.* Northvale, N.J.: Jason Aronson, 1990.

404

Chasidah, R. Yisrael Yitzchak Yishai. *Encyclopedia of Biblical Personalities, Ishei HaTanach, Anthologized from the Talmud, Midrash, and Rabbinic Writings.* Jerusalem: Shaar Press Publications, 1994.

Chaviv, R. Yaakov Ibn. *Ein Yaakov: The Ethical and Inspirational Teachings of the Talmud.* Translated by Avraham Yaakov Finkel. Lanham, Md.: Rowman and Littlefield Publishers, 2004.

Clark, Matityahu. *Etymological Dictionary of Biblical Hebrew.* New York: Feldheim Publishers, 1999.

Cordovero, R. Moshe. *The Palm Tree of Devorah (Tomer Devorah).* Translated by R. Moshe Miller. New York: Targum/Feldheim, 1993.

Davis, R. Menachem, ed. *The Pirkei Avot: Ethics of the Fathers.* New York: Artscroll, Mesorah Publications, 1995.

De Fano, R. Menachem Azariah. *Asarah Ma'amarot, Ma'amar Em Kol Hai.* Venice: n.p., 1597.

Encyclopedia Judaica. Jerusalem: Keter Publishing, 1971.

Feuer, R. Avrohom Chaim. *The Shemoneh Esrei.* New York: Artscroll, Mesorah Publications, 1990.

Finkelman, R. Shimon, and R. Nosson Scherman, eds. *Lag Ba' Omer: Its Observance, Laws and Significance.* New York: Artscroll, Mesorah Publications, 1999.

Frankel, Ellen, and Betsy Platkin Teutsch. *The Encyclopedia of Jewish Symbols.* Northvale, N.J.: Jason Aronson, 1992.

Ginsburgh, R. Yitzchak. *The Alef-Beit: Jewish Thought Revealed through the Hebrew Letters.* Northvale, N.J.: Jason Aronson, 1991, 1995.

———. *Living in Divine Space: Kabbalah and Meditation.* Jerusalem: Linda Pinsky Publications, Gal Einai Institute, 2003.

Glazerson, R. Matityahu. *Building Blocks of the Soul: Studies on the Letters and Words of the Hebrew Language.* Northvale, N.J.: Jason Aronson, 1997.

———. *Sparks of the Holy Tongue: The Secret Behind Words and Letters in the Hebrew Language.* New York: Feldheim Publishers, 1980.

Greenbaum, Avraham, comp. and trans. *Rabbi Nachman's Tikkun: The Comprehensive Remedy (Tikkun Hakali with Shemot Hatzaddikim)* (Names of the Tzaddikim). New York: Breslov Research Institute, 1984.

Haralick, Robert M. *The Inner Meaning of the Hebrew Letters.* Northvale, N.J.: Jason Aronson, 1995.

Jacobson, Simon. *The Counting of the Omer.* New York: Vaad Hanochos Hatmimim, 1996.

———. *The Spiritual Guide to Counting the Omer.* New York: The Meaningful Life Center, 2007.

Kaplan, R. Aryeh. *Handbook of Jewish Thought,* two volumes. Edited by R. Avraham Sutton. New York: Maznaim Publishing Corporation, 1979.

———. *Immortality, Resurrection, and the Age of the Universe: A Kabbalistic View.* Hoboken, N.J.: KTAV Publishing House and Association of Orthodox Jewish Scientists, 1993.

———. *Inner Space: Introduction to Kabbalah, Meditation and Prophecy.* New York: Moznaim Publishing Corporation, 1990.

———. *Sefer Yetzirah: The Book of Creation in Theory and Practice.* Boston: Red Wheel/Weiser, 1997.

Kramer, R. Chaim, and R. Avraham Sutton. *Anatomy of the Soul: Rebbe Nachman of Breslov.* New York: Breslove Research Institute, 1998.

Lieber, R. Moshe, and R. Nosson Scherman, eds. *The Pirkei Avos: Ethics of the Fathers, The Sages Guide to Living.* New York: Mesorah Publications, 1995.

Locks, Gutman. *The Spice of Torah—Gematria.* New York: Judaica Press, 1985.

Luria, R. Yitzchak (Isaac). *Sefer Halikutim.* Edited by R. Mordechai Scheinberger. Jerusalem: R. Avraham Brandwein, 1988.

Luzzatto, R. Moshe Chaim. *Secrets of Redemption.* Translated by R. Mordechai Nissim. New York: Feldheim Publishers, 2004.

———. *The Path of the Just* (Mesillas Yesharim). Translated by R. Yosef Leibler. New York: Feldheim Publishers, 2004.

———. *The Path of the Just* (Mesillat Yesharim). Translated by R. Shraga Silverstein. New York: Feldheim Publishers, 1966.

———. *The Way of God* (Derech HaShem). Translated by R. Aryeh Kaplan. New York: Feldheim Publishers, 1983.

Maimonides (R. Moses Ben Maimon). *Mishneh Torah.* Translated by R. Eliyahu Touger. New York: Moznaim Publishing, 1990.

———. *Mishneh Torah: Hilchot Yesodei HaTorah,* vol. 1, *Hilchot Teshuvah,* vol. 4, and *Shaarei Kedusha.* Translated by R. Eliyahu Touger. New York: Moznaim Publishing, 1989.

———. *The Guide of the Perplexed.* Translated by Shlomo Pines. Chicago: University of Chicago Press, 1963.

Menzi, Donald Wilder, and Zwe Padeh, trans. *The Tree of Life: The Palace of Adam Kadmon, Chayyim Vital's Introduction to The Kabbalah of Isaac Luria.* Northvale, N.J.: Jason Aronson, 1999.

Miller, R. Moshe, trans. *The Chofetz Chaim on Awaiting Mashiach.* Southfield, Mich.: Targum Press, 1993.

Naor, Bezalel, *From a Kabbalist's Diary: Collected Essays.* Spring Valley, N.Y.: Orot, 2005.

———. *Lights of Prophecy.* New York: Union of Orthodox Jewish Congregations of America, 1990.

Paquda, R. Bachya Ben Joseph Ibn. *Duties of the Heart.* Translated by R. Yehudah Ibn Tibbon and Daniel Haberman. New York: Feldheim Publishers, 1996.

Rosenblatt, R. Yaakov. *The Maharal, Emerging Patterns: Ten Representative Essays Culled from the Works of Rabbi Yehudah Loew of Prague.* New York: Feldheim Publishers, 2001.

Scherman, R. Nosson, ed. *Perek Shira, The Song of the Universe.* New York: Artscroll, Mesorah Publications, 2005.

———. *Tanach: The Torah, Prophets, Writings—The Twenty-Four Books of the Bible.* New York: Artscroll, Mesorah Publications, 1996.

———. *Shabbos, The Sabbath: Its Essence and Signficance.* New York: Artscroll, Mesorah Publications, 2002.

Scherman, R. Nosson, and R. Meir Zlotowitz, eds. *The Complete Artscroll Siddur.* New York: Artscroll, Mesorah Publications, 1985.

Schneider, Sarah. *Kabbalistic Writings on the Nature of Masculine and Feminine.* Northvale, N.J.: Jason Aronson, 2001.

Schneerson of Lubavitch, R. Shalom Dov Ber. *Forces in Creation, Yom Tov Shel.* New York: Kehot Publication Society, 2003.

Sivan, Reuven, and Edward A. Levenston. *Hebrew and English Dictionary, the New Bantam-Megiddo.* New York: Bantam, 1975.

Sokolovosky, Meir Simcha. *Prophecy and Providence: The Fulfillment of Torah Prophecies in the Course of Jewish History.* New York: Feldheim Publishers, 1991.

Wigoder, Geoffrey. *The Student's Encyclopedia of Judaism.* New York: New York University Press, 2004.

Yoshor, R. Moses M. *The Chafetz Chaim: The Life and Works of Rabbi Yisrael Meir Kagan of Radin.* New York: Artscroll, Mesorah Publications, 1994.

Zalman of Liadi, R. Schneur. *Likkutei Amarim Tanya.* New York: Kehot Publication Society, 1993.

Zaloshinsky, R. Gavriel, ed. *The Ways of the Tzaddikim.* Translated by R. Shraga Silverstein. New York: Feldheim Publishers, 1995.

Zlotowitz, R. Meir, ed. *Shir HaShirim, Song of Songs: An Allegorical Translation Based upon Rashi with a Commentary Anthologized from Talmudic, Midrashic and Rabbinic Sources.* Translated by R. Nosson Scherman. New York: Artscroll, Mesorah Publications, 1977.

Index

Page numbers followed by *f* indicate footnotes.